Los Angeles & D...
For Dummies, 2...

Disneyland: Two-Day Touring Plan for Teens & Adults

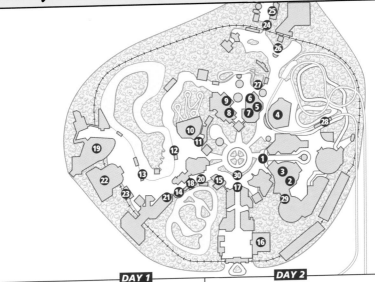

DAY 1

★ *Arrive 30-40 min. prior to opening.*
Line up at any gate with a short line.

1. Go to Tomorrowland.
2. Ride Space Mountain.
3. Ride Star Tours.
4. Ride the Matterhorn Bobsleds.
5. Ride Alice in Wonderland.
6. Ride Mr. Toad's Wild Ride.
7. Ride Peter Pan's Flight.
8. Ride Snow White's Scary Adventures.
9. Ride Pinocchio's Daring Journey.
10. Ride Big Thunder Mountain.
11. Eat lunch.
12. Ride the Mark Twain Riverboat or the Sailing Ship *Columbia*.
   (Work live shows and parades into the Touring Plan.)
13. Take a raft to Tom Sawyer Island.
14. Tour Tarzan's Treehouse.
15. See the *Enchanted Tiki Room* show.
16. See *The Walt Disney Story*.
17. See parades and live shows.

DAY 2

★ *Arrive 30-40 min. prior to opening.*
Line up at any gate with a short line.

18. Ride Indiana Jones.
19. Ride Splash Mountain.
20. Ride the Jungle Cruise.
21. Ride Pirates of the Caribbean.
22. See the Haunted Mansion.
23. Take the Train from New Orleans Square to the Fantasyland/Toontown Station.
24. Go to Mickey's Toontown.
25. Ride Roger Rabbit's Car Toon Spin (FASTPASS).
26. Ride It's a Small World.
27. Ride the Storybook Land Canal Boats.
28. Take a round-trip on the monorail.
29. Return to Tomorrowland on the monorail. See *Honey, I Shrunk the Audience*.
30. See parades and live shows.

Disney's California Adventure: One-Day Family Plan

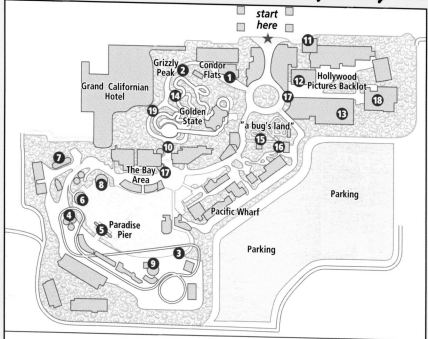

★ **Arrive 30-40 min. prior to opening.**

1 Ride Soarin' Over California.

2 Head for Paradise Pier.

3 Ride California Screamin'.

4 Ride Maliboomer.

5 Ride the Sun Wheel.

6 Ride the Orange Stinger.

7 Ride the Mulholland Madness.

8 Ride the Golden Zephyr.

9 If you have children, ride King Triton's Carousel.

10 Ride Grizzly River Run or obtain a FASTPASS to ride later.

11 See *Who Wants to Be a Millionaire?*

12 See *Muppet Vision 3-D.*

13 Check out Disney Animation.

14 If you have FASTPASSes, return to ride Grizzly River Run.

15 See *It's Tough to Be a Bug!*

16 Visit Flik's Fun Fair.

17 See *Golden Dreams* in the Bay Area or *Playhouse Disney* at Hollywood.

18 Check out the schedule for shows at the Hyperion Theater.

19 Try the Redwood Creek Challenge Trail if you have children.

Enjoy the parades and other live entertainment. Repeat attractions or see ones you missed.

FOR DUMMIES

The fun and easy way™ to travel!

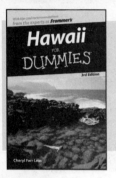 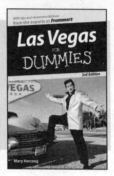

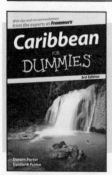 

Los Angeles & Disneyland®

FOR

DUMMIES

2ND EDITION

by Mary Herczog

WILEY

Wiley Publishing, Inc.

Los Angeles & Disneyland® For Dummies®, 2nd Edition

Published by
Wiley Publishing, Inc.
111 River St.
Hoboken, NJ 07030-5774
www.wiley.com

WILEY

About the Author

Mary Herczog is a relative anomaly in Los Angeles, a second-generation native. Her mom sat next to Norma Jean Baker in home room, and since Norma Jean went on to become Marilyn Monroe, this clearly gives Mary ample authority to talk about Los Angeles and, of course, celebrity scandals. She also writes *Frommer's New Orleans*, *Frommer's Las Legas*, and *Las Vegas For Dummies*, plus one half of *California For Dummies*, and when she's not doing that, she works in the film industry.

Dedication

To my father who moved here and my mother who lived here, and who together gave me this city.

Author's Acknowledgments

Extra special hardcore thanks to Lisa Derrick (for endlessly cheerful and ridiculously thorough research, and fine writing to boot) and Heidi Siegmund Cuda (for knowing and telling all about L.A. nightlife) — this book would not exist without them, or if it did, it wouldn't be as good.

Great thanks to Steve Bassman and Frommer's, for sweetly putting up with me and giving me the sort of job that makes others totally jealous.

Thanks to Rick Garman for always answering the phone.

Los Angeles glitters when I am there with Steve Hochman.

Publisher's Acknowledgments

We're proud of this book; please send us your comments through our Dummies online registration form located at www.dummies.com/register/.

Some of the people who helped bring this book to market include the following:

Acquisitions, Editorial, and Media Development

Development Editor: Stephen Bassman

Project Editor: Corbin Collins

Cartographer: Nick Trotter

Editorial Manager: Carmen Krikorian

Editorial Assistant: Nadine Bell

Senior Photo Editor: Richard Fox

Cover Photos: Front cover photo © Mike Powell, Allsport/Getty Images; back cover photo © Lee Foster/Lonely Planet Images

Cartoons: Rich Tennant, www.the5thwave.com

Composition

Project Coordinator: April Farling

Layout and Graphics: Lauren Goddard, Denny Hager, Joyce Haughey, Jacque Roth, Julie Trippetti

Special Art:

Proofreaders: Carl William Pierce, Charles Spencer, TECHBOOKS Production Services

Indexer: TECHBOOKS Production Services

Publishing and Editorial for Consumer Dummies

Diane Graves Steele, Vice President and Publisher, Consumer Dummies

Joyce Pepple, Acquisitions Director, Consumer Dummies

Kristin A. Cocks, Product Development Director, Consumer Dummies

Michael Spring, Vice President and Publisher, Travel

Brice Gosnell, Associate Publisher, Travel

Kelly Regan, Editorial Director, Travel

Publishing for Technology Dummies

Andy Cummings, Vice President and Publisher, Dummies Technology/ General User

Composition Services

Gerry Fahey, Vice President of Production Services

Debbie Stailey, Director of Composition Services

Contents at a Glance

Maps at a Glance

Table of Contents

Introduction

*L*otus Land. La-La Land. Swimming pools. Movie stars. Fruits, nuts, and flakes. And 350 cloudless days a year.

Face it: That's what you conjure up when you think of Los Angeles. You figure that everyone runs around sporting sunglasses and spouting New Age aphorisms while heading off to lunch on granola with Mel and Gwyneth. Well, that's just so untrue. For one thing, Mel and Gwyneth won't take our phone calls. For another, it's been weeks, *weeks,* since we were last at the Bodhi Tree (New Age bookstore nonpareil). And finally, we so hate granola.

But that's just us. In truth, all those things you think about L.A. aren't terribly far off the mark. Yet, mere clichés don't do the town justice. Let's add to your list, shall we? Los Angeles features bougainvillea and roses blooming year-round, pretty little Spanish and Craftsman bungalows, flea markets, sunsets and Sunset Boulevard, art at the Getty, hiking in Griffith Park, surfing at Zuma Beach, shopping on Third Street, first-run movies, palm trees, summer-evening concerts at the Santa Monica Pier, and all types of ethnic food from A (Armenian) to Z (zabaglione). And that's not even getting into in-line skating, UCLA, driving up Pacific Coast Highway, the Museum of Television and Radio and the Museum of Jurassic Technology, performance art at Highways and opera at the Dorothy Chandler Pavilion, the Rose Parade, baseball games at Dodger Stadium, wild parrots, celebrity grave hunting, author signings at Dutton's Books, concerts at the Greek Theater, nighttime club hopping, Zankou Chicken, and the Laurel Canyon dog park. Oh yeah, and the weather, which allows us to play softball in our T-shirts and shorts in January and go to the beach on Christmas Day.

There is, you see, quite a bit more to *El Pueblo de Nuestra Señora, la Reina de Los Angeles* ("The Town of Our Lady, the Queen of the Angels") — the full and proper name of the city — than you may first think. There is even more to its very name. If you follow us, here in *Los Angeles & Disneyland For Dummies,* you may not see it all, but you shall have a very good start. And we dare say you'll have a ripping good time in the process. Sure, there may be sunglasses, granola, and even a Mel or Gwyneth sighting involved (if you're lucky), but that certainly won't be the whole of it.

About This Book

This book is designed to quickly acclimate you to L.A. and provide you with the best, most essential ingredients for a great vacation. We've done the legwork for you, offering our expertise and frank opinions to

---

Dummies Post-it® Flags

As you're reading this book, you'll find information that you'll want to reference as you plan or enjoy your trip — whether it be a new hotel, a must-see attraction, or a must-try walking tour. Mark these pages with the handy Post-it® Flags included in this book to help make your trip planning easier!

---

help you make savvy, informed decisions while you plan your trip. What you *won't* find here is a numbing, phone-book-style directory of every place to eat, sleep, and do your laundry in L.A. or statistics of who has been satisfied with a particular restaurant or attraction. Frankly, those kinds of guidebooks make our eyes glaze over. In *Los Angeles & Disneyland For Dummies*, we cut to the chase. We chose our favorites in many categories and put them into a form you can easily access and use to make your own decisions.

 Please be advised that travel information is subject to change at any time and this is especially true of prices. We therefore suggest that you write or call ahead for confirmation when making travel plans. The author and publisher cannot be held responsible for the experiences of readers while traveling. Your safety is important to us, however, so we encourage you to stay alert and be aware of your surroundings. Keep a close eye on cameras, purses, and wallets, all favorite targets of thieves and pickpockets.

Conventions Used in This Book

In this book, we list hotels, restaurants, and attractions. As we describe each, we often include abbreviations for commonly accepted credit cards:

> AE: American Express
>
> DC: Diners Club
>
> DISC: Discover
>
> MC: MasterCard
>
> V: Visa

We also include some general pricing information to help you as you decide where to unpack your bags or dine on local cuisine. We have used a system of dollar signs to show a range of costs for one night in a hotel (the price refers to a double-occupancy room) or a meal at a restaurant (included in the cost of each meal is soup or salad, an entree, dessert, and a nonalcoholic drink). Check out the following table to decipher the dollar signs:

Cost	Hotel	Restaurant
$	Under $100	Under $20
$$	$100–$200	$20–$30
$$$	$200–$275	$30–$40
$$$$	$275 and up	$40–$50
$$$$$		over $50

Foolish Assumptions

In writing this book, we've made some of the following assumptions about you, the reader:

✔ You may be an inexperienced traveler who is interested in Los Angeles and wants a no-nonsense guide on when to go, how to arrange your trip, and what to expect.

✔ You may be an experienced traveler who has visited the region before, but you're looking for a guide full of lively, informed opinions to help you plan your vacation. You want to know what's new, and you want to be able to quickly access information with minimal fuss.

✔ You're a busy, on-the-go consumer, who doesn't want to waste time absorbing the mind-numbing details of traditional guides and micromanaging your trip. You want a book that gives you frank, informed opinions on planning the perfect, hassle-free trip.

If any of these ring a bell with you, then *Los Angeles & Disneyland For Dummies* will be an invaluable guide for your trip.

How This Book Is Organized

This book is divided into seven parts, and together they cover all of the major aspects of planning and enjoying your trip. The Table of Contents at a Glance and complete Table of Contents that preceded this chapter are perfect tools for finding general and specific information. At the back of the book, you'll find an Appendix of helpful service information and phone numbers, as well as the index, the most useful tool for navigating this book.

Part 1: Introducing Los Angeles

Here's where that old proverbial ball gets rolling with a few lists of the very best that L.A. has to offer, plus background history and architecture, plus a calendar of events and seasonal breakdown to help you decide when to visit.

Part II: Planning Your Trip to Los Angeles

Details, details. How can you get the best bang for your buck? Should you buy travel insurance? Do you need traveler's checks? Where can you find resources for special needs and interests? We discuss all the "before you go" essentials, including where to book your flight and the best deals on airfare.

Part III: Settling Into Los Angeles

Arriving in a new city and getting acclimated is one of the great joys of travel, and this section makes it easy. Here's where you really get to know the City of Angels, neighborhood by neighborhood. You'll discover myriad ways to get from the airport to your hotel, the smartest ways to get around the city, and where to get cash. And, perhaps most important, here is where you discover our favorite hotels and restaurants — the classic hotels, the best deals, the best quick bites, and places to spot celebs. We give you the lowdown and then break it down by category, price, and neighborhood.

Part IV: Exploring Los Angeles

Here you discover what we consider the best sights and attractions in Los Angeles, as well as the best museums, sports events, movie tours, kid-friendly venues, and downtown delights. Here, too, is a select shopper's guide to L.A., whether you're strolling in a glittering supermall or taking it to the streets at funky flea markets. For the reader looking for a variety of L.A. experiences, we offer unique itineraries and daytrips beyond L.A. plus tips on organizing your time to explore the city more efficiently.

Part V: Living It Up After Dark: Los Angeles Nightlife

Los Angeles has no dearth of nightlife, and here you get the lowdown on how to get tickets to hot shows, where to go to see theater, dance, and more, and where to find the nightclub or bar of your (L.A.) dreams.

Part VI: A Trip to Disneyland

Here we tell you how to get to Disneyland Drive, when to come to avoid the peak tourist season, how to avoid long lines, where to stay and dine in the Disneyland area, and what's new and exciting in the Disney park system.

Part VII: The Part of Tens

Here we have fun throwing our opinions around about places you probably can't afford, places to spot the city's celebrated celebrities, and venues where you can have an out-of-L.A. experience.

Icons Used in This Book

The icons alert you to special cases or particularly useful information.

 The Bargain Alert icon tells you when you're about to save a bundle or suggests ways that you can cut costs.

 Best of the Best icon highlights the best the destination has to offer in all categories: hotels, restaurants, attractions, activities, shopping, and nightlife.

 The Heads Up icon tells you when you should be especially aware of a potentially dangerous situation, a tourist trap, or, more likely, a rip-off. In other words, be especially alert when you encounter these situations.

 Families with kids in tow will appreciate the Kid Friendly icon, which identifies places that are welcoming and/or particularly suited to kids.

 Helpful hints to make your experience easier and/or less stressful are marked with the Remember icon.

 Especially created for this book, the Star Spotting icon directs you to those places where you have the best chance to spot celebrities.

 The Tip icon delivers some inside information and advice on things to do or ways to best handle a specific situation, helping you to save time or money.

Where to Go from Here

Fly, drive, run, or walk. Just come. The bougainvillea is in bloom. The sand is warm and tawny. The surf is up at Zuma. With *Los Angeles & Disneyland For Dummies* by your side, the City of Angels is yours for the taking.

Part I

Introducing Los Angeles

RODEO CLOWNS LOST IN LA

RODEO DR

"Here we go, boys. Heck-even if they can't help us at least we won't feel so dern out of place."

In this part . . .

This first part introduces you to Los Angeles — the sprawling, sparkling, scintillating City of Angels. In this part we list the best the city has to offer, give you some historical background information, and help you decide the best time to go. We include a calendar of the city's top events, festivals, and happenings as a reference.

Chapter 1

Discovering the Best of Los Angeles

●●●

●●●

> "This town is our town / It is so glamorous / Bet you'd live here if you could / And be one of us"
>
> —The Go-Go's, "This Town"

*W*e love L.A. — we really, really do, but that's because we know how best to find and experience its admittedly subtle charms. Yeah, it's got smog (though increasingly less), and yes, it's got traffic (alas, more than ever), and yes, much of the distinctive architecture has been torn down thanks to an utter disinterest in preservation. And yes, it's far-flung, and public transportation stinks, so you absolutely have to buck that aforementioned heavy traffic to get anywhere to enjoy anything.

But. Here's a place where you can surf and ski on the same day. Here's a place where your sightseeing is enhanced by cloudless skies. Here's a place where movie-star footprints are enshrined, and the Getty family gave a great deal of money to amass one of the finest art collections in the world. Here's a place where you can enjoy the L.A. Philharmonic (and other internationally known artists) out in the fragrant night air at the gorgeous Hollywood Bowl and in the new, state-of-the-art, visually delirious Disney Hall. Here's a place where just a 1-mile stretch of Hollywood Boulevard peacefully holds Thai, Mexican, Romanian, Armenian, Vietnamese, and Persian restaurants, all of them with some of the most wonderful food you've ever tasted, for bargain prices. Here's a place where weirdness and eccentricity are embraced — and of course, if you can turn it into a sitcom, so much the better. Here's a place where you can grocery shop right next to the actors who star in those very sitcoms, just like they were regular folks. Here's a place where you can take a ride in a spinning teacup.

To appreciate L.A. you need to look past the snarling traffic and the smog and the freeway signs and catch the city on one of those gin-clear days when you have an ideal view of the mountains. You'll catch yourself outside on a breezy morning, enjoying the sun in short sleeves and sipping some coffee, and you'll think to yourself, "It's January?" Those days usually win people over.

But all is not lost if you don't happen upon L.A. during perfect weather. Following is a list of our favorite itineraries, attractions, and experiences that should endear you to Los Angeles, smog and all.

The Best Itineraries

✔ **Best way to see Los Angeles in a day:** Drive **Sunset Boulevard** from start to finish. That most identifiable of Los Angeles streets takes you from the heart of Downtown, right next to the oldest extant street in the city, all the way to the Pacific Ocean. Along the way, you will see a little bit of everything that defines Los Angeles, from what the city council wants you to think to what residents know is the truth, for good and for bad. Even if you have a week here, take this drive. We've provided a gossipy, scandal-ridden tour on p. 176.

✔ **Best way to see L.A. without moving:** Park yourself on a towel on a hot summer day on a **Santa Monica** or **Venice beach.** It's not a true picture of Los Angeles, but we will join forces with the tourism commission on this one, and let it go. Bikini babes, surfer boys, some oddballs, miles of ocean blue, the nearby kook-filled Venice boardwalk, and family-filled Santa Monica pier — isn't it what you came here for? You could justly wonder why we would make you do anything else. See Chapter 11.

✔ **Best way to prove New York City doesn't have a monopoly on culture:** Hit any one of our Big Three museums: the **Los Angeles County Museum of Art** (p. 166) offers an encyclopedic museum collection that rivals New York's Metropolitan, and so has something for everyone, from antiquities to masters to Asian art to modern art and more. It's also in a shamefully ugly complex. That's why locals tend to steer people to the **Getty** (p. 165), which is housed in Los Angeles' version of an urban setting, which is to say way up on a hillside, preventing anyone from walking there, and offering views to make grown men weep. The collection is kind of boring, though few will admit that out loud, but it did cost a lot and that makes it very L.A. The downtown **Museum of Contemporary Art** (p. 167) manages to combine the best of both — a nifty, modern piece of architecture (its façade just turned up in a car commercial) with a sterling collection.

The Best Hotels

✔ **Best cheap hotel on the beach: The Cadillac Hotel** (p. 92) is currently undergoing a renovation to raise it from the depths of hostel-budget-land, so by the time you read this, the word "cheap" may no longer be strictly accurate. But it is just about as close to the beach as you can get, and the renovations will make stays in its basic-but-fine rooms that much nicer.

✔ **Best soft-focus-B&B-type hotel:** L.A. doesn't have much in the way of charming B&B places, the sort that show up in *Victorian* magazine, but both the steps-from-the-beach **Venice Beach House** (p. 107) and the up-the-hill-from-the-sea **Channel Road Inn** (p. 93) are magazine-layout-ready. Both are housed in lovingly restored Craftsman homes, and both offer the kind of personal service and attention to detail that those of us who prefer character over design crave. And both have very L.A.-specific, seriously pretty settings.

✔ **Best hotel for old Hollywood romance:** Mystery, scandal, and more lurk around the **Chateau Marmont** (p. 93), an old behemoth castle of a hotel, best known as the place where John Belushi died, but almost equally well known as the place any number of stars stay when they come to town, or even live. We think this gorgeous, slightly peeling old place just reeks of romance and intrigue.

✔ **Best romantic hotel: The Hotel Bel Air** (p. 99), with its gardens and ponds and swans and its luxurious guest rooms, some with fireplaces and patios and all with 400-thread-count sheets, is the best place in the city for an assignation or any other romantic intrigue you want to cook up. Too bad none of us can afford it.

✔ **Best Downtown hotels:** For the best classic old L.A. hotel, there's the Beaux Arts and Deco wonder that is the **Biltmore** (p. 103), where presidents stay or at least speak when they are in town. For the best classic old hotel that is more affordable, there is the Moroccan-and-Turkish-themed **Hotel Figueroa** (p. 99), where the owners are working hard to do it justice with newly done rooms. For a great weekend rate, it's hard to beat the $99 you can get at the **Checkers** (p. 97). And for the hippest crowd in L.A., try the **Standard** (p. 106).

✔ **Best hotels in Beverly Hills: The Maison 140** (p. 102) is sexy and sybaritic, whereas the **Beverly Hills Reeves** (p. 88) isn't, but the latter has clean rooms for such shockingly low prices at times that even a budget traveler can have the cachet of saying "I'm staying in Beverly Hills."

The Best Restaurants

✔ **Best high-end restaurant:** Opinion is sharply divided here among Mark Peel's defining work at **Campanille** (certainly the loveliest restaurant of the three: p. 124), the restaurant-empire-spawning

Patina (p. 138), and the French innovation creations at **Bastide** (p. 120). We've listed them in (more or less) escalating order of price, but please don't let that be your only deciding factor. All four are excellent and will demonstrate why Los Angeles cannot be overlooked when discussing foodie destinations.

✔ **Best reason to rejoice that L.A. is a melting pot:** Because it means the city teems with interesting hole-in-the-wall ethnic joints, that's why. Here are our favorites: The roast chicken at **Zankou** (p. 144) would be enough to bring us here regularly, but when combined with its garlic paste, we know what we would request for our last meal. The sampler platter at **Caroussel** (p. 127) is our favorite introduction to Armenian food (and our favorite way to overeat), whereas **Sanamluang Café** (p. 141) is the Thai restaurant we love the most. Can't decide? Go to the **Grand Central Market** (p. 130) in Downtown, where the food might not be the absolute best, but because it's laid out stall after stall in a semichaotic scene like no other in L.A., and the choices range from Thai to Japanese to Deli to Mexican and more that we've forgotten, the experience makes up for it.

✔ **Best sushi:** Apart from tired jokes about granola and sprouts, sushi is probably the food most closely identified with Los Angeles, if only because it seems so *dainty*. And silly. You can try some of the finest around, if you are willing to pay for it, at Matsuhisa (p. 137) and its somewhat cheaper sibling, Nobu, but frankly, we find the raw fish at **Sushi Gen** (p. 143) just about as good and considerably more affordable.

✔ **Best Mexican:** Of course, if you ask the locals, they will tell you that L.A.'s defining cuisine — the thing that gets us the most homesick when out of town — is Mexican. You will also start fights over what this means, exactly. For what most of us probably mean, and you too, when you think of Mexican food, which is to say the very specific, Southern California Mexican style, try the old school (we mean it — they've been around forever) **El Cholo** (p. 129). But if you want to know what real Mexicans think of when they think of what their mother made back home, then go to **Border Grill** (p. 122), where the chefs known as the Two Hot Tamales will show you what the real thing is. Or try yet another variation, the Yucatan-style, fast-food-doesn't-do-it-justice tacos and the like at **Yuca's Hut** (p. 144).

✔ **Best late-night hang:** You can't beat **Canter's Deli** (p. 126) for a scene. Old rockers, young rockers, Jewish grandmas, college kids on a budget, hipsters, and nobodies, they all come to Canter's, and a lot of them do it in the wee hours of the morning. Sometimes they play music in the Kibbitz Room, too.

✔ **Best cafe:** We hate to give any more press to **Clementine's** (p. 128) because it's hard enough to get a table there, but the lovely sandwiches, salads, and entrees that are always prepared with a strict eye to the season, plus the baked goods, are so delectable we have to tell you about it. But let us sit at your table if it's full when we all get there, okay?

✔ **Best "Now THIS is L.A." restaurant: Philippe's** (p. 139) has been around longer than just about any other restaurant, and deservedly so, with the still-divine French dip sandwiches they claim to have invented in the first place, the sawdust on the floors, and the long tables you have to share with strangers from the entire broad Los Angeles spectrum. And the 9¢ cup of coffee. You have to eat here at least once or you've missed out on the heart of L.A.

The Best Attractions

✔ **Best must-do:** Do you even have to be told to see **Disneyland** (Chapters 17–19)? Really? You've never been and weren't planning on going? Shame on you. Would you go to Rome and skip the Vatican?

✔ **Best way to guarantee getting within 6 feet of a star:** Go to **Forest Lawn, Hollywood Forever,** or **Westwood Memorial Park** (Chapter 13). Oh, did you want the star to be breathing? Sorry. Well, if you still want to see the resting places of the likes of Valentino, Marilyn Monroe, or Andy Gibb, you can.

✔ **Best touristy thing to do:** Go see the **stars on the Hollywood sidewalk,** see the **footprints at Grauman's,** and look up at the **Hollywood sign** (Chapter 11). Apart from the beach, why else did you come here? And once you've done it, wasn't it just a bit cooler than you thought it might be?

✔ **Best building to say things like "Wow" about: The Walt Disney Concert Hall** (p. 210) gleams and billows and looks different from every angle. By rights, this will become Los Angeles' Eiffel Tower, its Sydney Opera House, its Big Ben.

✔ **Best museum for L.A.: The Museum of Television & Radio** (p. 193) celebrates, well, television and radio. Those things (along with the flicks, of course) built this town. Going here means a great excuse to watch TV, including all sorts of rare and remarkable moments in media.

✔ **Best weirdest and most wonderful museum: The Museum of Jurassic Technology** (p. 192) is so great and so hard to explain that at least one person wrote a book about it (and came to no conclusion whatsoever). The focus is on the Lower Jurassic, but don't expect dinosaurs. It's small and strange, arty and informative, claustrophobic for some, utter heaven for others.

✔ **Best museum for our troubled times:** Kidding aside, there are lessons that we all need to learn at the **Museum of Tolerance** (p. 193).

Chapter 2

Digging Deeper into Los Angeles

- -

In This Chapter

▶ Taking in the scene at the beach
▶ Spotting the celebs
▶ Patronizing the arts
▶ Sleeping, eating, and clubbing
▶ Watching L.A. on the silver screen

- -

*N*ow that you know the best of the best, consider some background information about the city and its culture — and rent a movie or two.

The Beach Scene

To many people, Los Angeles is one big beach party, with Frankie and Annette riding an eternal surfboard against a picture-perfect blue sky. To some extent, you can find a piece of that *Beach Blanket Bingo* vibe at places like the **Santa Monica Pier,** where you can stroll among the motley collection of souvenir shops, old carny rides, and a 1930s-era merry-go-round, or the **Venice Ocean Front Walk,** where the boys preen at Muscle Beach and pony-tailed gals zoom by on their in-line skates — both genders have more tattoos than they did back in the '50s. But if you want to enjoy the ocean in a more pristine setting, head north into the **Pacific Palisades** and **Malibu,** where the waves get bigger and the houses get ritzier. North of that is **Zuma,** with its wild, cold waters. See "The top beaches," p. 171 for listings.

Celebrity Culture

The days of studio moguls such as Louis B. Mayer and his stable of MGM stars may be long gone, but the city of Los Angeles remains synonymous with high-wattage celebrity. Of course, these days Hollywood proper is more a state of mind than a place where movies are made and film stars prance around in ermine and silk. That's because the motion-picture industry isn't based in Hollywood, and truth be told, it never really was. If you want to see stars — and they're out there, to be sure — you need to trek to the nether reaches of Malibu coffee shops and Beverly Hills clothing stores.

You may not find filmmakers in Hollywood, but you still have a number of fine reasons to visit, such as **Grauman's Chinese Theatre** (p. 160). What began in 1927 as a publicity stunt (heck, it's still a publicity stunt) has gotten a facelift, which removed some of its more endearingly eccentric stylings (neon dragons!) but left the glorious interior (pomp and gilt!) intact. But of course, you go to see the footprints, handprints, and other body prints of stars past. Have fun comparing your foot size with that of Mary Pickford or your nose with Jimmy Durante's proboscis print. Shoppers and mall fanciers will want to head to the **Hollywood-Highland Complex** (p. 162), home of the Academy Awards (in the Kodak Theatre) and a mega shopping center with major shops, movie theaters, a couple of nightclubs, several restaurants, and the brand-new **Hollywood Motion Picture Museum** (p. 160), home of such Tinseltown artifacts as Dorothy's

History 101: El Pueblo de Los Angeles

El Pueblo de Nuestra Señora, la Reina de Los Angeles ("The Town of Our Lady, the Queen of the Angels") was founded by the Spanish in 1781 — and take that, all you Easterners who think L.A. doesn't have a history. But truth be told, L.A. really wasn't on the map until the movie folks came out here in search of outdoor locations that didn't suffer from snow. By World War I, the movie business had a hold on the town, and in the 1920s and '30s, folks came here in droves, seeking their fortunes on and off the silver screen. Very few of them were "discovered" sipping sodas in malt shops, à la Lana Turner, but that didn't stop anyone from trying.

That crush of people came with cars, and as early as 1940, the Arroyo Seco Parkway, the first freeway, was opened. The automobile business solidified L.A.'s total depend-ence on cars by crushing the then quite handy public transport (the "Little Red Cars" trolley system). More freeways followed, and more people came to work in the thriv-ing aerospace industry (led by McDonnell Douglas) and the new television industry. It didn't hurt that every year Pasadena put on the glorious Rose Parade under inevitably clear blue skies, causing snowbound Midwesterners and others to throw everything in the car and come to permanently join the balmy fun. In no time at all, L.A. became an urban sprawl of impossible dimensions.

And they keep on acomin', though a few events have quenched the migration enthu-siasm, at least briefly. In 1971, a 6.2 earthquake rocked nearby Sylmar, but though it loomed in legend for more than 20 years, it was nothing compared with the "Biggish One" in 1994, the 6.8 Northridge quake that left nearly 60 people dead and a portion of the 10 freeway collapsed. Riots in the wake of the Rodney King verdict shut the city down for several days, as homes and businesses burned and the National Guard came out to restore order. And then there was the O.J. trial. But thanks to its blessedly short memory, floods, fires, and even football players haven't managed to stop this town.

gingham dress from *The Wizard of Oz*. And of course, there's **Sunset Boulevard,** the city's main artery and witness to any number of sordid "Hollywood Babylon" stories (see "The Sensational, Star-Studded, Scandalous Sunset Boulevard Tour, p. 176). And it goes without saying that savvy shoppers will want to head to **Melrose Avenue,** where funky stores and hip dining spots abound.

See Chapter 20 and watch for the "Star Spotting" icon throughout the book.

Best of the Museums

L.A. has a number of museums with very high quality collections, along with a few of the quirkier sort that folks like us tend to patronize. The big ones, of course, are the **Getty** (p. 165), which specializes in Greek and Roman antiquities and European paintings; the **Los Angeles County Museum of Art (L.A.CMA),** which holds masterpieces by Rembrandt, Degas, and Magritte as well as one of the finest collections of Islamic art in the world (p. 166); and the **Museum of Contemporary Art (MOCA) at the Geffen Contemporary,** which has two locations and a collection that includes Warhol, Pollack, and De Kooning, plus conceptual installations.

Then there are the specialty museums, such as the **Autry Museum of Western Heritage** (p. 192), the legacy of the Singing Cowboy himself; the **Japanese American National Museum** (p. 192), which includes a moving reconstruction of an actual building from a Japanese relocation camp; the **Museum of Tolerance** (p. 193), which offers a look at prejudice and intolerance through the ages; the **California ScienCenter** (p. 189), a wonderful hands-on science museum; and the **Petersen Automotive Museum** (p. 195), a paean to the freeway's favorite accessory, the car. See "Museums galore" on p. 189 for listings.

The Hotel and Restaurant Scene

Los Angeles is spread out, so no matter where you stay, you'll probably be driving (or taking some other means of transportation) to get to the major sightseeing spots. Unlike quainter places, such as Santa Fe or New Orleans, Los Angeles has few atmospheric B&Bs or cunning little inns. What it does have are many standard-issue hotel rooms. You can find a measure of individuality, however, by staying at one of the venerable Old Hollywood establishments (such as the **Hollywood Roosevelt,** said to be haunted by Marilyn Monroe; see p. 98) or such hipster spots as West Hollywood's **The Standard** (where you can schedule a tattoo; see p. 106). Or, if you have buckets of money, you can stay where the movie stars stay, in the cream-colored suites with the champagne on ice, the 300-thread-count sheets, and the Egyptian-cotton towels. Or not. See Chapter 9 for complete listings.

As for food, we are pleased as punch to tell you that you don't have to *spend* like a movie star to eat like a movie star. Oh, sure, you can spring for a four-star meal at **Spago Beverly Hills** (p. 142), or **Matsuhisa** (p. 329), but you can eat very well in any number of inexpensive places all over the city — and often brilliantly. Among our favorites are **Zankou Chicken** (p. 144), a hole-in-the-wall joint with perfect roast chicken, **Sanamluang Cafe,** for scrumptious Thai noodles, and **Pink's,** a famously dumpy little hot-dog stand in West Hollywood, where a line of people stand day and night to get their hands on one of the divine hot dogs. And L.A. wouldn't be L.A. without the quintessential **old-school restaurants,** where you can order a ring-a-ding-ding martini and a slab of red meat from crusty old waiters in dark wood-paneled environs. Need we say: Meet us at **Musso & Frank**.

Nightlife Highlights

L.A. truly rocks. Nightlife in the City of Angels ranges from family-style sporting events such as an evening at the **Staples Center** (p. 269) cheering on the world-champion L.A. Lakers, to classical concerts under the stars at the **Hollywood Bowl** (the Beatles played here! See p. 268), to finding your way past the velvet ropes into club land. Rock historians will have a field day in L.A., visiting such seminal '60s and '70s clubs as the **Roxy** (p. 272), **the Whisky a Go-Go** (p. 185), and **the Troubadour** (p. 273). You'll find saucy places to dance to any kind of music as well as elegant cocktail lounges and real dive bars (but look who's sitting on the barstool next to you!). And don't forget the opportunities to see major plays and musicals (**the Music Center** (p. 265), **the Mark Taper Forum** (p. 267, **the Actors' Gang** (p. 267)), symphony (**the Los Angeles Philharmonic,** in its new home at the Walt Disney Concert Hall, p. 267), and opera (**the Los Angeles Opera,** at the Dorothy Chandler Pavilion, p. 268). See Chapter 16 for complete listings.

Hollywood goes Hollywood: L.A. movies

L.A. is all about moving pictures, and you could do worse to get revved up for your trip than screen *Gidget* (1965), in which perky Sally Field is the ultimate California beach girl in the ultimate California beach movie. *Chinatown* (1974) is possibly the finest noir ever committed to film, using L.A. in the '70s to re-create L.A. in the '30s impeccably. Its modern-day successor is the Oscar-winning *L.A. Confidential* (1997). *The Player* (1992) all-too-realistically captures the seedy underbelly and soul-selling seductive power of Hollywood influence and celebrity. *The Big Picture* (1989) is director Christopher Guest's first feature, a dead-on satire of the movie industry, filmed presumably on a shoestring around Hollywood. David Lynch's *Mulholland Drive* (2001) may be too weird for some, but it sticks in the brain like a vivid, curious dream about Tinseltown. Steve Martin's *L.A. Story* (1991) is a romantic look at everything that's wonderfully silly about city life. *Valley Girl* (1983), starring teenage Nicolas Cage, is a New-Wave-Boy-meets-mall-lovin'-Valley-Girl love story at the height of Valley Girl mania. Need a guilty pleasure? Check out any movie with "Beverly Hills" in the title (*Slums of Beverly Hills, Down and Out in Beverly Hills, Beverly Hills Cop,* etc.)

Chapter 3

Deciding When to Go

. . . .

In This Chapter

▶ Weighing the pros and cons of each season
▶ Considering the average monthly temperatures
▶ Planning around the Los Angeles calendar of events

. . . .

*T*here really isn't a bad time to visit L.A. — you can expect 350 cloudless, comfortable days a year. But deciding *when* to visit likely depends on factors other than mere weather conditions. You may want to breeze into town when the big events are held, or when hotel rates are at their most reasonable, or when you simply need a respite from the winter blahs. But no matter when you come to L.A., you'll have no trouble finding activities and events to entertain you.

The Secrets of the Seasons

People are fond of complaining that Los Angeles has no seasons. Sure, certain flowers bloom all year long, but the seasonal changes are there — they're just subtle, that's all. In the winter, the trees are bare (well, not the palm trees), and spring looks like spring almost anywhere (see Table 3-1).

If it's going to rain — and odds are, it won't, unless another El Niño snakes its way out of the Tropics — it's most likely going to happen in the spring. Even then, heavy rainstorms are unusual.

It can get nippy in winter — not Minnesota, 40-below-zero nippy — but it can get down in the 20s at night, so bring a coat if you visit in the cool months. A light wrap is always a good idea, thanks to temperatures that can flit annoyingly from 80 during the day to 50 at night.

Fall can bring the Santa Anas, the surprisingly strong, warm winds that are a bane to firefighters. And summer brings the real heat, and with that the smog. Get in the car and head to the beach along with everyone else.

Note also that the Westside neighborhoods (Santa Monica, Brentwood, Pacific Palisades, and even Westwood) always seem to be 20 degrees (or more) cooler than Hollywood, Pasadena, and the Valley (the latter two are the hottest places in the metropolitan area). We've spent many a day sweltering in 90-degree weather on the Eastside and then traveled west, only to find it 62 and foggy. Go figure. Thank the ocean breezes.

Table 3-1	Los Angeles' Average Temperatures											
	Jan	Feb	Mar	Apr	May	June	July	Aug	Sep	Oct	Nov	Dec
High (°F/°C)	66/19	68/20	69/21	71/22	73/23	77/25	82/28	84/29	82/28	78/26	73/23	68/20
Low (°F/°C)	48/9	50/10	51/11	54/12	57/14	60/16	63/17	64/18	63/17	59/15	53/12	50/10

Autumn serenade

Autumn is a fine time to consider a trip to Los Angeles because

- ✔ The tourist season slows down around the end of September and remains that way for some months to come.
- ✔ Rain is virtually nonexistent.

But on the other hand

- ✔ Summer doesn't really end until after September (and sometimes it pops up again in October), so it can be quite hot. We mean triple-digit hot — sometimes 115 degrees.
- ✔ Fall brings the strong Santa Ana winds, which play havoc with fire.

Winter wonderland

Winter is an absolutely wonderful time to come to Los Angeles because

- ✔ It's Oscar time! The Academy Awards, now held in February at the Kodak Theatre, honors the best in film every year with a high-wattage display of star power.
- ✔ Oscar week aside, it's a slow time, tourist-wise, and hotel rates can be a bargain.
- ✔ The weather is fabulous: crisp and clear. It may rain, and there can be wind, but those elements just blow away the smog and haze, leaving the landscape looking crisp and perfect.
- ✔ The mountains appear to be cut from glass, and the palm trees stand stark against the sky, which is blue blue blue, except when puffy cloud formations add to the extraordinary look of things. This is the time for mountains-to-the-sea views.
- ✔ It can get a bit nippy, yes, but that's relative, and besides, within a day or two, it might be in the 80s again. Or at least in the 70s. If you

experience an L.A. winter, you'll understand why so many people moved here in the first place and why they are loathe to leave.

✔ It's whale-watching season! The Pacific gray whales make their annual migration, providing many opportunities to watch 'em frolic.

✔ Cold or even drizzly weekdays are the best time to avoid crowds at theme parks like Disneyland.

But keep in mind that

✔ The notorious Santa Ana winds, which crop up from October through February, are likely to hit their peak during this season, with gusts of up to 50 mph in some places and maybe even higher in the Santa Ana Mountain foothills. The winds drive some people nuts because they're warm yet breezy and can make travel into other parts of Southern California tricky. In fact, they've been known to knock over semis in certain mountain passes.

✔ The Pacific is never very temperate, but that matters more on cold days than when steamy triple-digit temperatures are in play. And the winter ocean may well be fogbound much of the day anyway. You can forget about swimming in the ocean.

✔ Although the tourist season is slow, it does pick up during Christmas and the New Year's holidays (when you may be more likely to travel, especially if you have kids) because lots of people come to town for the Tournament of Roses Parade (p. 21) and the Rose Bowl. And you will likely have to contend with passels of schoolchildren visiting museums and so forth.

Spring in your step

Spring is another delightful time in Los Angeles because

✔ Temperatures are moderate, and so are the crowds.

✔ Blooms are bustin' out all over, not the least of which are the jacaranda trees with their light-purple blossoms. They bloom in May, turning into purple puffballs and raining purple snow, a sight that regularly pacifies even the grouchiest driver during a slow commute. Plus, the hills are green, and birds are out in abundance.

✔ There still can be snow up in the mountains, which means that you can ski in your bikini. Really. Or you can just go to watch snow bunnies ski in their bikinis. Really.

On the other hand

✔ It never rains in Southern California, except when it *does,* and when it does, the streets can (and often do) flood, traffic snarls, and it's darn wet. Rain is more likely to happen at this time of year.

✔ Speaking of weather, because summer lasts so long, it's only reasonable that it shouldn't start too soon, and many unsuspecting tourists may find themselves shivering in what locals call the "June gloom." It's cold. Foggy. Unfair.

Summer in the city

Summer is our least favorite time but perhaps the best for families because

✔ The kids are out of school, and when else can you travel?

✔ It's warm, and you probably want to go to the beach.

But then again:

✔ Heavens above, it's hot. Extreme heat isn't predictable, and it may only be a few days during the entire summer, but sheesh. . . .

✔ With summer comes the smog — in inescapable layers. Blech. In fact, entire mountain ranges can disappear in the haze. Los Angeles looks pretty tawdry this time of year.

✔ Almost everyone heads to the beach to escape the heat. Expect to battle for towel space on the sand.

✔ Speaking of everyone, that includes everyone with kids. Crowds. Lots of 'em.

Los Angeles Calendar of Events

Los Angeles is a festive place any time of year, but some extra-special occasions stand out. Here are some of the city's biggest events to mark on your calendar.

January

The granddaddy of all parades is the **Tournament of Roses Parade,** and New Year's Day is Pasadena's moment to shine — and bloom — because all the floats are constructed out of natural products, mostly flowers. The parade features marching bands, costumed horseback riders, and other entries, but it's the floats that matter. And if you've seen them only on TV, honestly, you've never really seen them. It's well worth coming to L.A. just to witness this spectacle in person. But you won't be alone: A million or more folks line up on the parade route, many of them spending the night to secure their patches of sidewalk, which makes for one noisy, memorable New Year's Eve party. Call ☎ **626-449-4100** or check out www.tournamentofroses.com for more details. January 1.

February

The **Academy of Motion Picture Arts and Sciences Awards** — that's the Oscars to you and me — is now held in February. (The Academy moved up their big bash in 2004, attempting to beat the other award shows. But then all the other award shows moved up *their* shows. So although the plan is for February in 2005, by 2006 it could be moved back to the traditional last Sunday in March.) For its biggest, most self-congratulatory day, the town turns topsy-turvy, so don't expect to get attention from any serious facialist, manicurist, stylist, or clothier, and don't look to get a really good hotel room, either (if you do find one, you can bet that you'll have some cover-boy neighbors). The Academy's new home is the Kodak Theatre in the Hollywood-Highland Complex. Go to www.oscars.org for more details. Last Sunday in February.

March

Twenty-six miles and it's a hoot; sure, the guys (and gals) out front are streamlined and serious, but behind them are thousands of participants, some dressed like Elvis or in other pieces of whimsy. You can run or walk the **Los Angeles Marathon**; some even bike it or just line the route (which starts in downtown L.A. and hits most of Hollywood and other scenic bits) and cheer everyone on. Call ☎ **310-444-5544** or go to www.lamarathon.com for information. Early March.

Just an hour or so north of L.A. lies the Antelope Valley California Poppy Reserve, where, during the springtime **California Poppy Blooming Season,** miles of hillside blaze with vibrant, dazzling color. Visit during the **California Poppy Festival,** usually held in April. For information and directions, call ☎ **661-723-6077** or go to www.poppyfestival.com. Mid-March through mid-May.

April

Dogs, cats, horses, hamsters, tortoises, and turtledoves all gather, bleating and barking, at the plaza entrance to Olvera Street for the Archdiocese of Los Angeles' annual **Blessing of the Animals.** Angelenos bring their pets, some of them dressed to the nines in rhinestone collars and top hats, and line up to have Cardinal Roger Mahoney splash holy water on them. Mariachis play, snacks are served, goats and girls giggle. Gathering begins at noon, and ceremonies start around 2 p.m. For information, try www.olvera-street.com or call ☎ **213-628-7164.** Easter Sunday, usually in April.

Look both ways before you cross the street in Long Beach during the **Toyota Grand Prix.** Indy-level drivers from around the world race through the streets for several days. For information, call ☎ **888-82-SPEED** (888-827-7333) or ☎ **562-436-9953** or go to www.longbeachgp.com. Mid-April.

May

The **Venice Art Walk** is a festival of art and music, with self- and docent-guided tours of local studios, galleries, and even collectors' homes, plus installations, auctions, and receptions. Proceeds benefit the Venice Family Clinic. Call ☎ **310-392-8630** or go to www.venicefamilyclinic. org. Mid-May.

June

West Hollywood, also known as "Christopher Street West," rivals the Castro in San Francisco for the size of its gay and lesbian community. For more than 30 years, the celebration of **Gay & Lesbian Pride Day** has gotten bigger and bigger. (Local gays observe that it's turned into Gay Pride Week.) The parades, dance tents, food booths, costumes, and general revelry must be seen to be believed. Call ☎ **323-658-8700** or visit www.lapride.org (and be prepared for pounding disco/house music from your computer's speakers). Third or fourth weekend in June.

July

For more than 60 years, the **Festival of the Arts** and **Pageant of the Masters** have been held in Laguna Beach. The incredible Pageant of the Masters re-creates works of art using live people; it sounds goofy, but it's astonishing. The Festival of the Arts is a juried (meaning artists are chosen by a committee) fine-arts show with 150 exhibitors.

Across the street, local artists and craftspeople are showcased all summer long at the **Sawdust Art Festival** (www.sawdustartfestival. org). Tickets for the Festival of the Arts and the Pageant of the Masters must be arranged in advance; call ☎ **800-487-FEST** (800-487-3378) or 949-494-3030 or go to www.foapom.com. July through August.

The lotus flower is valued throughout Asia as medicine, food, and a symbol of purity, so the **Lotus Festival** in Echo Park is as good a reason as any for a celebration of Asian culture. Echo Park contains the largest lotus-flower bed in the United States and is close to neighborhoods like Little Tokyo, Chinatown, Koreatown, and Filipino and other local Asian-Pacific communities, including Vietnamese, Laotian, Indonesian, and many more. Thousands come to celebrate their cultures or experience new ones though music, art, dragon-boat races, carnival games and rides, and a vast array of food in one of the city's oldest and prettiest parks. Call ☎ **213-485-8743** or go to www.laparks.org/grifmet/lotus.htm. On Park Avenue between Glendale and Echo Park Boulevards. Mid-July.

August

For more than 30 years, in an effort to promote neighborhood harmony, the **Sunset Junction Street Fair** (located at 3600 through 4200 Sunset Blvd.) has brought together all the disparate elements of Silver Lake into one music-loving, snack-chewing, mingling, sweaty, harmonious whole. The Latino gang members and homosexual leather boys, not to mention artists, punks, and ordinary families, all come together for two days to enjoy three stages of local music, carnival rides, and 200 booths of crafts, food (fabulous Mexican, wonderful Thai, and our favorite, bacon-wrapped hot dogs; see Chapter 10), and community service and outreach. It's usually hot and crowded (and gets more crowded as the day goes on), but it's a hoot. Note that street parking fills up, so you may have a hike to the actual site. For more information, call ☎ 323-661-7771 or go to www.sunsetjunction.org. Toward the end of August.

September

It's got pig races. **The Los Angeles County Fair,** one of the largest county fairs in the world, also has agriculture and cake-baking contests and all that sort of thing, only on a massive scale. It's held in Pomona, 30 miles east of downtown Los Angeles. Call ☎ 909-623-3111 or go to www.fairplex.com. Throughout September.

October

The American Film Institute's **Los Angeles International Film Festival** is not quite as prestigious or groundbreaking as it used to be (or so hardcore film buffs sniff), but it's still a must for those with an interest in cinema and usually features early viewings of major works. Call ☎ 323-856-7707 or go to www.afifest.com. Late October or early November.

November

Los Angeles' ties to Hispanic culture are never more evident than on the **Dia De Los Muertos,** or **Day of the Dead.** Once a year, ancestors are honored with the construction of colorful and elaborate altars on or around family graves, while special meals (including candy skulls and *pan de muerto*) are prepared and eaten at the cemetery. Art and other special events pop up around town at this time, but the best formal celebration is held at Hollywood Forever Cemetery. Many compete for prizes for the best altar, and observers enjoy the snacks and folklore performances. Check ahead; the celebration was held a week early in 2004. Go to www.hollywoodforever.com or www.olvera-street.com. November 1, though events can begin mid-October.

It's the *other* Pasadena parade. Started as a response to the Tournament of Roses Parade on New Year's Day, the **Doo Dah Parade** features such memorable entries as the Synchronized Marching Briefcase Drill Team, the Precision BBQ Team, the Hello Dalai Lamas, Queen Tequila Mockingbird, and the Little Old Ladies from Hooters. An utter, utter hoot. Call ☎ 626-440-7379 or visit www.pasadenadoodahparade.com. Usually Thanksgiving weekend.

As kids, we would stay up late to catch Santa, who always brought up the rear of the **Hollywood Christmas Parade.** Now we watch the parade to mock the B-level celebs who ride in it. Call ☎ 323-962-8400. Sunday after Thanksgiving.

Part II
Planning Your Trip to Los Angeles

The 5th Wave   By Rich Tennant

"The closest hotel room to the Santa Monica Pier I can get you for that price is in Bakersfield."

In this part . . .

*H*ere we discuss all your travel planning: Choosing a method of transportation, working with a travel agent, deciding whether to go the package-tour route, managing your money, and finalizing those little last-minute details like making dinner reservations at hot local restaurants, packing the right clothes, and weighing your travel insurance options. We also provide extra planning tips for families, people with disabilities, and gay and lesbian travelers.

Chapter 4

Managing Your Money

● ●

In This Chapter

▶ Gauging how you'll spend your money
▶ Using traveler's checks and credit cards
▶ Cutting costs from your trip
▶ Dealing with a lost or stolen wallet

● ●

*L*os Angeles isn't a breathtakingly expensive town. But hotel rooms can be costly, and dining can take a bite out of your wallet (see Chapters 9 and 10 for some budget alternatives). In this chapter, we lay out the major expenditures for your trip to Los Angeles.

Planning Your Budget

Your major, hard-to-avoid costs come in the form of hotel rooms, transportation, restaurants, and admissions to high-priced attractions.

Lodging

A mantra for your trip planning should be: "The Internet is my friend." Many hotels (and other establishments) offer special deals available only through the Web, and we suggest you check there before booking a room. You can also use the information you find to bargain down a room price, especially during the slow seasons, when prices drop dramatically. If you aren't bringing children along, you may want to consider staying Downtown, where very nice hotel rooms go for considerably less than rooms in other areas on weekend nights.

Transportation

The costs for getting into the city vary according to your mode of transportation. From Los Angeles International Airport (LAX), you can either drive yourself in a **rental car,** take a **cab, car service,** or **shuttle,** or take **public transportation.** Cabs charge an airport fee of $2.50 in addition to a $2 pickup fee and $2 per mile (plus tip). The shuttles and vans that operate to and from the airport charge on a per-person basis: From LAX to Santa Monica, for example, it's $18 (plus a $2 tip). A car service typically charges fares of around $40 to $45 (including a

$1.50 airport pickup fee), depending on where you are dropped off. You can also take public transportation on the Metropolitan Transit Authority (MTA) combination light rail/bus system to and from LAX for less than $2.

Transportation around the city is a little tricky. We recommend **renting a car.** Finding the best rental-car deal just means putting in some time — call travel agents, search the Web, call car-rental companies yourself, and pit them all against each other.

But even if you get a good deal, you're still going to have **parking costs** — lots around town charge from $2 to $20, depending on location and time of day or night. Keep in mind that some lots, near or directly connected with certain attractions, offer discounts in the form of rebates: If you bring back a ticket from the attraction, you can get $2 or so back. (For example, a lot north of Hollywood on Las Palmas, on the west side of the street, offers rebates following screenings at the Egyptian Theatre.)

Public transportation is a fine idea if you plan on doing limited travel around the city; the bus system is great in Santa Monica, and the subway works well between Hollywood, Universal City, and Downtown. You can also do some advance trip planning through the Metropolitan Transit Authority's Web site (www.mta.net) or by giving them a call (☎ 800-COMMUTE/266-6883). On the Web site, just plug in when and where you want to go, and your designated route pops up, complete with bus and subway lines. In Downtown, in addition to the subway, you can take the DASH, a commuter bus that flits around the entire area and costs only 25¢ one way, including one transfer.

If you intend to rely on cabs to get around, keep in mind that cabs charge a $2 pickup fee and then $2 per mile, and the meter keeps ticking if you get stuck in traffic, a common occurrence. A 10-percent to 15-percent tip is standard.

Dining

Food in L.A. need not set your budget back; we constantly assert that the best food in town comes in the form of cheap ethnic places and other hole-in-the-wall joints. We've made a number of suggestions in Chapter 10, but you can also consider purchasing *Hungry? Los Angeles: A Guide to the City's Greatest Diners, Dives, Cafeterias and Coffee Shops!*, edited by Kristin L. Petersen (Really Great Books), a handy guide to all the eateries that are affordable and savory in a town that has an incredible variety of dining cultures.

Sightseeing

Prices for attractions vary, of course. The behemoth **Disneyland** is pretty costly (see Chapters 17–19), but check the park Web site at www.disneyland.com before you go. Multiday "Hopper Passes" are offered at a substantial discount, and other offers come up all the time. It's practically worth designing a trip around the times these great deals come up. Package tours can help with that expense as well. Also, **Universal Studios** (www.universalstudioshollywood.com), itself none too cheap, offers a number of deals through its Web site, including multivisit passes and combo offers with other Southern California area attractions.

But not all local attractions hit the middle double digits. In fact, some are downright cheap. One of the city's top attractions, the **Getty Museum,** is free, though there is a $5-per-car parking fee. Only the fit can walk up to the museum, but you can take advantage of the free park-and-ride service from a lot at Sepulveda Boulevard and Constitution Avenue (located just north of Wilshire Boulevard). A couple of local bus lines also service it (but by then, depending on how many people you're paying for, you may as well take your car in). The **California ScienCenter** is free, and so are the **La Brea Tar Pits,** though the museum attached is not. The **Museum of Jurassic Technology** costs a mere $5 for adults over 21, and kids under 18 get into the **Los Angeles County Museum of Art** for free.

And speaking of free, the **beach** is, though nearby parking is usually around $5. So just walk from your hotel or your street parking a few blocks away. The **Venice Boardwalk** and **Santa Monica Pier** are also free, and Thursday nights during the summer free concerts are held at the latter. All summer long, mostly at night, but not exclusively, free concerts are held at the **California Plaza** near the Museum of Contemporary Art. Again, parking will likely be problematic, so just take the MetroRail. And way-high-up seats for many summertime **Hollywood Bowl** concerts go for as little as $1. (All these prices are subject to change, of course, but not by too terribly much.)

Shopping

This category depends entirely on you, your budget, and those things you absolutely can't live without. You can pay full price here almost any time of the year, but know that the major department stores and malls tend to have sales during most holiday weekends (Labor Day, Presidents' Day, Memorial Day, and so forth) and back-to-school events beginning mid-August. The *Los Angeles Times* is crammed with full-page ads just before these events, often with coupons that promise still more discounts.

The biggest shopping event of the year is the **Divine Design sale,** held the first week in December to benefit Project Angel Food, a Los Angeles–based organization that delivers food and necessities to homebound people with chronic illnesses. Hundreds of clothing, housewares, and accessory designers donate extra goods and samples, which are then offered to the public at steep discounts that sharply decline each day. Nervy shoppers try to stick it out as long as they can, watching the prices plummet from 20-percent discounts to 75 percent off by the last day; call Project Angel Food (☎ 323-845-1800) or visit its Web site at www.angelfood.org for more information.

If you're looking for unique bargains, check out the flea markets and vintage-wear shops throughout the city (see Chapter 12). **The Farmer's Market** (see p. 200) has many stands that feature wonderful fresh breads, prepared foods, and even clothing at low prices.

Nightlife

If you plan to attend any big events, such as the symphony, opera, or major theater offerings, keep in mind that if you purchase your tickets through Ticketmaster, you pay a hefty per-ticket handling fee that can be anywhere from $2 to $15 extra per ticket.

Cover prices vary from nightclub to nightclub (from $5 to $20), but remember that parking rates get steeper as the week progresses, and you can expect to pay up to $30 on the Sunset Strip Friday and Saturday nights. Taking a cab might be the smarter way to visit club land.

Cutting Costs — but Not the Fun

Even those with very deep pockets don't like to throw money away. There's a little cost cutter in everyone. Here are some savvy money-saving tips for chipping away at your vacation budget.

- ✔ **Go off-season.** If you can travel at nonpeak times (winter, unless it's during a convention, or Oscar weekend, for example), you'll find hotel prices almost half the price of peak months.

- ✔ **Travel midweek.** If you can travel on a Tuesday, Wednesday, or Thursday, you may find cheaper flights to your destination. When you ask about airfares, see if you can get a cheaper rate by flying on a different day. For more tips on getting a good fare, see Chapter 5.

- ✔ **Try a package tour.** For many destinations, you can book airfare, hotel, ground transportation, and even some sightseeing just by making one call to a travel agent or packager, for a price much less than if you put the trip together yourself. (See Chapter 5 for more on package tours.)

- ✔ **Reserve a room with a refrigerator and coffee maker.** You don't have to slave over a hot stove to cut a few costs; several motels have minifridges and coffee makers. Buying supplies for breakfast will save you money — and probably calories.

- ✔ **Always ask for discount rates.** Membership in AAA, frequent-flier plans, trade unions, AARP, or other groups may qualify you for savings on car rentals, plane tickets, hotel rooms, and even meals. Ask about everything; you may be pleasantly surprised.

- ✔ **Ask if your kids can stay in the room with you.** A room with two double beds usually doesn't cost any more than one with a queen-size bed. And many hotels won't charge you the additional-person rate if the additional person is pint-size and related to you. Even if you have to pay $10 or $15 extra for a rollaway bed, you'll save hundreds by not taking two rooms.

✔ **Try expensive restaurants at lunch instead of dinner.** Lunch tabs are usually a fraction of what dinner would cost at a top restaurant, and the menu often boasts many of the same specialties. And Chapter 10 suggests a number of cheap eats — the best food in L.A. is found at inexpensive ethnic restaurants, though we also suggest a number of takeout places.

✔ **Get out of town.** In many places, big savings are just a short drive or taxi ride away. Hotels in the San Fernando Valley often are cheaper than in the heart of L.A. You'll need a rental car to go anywhere, though. See Chapter 9 for more on hotels.

✔ **Don't rent a gas guzzler.** Renting a smaller car is cheaper, and you save on gas to boot. Unless you're traveling with kids and need lots of space, don't go beyond the economy size. For more on car rentals, see Chapter 7.

✔ **Skip the souvenirs.** Your photographs and your memories could be the best mementos of your trip. If you're concerned about money, you can do without the T-shirts, key chains, salt-and-pepper shakers, mouse ears, and other trinkets.

Handling Money

Most travelers these days use a combination of traveler's checks, plastic, and cash to cover their expenses in L.A. Certainly, having a credit card makes sense if you plan to reserve a hotel room or rent a car (although we list some rental-car companies that don't require credit cards; see Chapter 7). And with the prevalence of ATMs throughout the city, cash is easy to access on the spot. This section gives a quick look at your best options when paying for your vacation. (For more on ATMs and getting cash where you need it in Los Angeles, see Chapter 4.)

You're the best judge of how much cash you feel comfortable carrying, or what alternative form of currency is your favorite. That's not going to change much on your vacation. True, you'll probably be moving around more and incurring more expenses than you generally do (unless you happen to eat out every meal when you're at home), and you may let your mind slip into vacation gear and not be as vigilant about your safety as when you're in work mode. But, those factors aside, the only type of payment that won't be quite as available to you away from home is your personal checkbook.

Using ATMs and carrying cash

The **Cirrus** (☎ 800-424-7787; www.mastercard.com) and **PLUS** (☎ 800-843-7587; www.visa.com) networks span the globe; look at the back of your bank card to see which network you're on, then call or check online for ATM locations at your destination. Be sure you know your personal identification number (PIN) before you leave home and be sure to find out your daily withdrawal limit before you depart. Also keep in mind that many banks impose a fee every time your card is used at a different bank's ATM, and that fee can be higher for international transactions (up to $5 or more) than for domestic ones (where they're rarely more than $1.50). On top of this, the bank from which you withdraw cash may charge its own fee. To compare banks' ATM fees within the United States, use www.bankrate.com. For international withdrawal fees, ask your bank.

Los Angeles is rife with ATMs. Banks like **Wells Fargo** (☎ 800-956-4442; www.wellsfargo.com), **Bank of America** (www.bankofamerica.com), and **Washington Mutual** (www.wamu.com) are everywhere, mostly linked by Cirrus, Star, and Maestro, as well as bank links. Malls and convenience marts like 7-11 have ATMs and charge a fee for their use.

If you want the safest ATM in town, especially in the wee hours of the morning, drop in on the friendly folks at the **Hollywood Division of the Los Angeles Police Department** (1358 N. Wilcox Ave.). You will be charged unless you're a member of Co-Op Network, but it's open 24/7 and has plenty of free parking.

Charging ahead with credit cards

Credit cards are a safe way to carry money: They also provide a convenient record of all your expenses and generally offer relatively good exchange rates. You can also withdraw cash advances from your credit cards at banks or ATMs, provided you know your PIN. If you've forgotten yours, or didn't know you had one, call the number on the back of your credit card and ask the bank to send it to you. It usually takes five to seven business days, though some banks will provide the number over the phone if you tell them your mother's maiden name or some other personal information.

Some credit-card companies recommend that you notify them of any impending trip abroad so that they don't become suspicious when the card is used numerous times in a foreign destination and block your charges. Even if you don't call your credit-card company in advance, you can always call the card's toll-free emergency number if a charge is refused — a good reason to carry the number with you (it's often printed on the back). But perhaps the most important lesson here is to carry more than one card with you on your trip; a card might not work for any number of reasons, so having a backup is the smart way to go.

Toting traveler's checks

These days, traveler's checks are less necessary because most cities have 24-hour ATMs that allow you to withdraw small amounts of cash as needed. However, keep in mind that you will likely be charged an ATM withdrawal fee if the bank is not your own, so if you're withdrawing money every day, you might be better off with traveler's checks — provided you don't mind showing identification every time you want to cash one.

You can get traveler's checks at almost any bank. **American Express** offers denominations of $20, $50, $100, $500, and (for cardholders only) $1,000. You'll pay a service charge ranging from 1 percent to 4 percent. You can also get American Express traveler's checks over the phone by calling ☎ 800-221-7282; Amex gold and platinum cardholders who use this number are exempt from the 1-percent fee.

Visa offers traveler's checks at Citibank locations nationwide as well as at several other banks. The service charge ranges between 1.5 percent and 2 percent; checks come in denominations of $20, $50, $100, $500, and $1,000. Call ☎ 800-732-1322 for information. AAA members can obtain Visa checks without a fee at most AAA offices or by calling ☎ 866-339-3378. **MasterCard** also offers traveler's checks. Call ☎ 800-223-9920 for a location near you.

 If you choose to carry traveler's checks, be sure to keep a record of their serial numbers separate from your checks in the event that they are stolen or lost. You'll get a refund faster if you know the numbers.

Dealing with a lost or stolen wallet

Be sure to contact all of your credit-card companies the minute you discover your wallet has been lost or stolen, and file a report at the nearest police precinct. Your credit-card company or insurer may require a police-report number or record of the loss. Most credit-card companies have an emergency toll-free number to call if your card is lost or stolen; they may be able to wire you a cash advance immediately or deliver an emergency credit card within a day or two. Call the following emergency numbers in the United States:

- ✔ **American Express:** ☎ 800-221-7282 (for cardholders and traveler's check holders)
- ✔ **MasterCard:** ☎ 800-307-7309 or 636-722-7111
- ✔ **Visa:** ☎ 800-847-2911 or 410-581-9994

For other credit cards, call the toll-free number directory at ☎ 800-555-1212.

If you need emergency cash over the weekend when all banks and American Express offices are closed, you can have money wired to you via **Western Union** (☎ 800-325-6000; www.westernunion.com).

Identity theft or fraud is a potential complication of losing your wallet, especially if you've lost your driver's license along with your cash and credit cards. Notify the major credit-reporting bureaus immediately;

placing a fraud alert on your records may protect you against liability for criminal activity. The three major U.S. credit-reporting agencies are **Equifax** (☎ 800-766-0008; www.equifax.com), **Experian** (☎ 888-397-3742; www.experian.com), and **TransUnion** (☎ 800-680-7289; www.transunion.com). Finally, if you've lost all forms of photo ID, call your airline and explain the situation; they might allow you to board the plane if you have a copy of your passport or birth certificate and a copy of the police report you've filed.

Taxing Matters

The sales tax on most commonly purchased items (except for snack foods) is 8.25 percent in all of Los Angeles County. For hotels, the tax is 14 percent; for rental cars, 8.25 percent plus $1.25 per day.

Chapter 5

Getting to Los Angeles

*Y*ou've bought the *Risky Business* shades, perfected the hipster slouch, and even changed your name to oh, say, Stone or Tiffany. Now all you have to do is get here!

Flying to Los Angeles

Package tours work for some, but if you're a plan-it-yourselfer, the following information can help you plot the perfect trip on your own.

The City of Angels is an international hub and thus is served by most major commercial airlines. Of the five airports in the Los Angeles area, most visitors fly into Los Angeles International Airport (LAX) (☎ 310-646-5252; www.lawa.org/lax).

Within North America

Airlines that fly within North America on regularly scheduled flights to and from Los Angeles at LAX are

- ✔ **Air Canada** (☎ 888-247-2262; www.aircanada.ca), which flies from Vancouver, Toronto, and Montreal.

- ✔ **Alaska Airlines** (☎ 800-426-0333; www.alaskaair.com).

- ✔ **American Airlines** (☎ 800-433-7300; www.aa.com).

- ✔ **American Trans Air** (☎ 800-225-2995; www.ata.com).

- ✔ **America West Airlines** (☎ 800-235-9292; www.americawest.com).

- ✔ **Continental Airlines** (☎ 800-525-0280; www.continental.com).

- ✔ **Delta Air Lines** (☎ 800-221-1212; www.delta.com).

✔ **Frontier Airlines** (☎ **800-432-1359;** www.frontierairlines.com).

✔ **Hawaiian Airlines** (☎ **800-367-5320;** www.hawaiianair.com).

✔ **Midwest Express** (☎ **800-452-2022;** www.midwestexpress.com).

✔ **Northwest Airlines** (☎ **800-225-2525;** www.nwa.com).

✔ **Southwest Airlines** (☎ **800-435-9792;** www.southwest.com).

✔ **Spirit Airlines** (☎ **800-772-7117;** www.spiritair.com).

✔ **United Airlines** (☎ **800-241-6522;** www.united.com).

✔ **US Airways** (☎ **800-428-4322;** www.usairways.com).

International flights

From **Great Britain,** you can get regularly scheduled flights to Los Angeles on **American Airlines** and **United** (contact information for both is in the preceding section), as well as the following:

✔ **British Airways** (☎ **800-247-9297** in the continental United States and ☎ **0345/222-111** or 0845/77-333-77 in Britain; www.british-airways.com)

✔ **Virgin Atlantic Airways** (☎ **800-862-8621** in the continental United States and ☎ **0293/747-747** in Britain; www.virgin-atlantic.com)

✔ **Air New Zealand** (☎ **800-262-1234** or 800-262-2468 in the United States; ☎ **800-663-5494** in Canada; ☎ **0800/737-767** in New Zealand; www.airnewzealand.com)

From **Australia,** you can get regularly scheduled flights to Los Angeles from **Sydney** on carriers mentioned previously in this chapter, such as **American Airlines, United,** and **Air New Zealand,** as well as **Qantas** (☎ **800-227-4500** in the United States and ☎ **612/9691-3636** in Australia; www.qantas.com). From Melbourne, you can take **American Airlines** and **Qantas.** From **New Zealand,** you can get regularly scheduled flights to Los Angeles on **Air New Zealand, United,** and **Qantas.**

From **Canada,** you can get regularly scheduled flights to Los Angeles from **Vancouver** on **Air Canada, United, Alaska,** and **Northwest**. From **Toronto,** you can take **American Airlines** and **Air Canada.** From **Montreal,** you can take **Air Canada.** (Contact information for all these carriers is listed earlier in this chapter.)

Getting the best deal on your airfare

Competition among the major U.S. airlines is unlike that of any other industry. Every airline offers virtually the same product (a coach seat is a coach seat is a coach seat), yet prices can vary by hundreds of dollars.

Business travelers who need the flexibility to buy their tickets at the last minute and change their itineraries at a moment's notice — and who want to get home before the weekend — pay (or at least their companies pay) the premium rate, known as the *full fare.* But if you can book your ticket far in advance, stay over Saturday night, and are willing to travel midweek (Tuesday, Wednesday, or Thursday), you can qualify for the least expensive price — usually a fraction of the full fare. On most flights, even the shortest hops within the United States, the full fare is close to $1,000 or more, but a 7- or 14-day advance purchase ticket may cost less than half of that amount. Obviously, planning ahead pays.

The airlines also periodically hold sales, in which they lower the prices on their most popular routes. These fares have advance purchase requirements and date-of-travel restrictions, but you can't beat the prices. As you plan your vacation, keep your eyes open for sales, usually in seasons of low travel volume. You almost never see a sale around the peak summer vacation months of July and August, or around Thanksgiving or Christmas.

Consolidators, also known as *bucket shops,* are great sources for international tickets, although they usually can't beat the Internet on fares within North America. Start by looking in Sunday newspaper travel sections; U.S. travelers should focus on the *New York Times, Los Angeles Times,* and *Miami Herald.* For less-developed destinations, small travel agents who cater to immigrant communities in large cities often have the best deals.

Bucket-shop tickets are usually nonrefundable or rigged with stiff cancellation penalties, often as high as 50 percent to 75 percent of the ticket price, and some put you on charter airlines with questionable safety records.

Several reliable consolidators are worldwide and available on the Net. **STA Travel** (☎ 800-781-4040; www.statravel.com), the world's leader in student travel, offers good fares for travelers of all ages. **ELTExpress** (☎ 800-TRAV-800; www.flights.com) started in Europe and has excellent fares worldwide but particularly to that continent. Flights.com also has "local" Web sites in 12 countries. **FlyCheap** (☎ 800-FLY-CHEAP; www.1800fly cheap.com) is owned by package-holiday megalith MyTravel and so has especially good access to fares for sunny destinations. **Air Tickets Direct** (☎ 800-778-3447; www.airticketsdirect.com) is based in Montreal and leverages the currently weak Canadian dollar for low fares; it'll also book trips to places that U.S. travel agents won't touch, such as Cuba.

Booking your flight online

The "big three" online travel agencies, **Expedia** (www.expedia.com), **Travelocity** (www.travelocity.com), and **Orbitz** (www.orbitz.com) sell most of the air tickets bought on the Internet. (Canadian travelers should try www.expedia.ca and www.travelocity.ca; United Kingdom residents can go for expedia.co.uk and opodo.co.uk.) Each has different business deals with the airlines and may offer different fares on the same flights, so shopping around is wise. Expedia and Travelocity will also send you a **notification** when a cheap fare becomes available to your favorite destination. Of the smaller travel agency Web sites, **SideStep** (www.side step.com) receives good reviews from users. It's a browser add-on that purports to "search 140 sites at once" but in reality only beats competitors' fares as often as other sites do.

Great **last-minute deals** are available through free weekly services provided directly by the airlines. Most of these deals are announced on Tuesdays or Wednesdays and must be purchased online. Most are only valid for travel that weekend, but some (such as Southwest's) can be booked weeks or months in advance. Sign up for weekly alerts at airline Web sites or check megasites that compile comprehensive lists of last-minute specials, such as **Smarter Living** (smarterliving.com). For last-minute trips, www.site59.com in the United States and www.last minute.com in Europe often have better deals than the major-label sites.

If you're willing to give up some control over your flight details, use an *opaque fare service* like **Priceline** (www.priceline.com) or **Hotwire** (www.hotwire.com). Both offer rock-bottom prices in exchange for travel on a "mystery airline" at a mysterious time of day, often with a mysterious change of planes en route. The mystery airlines are all major, well-known carriers — and the possibility of being sent from Philadelphia to Chicago via Tampa is remote. But your chances of getting a 6 a.m. or 11 p.m. flight are pretty high. Hotwire tells you flight prices before you buy; Priceline usually has better deals than Hotwire, but you have to play their "name your price" game. See **Bidding For Travel** (www.biddingfortravel.com) for tips on playing the opaque fare game. *Note:* In 2004, Priceline added nonopaque service to its roster. You now have the option to pick exact flights, times, and airlines from a list of offers — or opt to bid on opaque fares as before.

 Great last-minute deals are also available directly from the airlines themselves through a free service called *E-savers*. Each week, the airline sends you a list of discounted flights, usually leaving the upcoming Friday or Saturday and returning the following Monday or Tuesday. You can sign up for all the major airlines at one time by logging on to **Smarter Living** (www.smarterliving.com), or you can go to each individual airline's Web site. Airline sites also offer schedules, flight booking, and information on late-breaking bargains.

One more Web site: We're a bit biased, but we think **Frommer's** (www. frommers.com) is an excellent and comprehensive travel-planning resource, with daily travel tips and bargains, reviews, monthly vacation giveaways, and a popular message-board section where readers post queries and share advice.

Driving to Los Angeles

Los Angeles is accessible from a number of freeways — after all, it was once on the much-missed Route 66 and is still on the Christopher Columbus Trans-Continental Highway, otherwise known as the 10, which runs pretty much straight across the southern part of the United States. Just point your car west and be sure to hit the brakes when you see the ocean. See map on p. 62.

Arriving by Other Means

By train

But now that you've thought of planes and automobiles, you want to remember trains. Los Angeles is serviced by the national passenger railway **Amtrak** and is accessible from any U.S. city that has rail service. For schedules and rate information, call ☎ **800-USA-RAIL** (800-872-7245) or check online at www.amtrak.com.

By bus

Greyhound serves Los Angeles, with connections to other cities throughout the country. The main station for arriving buses is downtown at 1716 E. Seventh St., east of Alameda (☎ **800-231-2222;** www.greyhound.com).

Choosing a Package Tour

Package tours are not the same thing as escorted tours. *Package tours* are simply a way to buy the airfare, accommodations, and other elements of your trip (such as car rentals, airport transfers, and sometimes even activities) at the same time and often at discounted prices — kind of like one-stop shopping.

Package tours do have their advantages — someone else does most of the arranging for you, and you almost always save money. But among the disadvantages are limited choices, such as unremarkable hotels or a fixed itinerary that doesn't allow for an extra day of shopping.

How to tell the deals from the duds

Once you start looking at packages, you're going to find that the sheer number of choices may overwhelm you — but don't let them. Use these tips to help you figure out the right package for you.

✔ **Do your homework.** Read through this guide and decide what attractions you want to visit and what type of accommodations you think you'll like. Compare the rack rates that we list in Chapter 9 against the discounted rates being offered by the packagers to see whether you're actually being given a substantial savings.

✔ **Read the fine print.** Make sure you know exactly what's included in the price you're being quoted and what's not. Some packagers include airfare plus lots of extra discounts on restaurants and activities, but others don't even include airfare in the price.

✔ **Know what you're getting yourself into — and if you can get yourself out of it.** Before you commit to a package, make sure that you know how much flexibility you have. Some packagers require ironclad commitments, whereas others charge minimal fees for changes or cancellations. Ask about the packagers' restrictions and cancellations policies up front.

Where to find the packager for you

The best place to start looking is the **travel section of your local Sunday newspaper.** Also check the ads in the back of **national travel magazines** such as *Travel & Leisure, National Geographic Traveler,* and *Condé Nast Traveler.* Then call a few package tour companies and ask them to send you their brochures. The biggest **hotel chains** also offer packages. If you already know where you want to stay, call the hotel and ask if it offers land/air packages.

Airlines also often package their flights together with accommodations. Although you can book most airline packages directly with the airline itself, your local travel agent can also do it for you. Prices are usually comparable to what you can get from other packagers.

Most airline packages reward you with miles based not only on the flight but on all the dollars you spend — which can really add up and earn you credit toward your next vacation. Call the airlines or check their Web sites for the latest offers (see Table 5-1).

Table 5-1	Major Airlines' Frequent-Flier Service Numbers and Web Sites	
Airline	*Phone Number*	*Web Site*
Alaska	☎ 800-654-5669	http://mileageplan.alaskaair.com
American	☎ 800-882-8880	www.aa.com/aadvantage
Continental	☎ 800-621-7467	http://onepass.continental.com
Delta	☎ 800-323-2323	www.delta.com/skymiles
Northwest	☎ 800-447-3757	www.nwa.com/freqfly
Southwest	☎ 800-248-4377	www.southwest.com/rapid_rewards
United	☎ 800-421-2655	www.mileageplus.com
US Airways	☎ 800-428-4322	www.usairways.com/dividend miles

Package deals to Los Angeles

For lots of destinations, a package tour that includes airfare, hotel, and transportation to and from the airport costs less than the hotel alone on a tour you book yourself. That's because packages are sold in bulk to tour operators, who resell them to the public. It's kind of like buying your vacation at a buy-in-bulk store — except the tour operator is the one who buys the 1,000-count box of garbage bags and resells them 10 at a time at a cost that undercuts the local supermarket.

Package tours can vary. Some offer a better class of hotels than others; others provide the same hotels for lower prices. Some book flights on scheduled airlines; others sell charters. In some packages, your choice of accommodations and travel days may be limited. Some let you choose between escorted vacations and independent vacations; others allow you to add on just a few excursions or escorted daytrips (also at discounted prices) without booking an entirely escorted tour.

To find package tours, check out the travel section of your local Sunday newspaper or the ads in the back of national travel magazines such as *Travel & Leisure, Condé Nast Traveler,* and *Frommer's Budget Travel Magazine.* **Liberty Travel** (call ☎ **888-271-1584** to find the store nearest you; www.libertytravel.com) is one of the biggest packagers in the Northeast and usually boasts a full-page ad in Sunday papers.

Another good source of package deals is the airlines themselves. Most major airlines offer air/land packages, including **American Airlines Vacations** (☎ 800-321-2121; www.aavacations.com), **Delta Vacations** (☎ 800-221-6666; www.deltavacations.com), **Continental Airlines Vacations** (☎ 800-301-3800; www.covacations.com), and **United Vacations** (☎ 888-854-3899; www.unitedvacations.com). Several big **online travel agencies** — Expedia, Travelocity, Orbitz, Site59, and Lastminute.com — also do a brisk business in packages. If you're unsure about the pedigree of a smaller packager, check with the Better Business Bureau in the city where the company is based or go online at www.bbb.org. If a packager won't tell you where it's based, don't fly with them.

The following offer specific L.A. package deals. Always call and find out rates beforehand to make sure that the package is the more economical way to go.

✔ **American Airlines Vacations:** California packages have included Los Angeles and the beaches, with accommodations for two or more nights and optional sightseeing tours of Disneyland, Catalina, and Hollywood. Car rental and airport/hotel transfers are available (☎ **800-321-2121;** www.aavacations.com).

✔ **American Express Vacation Packages:** American Express offers custom packaging through any of its retail outlets, or you can ask your American Express agent about special Southern California packages (☎ **800-346-3607;** www.americanexpress.com/travel).

✔ **Amtrak Vacations:** L.A. package includes round-trip Amtrak coach rail, moderate lodging for two nights, and a four-hour sightseeing tour. Available options include Universal Studios Hollywood, Disneyland, and rental car (☎ **877-YES-RAIL** (877-937-7245); www.amtrak.com).

✔ **Continental Airlines Vacations:** Includes round-trip airfare from select cities, hotel accommodations, economy rental car, plus discounts on admission to Autry Museum of Western Heritage, Movieland Wax Museum, and Ripley's Believe It or Not Museum. Optional features include Catalina Island Adventure Tour and admission to Universal Studios Hollywood, Disneyland, and Knott's Berry Farm (☎ **800-634-5555**; www.coolvacations.com).

✔ **Southwest Airlines Vacations:** Packages include round-trip airfare, hotel accommodations for 2 to 14 nights, an Alamo economy rental car, and a FunBook discount coupon booklet. Optional features include airport/hotel transfers and passes for Universal Studios Hollywood and Disneyland (☎ **800-243-8372**; www.swavacations.com).

✔ **United Vacations:** United Vacations offers a wide array of lodging options to fit individual taste and budget. California vacation packages include hotel accommodations, Alamo two-door economy car rental, 10 percent off food, beverages, and merchandise, plus VIP seating at Planet Hollywood. Optional features include airport/hotel transfers and admission to Universal Studios Hollywood and Disneyland (☎ **888-854-3899**; www.unitedvacations.com).

✔ **Universal Studios Hollywood Vacations:** Each package includes unlimited admission to Universal Studios Hollywood (☎ **800-224-3838**; www.universalstudios.com) for the entire length of your stay; VIP priority entrance to Jurassic Park: The Ride, Back to the Future: The Ride, Backdraft, The E.T. Adventure, and the Backlot Tram Tour; hotel accommodations; and a Universal City Coupon Book. Optional airfare and rental car features are available.

✔ **US Airways Vacations:** Southern California packages include round-trip airfare, hotel accommodations for 2 to 21 nights, an Alamo rental car with upgrade, and lunch at Planet Hollywood with VIP seating (☎ **800-455-0123**; www.usairwaysvacations.com).

Chapter 6

Catering to Special Travel Needs or Interests

● ●

In This Chapter

▶ Traveling with kids in tow

▶ Discovering special deals for seniors

▶ Enabling the disabled

▶ Finding gay-friendly resources and communities

● ●

*L*os Angeles puts out the welcome mat for visitors of all stripes, sizes, and ages. This chapter gives you some travel tips and resource information for travelers with specific needs or preferences.

Traveling with the Brood: Advice for Families

You can relax; Los Angeles is a fine place to bring children. The city offers, among so many other things, a huge beach, a pier, a few amusement parks (including one called Disneyland), a zoo, and recreational parks galore. Yes, L.A. is kid friendly, and if you bring children, you won't be alone; babies are the new hip accessories here!

Note: Throughout this book, we mark the best hotels, restaurants, and activities for children with a Kid Friendly icon.

Most kids, unless they loathe water, will want to spend a great deal of time at the **beach.** You can vary this potentially dull routine with jaunts to the **Santa Monica Pier,** with its shops, food stalls, and mini-amusement park, plus one delightful merry-go-round. You can also stroll on the **Venice Ocean Front Walk,** which does have its freak quotient (from street musicians to hippies hawking wares), but the oddballs are usually harmless and they add to the people-watching fun. Plus, it's a great place for roller/in-line skating, biking, and more.

Los Angeles has quite a few **parks,** from small municipal ones (the best are in Santa Monica and Beverly Hills) to giant places like Griffith

Park, the largest municipal park in the country. In addition to acres of Santa Monica mountains to hike through, Griffith Park has a lovely merry-go-round and Travel Town, a place where kids ride little trains and sometimes ponies. Try www.citysearch.com for a complete list of options or go to www.ci.la.ca.us/RAP for the City of Los Angeles' Department of Recreation and Parks' individual listings.

Of course, there is **Disneyland;** its appeal to kids is so massive and legendary that it's hard to sum up in a few pithy words. Suffice it to say that every kid ought to go at least once, as part of his or her birthright. (See Chapters 17–19.)

Your kid may or may not be into **museums,** but keep in mind that the Getty has an *entire section* devoted to children's activities (some hands-on approaches to art), while the California Science Center is designed just for kids. The Natural History Museum is getting a bit musty, but the Discovery Room is still great fun and contains live snakes.

Families are probably better off basing themselves in **Santa Monica;** it's more pedestrian friendly (to say nothing of beach accessible), and you'll see as many locals (accompanied by kids themselves, as likely as not) as tourists, whereas Hollywood is mostly tourists (and few kids), and West Hollywood is more for the shopper or well-dressed mom seeking her yoga and cappuccino fix. Downtown really isn't for families.

Keep in mind that L.A. is spread out, and it does take a bit of driving to get from, say, Santa Monica to Hollywood (and Disneyland takes at least an hour), distances that can seem like an eternity to kids. So prep them for a certain amount of driving time as best you can, and be sure to have on hand their favorite toys, games, and road snacks. If you need car seats for the little ones, you can rent from **Babyland,** 1782 S. La Cienega Blvd., north of I-10 (☎ 310-836-2222), or 7134 Topanga Canyon Blvd., Woodland Hills (☎ 818-704-7848), which also rents strollers and cribs.

For babysitting services, try the **Baby-Sitters Guild** (☎ 323-938-8372 or 818-552-2229), or ask your hotel concierge for a local recommendation.

Familyhostel (☎ 800-733-9753; www.learn.unh.edu/familyhostel) takes the whole family, including kids ages 8 to 15, on moderately priced domestic and international learning vacations. Lectures, field trips, and sightseeing are guided by a team of academics.

You can find good family-oriented vacation advice on the Internet from sites like the **Family Travel Forum** (www.familytravelforum.com), a comprehensive site that offers customized trip planning; **Family Travel Network** (www.familytravelnetwork.com), an award-winning site that offers travel features, deals, and tips; **Traveling Internationally with Your Kids** (www.travelwithyourkids.com), a comprehensive site that offers customized trip planning; and **Family Travel Files** (www.the familytravelfiles.com), which offers an online magazine and a directory of off-the-beaten-path tours and tour operators for families.

If you have enough trouble getting your kids out of the house in the morning, dragging them thousands of miles away may seem like an insurmountable challenge. But family travel can be immensely rewarding, giving you new ways of seeing the world through smaller pairs of eyes.

Making Age Work for You: Advice for Seniors

Oh, the jokes we can make about seniors in L.A. (like "they were outlawed along with smoking"), but we won't. It's true that people here don't seem to age properly, thanks in part to a religious commitment to exercise and healthy diet, but even more so to an affinity for plastic surgeons. You may feel that you're the oldest person in L.A., but that's only because the woman next to you, who looks 40, is keeping up appearances through the magic of special effects. She's really 80.

But by and large, L.A. is a perfectly enjoyable destination for the visiting senior, apart from the heartbreak of how the town has neglected its heritage. Too many fantastic monuments to the Golden Age of Hollywood are gone, and you'll have a moment of shock as you read off names on the Walk of Fame or slip your foot into a cement print at Grauman's, only to hear a teen or twentysomething ask, "So who's John Wayne?" But then you notice how good it feels to be out in the sun, and you think, "Oh, whatever."

Seniors have a wealth of travel resources to choose from in Los Angeles. Most attractions in the city offer senior discounts, as do public transportation and movie theaters. Members of **AARP** (formerly known as the American Association of Retired Persons), 601 E St. NW, Washington, DC 20049 (☎ **888-687-2277** or 202-434-2277; www.aarp.org), get discounts on hotels, airfares, and car rentals. AARP offers members a wide range of benefits, including *AARP: The Magazine* and a monthly newsletter. Anyone over 50 can join.

Many reliable agencies and organizations target the 50-plus market. **Elderhostel** (☎ 877-426-8056; www.elderhostel.org) arranges study programs for those aged 55 and over (and a spouse or companion of any age) in the United States and in more than 80 countries around the world. Most courses last five to seven days in the United States (two to four weeks abroad), and many include airfare, accommodations in university dormitories or modest inns, meals, and tuition. **ElderTreks** (☎ **800-741-7956;** www.eldertreks.com) offers small-group tours to off-the-beaten-path or adventure-travel locations, restricted to travelers 50 and older. **INTRAV** (☎ **800-456-8100;** www.intrav.com) is a high-end tour operator that caters to the mature, discerning traveler, not specifically seniors, with trips around the world that include guided safaris, polar expeditions, private-jet adventures, and small-boat cruises down jungle rivers.

Recommended publications offering travel resources and discounts for seniors include the quarterly magazine *Travel 50 & Beyond* (www.travel50andbeyond.com); *Travel Unlimited: Uncommon Adventures for the Mature Traveler* (Avalon); *101 Tips for Mature Travelers,* available from Grand Circle Travel (☎ 800-221-2610 or 617-350-7500; www.gct.com); *The 50+ Traveler's Guidebook* (St. Martin's Press); and *Unbelievably Good Deals and Great Adventures That You Absolutely Can't Get Unless You're Over 50* (McGraw-Hill), by Joann Rattner Heilman.

Accessing Los Angeles: Advice for Travelers with Disabilities

Los Angeles is a very, *very* politically correct town, so fortunately every place is handicap accessible. (Okay, maybe not certain seedy bars. But you'd be surprised.) Sidewalks have dips at the curb to ease wheelchair movement, and restaurants and hotels all come properly equipped.

The main problem is that this is not a pedestrian-friendly town; you have to rely on a car to get everywhere. To this end, we suggest staying in Santa Monica or Beverly Hills, where the sightseeing is less reliant on cars. The Third Street Promenade in Santa Monica is an outdoor street closed to vehicular traffic, and most pleasant to be on, while both Santa Monica and Venice have sidewalks and pathways along the beaches.

Many travel agencies offer customized tours and itineraries for travelers with disabilities. **Flying Wheels Travel** (☎ 507-451-5005; www.flyingwheelstravel.com) offers escorted tours and cruises that emphasize sports and private tours in minivans with lifts. **Access-Able Travel Source** (☎ 303-232-2979; www.access-able.com) offers extensive access information and advice for traveling around the world with disabilities. **Accessible Journeys** (☎ 800-846-4537 or 610-521-0339; www.disabilitytravel.com) is a valuable resource for wheelchair travelers and their families and friends.

Avis Rent-a-Car has an "Avis Access" program that offers such services as a dedicated 24-hour toll-free number (☎ 888-879-4273) for customers with special travel needs; special car features such as swivel seats, spinner knobs, and hand controls; and accessible bus service.

Organizations that offer assistance to disabled travelers include the **MossRehab** (www.mossresourcenet.org), which provides a library of accessible-travel resources online; **SATH (Society for Accessible Travel and Hospitality)** (☎ 212-447-7284; www.sath.org; annual membership fees: $45 adults, $30 seniors and students), a valuable Web site with informed recommendations on destinations, access guides, travel agents, tour operators, vehicle rentals, and companion services; and the **American Foundation for the Blind** (AFB) (☎ 800-232-5463;

www.afb.org), a referral resource for the blind or visually impaired that includes information on traveling with Seeing Eye dogs.

For more information specifically targeted to travelers with disabilities, the community Web site **iCan** (www.icanonline.net/channels/travel/index.cfm) has destination guides and several regular columns on accessible travel. Also check out the quarterly magazine *Emerging Horizons* ($14.95 per year, $19.95 outside the United States; www.emerginghorizons.com); **Twin Peaks Press** (☎ 360-694-2462; http://disabilitybookshop.virtualave.net/blist84.htm), offering travel-related books for travelers with special needs; and *Open World Magazine,* published by SATH (subscription: $13 per year, $21 outside the United States).

Out and About: Advice for Gay and Lesbian Travelers

Los Angeles probably ranks behind only New York City and San Francisco (and then only barely) on the gay-friendly meter. In fact, **West Hollywood,** located right in the heart of Los Angeles, is predominantly gay (and known as Christopher Street West, after the longtime heart of gay Manhattan). Here you find the bulk of the gay bars, restaurants, shopping, and other resources, plus an annual Gay Pride Parade of considerable dimensions in June. The nightlife in West Hollywood is quite fabulous, as you can well imagine.

Other gay-friendly neighborhoods include the **Silverlake** area, just east of Hollywood and north of Downtown; **Studio City/North Hollywood,** in the San Fernando Valley; and portions of **Long Beach.** But really, you can feel free to hold hands anywhere you're likely to go in the city.

The **Los Angeles Gay and Lesbian Center** (1625 N. Schrader Blvd., Los Angeles; ☎ **323-993-7400;** www.laglc.org; open from 9 a.m. to 9 p.m. weekdays) can provide a full range of services, from finding the most popular nightclub to counseling and HIV assistance.

After that, your best bet for finding out what's going on in Los Angeles is to pick up one of the free local gay publications such as *Frontiers, In,* and *Odyssey.* They're packed with directories, events, maps, and more, and you can find them at most of the gay bars in town.

Online, start at www.westhollywood.com, a fairly comprehensive compendium of events, directories, classifieds, and more. You can also visit the *Los Angeles Times* at www.latimes.com/extras/outinla/index.html. The paper's "Out in LA" section is certainly not as "complete" as they bill it to be, but it's a good place to start.

For more general travel information and packages, **The International Gay and Lesbian Travel Association (IGLTA)** (☎ **800-448-8550** or

954-776-2626; www.iglta.org) is the trade association for the gay and lesbian travel industry and offers an online directory of gay- and lesbian-friendly travel businesses; go to the Web site and click on "Members."

Many agencies offer tours and travel itineraries specifically for gay and lesbian travelers. **Above and Beyond Tours** (☎ **800-397-2681;** www.abovebeyondtours.com) is the exclusive gay and lesbian tour operator for United Airlines. **Now, Voyager** (☎ **800-255-6951;** www.nowvoyager.com) is a well-known San Francisco–based, gay-owned and -operated travel service. **Olivia Cruises & Resorts** (☎ **800-631-6277** or 510-655-0364; www.olivia.com) charters entire resorts and ships for exclusive lesbian vacations and offers smaller group experiences for gay and lesbian travelers.

The following travel guides are available at most travel bookstores and gay and lesbian bookstores, or you can order them from **Giovanni's Room** bookstore, 1145 Pine St., Philadelphia, PA 19107 (☎ **215-923-2960;** www.giovannisroom.com) or locally at **A Different Light Bookstore,** 8853 Santa Monica Blvd. (☎ **310-854-6601;** www.adlbooks.com): *Frommer's Gay & Lesbian Europe,* an excellent travel resource (www.frommers.com); *Out and About* (☎ **800-929-2268** or 415-644-8044; www.outandabout.com), which offers guidebooks and a newsletter ($20/year; ten issues) packed with solid information on the global gay and lesbian scene; *Spartacus International Gay Guide* (Bruno Gmünder Verlag; www.spartacusworld.com/gayguide/) and *Odysseus,* both good, annual English-language guidebooks focused on gay men; the *Damron* guides (www.damron.com), with separate, annual books for gay men and lesbians; and *Gay Travel A to Z: The World of Gay & Lesbian Travel Options at Your Fingertips* by Marianne Ferrari (Ferrari International; Box 35575, Phoenix, AZ 85069), a very good gay and lesbian guidebook series.

Chapter 7

Taking Care of the Remaining Details

. . . .

In This Chapter

▶ Getting the lowdown on rental cars and travel insurance

▶ Staying healthy on your trip

▶ Accessing the Internet and using your cell phone

▶ Planning ahead for the latest airline security measures

. . . .

*Y*ou've purchased your ticket, reserved your hotel room, and even plotted out a day-to-day itinerary for your trip to Los Angeles. Now is the time to attend to the little details of your trip, from renting a car to reserving a table at a hot restaurant to deciding what clothes, shoes, assorted gear, and bare necessities to pack.

Renting a Car: Weighing Your Options

Here we have a true paradox. Los Angeles is miserable to drive in, through, and around. Car culture here is second only to Detroit's. It's bad to drive here. Oh, not Manhattan-at-rush-hour bad, but bad.

And yet, you have to drive for two related reasons:

▶ Los Angeles is a sprawling locale; it's the largest city, in terms of land mass and sheer geographical dimensions, in the United States — and that's not taking into account the cities attached to it, such as Pasadena, or cities just to the south of it, such as Anaheim (home to a little place called Disneyland), places that you, the visitor, will surely want to visit.

▶ The size and the ring of interrelated cities would lead you to assume that L.A. must have a fabulous public transportation system, right? Pardon us while we fall to the floor laughing. Yes, we have a bus system and a subway, but neither is up to par. You can find more details about getting around the city in Chapter 8, but for now, just accept that you're going to be part of the traffic problem in L.A. Unless, of course, you plan to be here for only a couple of days and stay in a highly central location (like Downtown or Hollywood) and don't plan to leave that neighborhood much, if at all.

With that in mind, you may indeed decide to rent a car during your stay in Los Angeles. Luckily, doing so is a snap. All major car-rental agencies have offices in the city; many can be found at the airport or in major hotels. For a complete listing of **major car-rental agencies,** with phone numbers and Web sites, go to the Quick Concierge appendix at the back of the book.

- ✔ In general, car-rental rates in Los Angeles are more reasonable than those found in other U.S. markets. Still, you'll find that prices can vary greatly, depending on the size of the car, the length of time you keep it, where and when you pick it up and drop it off, and a host of other factors. Asking a few key questions may save you hundreds of dollars.

- ✔ Weekend rates may be lower than weekday rates. If you're keeping the car five or more days, a weekly rate may be cheaper than the daily rate. Ask if the rate is the same for pickup Friday morning as it is Thursday night.

- ✔ Some companies may assess a drop-off charge if you don't return the car to the same rental location; others, notably National, don't.

- ✔ Check whether the rate is cheaper if you pick up the car at a location in town rather than at the airport

- ✔ Find out whether age is an issue. Many car-rental companies add on a fee for drivers under 25, while some don't rent to them at all.

- ✔ If you see an advertised price in your local newspaper, be sure to ask for that specific rate; otherwise, you may be charged the standard (higher) rate. Don't forget to mention membership in AAA, AARP, and trade unions. These memberships usually entitle you to discounts ranging from 5 percent to 30 percent.

- ✔ Check your frequent-flier accounts. Not only are your favorite (or at least the most frequently used) airlines likely to have sent you discount coupons, but most car rentals add at least 500 miles to your account.

- ✔ As with other aspects of planning your trip, using the Internet can make comparison shopping for a car rental much easier. You can check rates at most of the major agencies' Web sites. Plus, all the major travel sites — **Travelocity** (www.travelocity.com), **Expedia** (www.expedia.com), **Orbitz** (www.orbitz.com), and **Smarter Living** (www.smarterliving.com), for example — have search engines that can dig up discounted car-rental rates. Just enter the car size you want, the pickup and return dates, and location, and the server returns a price. You can even make the reservation through any of these sites.

In addition to the standard rental prices, other optional charges apply to most car rentals (and some not-so-optional charges, such as taxes). The *Collision Damage Waiver* (CDW), which requires you to pay for damage to the car in a collision, is covered by many credit-card companies. Check with your credit-card company before you go so you can avoid paying this hefty fee (as much as $20 a day).

The car-rental companies also offer additional *liability insurance* (if you harm others in an accident), *personal accident insurance* (if you harm yourself or your passengers), and *personal effects insurance* (if your luggage is stolen from your car). Your insurance policy on your car at home probably covers most of these unlikely occurrences. However, if your own insurance doesn't cover you for rentals, or if you don't have auto insurance, definitely consider the additional coverage (ask your car-rental agent for more information). Unless you're toting around the Hope Diamond and don't want to leave it in your car trunk anyway, you can probably skip the personal-effects insurance, but driving around without liability or personal accident coverage is never a good idea.

Some companies also offer *refueling packages,* in which you pay for your initial full tank of gas up front and can return the car with an empty gas tank. The prices can be competitive with local gas prices, but you don't get credit for any gas remaining in the tank. If you reject this option, you pay only for the gas you use, but you have to return the car with a full tank or face charges of $3 to $4 a gallon for any shortfall. If you usually run late, and a fueling stop may make you miss your plane, you're a perfect candidate for the refueling package option.

For tips on driving in Los Angeles, see p. 38.

Playing It Safe with Travel and Medical Insurance

Three kinds of travel insurance are available: trip-cancellation insurance, medical insurance, and lost-luggage insurance. The cost of travel insurance varies widely, depending on the cost and length of your trip, your age and health, and the type of trip you're taking, but expect to pay between 5 percent and 8 percent of the vacation itself. Here is our advice on all three.

- ✔ **Trip-cancellation insurance** helps you get your money back if you have to back out of a trip, if you have to go home early, or if your travel supplier goes bankrupt. Allowed reasons for cancellation can range from sickness to natural disasters to the State Department's declaring your destination unsafe for travel.

- ✔ A good resource is **Travel Guard Alerts,** a list of companies considered high-risk by Travel Guard International (www.travelinsured. com). Protect yourself further by paying for the insurance with a credit card — by law, consumers can get their money back on goods and services not received if they report the loss within 60 days after the charge is listed on their credit-card statement.

Note: Many tour operators include insurance in the cost of the trip or can arrange insurance policies through a partnering provider. Make sure the tour company is a reputable one. Some experts suggest you avoid buying insurance from the tour or cruise company you're traveling with, reasoning it's better to buy from a third-party insurer than to put all your money in one place.

✔ For domestic travel, buying **medical insurance** for your trip doesn't make sense for most travelers. Most existing health policies cover you if you get sick away from home — but check before you go, particularly if you're insured by an HMO.

✔ **Lost luggage insurance** is not necessary for most travelers. On domestic flights, checked baggage is covered up to $2,500 per ticketed passenger. On international flights (including U.S. portions of international trips), baggage coverage is limited to approximately $9.07 per pound, up to approximately $635 per checked bag. If you plan to check items more valuable than the standard liability, see if your valuables are covered by your homeowner's policy, get baggage insurance as part of your comprehensive travel-insurance package, or buy Travel Guard's "BagTrak" product. Don't buy insurance at the airport because it's usually overpriced. Be sure to take any valuables or irreplaceable items with you in your carry-on luggage because many valuables (including books, money, and electronics) aren't covered by airline policies.

✔ If your luggage is lost, immediately file a lost-luggage claim at the airport, detailing the luggage contents. For most airlines, you must report delayed, damaged, or lost baggage within four hours of arrival. The airlines are required to deliver luggage, once found, directly to your house or destination free of charge.

For more information, contact one of the following recommended insurers: **Access America** (☎ 866-807-3982; www.accessamerica.com); **Travel Guard International** (☎ 800-826-4919; www.travelguard.com); **Travel Insured International** (☎ 800-243-3174; www.travelinsured.com); and **Travelex Insurance Services** (☎ 888-457-4602; www.travelex-insurance.com).

Staying Healthy When You Travel

Getting sick will ruin your vacation, so we *strongly* advise against it, of course.

For domestic trips, most reliable health-care plans provide coverage if you get sick away from home. For travel abroad, you may have to pay all medical costs up front and be reimbursed later. For information on purchasing additional medical insurance for your trip, see the previous section.

Talk to your doctor before leaving on a trip if you have a serious and/or chronic illness. For conditions such as epilepsy, diabetes, or heart problems, wear a **MedicAlert identification tag** (☎ **888-633-4298;** www.medic alert.org), which immediately alerts doctors to your condition and gives them access to your records through Medic Alert's 24-hour hotline. Contact the **International Association for Medical Assistance to Travelers (IAMAT)** (☎ **716-754-4883** or, in Canada, 416-652-0137; www. iamat.org) for tips on travel and health concerns in the countries you're visiting, and lists of local, English-speaking doctors. The United States's **Centers for Disease Control and Prevention** (☎ **800-311-3435;** www.cdc.gov) provides up-to-date information on health hazards by region or country and offers tips on food safety.

Staying Connected by Cell Phone or E-Mail

Using a cell phone across the United States

Just because your cell phone works at home doesn't mean it'll work elsewhere in the country (thanks to our nation's fragmented cell phone system). It's a good bet that your phone will work in major cities, though our personal cell phone conks out all over L.A. But take a look at your wireless company's coverage map on its Web site before heading out — T-Mobile, Sprint, and Nextel are particularly weak in rural areas. If you need to stay in touch at a destination where you know your phone won't work, **rent** a phone from **InTouch USA** (☎ **800-872-7626;** www.intouch global.com) or a rental car location, but beware that you'll pay $1 a minute or more for airtime.

If you're venturing deep into national parks, you may want to consider renting a **satellite phone** *(satphone),* which is different from a cell phone in that it connects to satellites rather than ground-based towers. A satphone is more costly than a cell phone but works where there's no cellular signal and no towers. Unfortunately, you'll pay at least $2 per minute to use one, and it only works where you can see the horizon (that is, usually not indoors). In North America, you can rent Iridium satellite phones from **RoadPost** (☎ **888-290-1606** or 905-272-5665; www. roadpost.com). InTouch USA offers a wider range of satphones but at higher rates. As of this writing, satphones are very expensive to buy.

If you're not from the United States, you'll be appalled at the poor reach of our **GSM (Global System for Mobiles) wireless network,** which is used by much of the rest of the world. Your phone will probably work in most major U.S. cities; it definitely won't work in many rural areas. (To see where GSM phones work in the United States, check out www. t-mobile.com/coverage/national_popup.asp.) You may or may not be able to send SMS (text messaging) home. Assume nothing — call your wireless provider and get the full scoop. In a worst-case scenario, you can always rent a phone; InTouch USA delivers to hotels.

Accessing the Internet away from home

Travelers have any number of ways to check their e-mail and access the Internet on the road. Of course, using your own laptop — or even a PDA (personal digital assistant) or electronic organizer with a modem — gives you the most flexibility. But even if you don't have a computer, you can still access your e-mail and even your office computer from cybercafes.

It's hard nowadays to find a city that *doesn't* have a few cybercafes. Although there's no definitive directory for cybercafes — these are independent businesses, after all — two places to start looking are at www.cybercaptive.com and www.cybercafe.com.

Aside from formal cybercafes, most **youth hostels** nowadays have at least one computer connected to the Internet. And most **public libraries** across the world offer Internet access free or for a small charge. Avoid **hotel business centers** unless you're willing to pay exorbitant rates.

Most major airports now have **Internet kiosks** scattered throughout their gates. The kiosks' clunkiness and high price mean they should be avoided whenever possible.

To retrieve your e-mail, ask your **Internet Service Provider (ISP)** if it has a Web-based interface tied to your existing e-mail account. If your ISP doesn't have such an interface, you can use the free **mail2web** service (www.mail2web.com) to view and reply to your home e-mail. For more flexibility, you may want to open a free, Web-based e-mail account with **Yahoo! Mail** (http://mail.yahoo.com). (Microsoft's Hotmail is another popular option, but Hotmail has severe spam problems.) Your home ISP may be able to forward your e-mail to the Web-based account automatically.

If you need to access files on your office computer, look into a service called **GoToMyPC** (www.gotomypc.com). The service provides a Web-based interface for you to access and manipulate a distant PC from anywhere — even a cybercafe — provided your "target" PC is on and has an always-on connection to the Internet (such as with Road Runner cable). The service offers top-quality security, but if you're worried about hackers, use your own laptop rather than a cybercafe computer to access the GoToMyPC system.

If you are bringing your own computer, the buzzword in computer access to familiarize yourself with is **wi-fi** (wireless fidelity). More and more hotels, cafes, and retailers are signing on as wireless "hotspots" where you can get high-speed connection without cable wires, networking hardware, or a phone line. You can get wi-fi connection one of several ways. Many laptops sold in the last year have built-in wi-fi capability (an 802.11b wireless Ethernet connection). Mac owners have their own networking technology called Apple AirPort. For those with older computers, an 802.11b/**wi-fi card** (around $50) can be plugged into your laptop. You sign up for wireless access service much as you do cell phone service, through a plan offered by one of several commercial companies that have made wireless service available in airports, hotel lobbies, and coffee shops, primarily in the United States (followed by the United Kingdom and Japan). **T-Mobile Hotspot** (www.t-mobile.com/hotspot) serves up wireless connections at more than 1,000 Starbucks coffee shops nationwide. **Boingo** (www.boingo.com) and **Wayport** (www.wayport.com) have set up networks in airports and high-class hotel lobbies. **IPass** providers also give you access to a few hundred wireless hotel-lobby setups. Best of all, you don't need to be staying at the Four Seasons to use the hotel's network; just set yourself up on a nice couch in the lobby. The companies' pricing policies can be byzantine, with a variety of monthly, per-connection, and per-minute plans, but in general you pay around $30 a month for limited access — and prices are likely to get even more competitive as more and more companies jump on the wireless bandwagon.

To locate **free wireless networks** in cities around the world, go to www.personaltelco.net/index.cgi/WirelessCommunities.

If wi-fi is not available at your destination, most business-class hotels throughout the world offer dataports for laptop modems, and a few thousand hotels in the United States and Europe now offer free high-speed Internet access using an Ethernet network cable. It's usually cheaper to bring your own cable because most hotels rent them for around $10. **Call your hotel in advance** to see what your options are.

In addition, major Internet Service Providers have **local access numbers** around the world, allowing you to go online by simply placing a local call. Check your ISP's Web site or call its toll-free number and ask how to use your current account away from home and how much it will cost. If you're traveling outside the reach of your ISP, the **iPass** network has dial-up numbers in most of the world's countries. You'll have to sign up with an iPass provider, who will then tell you how to set up your computer for your destination(s). For a list of iPass providers, go to www.ipass.com and click on "Individual Purchase." One solid provider is **i2roam** (☎ **866-811-6209** or 920-235-0475; www.i2roam.com).

Wherever you go, bring a **connection kit** of the right power and phone adapters, a spare phone cord, and a spare Ethernet network cable — or find out whether your hotel supplies them to guests.

Keeping Up with Airline Security Measures

With the federalization of airport security, security procedures at U.S. airports are more stable and consistent than ever. Generally, you'll be fine if you arrive at the airport **one hour** before a domestic flight and **two hours** before an international flight; if you show up late, tell an airline employee, and she'll probably whisk you to the front of the line.

Bring a **current, government-issued photo ID** such as a driver's license or passport. Keep your ID at the ready to show at check-in, the security checkpoint, and sometimes even the gate. (Children under 18 do not need government-issued photo IDs for domestic flights, but they do for international flights to most countries.)

In 2003, the Transportation Security Administration (TSA) phased out **gate check-in** at all U.S. airports. And **e-tickets** have made paper tickets nearly obsolete. Passengers with e-tickets can beat the ticket-counter lines by using airport **electronic kiosks** or even **online check-in** from your home computer. Online check-in involves logging on to your airline's Web site, accessing your reservation, and printing out your boarding pass — and the airline may even offer you bonus miles to do so! If you're using a kiosk at the airport, bring the credit card you used to book the ticket or your frequent-flier card. Print out your boarding pass from the kiosk and simply proceed to the security checkpoint with your pass and a photo ID. If you're checking bags or looking to snag an exit-row seat, you will be able to do so using most airline kiosks. Even the smaller airlines are employing the kiosk system, but always call your airline to make sure these alternatives are available. **Curbside check-in** is also a good way to avoid lines, although a few airlines still ban curbside check-in; call before you go.

Security checkpoint lines are getting shorter than they were during 2001 and 2002, but some doozies remain. If you have trouble standing for long periods of time, tell an airline employee; the airline will provide a wheelchair. Speed up security by **not wearing metal objects** such as big belt buckles. If you've got metallic body parts, a note from your doctor can prevent a long chat with the security screeners. Keep in mind that only **ticketed passengers** are allowed past security except for folks escorting disabled passengers or children.

Federalization has stabilized **what you can carry on** and **what you can't.** The general rule is that sharp things are out, nail clippers are okay, and food and beverages must be passed through the X-ray machine — but that security screeners can't make you drink from your coffee cup. Bring food in your carryon rather than checking itbecause explosive-detection machines used on checked luggage have been known to mistake food (especially chocolate, for some reason) for bombs. Travelers in the United States are allowed one carry-on bag, plus a "personal item" such as a purse, briefcase, or laptop bag. Carry-on hoarders can stuff all sorts of things into a laptop bag; as long as it has a laptop in it, it's still considered a personal item. The TSA has issued a list of restricted items; check its Web site (www.tsa.gov/public/index.jsp) for details.

Look for Travel Sentry certified **luggage locks** at luggage or travel shops and Brookstone stores (you can buy them online at www.brookstone.com). These locks, approved by the TSA, can be opened by luggage inspectors with a special code or key. For more information on the locks, visit www.travelsentry.org. If you use something other than TSA-approved locks, your lock will be cut off your suitcase if a TSA agent needs to hand-search your luggage.

Part III
Settling Into Los Angeles

The 5th Wave   By Rich Tennant

In this part . . .

This section helps you orient yourself in the city, whether you arrive by plane, train, bus, or car. We tell you the best ways to get from the airport to your hotel. And which hotel will that be? We give you a list of the city's best, from classic to chic to family friendly. Then, we move on to all the tasty details of where to dine on highbrow cuisine, snacks on the go, and locals' favorite dishes. For those of you on a budget, we list cost-cutting tips and budget alternatives.

Chapter 8

Arriving and Getting Oriented

. . . .

In This Chapter

▶ Getting there by plane, train, or automobile
▶ Getting from the airport to your hotel
▶ Discovering L.A. neighborhoods
▶ Making your way around the city

. . . .

*Y*ou've arrived, in the most literal sense, in a sprawling, steaming caldron of light and energy. What, pray tell, do you do next? In this chapter, we tell you how to get to your hotel with ease and confidence as well as give you a concise orientation of Los Angeles neighborhoods.

Arriving by Plane

Los Angeles International Airport — more familiarly known as LAX — is the third busiest airport in the world (☎ 310-646-5252; www.lawa.org/lax). But you don't need to sit down and sob. The airport got a fine redesign for the 1984 Olympics, one that put departing traffic on an upper level and arriving traffic on a lower level, so that helped with traffic in and out. Signage is good; arriving travelers are clearly directed to baggage claim, taxis, and so forth. One bit of confusion is directly outside, where there are a number of shuttle stops for shuttles to hotels, airport parking lots (for long-term parking), the city, and so on. Read the signs on the shuttles carefully, or just ask someone. The airport is 9½ miles from Santa Monica and 16 miles from Hollywood. From the airport, it's approximately a half-hour drive to Downtown, and a 40-minute drive to West Hollywood, depending on the traffic.

You may arrive at the small but busy **Burbank-Glendale-Pasadena Airport,** some 8 miles northeast of Hollywood (☎ 818-840-8840; www.burbankairport.com). It has only two terminals and is easy to get around — everyone is filtered to the same stretch of a few-yards-long sidewalk. From the airport, it's about a 25-minute drive to Downtown, and a 20-minute drive to West Hollywood, depending on the traffic.

Getting to your hotel by taxi

The easiest way to get to your hotel is probably by **cab.** Taxis can be found curbside on the Lower/Arrival Level islands in front of each terminal at LAX under the yellow sign indicating "Taxis." Cabs charge an airport fee of $2.50, in addition to a $2 pickup fee, and $2 per mile, plus additional charges when you get stuck in traffic, a common occurrence. Tipping your cab driver 10 percent to 15 percent is customary. Expect to pay between $31 and $40 (plus tip), depending on your destination. Taxis can accommodate up to five passengers.

At Burbank, you find cab racks on the island in front of each terminal, with clearly marked signs and a cab coordinator. Taxi fare will depend on your final destination, but expect to pay between $20 and $30 to Hollywood.

Getting to your hotel by rental car

All the major car-rental agencies have branches at the airport (for a listing of agencies with phone numbers and Web sites, go to the Appendix in the back of the book). Each company provides shuttle service between the terminals and its off-site lot.

For tips on getting the best car-rental rates and information on car-rental insurance options, see Chapter 7.

Getting to your hotel by public transportation

You can also take the **Metropolitan Transit Authority** (**MTA**) Metro Rail public transportation from the airport; a combination **light rail/bus system** runs to and from an outer parking lot at LAX. Free shuttle service is provided from the airport to the MTA Aviation Station; wait for the shuttle under the LAX Shuttle & Airline Connections sign on the Lower/Arrival Level island in front of each terminal and board the G shuttle to the Aviation Station to board light rail.

It's a long and tedious but cheap journey — less than $2 ($1.25 plus 25¢ for transfers) — and it involves transferring buses in fairly marginal, sort-of-dicey neighborhoods. It's not for the faint of heart, either, because one portion of the light rail trip involves standing on a platform right next to the fast-moving freeway, with only a cement barrier and chain-link fence between you and a slew of BMWs and big rigs.

For details, call ☎ **800-COMMUTE** (or 808-266-6883) or go to the MTA Web site at www.mta.net, which provides a handy click-through trip planner with directions on planning your commute by public transport.

The **Metro Green Line** also goes *to* the airport; you catch it by transferring from the Hollywood Red Line westbound to the Green Line. But relying on public transport to get you to the airport when you depart the

City of Angels is fraught with the possibility of missing your flight if there are delays, missed connections, or other man-made disasters.

Burbank Airport is serviced by Metro Rail Monday through Friday and MTA buses daily. The Burbank Airport Web site (www.burbankairport.com) offers links to Metro schedules.

Getting to your hotel by shuttle or van

If you're traveling alone, **Prime Time Shuttle** or **Super Shuttle** may be the right choice because prices are on a per-person basis. From either LAX or Burbank, claim your bags, then step out to the clearly marked shuttle-stop island and contact the Shuttle Guest Service Representative.

 With shuttles, you travel with others who are going to the same approximate area, so if the van is crowded, it may take a while to get to your location. Also, you must wait until a van going to your destination comes around.

 Schedule return trips at least 24 hours in advance, and be sure to call to confirm. The agent will tell you what time you'll be picked up, usually several hours before your flight.

Typical approximate fares from LAX are $18 to Santa Monica and $22 to Beverly Hills or Hollywood. Rates are the same for returns to the airport. Tipping the driver $2 is customary. (**Super Shuttle** ☎ **800-258-3826** or 310-782-6600 in Los Angeles; **Prime Time Shuttle** ☎ **800-RED-VANS** (800-733-8267) or 310-342-7200, which is usually the cheaper of the two.)

Getting to your hotel by car service

For groups of two or more, a **car service** may be the most pleasant and reasonable alternative. Make reservations with your credit card. After you land, get your luggage, and once you arrive curbside, call the 800 number from a pay phone or from your cell phone, giving your location and description. A Lincoln Towncar, which seats up to four passengers, will appear shortly and take you to your destination.

Typical fares from LAX are $50 to Santa Monica, $60 to Beverly Hills, and $65 to Hollywood. For an additional $15 to $25, you'll be met in the baggage-carousel arrival section, with your name on a placard. Tipping 15 percent to 20 percent is customary. The rates are the same for returns to the airport. For car service, call **ExecuCar** (☎ **800-413-4020**) or join every single entertainment exec we know and try **Music Express** (☎ **818-526-0211**) or join the likes of the American Idol contestants and various rock stars by calling **Diva Limousines** (☎ **800-427-DIVA** or 310-278-3482).

Arriving by Car

As you may expect from the unofficial "car capital of the world," Los Angeles is accessible via a variety of freeways. From the north, take

Los Angeles Freeways

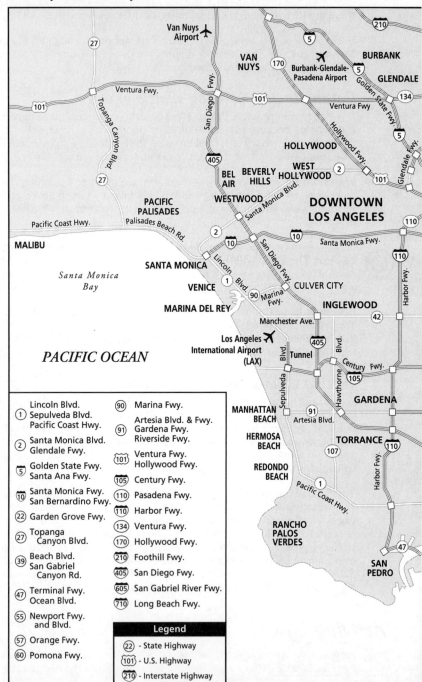

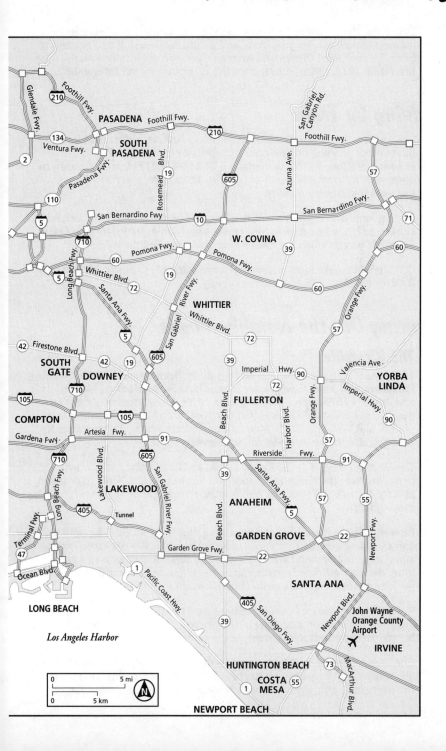

either the **101 Freeway** or **Interstate 5** into Los Angeles. **Interstate 15** connects you from Nevada, Utah, and points northeast. If you're coming from the southeast (Texas and Arizona), you can get into Los Angeles via **Interstate 10.** Arriving from the south? Enter the city via **Interstate 5.**

Arriving by Train

Los Angeles is a major destination for many Amtrak routes, and fares fluctuate depending on seasonal and special promotions. Trains arrive at **Union Station,** 800 N. Alameda St. (☎ **213-624-0171**), on the northern edge of Downtown just north of U.S. 101. From here, you can take one of the taxis that line up outside.

Among Amtrak's regular routes, the *Sunset Limited* travels from Orlando, Florida, to L.A. with stops in New Orleans and San Antonio, and the *Coast Starlight* travels along the Pacific Coast between Seattle and L.A.

Call ahead to make sure that services are available (Amtrak: ☎ **800-USA-RAIL** or 800-872-7245; www.amtrak.com).

Figuring Out the Neighborhoods

The Westside

This area is actually several neighborhoods: **Brentwood, Bel Air, Pacific Palisades,** and **Venice,** which are part of L.A.; **Santa Monica, Malibu,** and **Beverly Hills,** which are their own cities. Santa Monica is right on the ocean. Pacific Palisades is just north of Santa Monica, Malibu north of that, and Venice to Santa Monica's immediate south. Brentwood is to the east, and then comes Bel Air and Beverly Hills.

The Westside begins at the Pacific Ocean and heads east until Doheny Drive, north to the mountains (once you hit the top, you begin to descend into the Valley), and south to Pico Boulevard (except for Venice, which keeps going).

Beverly Hills is expensive and excessive, but it's wonderful for walking and snooping outside the homes of legendary (usually deceased) movie stars on palm-tree-lined streets. It also has several very nice (if a bit intimidatingly groomed) parks and is one of the safest neighborhoods in the city, thanks to a most zealous police force.

Hotels and restaurants cost more here (and the dining isn't that interesting), and the shopping is some of the priciest in the world (you have heard, perhaps, of Rodeo Drive?).

The area around **Santa Monica** and **Venice** is the number-one area for any tourist, and why not? It's the beach, for Pete's sake. The weather is the best in the city, with mostly clear skies and moderate temperatures.

And here you'll find the nicest walking opportunities — pretty residential neighborhoods full of palm trees and Spanish architecture, great shopping (especially on the pedestrian, blocks-long Third Street Promenade), and outdoor dining options galore.

It's lovely, for sure, but it does have its drawbacks, not the least of which is hotel price and the occasional outburst of foggy, chilly weather. Except for certain chic locales, you find the highest hotel rates here — and the closer you get to the water, the more you'll pay.

West Hollywood

West Hollywood (WeHo) is an interesting mix. It's inhabited in part by Orthodox and Conservative Jews, for which this has been a longtime central location, in a neighborhood that stretches into the area immediately south of Beverly Hills, along Pico Boulevard.

But that identity has long since been eclipsed by its "Christopher Street West" nickname; this is the heart of L.A. gay life, especially around Santa Monica Boulevard east of La Cienega Boulevard. South of here (through 6th Street) is a healthy dose of shops and cafes, catering to the beautiful but less-stodgy, more-hip people.

Parts of West Hollywood are visually dull but trendy and thus expensive. Nearly all are within walking distance of great shopping and dining. Several streets (most notably Melrose and Third) are full of cafes and boutiques, which makes for great strolling.

Hollywood

Let's clear up any misconceptions: There are no studios, and few movie stars, in Hollywood. Sure, Sony Pictures has a branch at Sunset Boulevard and Gower Street, but otherwise the movie-making business has long since retreated from Hollywood proper. Now it's just a name, but a name with such drawing power that the city has spent a great deal of money trying to clean up Hollywood Boulevard (long ago deteriorated into a bunch of junky shops and derelict buildings), mostly in the form of the brand-new Hollywood & Highland shopping and entertainment complex.

Hollywood begins more or less at La Brea Avenue to the west and ends around Vermont Avenue (where the hip Los Feliz and Silverlake neighborhoods take over, unless you just consider those East Hollywood, and you may) to the east, the Hollywood Hills to the north, and Melrose Avenue to the south.

You'll want to come here for the centrally located hotels with gorgeous hill and mountain views — and because it's Hollywood, darn it, even if the sights have less substance than myth attached to them. And Los Feliz and Silver Lake are constantly in style pages as the artistic and bohemian and hot-young-actor epicenter. You want to be a part of that scene, admit it.

Los Angeles Neighborhoods

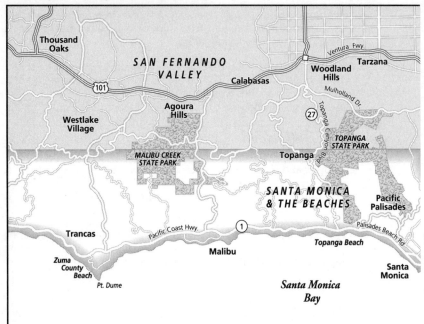

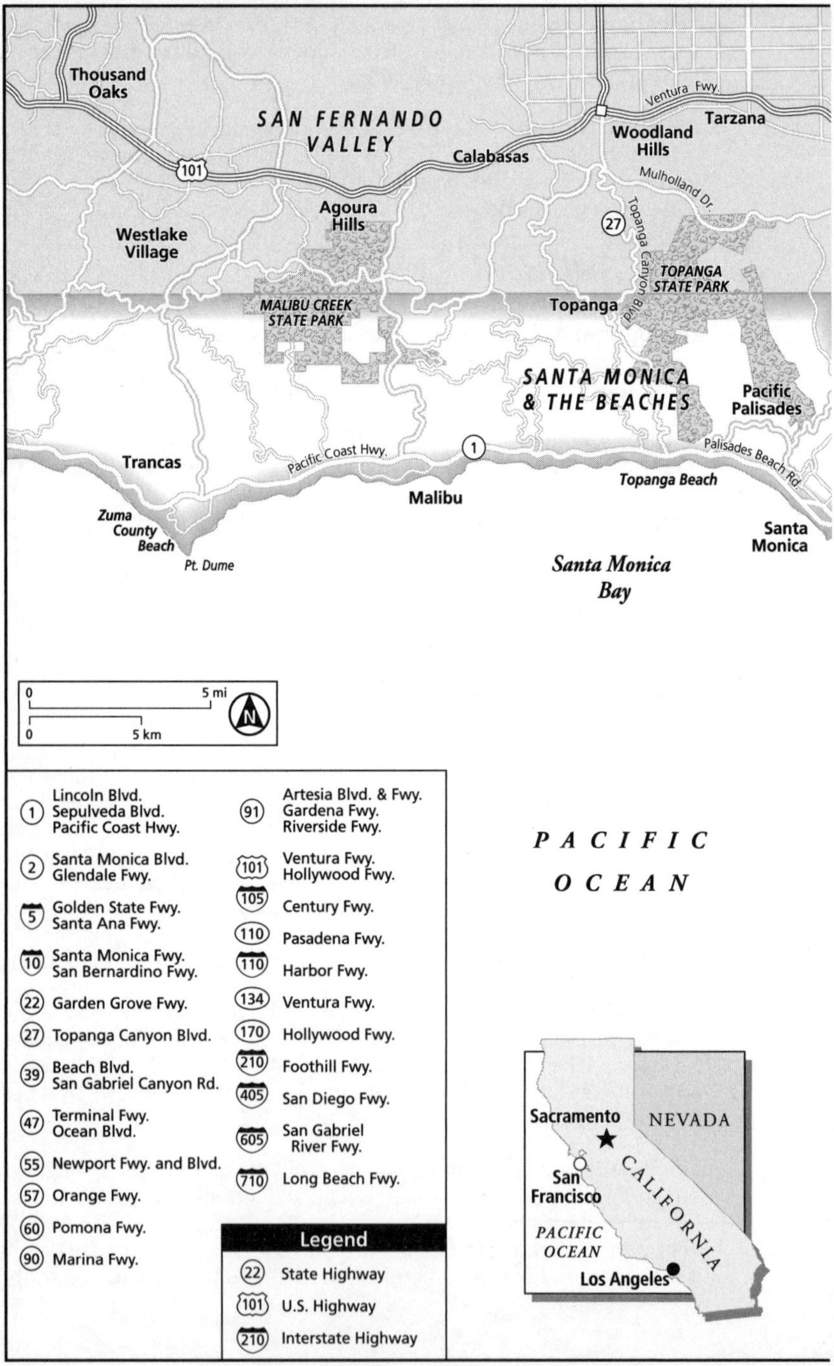

Thousand Oaks
SAN FERNANDO VALLEY
Ventura Fwy.
Tarzana
Woodland Hills
Calabasas
101
Mulholland Dr.
Agoura Hills
27
Topanga Canyon Blvd.
Westlake Village
TOPANGA STATE PARK
MALIBU CREEK STATE PARK
Topanga
SANTA MONICA & THE BEACHES
Pacific Palisades
Pacific Coast Hwy.
1
Palisades Beach Rd.
Trancas
Topanga Beach
Malibu
Zuma County Beach
Santa Monica
Pt. Dume
Santa Monica Bay
0
5 mi
0
5 km
N
1 Lincoln Blvd. Sepulveda Blvd. Pacific Coast Hwy.
2 Santa Monica Blvd. Glendale Fwy.
5 Golden State Fwy. Santa Ana Fwy.
10 Santa Monica Fwy. San Bernardino Fwy.
22 Garden Grove Fwy.
27 Topanga Canyon Blvd.
39 Beach Blvd. San Gabriel Canyon Rd.
47 Terminal Fwy. Ocean Blvd.
(55) Newport Fwy. and Blvd.
(57) Orange Fwy.
(60) Pomona Fwy.
(90) Marina Fwy.
(91) Artesia Blvd. & Fwy. Gardena Fwy. Riverside Fwy.
101 Ventura Fwy. Hollywood Fwy.
105 Century Fwy.
110 Pasadena Fwy.
110 Harbor Fwy.
134 Ventura Fwy.
170 Hollywood Fwy.
210 Foothill Fwy.
405 San Diego Fwy.
605 San Gabriel River Fwy.
710 Long Beach Fwy.
Legend
22 State Highway
101 U.S. Highway
210 Interstate Highway
PACIFIC OCEAN
Sacramento
NEVADA
San Francisco
CALIFORNIA
PACIFIC OCEAN
Los Angeles

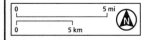

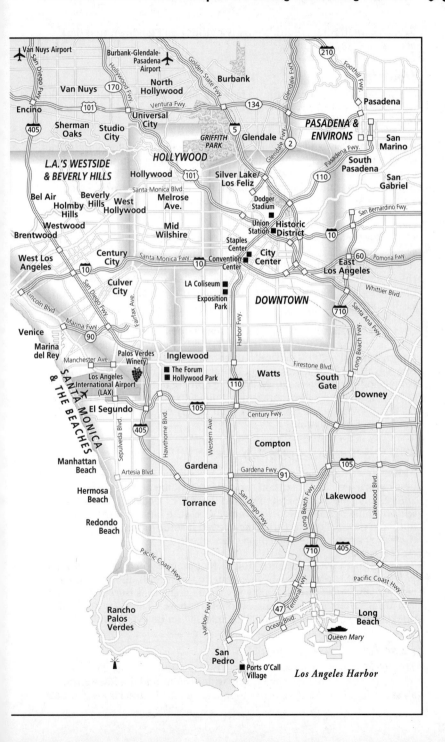

Crime is greater here, but it's mostly of the "don't go down that dark alley alone at night" sort.

Downtown

Los Angeles is too spread out to have a real urban center, but this is the de facto hub of the city, where you find the most skyscraper-type buildings, plus City Hall.

Downtown is a mixed bag, with staid offices and executives, immigrants, cheap clothing (the garment district is here), pricey restaurants, several fine museums, ethnic food, hustle and bustle of both the uniquely American sort and the type you might find in a big Third World city, and, unfortunately, a lot of homeless people.

Okay, so Downtown L.A. is seedy, and we don't walk around here at night. But the neighborhood is on the cusp of a renaissance, thanks to some very brisk development and renovations. You have several sights down here to see during the day (including the Walt Disney Hall, MOCA, the modern art museum, and the Music Center, for theater and symphony) plus Chinatown, Olvera Street (and other Hispanic areas), and Little Tokyo.

On weekends, hotel business drops tremendously, and so do the prices. We're talking quite nice hotel rooms for under (okay, in some cases, just under, but still) $100. The DASH, the downtown bus system, costs 25¢ one way and makes it easy to get around the area or travel over to Hollywood and Universal City. If you're coming to town for just a short stay, want to save some money, don't need an ocean or mountain view, prefer an urban setting, and don't want to rely on a car to get around, this is a perfect location.

The San Fernando Valley

Although we don't list many hotels or attractions in the Valley, we would be remiss if we didn't mention the ancestral home of Valley girls everywhere. Any true Angeleno knows that there are "locals" (those who live within a mile or so of the beach) and "Vals" (the intruders from over the hill), and never the twain shall meet, even if some locals had to move to the Valley because the housing is cheaper.

If you go north over the Santa Monica Mountains, you hit the Valley, and you can tell: Strip malls and other generic wastelands abound, and it's really, really hot. The only part you may be going to is Burbank because Warner Brothers and Universal Studios are there. (There are some nice pockets, for sure, but few you'll be exploring on this visit, probably.)

Pasadena

This jewel of a city lies just to the east of Los Angeles. It has gorgeous homes (thanks to old money), lovely wide streets, and the Rose Parade — all at the foot of the San Gabriel Mountains. It may be too far away for a brief L.A. visit (only half-hour or so on the freeway, but still). It does offer several major sights, however, including the Rose Bowl, the Huntington Library, and the Norton Simon Museum.

Burbank

For convenience to the main studios, the Metro rail, and Universal City, we tossed in a couple of hotels from Burbank in Chapter 9. But otherwise, it's dull.

Airport area

You stay here only because you want a place near the airport. It's ghastly, and there is nothing to see.

Finding Information After You Arrive

For more information and local maps, try the **Los Angeles Convention & Visitors Bureau's walk-in visitor center Downtown** (685 S. Figueroa St.). Or contact the LACVB directly (☎ **800-366-6116;** Events Hotline ☎ **213-689-8822;** www.lacvb.com) before you arrive, and it'll send you a free visitor kit.

Getting Around Los Angeles by Car

Learn to love the L.A. car fetish, or at least deal with it. Los Angeles is hooked on cars, and you have little choice in the matter. Angelenos think nothing of a 30-minute commute; some think nothing of a 2-hour commute. Traffic is usually bad, except when it's horrendous.

But as we continue to stress, you do have options — in the form of public transportation (see "Getting Around Without a Car," p. 74). Unfortunately, they aren't that desirable (though whenever you can take public transportation, please do so, if for no other reason than it makes traffic easier on the permanent residents!).

Driving in L.A. is like driving in any other major city; at times, it can be a dream, but much of the time, it's an ongoing frustration. Because L.A. is so spread out, you want to take the freeway as often as surface streets to get more efficiently from Point A to Point B because Point B may be miles away (hence, Angelenos often refer to places as "freeway close").

But keep in mind that if you're on the freeways during the evening rush hour (or in the morning on a lovely weekend day heading to the beach), you'll have much company. Still, if it's a nice day, driving can be pleasant, and you often have views of hills and mountains and palm trees. Ditto driving within the city; maybe the hills aren't so visible (though the palm trees are), and the buildings aren't as lovely as, say, those in San Francisco. But overall, the topography is less urban than such an urban place warrants. Just keep your cool, and build in enough time to get to your destination. Better to get somewhere early than miss out on valuable time by spending it in the car.

In theory, we simplify matters for you by suggesting hotels and restaurants more or less in all the same areas you'll be heading to anyway, for sightseeing or whatever. (Of course, we make exceptions for really special hotels or, more to the point, places where you just gotta eat.)

A basic map of L.A. demonstrates the easiest, if not most travel-time-efficient, way of getting to your destination. However, it never hurts to ask your concierge or to call the place in question; most institutes have an automated tape with directions, whereas any local hotel, concierge or no, probably has an opinion on the best way to get somewhere. You can also load up on maps at your local AAA before you come and use MapQuest.com (`www.mapquest.com`) to do some pretrip route planning.

Following the rules and making exceptions

Getting around in Los Angeles is pretty easy once you memorize a couple of basic rules and their huge exceptions.

- ✔ The mountains are always to the east and north *unless* you're in the Valley, where they're everywhere. That's one reason many people avoid going to the 818 (the area code), as the vast parcel of suburban sprawl is called.

- ✔ Freeways with odd numbers (5, 405, 101) run north/south; even numbered freeways run east/west, *except* the 110, which used to be the 11, and thus is a north/south with an extra zero at the end.

- ✔ The major east/west streets in Hollywood are **Sunset Boulevard, Santa Monica Boulevard, Melrose Avenue,** and **Beverly Boulevard.**

- ✔ After you hit Beverly Hills, **Wilshire Boulevard** begins to run north of **Santa Monica Boulevard,** other streets squish into a parallel northward direction, and **Beverly Boulevard** dissolves into **Santa Monica Boulevard;** thus your main east/west routes become **Sunset, Wilshire, Santa Monica,** and **Olympic boulevards.**

- ✔ Major north/south streets on the east side running to the west are **Vermont Avenue, Western Boulevard, Vine Street, Cahuenga Boulevard, Highland Avenue, La Brea Boulevard, Fairfax Avenue, Crescent Heights Boulevard, La Cienega Boulevard, Robertson Boulevard,** and **Doheny Drive.**

- ✔ Doheny Drive forms the dividing line into Beverly Hills. Once past Doheny, the major landmark streets are **Rexford Drive, Beverly Glen Boulevard, Veteran Avenue, the 405 Freeway, Barrington Avenue, 26th Street,** and **Lincoln Avenue.** The latter is eight blocks from the end of the road.

Like Atlanta, which has something like 14 streets named Peachtree, Los Angeles has a few streets that share the same name, with little else in common. This can be crucial and confusing. For example, L.A. has two Third streets, one in Santa Monica and the other in West Hollywood, and we can tell you from firsthand experience that if you're not sure which one you're going to, you may be very late, ahem, for dinner. Another duplicate is San Vicente Boulevard; one is on the Westside, and the other is in West Hollywood. Also make sure not to confuse Beverly Drive (in Beverly Hills) with Beverly Boulevard (in West Hollywood).

Great gridlock! Avoiding the slow, the snarling, and the stationary

We want you to see the sights with a minimum of fuss, so here are some specific tips on driving the streets of L.A.

✔ To get from the east side of Hollywood to West Hollywood during the afternoon, take **Melrose Avenue**, which has no left turn from 4 p.m. to 7 p.m. **Olympic Boulevard** provides a quick zip any time from Beverly Hills to Santa Monica. **Sunset Boulevard** is always lovely (if frequently slow), but **Santa Monica Boulevard** is just plain pokey, no matter what time of day, especially through Beverly Hills, where every street has a stoplight.

✔ **Vermont Avenue** is a particularly slow north/south street and should be avoided when commuting if possible — though you'll almost certainly have to take it if you're going north of Sunset Boulevard to get to Griffith Park, the Greek Theatre, and the Observatory.

✔ **Western Boulevard** is also notoriously bad, especially at the intersection of **Santa Monica Boulevard,** which can be so slow at times, it's actually in your best interest to go around it by making a series of left or right turns, forming a giant square. Better still, plan your travel west or east so that you are on **Fountain Avenue,** which is parallel to Santa Monica to the north.

✔ Avoid **Highland Avenue,** the major artery from Hollywood to Universal City/Burbank, on summer nights unless you know for sure that the Hollywood Bowl is dark and empty. Otherwise, you can get caught in massive traffic tie-ups.

✔ **Hope and Grand streets,** Downtown, can be tricky; they are elevated, so they are only accessible at their starts (around First Street) and ends (around Eighth Street) — all other streets pass under them. This can be a pain if you're trying to get to the Museum of Contemporary Art or the Disney Hall, which are on Grand, so read signs carefully.

A survival guide to driving L.A.

The longer your stay in L.A., the more driving yourself around is worth the grief. So how can you make it a little easier? We give you a few tricks on driving L.A. that will keep your road frustration to a minimum.

✔ **Don't drive from around 7 a.m. to 9:30 a.m., when the morning rush hour is at its most intense.**

✔ **Don't drive from 5 p.m. to 7 p.m., when the evening rush hour is at its thickest.**

✔ **Make sure that you build in about 40 minutes to get anywhere, just in case.**

✔ **Avoid the freeway, except in the middle of the day, and the 405 as much as you possibly can.** There was a time when the 405 was a fast thruway, but now, we swear it's crowded even at 3 a.m.

✔ **Avoid the High Occupancy Vehicle (HOV) lanes unless you have enough people in the car to qualify.** Fines are steep. Many L.A. freeways have designated carpool lanes, also known as HOV lanes. Some require two passengers; others, three.

✔ **When the light turns yellow, put a brake on it.** A number of L.A. intersections (such as the one at the corner of Fairfax and Fountain avenues) have cameras that flash right when the light turns red to catch people running through them. So you may think that you got away scot-free only to find a big fat ticket waiting in the mail. (Yes, they even trace rental-car license plates.)

✔ **Be like all natives and make sure that KFWB News Radio (980 AM) is on your car radio.** The station has traffic updates (that locals listen to religiously) every ten minutes, on the "ones" — 3:01, 3:11, and so on.

✔ **Above all, drive defensively!** Figure that the person next to you is not paying attention because he's talking on his cell phone or engaging in some other vehicular-inappropriate activity. (Yet, he will be angry if you cut him off; remember that the term "road rage" was coined here.)

Parking the car

Parking in L.A. is both easy and bothersome. Parking is relatively plentiful, both on the street and in paid lots, but parking enforcers are vigilant and merciless.

Parking restrictions vary from neighborhood to neighborhood and from city to city. In one block, you can leave L.A. and be in Beverly Hills or, worse, in West Hollywood, where much of the street parking is restricted to residents with permits.

In L.A., you may be able to park on the street (meter or free) most of the time, except during street cleaning and rush hour — from, say, 4 p.m. to

7 p.m. Monday to Friday, or Wednesday from 10 a.m. to noon — posted signs tell you what the restrictions are.

The moral of this story: *Read the street signs carefully.* Also, check your meter to see how much time is allowed; some offer only an hour, others much, much more. And prices vary; a quarter can buy you a measly eight minutes on the UCLA campus and an hour in other parts of the Westside. Have lots of change handy; merchants aren't always helpful in making change.

During rush hour, many major streets, including La Cienega, La Brea, and Wilshire boulevards, have strict no-parking/tow-away signs. If you don't read them, you will weep! If you're in doubt trying to translate "Two Hour Parking M–F 8 a.m.–6 p.m. No Parking without Permit" — park somewhere with a more user-friendly description. It's worth an extra block's walk to avoid a hefty fine or having your car towed!

Parking is probably worst in Downtown, where street parking is rare, and lots can cost quite a bit. The farther from the center of Downtown action, the cheaper the lots, though some lots offer early-bird, all-day rates. If you don't have endless parking funds, or if you don't feel like keeping your eyes open for street parking, your best bet, probably, is to take the Metro Rail into Downtown and get around with the DASH (see the section "By bus" later in this chapter).

West Hollywood at night, when the local streets go into resident-only parking, is the second worst; you may want to consider parking in lots wherever and as often as you can, or just taking taxis.

Renting a car

So we talked you into renting a car. Here's help in doing so. All the major car-rental agencies have offices in L.A., particularly at the airport and in major hotels; for a listing of agencies with phone numbers and Web sites, go to the Appendix in the back of the book.

The restaurant-shuttle-Music Center connection

Many downtown restaurants are on a free shuttle route that transfers patrons to the Music Center, making it relatively inexpensive to park your car at a restaurant, pay the minimal parking fee, take the shuttle to your play/opera/symphony, and then return by shuttle to your car. It's a very nice service; among the restaurants on the route are Cuidad, Cafe Pinot, and Nick & Stef's. Call to see whether you can catch a ride from the restaurant of your choice.

Internet sites for travel and car-rental agencies often offer specials and discounts. Another ongoing discount can be found at the Enterprise agency at the Ramada West Hollywood, which offers a 10-percent discount on rentals for guests at the hotel.

If you want to rent a car but lack a credit card, don't despair; check out these agencies:

- ✔ **Dollar Rent A Car** (☎ **800-800-4000**), which has a location at Los Angeles Airport as well as at the Bonaventure Hotel in downtown Los Angeles, will rent you a car on your debit card after they run a credit check on you and verify a high enough credit-rating score. They take a deposit for the cost of the rental plus 15 percent (or $250, whichever is higher), and, of course, you must have a valid driver's license.

- ✔ At **Cash Car Rent,** also known as **Hollywood Car Rental** (1600 La Brea Blvd.; ☎ **323-464-1657** or 323-464-4147), you can rent a car for a $300-per-week deposit — no plastic required. Return the car sooner, and you get a refund, based on an approximately $35-a-day rental. You must be over 21 with a valid driver's license and proof of where you're staying while in town; a return ticket also helps.

- ✔ **AA'A Rent A Car** (8820 Sepulveda #111; ☎ **310-348-1111;** www.aa-a rentacar.com), located three minutes from LAX (with a shuttle to take you to the rental lots), requires a return ticket. Rentals start at $29 per day, and a $450 deposit is required along with a valid license and a return ticket. California residents may also want to bring a copy of a utility bill from home to assuage the rental agent.

Getting Around without a Car

Yes, it can be done. But the Los Angeles public transportation system has, shall we say, limitations.

By bus

Ah, the MTA (that's Metropolitan Transit Authority): the bane of the car-less, the joke of the smug and fully automobiled. We love L.A., we really do, but for pity's sake, it's the only major, bustling, industrialized city we can think of with such a lousy public transportation system.

To be fair, plenty of people take the bus in L.A., and some even do so by choice rather than necessity. You can, too, though you must be patient and flexible. Some bus lines really do go (more or less) where you want to go, and when they do, it's a great pleasure.

You can check the MTA Web site (www.mta.net), which is, we have to admit, nicely and helpfully laid out, and see whether any of the routes cover your needs, for it certainly is nice to occasionally pretend that

L.A. is like other cities where residents aren't so dependent on cars. Plus, the bus only costs $1.25 one way.

Also note that Santa Monica is serviced by the somewhat less laughable **Big Blue Buses** (www.bigbluebus.com), which are swifter, cleaner, and more reliable than the MTA buses. Downtown has the **DASH** (www.ladot transit.com), a commuter bus that runs at frequent intervals throughout Downtown and costs just 25¢ one way. The latter is a particularly fine way to get around Downtown, which has miserable parking. We highly recommend it.

By subway

It still makes us laugh to refer to this two-mile, four-stop wonder as a subway. No, really, the **Metro Rail** is longer than that, though it hardly seems it. A multibillion-dollar public scandal, years in the making and days in the discarding, it's big, clean, and bright, and it goes almost no place useful (it seems). And if being the only person standing in one of the big, clean, bright terminals doesn't give you one of those "last one standing after the Apocalypse" feelings, nothing will.

Joking aside, the Metro Rail has some truly handy uses, and locals are gradually taking advantage of it. The rail travels tidily between the center of Hollywood and Universal Studios (the Red Line), and somewhat less tidily between Hollywood and Downtown (parts of Downtown require a transfer from the Red Line to the Blue Line). A trip from Hollywood and Vine to Staples Center, even with the transfer, is about 20 minutes. You can also take the rail (though it becomes an elevated train and costs more) to Anaheim and Disneyland (see Chapter 17) or Pasadena (via the new Gold Line), though those stops require a transfer at Union Station downtown.

We encourage you, in all seriousness, to use the itty-bitty "subway" as much as possible because it can make sightseeing a bit easier. It costs $1.25 one way, and one transfer is free. You buy your tickets from service machines in each station, though some people skip this part. You probably shouldn't; plainclothes agents wait at some stations and may demand to see your (up-to-date, so don't try to use an old one) ticket. Get caught without it, and pay a hefty ($250) fine. A weekly pass is $14. The Web site (www.mta.net) and toll-free number (☎ **800-COMMUTE/ 266-6883**) provide trip planning; give your departure and desired arrival point, and the services will tell you how to best get to where you want to go.

By taxi

The cab alternative isn't a bad one, but taxis in Los Angeles don't have cabstands, except at the airport and outside Santa Monica Place Mall and the Beverly Center. Plus, they don't drive by with the same frequency you find in other major cities.

To hire a cab, get your hotel to call one for you or use one of the main cab services in the city (which we list in this section). Cabs charge a $2 pickup fee and then $2 per mile, plus additional charges when you get stuck in traffic, a common occurrence. Tipping your cab driver 10 percent to 15 percent is customary.

 A word of warning: Pirate cabbies sometimes try to intercept your ride, and you may find yourself being transported in an unlicensed cab and paying way too much for a ride. We know; it once happened to us. Make sure that before you get in the cab has license stickers displayed and that the color and name of the cab matches the one you called.

With that in mind, here are a few of the cab companies that run the streets (and ones we've actually used), all of which are licensed:

- ✔ **Yellow Cab** (☎ 877-733-3305): Yes, they're yellow.

- ✔ **United Independent** (☎ 800-822-8294): Green-and-white cabs

- ✔ **Independent Taxi** (☎ 800-521-8294): White, with red-and-blue lettering

- ✔ **Checker Cabs** (☎ 800-300-5007): Yellow and blue, with yellow-and-blue checkerboard trim

On foot

It's not true that nobody walks in L.A., but heavens, it feels like it at times. The best areas of town to walk in are Santa Monica and Beverly Hills, both flat, pretty neighborhoods with lots of scenic stuff (both commercial and residential), palm trees, and, in the case of Santa Monica, the ocean.

Downtown and Hollywood are walkable areas, but sights and such are sporadically placed; for every few good blocks, there are a few icky ones to get through before the next set. Melrose and Third Street in West Hollywood are fun to meander down, thanks to a plethora of shops and cafes.

Chapter 9

Checking In at Los Angeles' Best Hotels

•••

In This Chapter

▶ Breaking down the price and saving some cash
▶ Booking online
▶ Choosing your hotel from an A–Z list
▶ Narrowing your hotel choices by price and location indexes

•••

*I*n this chapter we send you directly to our favorite places to stay — providing a range of choices in cost, location, and amenities — and tell you how and where to book them.

If you're coming to L.A. with children in tow, look for the Kid Friendly icons throughout the chapter, which point out the lodgings that are especially good for families.

Getting to Know Your Options

Los Angeles has two kinds of hotels: expensive and basic. This isn't New Orleans, where you have dozens of atmospheric or quaint old B&Bs and small hotels, or Las Vegas, which has behemoth themed hotels. If you're willing to drop some money, you have quite a range to choose from — discreet luxury, quiet luxury, unctuous luxury, hip luxury, or eccentric luxury. For budget travelers, there are basic brand-name hotels.

The absence of cunning B&Bs is probably due to Los Angeles' lack of reverence for its original architecture (so many likely B&B candidates have long ago been turned into parking lots) and equal lack of reverence for commercial zoning laws. Plus, the most interesting hotels have to charge quite a bit in order to support their prime locations and interior-design costs. But we've tried, really tried, to locate those little gems and sensible spots where you trade a certain level of glitz and glamour for reasonable rates — and, believe it or not, we found a few.

Finding the Best Room at the Best Rate

Frankly, rates around Los Angeles seem so willy-nilly — with rack rates at certain chain hotels equal to the ones at posher places — that trying to figure out rhyme and reason behind them is exhausting. Think instead about what is important to you: Character? Location? Hip-quotient? Room size? Go from there and pay accordingly, using the following tips to help find the best rates:

- ✔ **Don't be afraid to bargain.** Most rack rates include commissions of 10 percent to 25 percent for travel agents, which some hotels may be willing to reduce if you make your own reservations and haggle a bit. Always ask whether a room that is less expensive than the first one quoted is available, or whether any special rates apply to you. You may qualify for corporate, student, military, senior citizen, or other discounts. Be sure to mention membership in **AAA, AARP, frequent-flier programs, or trade unions,** which may entitle you to special deals as well. Find out the hotel policy on children, if necessary. Do kids stay free in the room, or does the hotel offer a special rate?

- ✔ **Use the Internet.** Many hotels offer discounted rates if you book directly from their Web sites or online reservations services.

- ✔ **Dial direct.** When booking a room in a chain hotel, compare the rates offered by the hotel's local line with that of the toll-free number. Also check with an agent and online. A hotel makes nothing on a room that stays empty, so the local hotel reservations desk may be willing to offer a special rate unavailable elsewhere.

- ✔ **Rely on a qualified professional.** Certain hotels give travel agents discounts in exchange for steering business their way, so if you're shy about bargaining, an agent may be better equipped to negotiate discounts for you.

- ✔ **Remember the law of supply and demand.** Resort hotels are most crowded, and therefore most expensive, on weekends, so discounts are usually available for midweek stays. Business hotels in Downtown locations are busiest during the week, so you can expect big discounts over the weekend. Avoid high-season stays whenever you can: Planning your vacation just a week before or after official peak season can mean big savings.

- ✔ **Look into group or long-stay discounts.** If you come as part of a large group, you should be able to negotiate a bargain rate because the hotel can then guarantee occupancy in a number of rooms. Likewise, if you're planning a long stay (at least five days), you may qualify for a discount. As a general rule, expect one night free after a seven-night stay.

- ✔ **Avoid excess charges.** When you book a room, ask whether the hotel charges for parking. Many hotels charge a fee just for dialing out on the phone in your room. Find out whether your hotel imposes a surcharge on local and long-distance calls. A pay phone, however inconvenient, may save you money, though many calling cards charge a fee when you use them on pay phones. Finally, ask about local taxes and service charges, which can increase the cost of a room by 25 percent or more.

✔ **Watch for coupons and advertised discounts.** Scan ads in the travel section of your local Sunday newspaper, an excellent source for up-to-the-minute hotel deals.

✔ **Consider a suite.** If you're traveling with your family or another couple, you can pack more people into a suite (which usually comes with a sofa bed) and thereby reduce your per-person rate. Keep in mind that some places charge for extra guests.

✔ **Book an efficiency.** A room with a kitchenette allows you to shop for groceries and cook your own meals. This is a big money saver, especially for families on long stays.

✔ **Join hotel frequent-visitor clubs.** Even if you don't stay in the hotels much, you'll be more likely to get upgrades and other perks.

✔ **Ask about frequent-flier points.** Many hotels offer frequent-flier points, so ask for yours when you check in.

Surfing the Web for hotel deals

Shopping online for hotels is generally done one of two ways: by booking through the hotel's own Web site or through an independent booking agency (or a fare-service agency such as Priceline). These Internet hotel agencies have multiplied in mind-boggling numbers of late, competing for the business of millions of consumers surfing for accommodations around the world. This competitiveness can be a boon to consumers who have the patience and time to shop and compare the online sites for good deals — but shop they must, for prices can vary considerably from site to site. And keep in mind that hotels at the top of a site's listing may be there for no other reason than that they paid money to get the placement.

Of the "big three" sites, **Expedia** (www.expedia.com) offers a long list of special deals and "virtual tours" or photos of available rooms so you can see what you're paying for (a feature that helps counter the claims that the best rooms are often held back from bargain booking Web sites). **Travelocity** (www.travelocity.com) posts unvarnished customer reviews and ranks its properties according to the AAA rating system. Also reliable are **Hotels.com** and **Quikbook.com.** An excellent free program, **TravelAxe** (www.travelaxe.net), can help you search multiple hotel sites at once, even ones you may never have heard of, and conveniently lists the total price of the room, including the taxes and service charges. Another booking site, **Travelweb** (www.travelweb.com), is partly owned by the hotels it represents (including the Hilton, Hyatt, and Starwood chains) and is therefore plugged directly into the hotels' reservations systems — unlike independent online agencies, which have to fax or e-mail reservation requests to the hotel, a good portion of which get misplaced in the shuffle. More than once, travelers have arrived at the hotel, only to be told that they have no reservation. To be fair, many of the major sites are undergoing improvements in service and ease of use, and Expedia will soon be able to plug directly into the reservations systems of many hotel chains — none of which can be bad news for consumers. In the meantime, it's a good idea to **get a confirmation number** and **make a printout** of any online booking transaction.

In the opaque Web site category, **Priceline** (www.priceline.com) and **Hotwire** (www.hotwire.com) are even better for hotels than for airfares; with both, you're allowed to pick the neighborhood and quality level of your hotel before naming your price. Priceline's hotel service even covers Europe and Asia, though it's much better at getting five-star lodging for three-star prices than at finding anything at the bottom of the scale. On the down side, many hotels stick Priceline guests in their least desirable rooms. Be sure to go to the **BiddingforTravel** Web site (www.biddingfortravel.com) before bidding on a hotel room on Priceline; it features a fairly up-to-date list of hotels that Priceline uses in major cities. For both Priceline and Hotwire, you pay up front, and the fee is nonrefundable. *Note:* Some hotels do not provide loyalty program credits or points or other frequent-stay amenities when you book a room through opaque online services.

Reserving the best room

After you make your reservation, asking one or two more pointed questions can go a long way toward getting the best room in the house. Always ask for a corner room. They're usually larger, quieter, and have more windows and light than standard rooms, and they don't always cost more. Also ask if the hotel is renovating; if it is, request a room away from the renovation work. Inquire, too, about the location of the restaurants, bars, and discos in the hotel — all sources of annoying noise. And if you aren't happy with your room when you arrive, talk to the front desk. If they have another room, they should be happy to accommodate you, within reason.

Using reservations services

Reservations services usually work as consolidators, buying up or reserving rooms in bulk and then dealing them out to customers at a profit. You can get 10 percent to 50 percent off, but remember that these discounts apply to inflated rack rates that savvy travelers rarely end up paying. You may get a decent rate, but always call the hotel as well to see if you can do better.

Among the more reputable reservations services, offering both telephone and online bookings, are **Hotel Reservations Network** (☎ 800-715-7666; www.hoteldiscounts.com or www.180096HOTEL.com) and **Quikbook** (☎ 800-789-9887, includes fax-on-demand service; www.quikbook.com). Online, try booking your hotel through us at **Frommer's** (www.frommers.com). **Microsoft Expedia** (www.expedia.com) features a "travel agent" that will also direct you to affordable lodgings.

The truth about rack rates

The **rack rate** is the maximum rate a hotel charges for a room. It's the rate you get if you walk in off the street and ask for a room for the night. You sometimes see these rates printed on the fire/emergency exit diagrams posted on the back of your door.

Hotels are happy to charge you the rack rate, but you can almost always do better. Perhaps the best way to avoid paying the rack rate is surprisingly simple: Just ask for a cheaper or discounted rate. You may be pleasantly surprised.

In all but the smallest accommodations, the rate you pay for a room depends on many factors — chief among them being how you make your reservation. A travel agent may be able to negotiate a better price with certain hotels than you can get by yourself. (The hotel often gives the agent a discount in exchange for steering his or her business toward that hotel.)

Reserving a room through the hotel's toll-free number may also result in a lower rate than calling the hotel directly. On the other hand, the central reservations number may not know about discount rates at specific locations. For example, local franchises may offer a special group rate for a wedding or family reunion, but they may neglect to tell the central booking line. Your best bet is to call both the local number and the toll-free number and see which one gives you a better deal.

Room rates (even rack rates) change with the season as occupancy rates rise and fall. But even within a given season, room prices are subject to change without notice, so the rates quoted in this book may be different from the actual rate you receive when you make your reservation. Be sure to mention membership in AAA, AARP, frequent-flyer programs, and any other corporate rewards programs you can think of — even your Uncle Joe's Elks lodge in which you're an honorary inductee — when you call to book. You never know when the affiliation may be worth a few dollars off your room rate.

We can't stress this enough: Rack rates are just a guideline. For the most part, you won't have to pay them. How to avoid paying rack rates? Start by planning your trip during the off-season — early December, January, and February. Be sure to check the Internet, starting with hotel Web sites, because most establishments have their best rates available there. For Downtown-area hotels, go on the weekends; prices drop precipitously because it's a business-oriented neighborhood and many hotels have rooms begging for guests when the workweek ends.

What the prices mean

The $ symbols accompanying each listing in this chapter are based on the hotel's posted rack rates for a standard room. (Suites are more expensive.) Keep in mind that rates fluctuate, and rack rates are generally at the top of a hotel's price schedule.

✔ **$ (Under $100).** This gets you basically a bed and motel-room furniture — unless, of course, you scored a good deal on an otherwise pricey room usually found in a higher category. Towels are likely to be of the depressingly thin variety, and don't expect top-brand toiletries. Remind yourself that you are there for the sunshine.

✔ **$$ ($100–$200).** This is a mixed-bag category. You could have a very nice (though perhaps generic-looking) hotel room, in a fine establishment with all the amenities. Or it could be even posher. Or it could be less so. *Check each listing carefully.*

✔ **$$$ ($200–$275).** Now we're talkin'. The service may be snooty, but the linens are soft, plus you get bathrobes and high-end amenities (nice shampoo, lotion, shoe buffer). And we bet the grounds are fabulously landscaped.

✔ **$$$$ ($275 and up).** In theory, you should have everything your little heart could desire in this category, but this is L.A., and sometimes you pay that price just for the privilege of staying somewhere that pampers Jennifer Lopez. You not being Jennifer Lopez, you may wonder what the fuss is all about.

Los Angeles' Best Hotels from A to Z

These are the best of the best in alphabetical order. If you're working around a fixed price range or neighborhood, your best bet is to start with the price and location indexes at the end of this chapter. See p. 110.

Alta Cienega Motel
$ West Hollywood

The Alta Cienega is famous around the world as the spot where Doors singer Jim Morrison often crashed in bacchanalian contemplation in a room above the motel driveway. This room, number 32, now bears a plaque on the door stating "Home of Jim Morrison" and is available for a maximum of $58 per night, plus tax — the same rate you'd pay for any other room at this no-frills joint, which is painted in pea green, orange, and white. And what do you get for the lowest hotel rate in the city of West Hollywood? Not a lot. The soda and ice machines are vintage and may be the same ones the Lizard King used, if he was so inclined. The rooms have wood-toned Formica furniture, small TVs, and cable Internet access, which is odd considering there are no phones in the room, though there are two pay phones conveniently located in the parking lot. Morning coffee and pastries, served in the office, are free. The Alta Cienega is full during the summer months, when American and European rock fans haunt the motel, trying to relive and revive Jim's spirit, as demonstrated by the ghostly graffiti on the walls of room 32.

See map p. 87. 1005 N. La Cienega Blvd. (near the Sunset Strip). ☎ *310-652-5797. Fax: 310-652-5797. Rack rates: $55–$58. AE, DC, DISC, MC, V.*

Argyle
$$$$ West Hollywood

Built in 1929 as the Sunset Towers apartment house, this Art Deco masterpiece has had starring roles in movies, including *The Player, Get Shorty,* and *Wayne's World 2,* and has been mentioned in literary works by Raymond Chandler, among others. Howard Hughes, John Wayne, Marilyn Monroe, Paulette Goddard, Zasu Pitts, and gangster Bugsy Siegel kept apartments here. Now, as a hotel, the Argyle still hosts celebrities in well-appointed rooms and suites, with masterpieces of Deco perfection and meticulous historical detail that reflect the glamour that was Hollywood (the carpet was woven especially for the stars!). Of course, the glamour doesn't come cheap, and we spied at least one room that had evidence of shabby neglect, for shame. Still, when it's on, there are few other places we'd rather stay. The hotel has a health club, a classy roof-top pool with a glamorous view, as well as 24-hour room service, complimentary continental breakfast, and the restaurant Fenix, which becomes a club/lounge featuring hip-hop on Friday nights and jazz on Saturday nights. Luckily, the building is soundproofed and strikingly quiet, buffered from the noise of the club and the Sunset Strip.

See map p. 87. 8358 Sunset Blvd. (at Kings Road). ☎ **800-225-2637** *or 323-654-7100. Fax: 323-654-9287.* www.argylehotel.com. *Rack rates: $169–$695 per night. AE, DC, DISC, MC, V.*

Avalon Hotel
$$$ Beverly Hills

Mae West and Marilyn Monroe lived here when it was an apartment building, and Lucy and Ricky Ricardo stayed here when they went to Hollywood in *I Love Lucy.* Now, it's a small, chic hotel, aggressively styled and inadvertently harkening back to the '50s/Jetsons' futurism — look for the green polished concrete and atom-age emblems. Rooms are spare but oh so comfortable — Frette linens! Philosophy-brand bathroom amenities! VCRs and CD and DVD players! The bathrooms are smallish, with inexplicable bamboo poles (for stripper practice?). The pool demands a good bathing suit and a figure to match, and the on-site restaurant, **Blue on Blue**, has a signature drink that looks like a glass of toilet-bowl cleaner. Not too surprisingly, the Avalon looks for business and fashion-industry clientele.

See map p. 87. 9400 W. Olympic Blvd. (at Cañon Dr.). ☎ **800-535-4715** *or 310-277-5221. Fax: 310-277-4928.* www.Avalon-hotel.com. *Rack rates: $219–$475 double. AE, DC, DISC, MC, V.*

Best Western Hollywood Hills Hotel
$$ Hollywood

Famous for the huge sign declaring this to be the "Last Cappuccino before the 101" and for the coffee shop — the **101 Coffee Shop** (see p. 137) — that was featured in the movie *Swingers,* this motel is usually crowded with local musicians, actors, and lounge-abouts digging on the hearty, reasonably

Santa Monica Accommodations

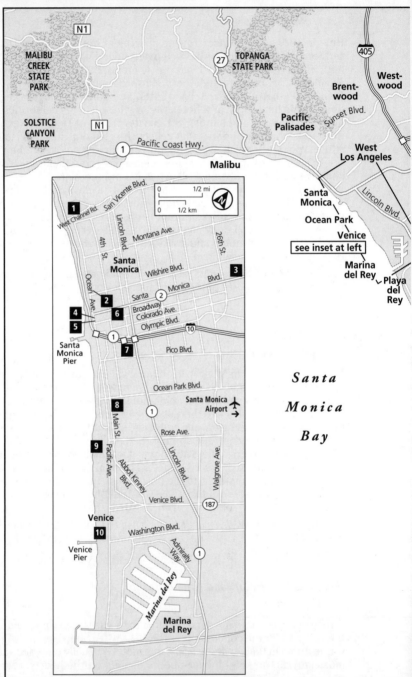

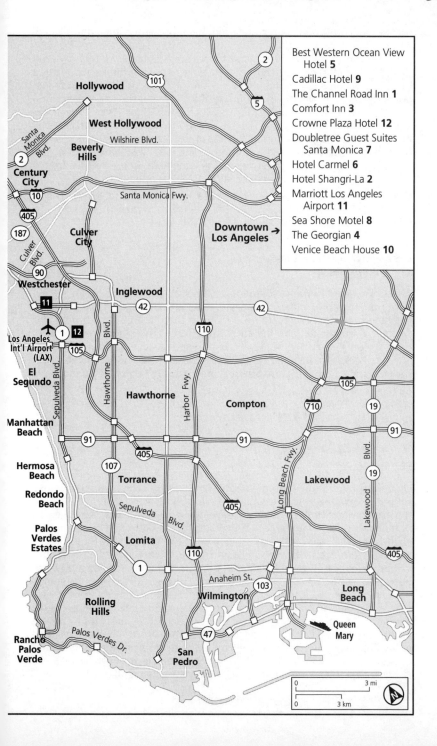

Best Western Ocean View Hotel **5**
Cadillac Hotel **9**
The Channel Road Inn **1**
Comfort Inn **3**
Crowne Plaza Hotel **12**
Doubletree Guest Suites Santa Monica **7**
Hotel Carmel **6**
Hotel Shangri-La **2**
Marriott Los Angeles Airport **11**
Sea Shore Motel **8**
The Georgian **4**
Venice Beach House **10**

priced food. The rooms are good-sized, the large pool is tiled and heated, and the location is good for public transportation and excellent for driving. There are star-spotting spots within walking distance (Victor's Deli and Café, Mayfair Market, Bourgeois Pig, and Cosmopolitan Books and Music), Universal Studios is five minutes away on the freeway, Hollywood is just down the hill, and Dodger Stadium, Griffith Park, and the Los Angeles Zoo are around the corner, making this a great choice for kids (even if the immediate neighbhorhood is not so much). The rooms are large, recently redone in shades of modern, but boring, tan and gray, with marble counters, comfy beds, and recently updated bathrooms. The most expensive rooms, the executive kings, feature a wet bar and seating area. Room service from 7 a.m. to midnight is from the coffee shop, which is open until 3 a.m.

See map p. 89. 6141 Franklin Ave. (between Vine and Gower sts.). ☎ *800-287-1700 or 323-464-5181. Fax: 323-962-0536.* www.bestwestern.com/hollywoodhills hotel. *Rack rates: $79–$169 double. AE, DC, DISC, MC, V.*

Best Western Ocean View Hotel
$$ Santa Monica

A Best Western, but a top-of-the-line one, so if you're looking for a standard modern hotel with a slippery marble foyer/lobby, this is it. Rooms are medium-sized, comfortable, heavy on the deep gold with blue and peach color scheme, and instantly forgettable (though some rooms do have ocean views, and some are handicapped accessible, which isn't always the case in the older Santa Monica hotels). Palisades Park is across the street; the Pier and Third Street Promenade are but a block or so away.

See map p. 85. 1447 Ocean Ave. (across the street from Palisades Park). ☎ *800-452-4888 or 310-458-4888. Fax: 310-458-0848.* www.bestwestern.com/oceanview hotel. *Rack rates: $99–$229 (depending on season).*

Beverly Garland Holiday Inn
$$ Burbank

Owned by, and named after, an actual movie and television star whose Hollywood Walk of Fame designation rests at Hollywood and Highland, the Beverly Garland Holiday Inn is a sprawling, comfortable ranchero-themed hotel located within minutes of Universal Studios. Although the rooms are slightly low-ceilinged with cinderblock walls (we like to think that's part of the ranchero feel), they're warmed up by deep red bedspreads and vaguely Western-themed furniture. A fireplace dominates the lobby, the large pool is heated, and unlike many L.A. hotels, there are tennis courts with an on-site pro. Family suites with special separate kids' rooms with twin bunks and PlayStation are a bonus, especially because kids twelve and under can eat and stay for free. Shuttles depart regularly for Universal Studios, and tours can be arranged to other attractions. The hotel's coffee shop, Paradise Cafe, is a funky retro joint with tropical-print booths and cocktails for grownups. Plus Miss Beverly Garland herself (*My Three Sons, Pretty Poison, D.O.A.,* and more) visits daily and hosts holiday brunches.

West Hollywood Accommodations

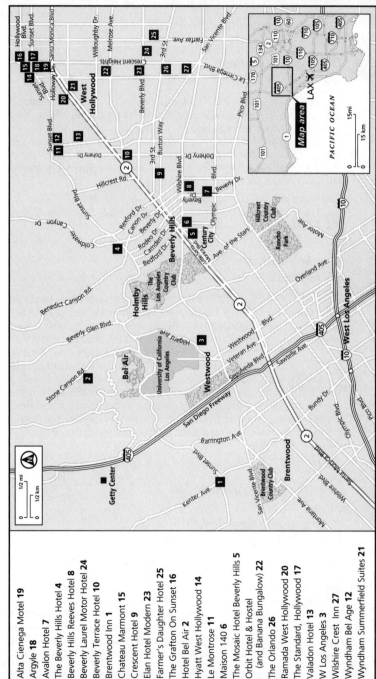

Alta Cienega Motel **19**
Argyle **18**
Avalon Hotel **7**
The Beverly Hills Hotel **4**
Beverly Hills Reeves Hotel **8**
Beverly Laurel Motor Hotel **24**
Beverly Terrace Hotel **10**
Brentwood Inn **1**
Chateau Marmont **15**
Crescent Hotel **9**
Elan Hotel Modern **23**
Farmer's Daughter Hotel **25**
The Grafton On Sunset **16**
Hotel Bel Air **2**
Hyatt West Hollywood **14**
Le Montrose **11**
Maison 140 **6**
The Mosaic Hotel Beverly Hills **5**
Orbit Hotel & Hostel
(and Banana Bungalow) **22**
The Orlando **26**
Ramada West Hollywood **20**
The Standard, Hollywood **17**
Valadon Hotel **13**
W Los Angeles **3**
Wilshire Crest Inn **27**
Wyndham Bel Age **12**
Wyndham Summerfield Suites **21**

See map p. 89. 4222 Vineland Ave., Burbank. ☎ *800-Beverly (800-238-3759) or 818-980-800. Fax: 818-766-0112.* www.beverlygarland.com. *Rack rates: $180 per night. AE, DC, DISC, MV, V.*

The Beverly Hills Hotel
$$$$ **Beverly Hills**

It's that enormous, faded-pink landmark on Sunset Boulevard. You've seen its spires on the cover of The Eagles' *Hotel California* album. You've heard tales of the **Polo Lounge** and those fabulous bungalows. You've heard of endless celebs who have stayed there. Should you? Probably not, we hate to say. Although it has had a major upgrade, the hotel is terribly pricey, and you likely won't get your money's worth. Unless you run into Liz or Mick — can you put a price on that?

See map p. 87. 9641 Sunset Blvd. (at Rodeo Dr.). ☎ *800-283-8885 or 310-276-2251. Fax: 310-887-2887.* www.beverlyhillshotel.com. *Rack rates: $375–$495 double. AE, DC, MC, V.*

Beverly Hills Reeves Hotel
$ **Beverly Hills**

Wow, talk about facelifts! This used to be a cheap place to stay in Beverly Hills; now it's a *nice* and cheap place to stay while vacationing in the 90210. Bought by a caring corporation, the Reeves has gotten a fresh coat of paint, new carpeting, an attractive lobby, and cleaner rooms thanks to the new owners. Yet the room rates remain shockingly low. There's no room service, but a decent continental breakfast is included, and each room has a small TV with cable. For daily and weekly guests, maid service and private bathrooms are included, though it's possible to rent rooms with shared baths (and that means sharing everything). Plus, the Reeves is walking distance from all the glitz and glitter of Rodeo Drive and points adjacent, so you can spend your savings shopping and dining and still say you stayed in Beverly Hills.

See map p. 87. 120 S. Reeves Dr. (half a block from Wilshire Blvd.). ☎ *310-271-3006. Fax: 310-271-2276.* www.bhreeveshotel.com. *Rack rates: $69–$99 per day, $259–$499 per week. AE, DC, DISC MC, V.*

Beverly Laurel Motor Hotel
$ **West Hollywood**

Built in 1964, the Beverly Laurel has plenty of kitschy charm, especially in the elevator, which is paneled with tiki-styled faux wood. It has a heated pool and cable TV; rooms — all of which face the pool — feature fridges and microwaves, along with Vargas prints and electric-blue walls. Larger rooms have kitchenettes with a ministove. Pets are welcome with a $10-per-day charge. There's no room service, but the hip diner **Swingers** is right downstairs. It's a favorite with porn stars, who actually sleep, not work, at the hotel! The motel has an arrangement with Easton's Gym

Hollywood Accommodations

Best Western Hollywood Hills Hotel **1**
Beverly Garland Holiday Inn **3**
Bevonshire Lodge **11**
Celebrity Hotel **7**
Graciela Burbank **2**
Hilton Los Angeles/Universal City **5**
Hollywood Roosevelt Hotel **10**
Magic Castle Hotel **6**
Orchid Suites Hotel **9**
Renaissance Hollywood Hotel **8**
Sheraton Universal Hotel **4**

across the street, and guests can get a reduced rate at the health club. Bus tours to see the sights can be arranged; it's close to the Farmers Market as well. Free parking.

See map p. 87. 8018 Beverly Blvd. (between Fairfax Ave. and La Cienega Blvd.). ☎ *800-962-3824 or 323-651-2441. Fax: 323-651-5225. Rack rates: $80–$84 double. AE, DC, MC, V.*

Beverly Terrace Hotel
$$ **Beverly Hills**

This is the best hotel deal in Beverly Hills in terms of a balance between price and quality (the Reeves is cheaper but not nearly as nice). It's located six (long) blocks from the heart of Beverly Hills and is about a quarter-mile steep hike from Sunset Strip. The exterior is fabulous '50s glamour; the interior has a cozy, tropical feel and a pair of cockatiels and has been recently redecorated with custom-made Chinoiserie furniture. The entire hotel is nonsmoking, though you can puff poolside under Indonesian-style canopies. The rooms, all of which come with refrigerators, are not large, and that's being kind, though the Oriental upgrades — rooms come in either muted jade green, neutrals, or sexy red and black — give an airy feel. Most rooms feature showers only, though you can request a tub room. Complimentary continental breakfast is served poolside daily, and the restaurant **Trattoria Amici** is located on-site.

See map p. 87. 469 N. Doheny Dr. (at Santa Monica Blvd.). ☎ *800-421-7223 or 310-274-8141. Fax: 310-385-1998.* www.beverlyterracehotel.com *Rack rates: $105–$145. AE, DISC, MC, V.*

Bevonshire Lodge
$ **Hollywood**

Oh, this motel is very inexpensive, the pool is unheated year-round, which can make for a really brisk morning swim, and rooms are basic and unfancy. But each room has a fridge, and some come with kitchenettes. A huge, famous rubber tree — taking up a ridiculous amount of space, bless it — grows in the lobby. The owner is a former employee who saved up money and bought the place; he also owns the (slightly) pricier **Beverly Inn** (7701 Beverly Blvd.; ☎ 323-931-8109) a block west, which is a fine but utterly basic value given the price and easy access to the Farmers Market and CBS. If you're looking for function over form, and a convenient location (with free parking!), the Bevonshire is the motel for you.

See map p. 89. 7575 Beverly Blvd. (at Curson Ave.). ☎ *323-936-6154. Fax: 323-934-6640. Rack rates: $50–$69. AE, DC, DISC, MC, V.*

Brentwood Inn
$$$ **Santa Monica**

Though technically not in Santa Monica, this venerable motor hotel turned upscale inn is located just five minutes from the ocean and ten from the Getty Center and UCLA. O.J. Simpson's old house was just down the street

Downtown Accommodations

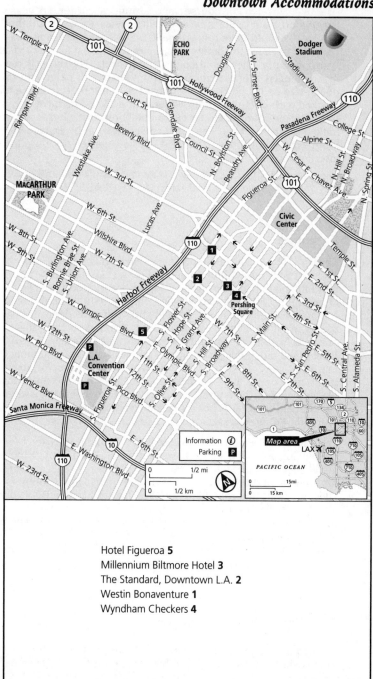

Hotel Figueroa **5**
Millennium Biltmore Hotel **3**
The Standard, Downtown L.A. **2**
Westin Bonaventure **1**
Wyndham Checkers **4**

(it's been leveled, of course) and around a corner, so yes, you're in Brentwood, a very affluent area of Los Angeles. Rumor has it that decades ago locals would have their romantic, adulterous assignations here, but really for decades the family-owned Brentwood Inn has served as a spare bedroom for families and friends visiting locals. The recently redecorated high-ceilinged rooms feature soothing shades of beige and cream and queen-size beds and come with high-speed Internet access, a minifridge stocked with complimentary water, and a TV. Baths have only showers, but the room charge includes continental breakfast, afternoon cookies and milk, and free parking. The office area will soon be expanded into a full lobby with an outdoor patio, and the new garden is set up for wireless Internet access.

See map p. 87. 12200 Sunset Blvd. (at Kenter). ☎ *800-840-3808 or 310-476-9981.* www.thebrentwood.com. *Rack rates: $139 –$169. AE,DC, DISC, MC, V.*

Cadillac Hotel
$ Venice

Built in 1905 as Charlie Chaplin's residence, this hotel is funky but cheap, a sort of Southern California version of the classic European pensione. A multimillion-dollar renovation, a top to bottom redo, was just beginning at press time. All the rooms will be stripped to the walls and redesigned in "complete Art Deco style," with slightly different décor for each of the rooms. We'll be the judge of that, but the goal is to bring this up at least one level from its current budget position, and it is a nice old building, with a fun grand old lobby. Plans include wireless access throughout the building. The two-room suite at the top, with beach views, for around $130 a night, may be the best bargain in town. The rooftop (unfortunately, no plans to change the tar-paper surface, but who looks down when you can look out at the ocean?) has a sweeping view of the bay (you can see up to four different fireworks shows from here on July 4).

Yes, there can be homeless people lurking around the (don't forget free!) parking lot; yes, services are basic, but the staff will arrange tours for you, and the location is right on the beach. Right there. We mean, *Baywatch* has filmed here. And there's a piece of the Berlin Wall in the lobby — we don't know why, but isn't that charming? The hotel's location is wonderful, on a sweet little alley street with three good cafes and a couple shops. Oh, and the beach. Exercise machines are in the basement next to the laundry, which tells you a lot, but the hotel is also just a couple blocks from the happening part of Main Street — and did we mention that it's right on the beach?!

See map p. 85. 8 Dudley Ave. (at Speedway). ☎ *310-399-8876. Fax: 310-399-4536.* www.thecadillachotel.com. *Rack rates: $79–$150. AE, MC, V.*

Celebrity Hotel
$ Hollywood

Smack dab in the heart of what the Chamber of Commerce desperately hopes will be a rejuvenated Hollywood, and dwarfed by the backside of the Renaissance Hotel, the Celebrity is, at press time, undergoing a massive renovation, including a new façade, marble lobby, and completely redecorated rooms. Say goodbye to the old gray-and-maroon murals and hello to a more classic contemporary look. Despite the upgrades, the hotel maintains its reasonable prices, making it a great place to stay if you prefer to spend your money on souvenirs. Its location is also a plus — just around the corner from the fabulous Hollywood & Highland Mall and Hollywood Boulevard itself. After dark, walk in groups.

See map p. 89. 1775 Orchid Ave. (between Hollywood Blvd. and Franklin Ave.). ☎ **800-222-7090** *or 323-850-6464. Fax: 323-850-7667.* www.hotelcelebrity.com. *Rack rates: $69–$105. AE, DISC, MC, V.*

The Channel Road Inn
$$$ **Santa Monica**

Nestled in Santa Monica Canyon less than two blocks from the beach, this three-story Colonial Revival Craftsman has been lovingly restored by owner Suzanne Zolla. Transformed into a period-perfect bed and breakfast (with all the modern conveniences, including in-room TVs and VCRs and a business center), the Channel Road Inn features 14 unique, circa-1920 rooms where fresh-baked cookies and handwritten notes greet arriving guests. Each room has its own private bath, and suites include a Jacuzzi tub. Homemade lemonade sits on the sideboard in the relaxed, wicker-filled breakfast room. You can relax in the living room, play piano, or take advantage of the bicycles provided to guests and pedal through the bucolic streets. Breakfast includes award-winning egg soufflés, home-baked goodies, fresh fruit, apple pancakes, and home-baked scones. At sunset, cheese, wine, and iced tea are laid out for guests. Although the canyon section of Santa Monica is not loaded with shops, downtown Santa Monica and Montana Avenue shopping districts are just minutes away by car, and there is a steakhouse across the street.

See map p. 85. 219 W. Channel Rd. (off Pacific Coast Hiwy.). ☎ **310-459-1920**. *Fax: 310-454-9920. Rack rates: $195–$375. AE, DC, DISC, MC, V.*

Chateau Marmont
$$$$ **Hollywood/West Hollywood**

Though its most notorious fame comes from John Belushi's overdose death (in Bungalow 2 in 1982), this is a fabulously romantic, slightly spooky old hotel much favored by celebs who value naturally acquired style and quirkiness. The whole place looks like a setting for a Raymond Chandler–style mystery, to say nothing of discreet assignations, which is probably why the legendary studio boss Harry Cohn famously said, "If you must get into trouble, do it at the Chateau Marmont." It was once a residence hotel (and many longtime occupants still live there), so the rooms can often be ridiculously large, especially the suites, which were originally intended as apartments. The furnishings and style in said rooms may put you in mind of the slighty faded Art Deco grandeur of the Coen Brothers' movie *Barton Fink* (though the beds are modern and comfortable). The tree-rimmed pool area is gorgeous and, along with the 1920s Spanish Mission lobby, is a hot spot for star spotting. The celebrity list, past and present, goes on and on, but suffice it to say that we were just there and so were Nicole Kidman and Ben Stiller. Jim Morrison once fell out of a window here. If the price is not in your budget, and your idea of honeymoon bliss requires more pristine, conventional surfaces, at least come by for a drink on the grounds.

See map p. 87. 8221 Sunset Blvd. (near Laurel Canyon Blvd.). ☎ *800-CHATEAU (800-242-8328) or 323-656-1010. Fax: 323-655-5311.* www.chateaumarmont.com. *Rack rates: $280 and up double. AE, DC, MC, V.*

Comfort Inn
$ Santa Monica

If you'd like to stay in Santa Monica but the high tariffs scare you off or you want a more central location, consider going a few miles east to the far edges of the city. The Comfort Inn is about 15 minutes from the beach and 20 from Beverly Hills in not the most glamorous part of the burg, though McDonald's and Carl's Jr. are just across the street. Rooms are, well, rooms, but really you want to be out sightseeing, don't you? There is a pool, parking is free, and muffins and coffee are served in the morning.

See map p. 85. 2815 Santa Monica Blvd. ☎ *800-228-5150 or 310 828-5517. Fax: 310-829-6084.* www.choicehotels.com. *Rack rates: $79–$129. AE, DC, DISC, MC, V.*

Crescent Hotel
$$ Beverly Hills

Originally used as an auxiliary building for Paramount Pictures (in the 1920s, when the studio was located in this area, actors used it for naps between scenes), this chic hotel — formerly the charming and serviceable Beverly Crescent — has undergone a major facelift. It's still charming, but now it's hip, sleek, *and* charming. Think concrete vanities in the bathrooms, flat-screen TVs, DVD players, and fluffy bathrobes and custom Italian linens in each room. **Boe,** the hotel's restaurant/lounge, draws the arty and powerful with its haute cuisine version of Asian "street food" and fusiony dishes (the room was designed by Dodd Mitchell, responsible for Linq, Koi, and other hot spots) and serves up an Oscar-themed signature cocktail, the Mystic River. Yet despite all the fabulosity and upscale accoutrements, the Crescent is still very reasonably priced for the neighborhood.

See map p. 87. 403 N. Crescent Dr. (at Brighton Way). ☎ *800-451-1566 or 310-247-0505. Fax: 310-247-9053.* www.beverlycrescenthotel.com. *Rack rates: $159–$250 (ask about discounts). AE, DC, DISC, MC, V.*

Crowne Plaza Hotel
$$$ Airport

The Crowne Plaza Hotel is situated a block closer to Los Angeles Airport than the Marriott, with slightly larger, perfectly pleasant rooms, Krispy Kreme doughnuts, and a fitness room that has a great view and plenty of equipment, doubles on all cardio machines, plus a free-weight bench and a weight machine. Rates are flexible, and there are suites as well as standard rooms with a king or two doubles. You won't find any room safes or minibars, but you can rent a fridge. The multilingual staff speaks Chinese, English, French, German, Italian, and Spanish. The hotel offers currency exchange, tours for sightseeing and to local attractions, room service, handicapped-accessible rooms, a pool, free transportation to and from the airport (including a great "park and fly" deal, perfect if you are making a fast jaunt up to San Francisco; you can park your car for free for several days if you pay a certain rate at the hotel for a night or two), and who can forget those Krispy Kreme doughnuts?

See map p. 85. 5985 W. Century Blvd. (near the airport). ☎ *800-315-3700 or 310-642-7500; TTY 310-348-9061. Fax: 310-417-3608.* www.crowneplaza.com. *Rack rates: $179–$450. AE, DC, DISC, MC, V.*

Doubletree Guest Suites Santa Monica
$$$$ **Santa Monica**

Don't be scared off by the rack rates at this hotel; Doubletree's Web site offers discounts of 40 percent or so, plus other specials. The location is prime: four blocks from both the beach and Santa Monica's Main Street. Plus, this is where all the heavyweights in the O.J. Simpson civil trial stayed.

See map p. 85. 1707 Fourth St. (four blocks from the beach). ☎ *800-222-TREE (800-222-8733) or 310-395-3332. Fax: 310-452-7399.* www.doubletree.com. *Rack rates: $199–$1,200. AE, DC, DISC, MC, V.*

Elan Hotel Modern
$$–$$$ **West Hollywood**

Just a block up from the Beverly Center, this strives for a very sleek and chic image, which is difficult to do when the lobby looks out at a Taco Bell and a (well-combed) Goodwill across the way. Still, it seems to bring in a lot of hip-hop business, so perhaps the image is successful enough. Rooms have essentially really nice versions of classic hotel/motel furniture, though the bathrooms are stylish, if small, with fruity-smelling amenities. Note that you can get some traffic noise if your room faces Beverly Boulevard. Beds have good sheets but not much in the way of a pad on the firm mattresses. Instead of calling room service, you can order from Jan's Coffee Shop across the street from 6 a.m. to 2 a.m., and they'll jaywalk it over for you. The hotel serves complimentary continental breakfast daily, and as of this writing, there's a nightly manager's wine and cheese reception for guests. The small on-site health club features free weights, a universal weight machine, a cross-trainer, and a treadmill; if that doesn't suit you, arrangements can be made for you at Beverly Hills Fitness just a few blocks away. Or just walk over to the Beverly Center and power shop. We wish a generic hotel had this much style (note the splashes of colored tile breaking up the otherwise all-white showers) or at least that this hotel had more-generic hotel prices.

See map p. 87. 8435 Beverly Blvd. (at La Cienega Blvd.). ☎ *888-661-0398 or 323-658-6663. Fax: 323-658-6640.* www.elanhotel.com. *Rack rates: $129–$215 double (ask about corporate discounts). AE, DC, DISC, MC.*

Farmer's Daughter Hotel
$$ West Hollywood

Stick a motel, an old family hotel, and a B&B into a blender, and then let 'er rip, and you have the Farmer's Daughter Hotel. For a long time, this was a rather notorious hot-sheets hotel, but a recent facelift made it a hip dive in the right way. You are just as likely to see gray-haired grandmothers staying here for college-graduation family gatherings as you are young movie execs having a naughty little tryst. The building still betrays its motel origins, though now it's tarted up in shades of bright blues and teals. Rooms, cute but not plush, are done in "His" and "Hers" style (just a change in color scheme, plus rooster wallpaper for the boys) and include rocking chairs, slightly dingy gingham curtains, CD players, and high-speed Internet access. Many rooms have balconies, though these overlook either busy Fairfax Avenue or parking lots. The slightly seedy pool area has blow-up pool toys, another example here of irony and whimsy run amuck. The concierge can arrange tours and TV-show taping tickets. Location, across from the Farmer's Market and Grove, near the Jewish Fairfax district, is optimal, full of shopping and eating opportunities for all budgets.

See map p. 87. 115 S. Fairfax Ave. (at Beverly Blvd.). ☎ *800-334-1658 or 323-937-3930. Fax: 323-932-1608.* www.farmersdaughterhotel.com. *Rack rates: $115–$125. AE, DC, DISC, MC, V.*

The Georgian
$$$ Santa Monica

For our money, because we value atmosphere above all, we find the blue-and-gold Georgian your best pricey bet in Santa Monica. Though it dates from the 1930s (it's a National Trust Historic Hotel), the hotel is more Edwardian than Georgian, and oh, is it stately. It's well maintained, too, by a polite staff. Basic rooms, in shades of rust and yellow, are good size (the difference in price depends on what sort of bed is within), romantic, and cozy thanks to furniture that seems to know its place. Suites are expensive but look almost straight out of a 1930s screwball comedy. Bathrooms veer towards quaint and/or vintage (read: not ultramodern), which doesn't bother us but may concern you. You'll find a bar and restaurant called the **Speakeasy** featuring American cuisine — Clark Gable ate here! — plus a health club, room service (for breakfast only, alas), an e-business center, and the ocean across the street. We initially want more, but then we look at the place and get over it.

See map p. 85. 1415 Ocean Ave. (across the street from Palisades Park). ☎ *800-538-8147 or 310-395-9945. Fax: 310-656-0904.* www.georgianhotel.com. *Rack rates: $150–$400 double (rates slightly higher in summer). AE, DC, DISC, MC, V.*

Graciela Burbank
$$$–$$$$ Burbank

This gorgeous luxury hotel is close to Burbank Airport, studios, and freeways and houses directors, actors, and other industry types while in town for meeting and shoots; some live there for the entire time their film is shooting. Over 60 percent of its elegant rooms are deluxe suites with fully equipped kitchenettes, complete with tableware, set in a polished-granite countertop. The smaller "superior" rooms are still huge (over 390 square feet), but the superior suites are gianormous — practically apartment-sized. All the sleek-yet-comfortable, blond-wood-furnished rooms come with Italian linen, down comforters, and marble bathrooms stocked with high-end amenities. Breakfast and dinner are served in the Library Lounge (it really is a library with a cool selection of art and film books), and room service is 24 hours. Rooftop spa, exercise room (with personal TVs on each treadmill), and sauna add to the luxury. The professional staff is genuine and kind, and the whole place has a boutique feel despite its size. Primarily a business hotel, the Graciela offers weekend discounts on its superior and deluxe suites.

See map p. 89. 322 N. Pass Ave., Burbank. ☎ *888-956-1900 or 818-842-8887. Fax: 818-260-8999.* www.thegraciela.com. *Rack rates: $199–$500. AE, DC, DISC, MV, V.*

The Grafton on Sunset
$$–$$$$ West Hollywood

A hotel designed with feng shui principles to give guests a delightful stay — it's just *so* L.A. You get round-the-clock room service and a beautiful city view from the pool. Best of all, the hotel's courtesy car is a lime-green PT Cruiser. The hip minimalist steakhouse **Balboa** is located on-site.

See map p. 87. 8462 W. Sunset Blvd. (near Beverly Hills). ☎ *800-821-3660 or 323-654-4600. Fax: 323-654-5918.* www.graftononsunset.com. *Rack rates: $179–$500 double. AE, DC, DISC, MC, V.*

Hilton Checkers
$$ Downtown

This hotel is housed in a gorgeous, sculptural-carved, limestone-façaded 1927 building (the renovated Mayflower) and is as well situated as a hotel in Downtown can be — it's right next to the Central Library; across from the plush Biltmore; an easy stroll to the Music Center and Walt Disney Concert Hall, MOCA, and the fashion and jewelry districts; and in a corner of L.A. that has a surprising Manhattan–San Francisco vibe. Newly renovated rooms feature great bedside lighting (a rarity), dark wood, built-in Chippendale-style cabinetry, comfortable mattresses, silky duvets, and lovely cove molding. Note that rooms ending in 02 are barely big enough to swing a cat in, while 07s are the largest. Warm peaches-and-cream marble is everywhere, even on the inlaid surfaces of the computer-ready desks. A tiny rooftop lap pool offers fantastic views of the downtown cityscape, which is visible from rooms on the eighth floor and up; others get views of office buildings. You get high-speed Internet access in your room, 24-hour room service, and complimentary downtown shuttle service from 7 a.m. to 9 p.m. Plus, the lovely restaurant serves one of the nicest afternoon teas in town. Service is personable, well informed, and friendly, and the special weekend rate of $99 makes this hotel a real and surprising bargain.

See map p. 91. 535 S. Grand Ave. (between Fifth and Sixth sts.). ☎ *800-423-5798 or 213-624-0000. Fax: 213-626-9906.* www.checkershotel.com. *Rack rates: $189 weekdays; $99 weekends double. AE, DISC, MC, V.*

Hilton Los Angeles/Universal City and Sheraton Universal Hotel
$$ Universal City

The only real reason to stay at these big, bland corporate hotels is that they're across the street from Universal Studios, CityWalk, and the Amphitheatre. Granted, these are perfectly decent upscale hotels, with all the amenities — including large, nicely decorated rooms, room service, in-room safes, coffee makers, minibars, valet parking, fitness rooms, and pools — but you can find more-centrally located hotels at the same or lower rates that feature way more personality, with no need to traverse the freeways to get around. Both hotels have efficient, professional staffs and not-cheap restaurants. (The Hilton features huge, pricey buffets daily for every meal.) Sure, it may be fun to say that you stayed at the same hotel where "guests of this show stayed" (that would be the Sheraton), and studios all over Hollywood do put up midlevel out-of-town actors at these hotels, so there's the chance of spotting someone who looks vaguely familar. Many rooms *do* have spectacular views of the city, but the only real pluses are the Universal tour packages and the sense of rich reliability offered by these hotels; both have huge two-bedroom suites available for similarly huge amounts of money. Fans of Beelzebub may want to request room number 666, available at both hotels, if only to say that they did.

See map p. 89. Hilton Universal City & Towers: 555 Universal Terrace Parkway. ☎ *800-445-8667 or 818-506-2500. Fax: 818-509-2058.* www.universalcity. hilton.com. *Rack rates: $150–$1,400 per night. AE, DC, DISC, MC, V. Sheraton Universal Hotel: 333 Universal Hollywood Dr.* ☎ *888-625-5144 or 818-980-1212. Fax: 818-985-4980.* www.sheraton.com. *Rack rates: $159–$1,000 per night. AE, DC, DISC, MC, V.*

Hollywood Roosevelt Hotel
$$$ Hollywood

This is a fabulous old Roaring Twenties Deco/Mission wonder, beautifully restored and reputedly haunted by Marilyn Monroe, amongst others. It lies smack in the middle of Hollywood Upgrade Central (across the street from Grauman's and down the street from the Hollywood & Highland Complex; the Walk of Fame runs right in front of it), and you won't get more style and a better Hollywood location at a cheaper price. Rooms have been recently upgraded with brushed-steel, haute moderne furniture that strikes a pose among Asian, space age, and Deco, Frette sheets, down duvets, and wireless Internet, the latter for a daily fee. There are views of mountains and the Hollywood sign from one side of the hotel and the rest of the city from the other side. The longtime jazz club, the Cinegrill, has reopened as Feinsteins's at the Cinegrill. The very first Academy Awards banquet was held here, and David Hockney just repainted the inside of the swimming pool, restoring his original mural. You may spot a big name or two here. Great for kids, too.

See map p. 89. 7000 Hollywood Blvd. (between La Brea and Highland aves.). ☎ *800-950-7667 or 323-466-7000. Fax: 323-469-7006.* www.hollywoodroosevelt.com. *Rack rates: $159–$299 double. AE, DC, DISC, MC, V.*

Hotel Bel Air
$$$$ Bel Air

This fabulous, 12-acre, lush hideaway — preferred by the well-heeled who love its discretion and creature comforts — is too expensive for most people who aren't on the *Forbes* 100 list. (Tom Cruise and Nicole Kidman *lived here,* if that tells you anything.) But if you can afford it — or better yet, expense it! — then by all means, go.

See map p. 87. 701 Stone Canyon Rd. (north of Sunset Blvd.). ☎ *800-648-4097 or 310-472-1211. Fax: 310-476-5890.* www.hotelbelair.com. *Rack rates: $385–$525 double. AE, DC, MC, V.*

Hotel Carmel
$$ Santa Monica

An almost 80-year-old veteran of the beachside hotel scene, this Italianate building is admittedly low on amenities (no room service or coffee makers), but has recently freshened up its furnishings with Mission Craftsman reproductions, rich burgundy down comforters, and new ultracomfy beds; dataports and laundry service are available. But the real reason we list the hotel here is that it's perfectly located between the beach (two blocks away) and the Third Street Promenade (one block away). Plus, though it's hardly hostel-cheap, the rates are very reasonable for beach-area accommodations, and you simply can't find a hotel this well situated.

See map p. 85. 201 Broadway (at Second St.). ☎ *800-445-8695 or 310-451-2469. Fax: 310-393-4180.* www.hotelcarmel.com. *Rack rates: $100–$190 suite. AE, DC, DISC, MC, V.*

Hotel Figueroa
$$ Downtown

Someone is taking great care with a lovely old hotel. The Figueroa has, hands down, the most gorgeous public spaces of any Downtown hotel: decor in a Moorish theme (think Moroccan meets Spanish), exotic fabrics, wrought-iron and wood furniture, tiles and other decorative bits of fancy, and soaring ceilings — how the heck did this place land here? Rooms are not quite as splashy, but boy, did somebody try, successfully tarting up what was probably a dumpy old hotel by painting the walls with bold faux-finish paint and adding more of that exotic furniture and fabric. Recently, they replaced the crappy old TVs and removed the acoustical tile, exposing some wonderful beamed ceilings. Rooms vary in size; 25s and 09s have cunning archways, and 30s are the biggest. With its desert succulents and splashing fountains, the pool area is *so* Palm Springs — who would expect to find such a quiet, secluded spot right in the middle of Downtown? The across-the-street location from the Staples Center sports complex means that this is a favorite meeting-up spot for Lakers and Clippers fans and generally happening spot most nights, so do pop in to the lobby for a drink or a bite at one of the two restaurants. There are plans for wireless access in the business center soon. Given that you can get similarly priced (at least on weekends), more up-to-date rooms at the Hilton Checkers, this may not be the place for you, but note that a former top executive with a national hotel chain volunteered that this is the only place he stays when he's in town, and that can tell you a great deal.

See map p. 91. 939 S. Figueroa St. (at Olympic Blvd.). ☎ *800-421-9092 or 213-627-8971. Fax: 213-689-0305.* www.figueroahotel.com. *Rack rates: $104–$136 double. AE, MC, V.*

Hotel Shangri-La
$$$ Santa Monica

Miami-Deco fabulous on the outside, the Shangri-La is a venerable Santa Monica establishment that is 90 percent one-bedroom suites, the majority of which have been retro-fitted with era-appropriate Heywood Wakefield furniture, including custom-built entertainment centers that match the original tables, desks, and armoires to give the rooms an authentic feel. Sadly, some of the ghastly 1970s repro-Deco stuff still floats around on the top floor. The often-upscale guests (rich musicians such as Madonna and a number of actors) doubtless enjoy the fact that they are staying directly across from Palisades Park and, thus, the ocean, access to which makes up for the lack of a pool. The gym has recently been moved and now has an oceanfront view. Continental breakfast and a simple afternoon tea are included in the price, as is parking, which is a real bonus.

See map p. 85. 1301 Ocean Ave. (two blocks from Third Street Promenade). ☎ *800-345-STAY (800-345-7829) or 310-394-2791. Fax: 310-451-3351.* www.shangrila-hotel.com. *Rack rates: $170–$550 double (ask about AAA discounts). AE, DISC, MC, V.*

Hyatt West Hollywood
$$$ West Hollywood

You've seen the rooftop pool in the movies *This is Spinal Tap* and *Almost Famous;* you've read the stories about the famous "Riot House" — no self-respecting 1970s rock star could claim that title unless he'd lobbed a TV out its windows. Nowadays the Hyatt is a bit more sedate, but it still vibrates with energy (and the occasional metal guitarist), much like the trippy op-art carpeting in the hallways. Many rooms (done up in good corporate hotel style, but rock-star hangovers could get a workout from all the patterns) have aquariums or balconies with hillside or Sunset Strip views. A fitness center has all the necessary equipment; the gift shop sells bathing suits in case you've left yours behind. You get room service from 6 a.m. till midnight, a bar, a restaurant with a chi-chi Chinese theme serving drinks and dim sum, money-exchange services, and fabulous views — though no longer of Robert Plant declaring that he is a golden god.

See map p. 87. 8401 Sunset Blvd. (at Kings Rd.). ☎ *323-656-1234. Fax: 323-650-7024.* www.hyatt.com. *Rack rates: $195–$390 double (ask about AAA and senior discounts). AE, DC, DISC, MC, V.*

Le Montrose
$$$ West Hollywood

Discreetly tucked onto a residential side street south of the Sunset Strip (which makes one feel a tad safer, especially with kids in tow) and one block from Beverly Hills, Le Montrose offers quiet European-style comfort amid Art Nouveau decor in the lobby and elevators (which are something to see, honest), plus a restaurant, a health club, and a rooftop tennis court and pool. All rooms are suites with sunken living rooms, fireplaces, fax machines, and twice-daily maid service; most come with kitchenettes. Free bicycles (adult size only) and tennis rackets are available for guests. Compared with equivalent places in the area, this is reasonably priced. Because it also has bed-and-breakfast packages, and children under 14 aren't generally charged, this isn't a bad upscale choice for families.

See map p. 87. 900 Hammond St. (at Sunset Blvd.). ☎ *800-766-0666 or 310-855-1115. Fax: 310-657-9192.* www.lemontrose.com. *Rack rates: $149–$950 per night. AE, DC, DISC, MC, V.*

Magic Castle Hotel
$$ Hollywood

The Magic Castle is a longtime clubhouse hangout for magicians and is impossible to get into unless you're a member (or invited by one) or unless you stay at this former dump now transformed into a respectable bit of lodging. The gray-and-green, spanking-clean, new rooms (embellished with magician showbills) have plenty of elbow room; many rooms even have kitchenettes (grocery-shopping services are available). The on-site pool is square and situated in the middle of the courtyard, but you have access to the curvy number at the hotel's sister establishment, the all-suites **Hollywood Hills Hotel Apartments** (1999 N. Sycamore; ☎ 323-874-5089; same rates and also worth checking out). The immediate surroundings are pulpy — as opposed to seedy — but it does have security parking, and you'll need a car; this hotel isn't walking distance to anything, though the Metro Station and the Hollywood & Highland Complex (with shops, movie theaters and cafes, and Ryan Seacrest live) are not too many blocks (depending on your perspective) away. It's not the most pleasant block; *however,* this area is ripe for transition, so take advantage of the charm and prices while they're reasonable.

See map p. 89. 7025 Franklin Ave. (between La Brea and Highland aves.). ☎ *800-741-4915 or 323-851-0800. Fax: 323-581-4926.* www.magiccastlehotel.com. *Rack rates: $99–$219. AE, DC, DISC, MC, V.*

Maison 140
$$ Beverly Hills

Once upon a time, Maison 140 was a boardinghouse owned by silent-screen star Lillian Gish. Now, it's the sexiest, most decadently decorated hotel in the greater Los Angeles area. From the all-black lobby with the most minimal touches of white and red to the smallish but luxe rooms stocked with Frette linens, chinoiserie furnishings, and Philosophy-brand bath products (most rooms have showers only; you can request one with a tub), this boutique hotel swathes you in glamorous, sybaritic elegance. The hotel's sitting area serves continental breakfast in the morning and then shifts into a full bar at cocktail hour. Twenty-four-hour room service is provided by an off-site kitchen, there's a small fitness center with clean new machines, and you're within walking distance of all of Beverly Hills. This place is as gorgeous as its glittering clientele.

See map p. 87. 140 S. Lasky Dr. (just south of Wilshire Blvd.). ☎ *800-432-5444 or 310-281-4000. Fax: 310-281-4001.* www.maison140.com. *Rack rates: $149–$229 (Internet discounts available). AE, DC, MC, V.*

Marriott Los Angeles Airport
$$ Airport

The Los Angeles Airport Marriott is just five minutes from Los Angeles International Airport (LAX) and ten minutes from Venice beach, and the friendly, helpful concierge can arrange tours and shuttles to tourist attractions. With two bars, two restaurants, a sports bar, a Starbucks, a car-rental outlet, handicapped-accessible rooms, an ATM, a gift shop, room service, a pool, a fitness room, a Kinko's business center, a notary public, a beauty shop, laundry and dry-cleaning services, and complimentary transportation to LAX, this is a fine way station or base camp from which to explore Los Angeles should you need to be close to the departure gates. Rooms can be hard to come by during Labor Day weekend, however, when the hotel is packed solid with guests of the Sweet & Hot Foundation's annual jazz festival; the hotel's warm relationship with the festival is demonstrated on the Jazz Walk of Fame around the pool. Rooms are nice (and can be discounted based on availability). The staff is relaxed and outgoing, and there's a calm, efficient vibe throughout.

See map p. 85. 5855 W. Century Blvd. (at the airport). ☎ *800-228-9290 or 310-641-5700. Fax: 310-337-5358.* www.marriott.com. *Rack rates: $194–$425. AE, DC, DISC, MC, V.*

Millennium Biltmore Hotel
$$$ **Downtown**

They just don't make 'em like this anymore. The Millennium Biltmore is a near masterpiece of a glorious old hotel — but though we swoon over the heavenly details (would you *look* at those ceilings?!), keep in mind the "old" aspect. If you require pristine, new, high-concept hotels, move down the listings to either of The Standard hotels and let us get on with it. Would you look at that tile in and around the indoor pool? All right, we'll stop. Here's what you need to know: This full-service hotel is centrally located in Downtown L.A. It has a good, Art Deco health club. The rooms (French Regency in appearance) vary in size (07s are usually largest, whereas 40s are the smallest, and the nicest rooms overlook Pershing Square), but all accommodations have windows that open, firm beds (but scratchy sheets), and dinky baths. It's a little frilly for the business traveler and a bit too staid and sedate for families. But we'd be thrilled to stay here.

See map p. 91. 506 S. Grand Ave. (between Fifth and Sixth sts.). ☎ *800-245-8673 or 213-624-1011. Fax: 213-612-1545.* www.millenniumhotels.com. *Rack rates: $199 and up double.*

The Mosaic Hotel Beverly Hills
$$$ **Beverly Hills**

What was once a nice, moderately priced, 49-room inn suddenly became very aware that it's perfectly located on a quiet street in Beverly Hills and turned itself into a boutique hotel. Think nouveau-Byzantine, glass mosaic tiling meets Oriental-moderne for the public areas and rooms with sleek black furniture upholstered in neutrals and mossy greens plus down comforters. Add in a bar with more black furniture and tiling off the lobby and a tapas restaurant, in the same décor, featuring global cuisine. The pool is lushily landscaped and heated year-round. Rack rates on suites are a deal for the area; for rooms, it's about even with other Bev Hills boutique and certain large hotels, but check out their Internet specials for some true deals.

See map p. 87. 125 S. Spalding Dr. (south of Wilshire Blvd.). ☎ *800-463-4466 or 310-278-0303. Fax: 310-278-1728.* www.innatbeverlyhills.com. *Rack rates: $189–$429 double. AE, DC, DISC, MC, V.*

Orbit Hotel & Hostel (and Banana Bungalow)
$ **West Hollywood**

This spartan yet comfortable accommodation is college-backpacker territory, though it may appeal to budget travelers accustomed to no-frills Euro lodgings (especially in the nicer parts of Eastern Europe). A former retirement home, it's gradually being turned into a youth-hostel-type place (Banana Bungalow has become a trademark for this), but there are definite style touches, from the bright colors used in the guest rooms to the Jetsons-type furniture in the public areas (which also include satellite TVs, a pool table, a "movie room," and two Internet-access computers). The rooms have dinky but good baths, TVs without cable but with DVD players, and clock radios, so they're a fine bargain at a fine location on Melrose. The hotel offers various city tours, shuttles, and even airport shuttles (pickup only). The average guests are in their twenties (which translates into serious parties), but don't be surprised to see some folks in their thirties, and even a few middle-aged Germans who know a good bargain when they see one.

See map p. 87. 7950 Melrose Ave. ☎ *877-ORBITUS or 323-655-1510.* www.orbit hotel.com. *Rack rates: $49–$112. Banana Bungalow:* ☎ *800-4-HOSTEL.* www. bananabungalow.com. *Rack rates: $15–$89. No credit cards.*

Orchid Suites Hotel
$ Hollywood

Located on the same cul de sac as the Celebrity Hotel, the Orchid Suites is a comfortable, no-nonsense place to stay. The majority of units are large one- or two-bedroom suites with full kitchens, while the four junior suites, each with twin beds, feature a kitchenette with stove, fridge, and coffee makers. There's a pool, and the friendly staff is happy to hook you up with discount tickets to nearby Universal Studios. Rates go up during the summer and up even more during the Oscars and the Playboy Jazz Festival but can actually be lower than rack depending on season and availablity.

See map p. 89. 1753 Orchid Ave. (off Franklin Ave.). ☎ *800-537-3052 or 323-874-9678. Fax: 323-874-9931.* www.orchidsuites.com. *Rack rates: $79–$209. AE, DC, DISC, MC, V.*

The Orlando
$$$ West Hollywood

Third Street in West Hollywood is a glorious riot of antiques shops, boutiques, and restaurants, and it's walking distance from the Beverly Center mall. Right there in the thick of it is the Orlando. Of course, at press time, they were undergoing a total redo, from the rooms to the public areas, and naturally, no one could tell us precisely how it was all going to look. But we got some hints, and it involved the use of a lot of brushed steel (a look guaranteed to age fast and badly, but no one ever checks with us first in their rush to hipster-ville). This also implies a possible increase in rack rates. So we just don't know. This could be one of the better boutique hotels in town, in one of the better locations, or it could be overpriced for what it is. Check the Internet for special rates and get a look at the photos of the finished product.

See map p. 87. 8384 Third St. (near the Beverly Center mall). ☎ *800-624-6835 or 323-658-6600. Fax: 323-653-3464.* www.beverlyplazahotel.com. *Rack rates: $219–$272. AE, DC, DISC, MC, V.*

Ramada West Hollywood
$$$ West Hollywood

The Ramada West Hollywood (locals call it the Big Gay Ramada, and not just because it's cheerful) has finally shed its party-boy looks and grown into a sophisticated gentleman — except for that eye-straining, candy-colored exterior. The lobby is all brushed metal and black, and the rooms have been upgraded with Art Deco-ish (emphasis on the "ish") furnishings in muted tones. Sadly, the headache-inducing '80s carpet still covers the hall floors, but eventually that too will be replaced. The Ramada is still as lively and gay-friendly as ever, and the hotel gets booked up early for summer, especially during the Gay Pride celebration (the second to last weekend in June) and Halloween, which also features a major parade. Litigants from the Judge Judy and Judge Joe Brown television shows stay here, and you can often hear them discussing the wacky points of their cases in the elevator. Room service comes from the on-site restaurant **Panini,** and you have Nintendo and wireless WebTV at your disposal, but the nightlife just outside the door is very tempting. The pool is huge with wireless access from the loungers; and long-term guests are welcome. Internet specials abound, so check out the Web site.

See map p. 87. 8585 Santa Monica Blvd. (near Sunset and La Cienega blvds.). ☎ *800-845-8585 or 310-652-6400. Fax: 310-652-4207.* www.ramada-wh.com. *Rack rates: $165–$275. AE, DC, DISC, MC, V.*

Renaissance Hollywood Hotel
$$$ Hollywood

A former dumpy Holiday Inn has been turned into the stylish neighbor of the new Hollywood & Highland Complex. "Midcentury modern" is the motto here; "too clever by half" is our response. The restaurant is called **Twist** "because it's a twist on things." (The menus are metal, that's all we noticed.) What do you expect from what is essentially the Marriott chain's response to the hip, neat, cool, and groovy W hotels (the hot, hip, happening hotels popping up all over the United States)? But still, we dig the cool Biedermeyer furniture in the rooms and the "good luck" bamboo in the bathrooms (to improve a room's feng shui and just generally promote good luck). Plus, all digs have Nintendo, WebTV, and CD players; higher-up rooms have their own Siamese fighting fish; and rooms facing north have lovely views of the Hollywood Hills. Shhh . . . it's totally booked up for the Oscars, probably by stars getting their hair done steps away from the red carpet.

See map p. 89. 1755 N. Highland Ave. (in the Hollywood & Highland Complex). ☎ *323-856-1200. Fax: 323-856-1205.* www.renaissancehollywood.com. *Rack rates: $199 and up double. AE, DC, DISC, MC, V.*

Sea Shore Motel
$$ Santa Monica

This family-owned and -operated establishment admittedly looks a little dumpy on the outside, but the rooms are better than that, though inexplicably Southwestern in theme (inspired, possibly, by the California Heritage Museum across the street), some with tile floors, and most with oddly roomy, very clean bathrooms. No room service is offered, but the beach is just a couple of blocks west, and free parking is provided in an area where spots are impossible to come by. Unless you absolutely need a posh place to rest your head, this is a fine bargain.

See map p. 85. 2637 Main St. (just south of Ocean Park Blvd.). ☎ *310-392-2787. Fax: 310-392-5167.* www.seashoremotel.com. *Rack rates: $75–$135 double (be sure to ask about discounts). AE, DISC, MC, V.*

The Standard, Downtown L.A.
$$–$$$ **Downtown**

Downtown's first hipster hotel was long overdue. The Standard in Downtown L.A. piles style on top of style in a self-consciously playful way, with live DJs spinning in the lobby at night as record company, rap industry, and film executive types check in. Design-conscious rooms have platform beds and "desks" that are really a wide shelf running under the entire 14-foot length of the windows. In the smallest rooms (not that small — 300 square feet — which is why room categories are called Huge, Gigantic, Enormous, and Wow!) the bathroom shower is separated from the sleeping area by a glass wall. Peekaboo! (The more modest can request rooms without this feature.) Bigger rooms have soaking tubs. TVs are large, and windows open, though not to great views. All rooms have complimentary high-speed Internet access, whereas the public areas have free wireless Internet access. The sexy pool area has a wonderful view of Downtown plus cabanas with round water beds and a bar. You can imagine the scene up here at night.

The coffee shop offers somewhat overpriced diner favorites and some unexpected treats (see p. 91). At press time, they were preparing to put in a sprawling, "playful and sexy" spa and health club, complete with "unisex" steam room. *Note:* The parking lot is owned by another company, so only park your car with the Standard valet parkers in red shirts or face an even larger parking fee.

See map p. 91. 550 S. Flower St. (at Sixth St.). ☎ *213- 892-8080. Fax: 213-892-8686.* www.standardhotel.com. *Rack rates: $99–$325. AE, MC, V.*

The Standard, Hollywood
$$$ **West Hollywood**

This high-style, high-concept, 1970s designer retro motor lodge comes complete with Warhol print fabrics, beanbag chairs in the rooms, and blue synthetic turf around the pool. This is hip hostelry at its most extreme. The barbershop can schedule a tattooist for you, and every night models writhe in the green glow of a glass booth behind the front desk. The pricey 24-hour coffee shop ($40 with tip for a two-person breakfast, yikes!) is a hot spot for clubgoers, and the lobby seethes with the sleek and chic. You can also stay in your room and enjoy the round-the-clock room service. No health club here, but your room key entitles you to half-price day rates at nearby Crunch Gym, where Leonardo DiCaprio and other stars get sweaty. Rooms that face the Strip are less expensive and noisier than those in the back, and all rooms come with CDs, WebTV, Nintendo, and T-1 lines, plus heaps of cool bath products. Pets of all sizes are welcome but require a $100 nonrefundable fee.

See map p. 87. 8300 Sunset Blvd. (east of La Cienega Blvd.). ☎ *323-650-9090. Fax: 323-650-2820.* www.standardhotel.com. *Rack rates: $135–$650 double. AE, DC, DISC, MC, V.*

Valadon
$$ West Hollywood

Located in a quiet residential neighborhood, a short walk up a steep hill from the Sunset Strip, this is a definite budget bargain but only if you don't have serious aesthetic needs. Not that there is anything wrong with this hotel, but from its mock-Spanish lobby (complete with faux timbers) that can smell of smoke and cooking, to room décor that is hopelessly stuck in the '80s, this is not going to wow you. (But do take a good look at the art lining the hallways. It only looks like hotel art — it's really quite valuable 1880s–1890s French Impressionist work from the owner's extensive collection.) But here's the thing: The smallest room (which can be had for less than the posted rack rates) has a decent amount of space, including a kitchenette or, at least, breakfast nook, whereas the next level up, the junior suite, has a sunken living/sitting area. And all accommodations have gas fireplaces (with remote controls, naturally), which just adds to the hilarity factor. The small rooftop pool has near-360° city views. When you see how these prices compare to some of the fancier and smaller digs around, the dated style probably won't bother you a bit. (The whole thing reminds us of dated "fancy" hotels in Eastern Europe.)

The only (minor) drawback is that the hotel is two blocks from the main fire station for the City of West Hollywood, so sirens may pierce your sleep. But the gamble is worth taking if you want a good hotel at a reasonable price (for Los Angeles) in a prime location. And golfers find the guaranteed tee times, transportation, and other golf amenities an extra bonus.

See map p. 87. 8822 Cynthia St. (off San Vicente Blvd.). ☎ *800-835-7997 or 310-854-1114. Fax: 310-657-2623.* www.lerevehotel.com. *Rack rates: $149–$290. AE, DC, DISC, MC, V.*

Venice Beach House
$$ Venice

If you were to take the best of what Los Angeles has to offer — what makes this city its own, and not some other random large city — and shrink it down and make it a B&B, it might look something like the Venice Beach House. An archetypal Craftsman home, steps away from the beach (the sandy part, anyway), surrounded by lawn (the front gate leads right to the walk to the beach), bougainvillea and other blooms — it's the dream of L.A., for sure. (The nightmare of L.A. is personified by the hideous modern apartment buildings that block the home's formerly perfect ocean views.) The interior has been well restored, though we wish all the rooms had hardwood floors and that the more modern-style baths weren't. The upstairs guest rooms have the most light and air. Each room has its own theme — from the tiny Tramps' Quarters (the smallest room) to the spacious Pier Suite (with a fireplace and sitting room) — and delights (like the wool-plaid-upholstered walls in the Abbot Kinney room and the fireplace in the James Peasgood room), as well as its own drawbacks (size varies, and four rooms share two bathrooms between them). So it's a good idea to check out the photos on the Web site. We love the Pier Suite (one of the most requested), with its pale-blue walls and many windows overlooking the area. (The only view of water, a sliver of blue, is from the upstairs hallway.) One of the two shared baths has two clawfoot tubs. Breakfast brings a different assortment daily of hot and cold items.

The good parts of Main Street are a serious hike away, and never mind the delights of Santa Monica, so plan on having a car (though there are restaurants within walking distance).

See map p. 85. 15 30th Ave. (at Speedway). ☎ *310-823-1966. Fax: 310-823-1842* www. venicebeachhouse.com. *Rack rates: $130–$195 (AAA discounts available). AE, MC, V.*

W Los Angeles
$$$ Westwood

The Westin people should be complimented on their successful experiment in combining the hipster hotel concept with the recognizable brandname concept. We've stayed in many Ws and we like them all because they are playful yet comfortable. This one, with its open, modern, chic spaces somewhere between techno and Zen, is probably our least favorite, though that may have less to do with reality than our perception of the kind of atmosphere that comes with an L.A. hotel full of beautiful people with attitude. But even by W standards these guest rooms seem a bit chilly, though they are also large — each is either a true suite or open studio style, with separate sitting and sleeping areas, and done in monochrome palates of tan, purple, and violet. That semi-Zen thing that the modern minimalist rooms have going extends throughout the hotel, to the pretty garden/cafe/ swimming-pool area (the pool itself is disappointing, small, and bland), complete with burbling rock waterfall. The gym is spacious and has attendants on duty to hand you fruit-soaked water. As with all Ws, the nightlife scene is as important as the actual guest accommodations, so expect the bars and lobby to be hopping. Note that all Ws take pets — and even encourage you to bring your pooch because, we suspect, many of the employees want to play with them.

See map p. 87. 930 Hilgard Ave. ☎ *310-208-8765. Fax: 310-824-0355.* www.whotel. com. *Rack rates: $200–$300. AE, MC, V.*

Westin Bonaventure
$$$ Downtown

When this five-cylinder-shaped glass tower went up in Downtown L.A. in 1976, some people found it appallingly hideous, while others thought it rather remarkable. It became an instant landmark, nonetheless. It's still a cheap thrill to take one of the fast-paced glass elevators to a room (not a good idea for folks with vertigo), each of which is shaped like a wedge of pie, making the somewhat small bathrooms more navigable than their size indicates. The largest hotel in Los Angeles (more than 1,300 units), it's a minicity, with bustling shops and restaurants galore, and a boon for families or anyone craving anonymity. The best rooms have the Westin's famed Heavenly Beds (top-of-the-line everything) or at least views (on clear days) of the Hollywood Hills, though every unit has floor-to-ceiling windows. The large outdoor pool can be quite the scene on warm days, and you get $10 passes to the handsome YWCA across the street.

See map p. 91. 404 S. Figueroa St. (between Fourth and Fifth sts.). ☎ *213-624-1000. Fax: 213-612-4800.* www.westin.com. *Rack rates: $219 and up double.*

Wilshire Crest Inn
$ Near Beverly Hills

Wilshire Boulevard is a major artery for Los Angeles, moving from Downtown to the beach, past museums and shopping areas, with regular, swift public transportation along its busy lanes. And the owner-operated Wilshire Crest Inn (which is actually right off Wilshire on a side street), a reasonably priced, attractive hotel, is perfectly situated to take advantage of all that the boulevard offers. Rooms are good sized and pale pink and green; the lobby/parlor is large, with couches and chairs; and you can relax on an outdoor courtyard and patio. Complimentary pastries, bagels, coffee, and tea offered in the lobby in the morning draw visiting staff from the nearby consulates and guest speakers and curators from the many museums down the road.

See map p. 87. 6301 Orange St. (off Wilshire Blvd.). ☎ *800-654-9951 or 323-936-5131. Fax: 323-936-2013.* www.wilshirecrestinn.com. *Rack rates: $89–$109 (senior citizen discounts available). AE, DC, DISC, MC, V.*

Wyndham Bel Age
$$$$ West Hollywood

Another Wyndham property, this hotel may be a favorite with pop stars and actors, but it still maintains a regal, luxurious elegance. Enjoy live jazz and California bistro cuisine in **TEN20** and fine Russian dining at **Diaghilev,** plus a gift shop, a pool, a florist, an art gallery, and handicapped-accessible rooms. You may remember this hotel from the *Beverly Hills 90210* prom night and Backstreet Boyz episodes. Deep discounts are available online.

See map p. 87. 1020 N. San Vincent Blvd. (between Sunset and Santa Monica blvds.). ☎ *877-999-3223 or 310-854-1111. Fax: 310-854-0926.* www.wyndham.com. *Rack rates: $300–$640. AE, DC, DISC, MC, V.*

Wyndham Summerfield Suites
$$$ West Hollywood

Located in the heart of West Hollywood, walking distance from Santa Monica Boulevard and the Sunset Strip, this Wyndham offers all-suites rooms, most with fireplaces and some with kitchenettes. You get a complimentary breakfast buffet and grocery shopping, plus a rooftop pool and Bath & Bodyworks toiletries.

See map p. 87. 1000 Westmount Dr. (one block west of La Cienega Blvd.). ☎ *877-999-3223 or 310-657-7400. Fax: 310-657-1535.* www.summerfieldsuites.com. *Rack rates: $219 and up double. AE, DC, DISC, MC, V.*

List of Accommodations by Neighborhood

Airport
Crowne Plaza Hotel ($$$)
Marriott Los Angeles Airport ($$)

Bel Air
Hotel Bel Air ($$$$)

Beverly Hills
Avalon Hotel ($$)
Beverly Crescent Hotel ($$)
Beverly Hills Hotel ($$$$)
Beverly Hills Reeves Hotel ($)
Beverly Terrace Hotel ($$)
Maison 140 ($$)
The Mosaic ($$$)

Burbank
Graciela Burbank ($$$)

Downtown
Hilton Checkers ($$)
Hotel Figueroa ($$)
Millennium Biltmore Hotel ($$$)
The Standard, Downtown L.A. ($$)
Westin Bonaventure ($$$)

Hollywood
Best Western Hollywood Hills Hotel ($$)
Bevonshire Lodge ($)
Celebrity Hotel ($)
Chateau Marmont ($$$$)
Hollywood Bungalows ($)
Hollywood Roosevelt Hotel ($$$)
Magic Castle Hotel ($$)
Renaissance Hollywood Hotel ($$$)

Santa Monica
Best Western Ocean View Hotel ($$)
Doubletree Guest Suites Santa Monica ($$$$)
The Georgian ($$$)
Hotel Carmel ($$)
Hotel Shangri-La ($$$)
Sea Shore Motel ($$)

Universal City
Hilton Los Angeles/Universal City ($$)
Sheraton Universal Hotel ($$)

Venice
Cadillac Hotel ($)
Venice Beach House ($$)

West Hollywood
Alta Cienega Motel ($)
Argyle ($$$$)
Beverly Laurel Motor Hotel ($)
Chateau Marmont ($$$$)
Elan Hotel Modern ($$)
Farmer's Daughter Hotel ($$)
The Grafton on Sunset ($$$)
Hyatt West Hollywood ($$$)
Le Montrose ($$$)
Orbit Hotel & Hostel and Banana Bungalow ($)
The Orlando ($$$)
Ramada West Hollywood ($$$)
The Standard, Hollywood ($$$)
Valadon Hotel ($$)
Wyndham Bel Age ($$$$)
Wyndham Summerfield Suites ($$$)

Westwood
W Los Angeles ($$$)

List of Accommodations by Price

$$$$

Argyle Hotel (West Hollywood)
Beverly Hills Hotel (Beverly Hills)
Chateau Marmont (Hollywood/
   West Hollywood)
Doubletree Guest Suites Santa Monica
   (Santa Monica)
Hotel Bel Air (Bel Air)
Wyndham Bel Age (West Hollywood)

$$$

Avalon Hotel (Beverly Hills)
Crowne Plaza Hotel (Airport)
The Georgian (Santa Monica)
Graciela Burbank (Burbank)
The Grafton on Sunset (West
   Hollywood)
Hollywood Roosevelt Hotel
   (Hollywood)
Hotel Shangri-La (Santa Monica)
Hyatt West Hollywood (West
   Hollywood)
Le Montrose (West
Hollywood)Millennium Biltmore Hotel
   (Downtown)
The Mosaic (Beverly Hills)
The Orlando (West Hollywood)
Ramada West Hollywood (West
   Hollywood)
Renaissance Hollywood Hotel
   (Hollywood)
The Standard, Hollywood (West
   Hollywood)
Westin Bonaventure (Downtown)
W Los Angeles (Westwood)
Wyndham Summerfield Suites
   (West Hollywood)

$$

Best Western Hollywood Hills Hotel
   (Hollywood)
Best Western Ocean View Hotel
   (Santa Monica)
Beverly Crescent Hotel (Beverly Hills)
Beverly Terrace Hotel (Beverly Hills)
Elan Hotel Modern (West Hollywood)
Hilton Checkers (Downtown)
Hilton Los Angeles/Universal City
   (Universal City)
Hotel Carmel (Santa Monica)
Hotel Figueroa (Downtown)
Farmer's Daughter Hotel (West
   Hollywood)
Magic Castle Hotel (Hollywood)
Maison 140 (Beverly Hills)
Marriott Los Angeles Airport (Airport)
Sea Shore Motel (Santa Monica)
Sheraton Universal Hotel (Universal
   City)
The Standard, Downtown L.A.
   (Downtown)
Valadon Hotel (West Hollywood)
Venice Beach House (Venice)

$

Alta Cienega Motel (West Hollywood)
Beverly Hills Reeves Hotel (Beverly
   Hills)
Beverly Laurel Motor Hotel (West
   Hollywood)
Bevonshire Lodge (Hollywood)
Cadillac Hotel (Venice)
Celebrity Hotel (Hollywood)
Hollywood Bungalows (Hollywood)
Orbit Hotel & Hostel and Banana
   Bungalow (West Hollywood)
Wilshire Crest Inn (near Beverly Hills)

Chapter 10

Dining and Snacking in Los Angeles

• •

In This Chapter

▶ Finding the top chefs and neighborhoods with the best food
▶ Learning dress codes and dining etiquette
▶ Cutting your meal costs
▶ Choosing your restaurants from an A–Z list
▶ Narrowing your restaurant choices with an index

• •

*L*os Angeles may not have the reputation for big-time dining that certain other cities claim (hello, New York), but we think that is entirely unfair. This is the city, after all, that gave the world chef Wolfgang Puck and his high-wattage culinary shrine, Spago, and, ubiquitous or not, Nouveau and California Cuisine followed in his wake.

As good as the city's three- and four-star restaurants are (and they are indeed worthy of your attention), it's the hole-in-the-wall ethnic spots that L.A. does best. (See "The Hotel and Restaurant Scene," p. 16, for a few suggestions.) Because it's such a melting pot of cultures, blessed with an extraordinarily diverse number of immigrants from all over the world, Los Angeles has a vast number of unprepossessing eateries, often found in ugly strip malls or in the farther reaches of the metropolis, in which you can pay a ridiculously small amount of money and dine on food the gods themselves would envy. L.A. has Thai, Vietnamese, Russian, Armenian, Romanian, and Mexican restaurants — and that's just a sample from a measly -mile stretch of Hollywood Boulevard.

Getting the Dish on the Local Scene

Celebrity chefs

Who's in the kitchen these days? Los Angeles has chefs who would shine in even the most hardcore restaurant scene: **Jochaim Splichal** of the Patina Group consortium of restaurants, including Patina, Nick

& Stef's, and the Pinot Bistro; **Susan Fennister** and **Mary Sue Milliken** of Border Grill and Ciudad (to say nothing of their popular Food Network show *Two Hot Tamales*); and **Mark Peel** and **Nancy Silverton** of Campanille and La Brea Bakery, to name but a few. L.A. has 'em all, and even a few more.

The top neighborhoods to dine in

Just as L.A. has no one main neighborhood, it also has no main dining area. Obviously, you find a greater number of seafood places closer to the ocean, but in this day of modern transportation and refrigeration, a few lousy miles is not going to stop anyone from serving up sole.

This chapter focuses on the three main areas: the **Westside** (especially Santa Monica and Beverly Hills), **West Hollywood/Hollywood,** and **Downtown.** Admittedly, the crowds change according to the neighborhood, but more often they change according to price range. Old money (pearls and suits) can generally be found in Beverly Hills, the hip-and-happening crowd is often seen in West Hollywood, and the funky-and-fun types gravitate to Hollywood.

Downtown sees business folks during the day and theatergoers and business travelers at night. Fox and Sony Studios are in the Westside, and Paramount is in Hollywood, so you're likely to see movie industry types — don't get excited, we are generally talking executives and agents here — in those neighborhoods during lunch.

If you're willing to travel a bit for outstanding ethnic food, head to the **San Gabriel Valley** (the towns of Alhambra, San Gabriel, and Rosemead), where the Chinese food will blow your mind, or **East L.A.,** where you find not just authentic Mexican but Cuban, El Salvadoran, and Honduran, as well.

For ethnic delights a tad closer to Los Angeles, there's **Little Tokyo** (the southeastern part of Downtown) — we are systematically working our way through every sushi bar we can find there. And although the official **Chinatown** (northeastern Downtown) doesn't have nearly the breadth and range of what's found in San Gabriel, it is considerably closer.

But don't stop at Chinatown for Asian food; the area south of Hollywood (Wilshire Boulevard to Olympic Boulevard north and south, and Crenshaw Boulevard to Vermont Avenue on the west-east borders) is called **Koreatown.** And don't forget **Thai Town** (Hollywood Boulevard, starting around Western Avenue to around Vermont Avenue) and **Little Armenia** (which overlaps a bit with Thai Town, beginning at Hollywood, Sunset, and Santa Monica boulevards at Wilton Drive and heading east until at least Virgil Avenue).

Although we focus on certain neighborhoods for most of our restaurant choices (neighborhoods you are most likely to either stay in or visit), there are other areas to keep in mind. **Melrose Avenue** (from Fairfax

Avenue to La Brea Boulevard) and **Third Street** (LaCienega Boulevard to Fairfax Avenue) both fairly jump with small cafes, as does the bohemian-trendy **Los Feliz/Silverlake** area just east of Hollywood (Sunset Boulevard east of Virgil Avenue, all the way down to where it becomes Cesar Chavez Boulevard).

Travel to **Vermont and Hillhurst avenues,** between Sunset and Los Feliz boulevards, where the food is likely to be cheaper and the clientele terrifyingly hip and cutting edge rather than forbiddingly chic.

When to make reservations

You should assume that you'll need to have a reservation for any high-end restaurant ($$$$ to $$$$$ in this guide). Make your reservations as far in advance as you can. If you can be flexible with your time, however, you stand a better chance of securing a reservation. Don't eat lunch between 1 p.m. and 2 p.m. for that is when movie industry folks tend to deal over meals, and avoid the popular dinner hours between 7:30 p.m. and 9:00 p.m. Weekends, naturally, are more crowded than weekdays.

Dress to dine, L.A. style

L.A. is a pretty informal town, so you will not need to pack gowns and pearls. Basic black always works, but even some of the nicest restaurants tolerate blue jeans (assuming, often correctly, that those blue jeans cost at least $100 a pair).

Cigarettes and cell phones

It is entirely illegal to smoke in restaurants in Los Angeles. This restriction does have a few bonuses: For nonsmokers, it means clothes that don't reek; for smokers, many restaurants offer pretty patio dining where smoking is allowed, and who knows what other famous nicotine addict you may end up standing with outside the restaurant, having a quick puff?

Cell phones aren't illegal, but they may as well be for the number of restaurants that ask you, with varying degrees of politeness, to please keep yours turned off. It's just as well; after you sit in a crowd of movie industry heavyweights or fanciers who are dripping with self-importance and talking loudly on their little toy phones, you'll applaud the movement to silence their noisy illusions of grandeur.

Where the locals eat

The well-heeled and timid are found in the Westside and the fine-dining establishments; everyone else is found everywhere else. If there is one place to consistently find locals, it's probably Starbucks or Coffee Bean and Tea Leaf. We shall ignore that and instead suggest the ethnic places we mention in the previous section. Do not fear modest, unprepossessing storefronts and interiors lacking any kind of taste or ambience. If the crowd is there, the food is likely to be a treat. Frankly, once the word is out, many an Angeleno will be seen chowing down in those food wagons the locals have cheekily dubbed "roach coaches" (especially in Hollywood, East L.A., and Koreatown) — for they know that some of the best tacos and such are found within.

If you're looking for curious cuisines, down-home diners, or cool cafes, we are going to urge two essential books on you:

- ✔ *Hungry? A Guide to L.A.'s Greatest Diners, Dives, Cafeterias and Coffee Shops* (edited by Kristin L. Petersen, published by Really Great Books) is a bright-green volume that more or less takes over where the Zagat Guide leaves off. It's opinionated and full of tips, such as how to avoid the crush, where the punks eat, and how to find the best parking space. No late-night spot or cheap meal deal goes undisclosed. It's essential for the budget-minded and well worth it for anyone who wants to find the real and the surreal in L.A. dining.

- ✔ *Counter Intelligence* by Jonathan Gold (published by L.A. Weekly Books for St. Martin's Press, Inc.) is just slightly less essential (and only because it covers fewer establishments but in much, much greater detail). Gold, the longtime guru of goat stew and anything else you never knew you wanted to eat until he described it, has a talent for sniffing out obscure culinary outposts and hole-in-the-wall establishments that feature sublime concoctions of often alarming ingredients. It's a talent that has earned him, via his regular "Counter Intelligence" column in the *L.A. Weekly* (one of two free weekly papers in L.A.) and his monthly column in *Gourmet* magazine, a rabid following of foodies who dote on his regular reports on where to find the best Thai dish, or who does the most with frog. But don't fear: Gold covers less-adventurous dining, too. Every time we've followed his lead to some locale and ordered what he recommended, we've been thrilled. His taste is to be trusted. But note that this book is many years old now, and so you have to call a restaurant to ensure they are still open.

The good news is that Gold is once again the restaurant critic for the *Weekly* (at least, as we write this). He also does a weekly "Ask Mr. Gold" tips column. We've rarely gone wrong by simply showing up at whatever obscure (or not so) locale he's reviewed that week (us, and many other loyal followers). You can check to see what he's covered in the past few weeks for some ideas for you own dining options by going to www.la weekly.com.

Where the celebs eat

Admit it: You love (or are at least mildly interested in) **star-spotting**. Well, you can find them preening and posing in any high-end restaurant, for sure, but keep your eyes peeled on the midrange restaurants as well. You may be able to find celebrities in spots such as Beverly Hills (more likely to be "old school" actors) and WeHo/Hollywood (anyone from Brad and Jen to WB stars). Again, if you patronize a restaurant in a neighborhood near the studios, you have a greater chance of spotting some bigwig being wooed by a studio head — though it is much more likely that such charm is being laid on in the relative privacy of a studio dining room. We will try, in appropriate reviews, to tip you off to the places where you will be most likely to spot a star (look for the Star Spotting icon), but, of course, it's hit and miss — sometimes *miss* if only because some of these folks, darn it, don't dress the part. See that pretty girl, with messy hair and no makeup, wearing blue jeans or sweats? Look carefully, for she may be Drew or Cameron.

Trimming the Fat from Your Budget

Even if you've made up your mind to patronize primarily those places that fall into the "cheap" category, you may want to have a couple of fancy meals. What can you do?

- ✔ **Visit the high-end places for lunch.** Many of these restaurants offer a cheaper menu at midday. The lunch menus may have several of the same items as the dinner menus, or they may even have something special that you can't get at dinnertime (as is the case at Angelini Osteria).

- ✔ **Order judiciously.** Skip wine — it can really drive up a bill — or dessert if you can; go to a good coffee shop or bakery early in the day and buy a treat for later. (See "All things sweet," p. 148.) You may also want to consider ordering just appetizers; a couple can make a meal by dining on appetizers alone, sometimes enjoying more interesting fare than the entrees offer.

- ✔ **Take advantage of the continental breakfast** if your hotel offers one. If you have kids in tow, keep in mind that they may be perfectly happy with a bowl of cereal and milk rather than some big, expensive breakfast out.

- ✔ **Eat one of your daily meals on the cheap.** Enjoy a hearty, full-course ethnic meal for peanuts or grab a specialty sandwich for a picnic meal (see "Great, cheap ethnic eats," p. 145, and "The earls (and kings) of sandwich," p. 146).

What the prices mean

Each listing in this chapter includes a main-course price range and a dollar-sign icon. Prices per person include standard entrees, along with appetizer, dessert, beverage, and tip. Here's a breakdown of the symbols:

Cost	Price Range
$	Under $20
$$	$20–$30
$$$	$30–$40
$$$$	$40–$50
$$$$$	Over $50

Los Angeles' Best Restaurants from A to Z

These are the best of the best in alphabetical order. If you're choosing your restaurant based solely on neighborhood, cuisine, or price, start with the indexes at the end of this chapter. See p. 152.

The Abbey
$$ West Hollywood   AMERICAN

Noted mostly for its scene, which is very, very gay — and we don't mean cheerful, though it's that, too— this semigothic coffeehouse/bar is included here because it serves affordable, quite tasty food. Sandwiches, pastas, and salads are all made to order, so don't be in a big rush. But you don't want to hurry, no siree, because there is much people-watching to be had here (oh, the psychodramas you are likely to witness) — especially at night, and even more so on weekend nights. Plus, with a full, full dessert case (which flaunts the Tuxedo Cake, a confection containing more white and chocolate frosting than any one piece of cake ought to have; we are so in favor of it), you need the time to work through it all. Grab a seat on the patio if the weather permits, as it usually does (and space heaters are there when it doesn't), or inside the gloomy interior, and enjoy yourself.

See map p. 121. 692 N. Robertson Blvd. (near Santa Monica Blvd.). ☎ *310-289-8410.* www.abbeyfoodandbar.com. *Main courses: $8–$14. Open: daily 8 a.m.–2 a.m. AE, DC, DISC, MC, V.*

Amuse Café
$ Venice Beach   AMERICAN

The chef-co-owner of this charming Venice cafe has been hailed as one of L.A.'s shining culinary lights, having started in her first executive chef job at 23. In this sweet old house painted bright yellow (it's so Southern California, particularly when you sit upstairs as the light pours in and through the cobalt-blue glassware on the table), she serves "small plates" of prettily prepared goodies like onion tart (the crust is phyllo), with a fresh salad, or buttery yellowtail on pearl barley salad, or falling-off-the-bone short ribs. Split three plates between two, and you have a nice, light lunch. Her sandwiches are heartier (try the Croque Madame with prosciutto and Gruyère with a fried egg) and just as carefully prepared, demonstrating that good, inventive cooking need not be of the showy, silly construction sort. (The menu can and will change periodically, but you get the idea.) Desserts are simple, too: an infused panna cotta or a thick, bittersweet brownie drenched in more melted chocolate, topped with home-made vanilla ice cream. A delightful breakfast and lunch spot, but don't forget about them for weekend dinner.

See map p. 119. 396 Main St. ☎ *310-450-1956.* www.amusecafe.com. *Everything under $15. Open: Hours unavailable at press time. Call ahead. AE, MC, V.*

Angeli Caffe
$$ West Hollywood   RUSTIC REGIONAL ITALIAN

Evan Kleiman, the chef-owner of this much-beloved near-institution, is known for haunting the local farmers' markets to ensure that her menu always reflects the seasons. Curious experiments with produce aside, this restaurant offers dedicatedly authentic Italian; the pizza is thin, the pasta fresh, and you can bet that if something has tomatoes in it, it's because tomatoes are in season, and they're ripe and perfect. *Note:* This may seem like a chic cafe, but it's quite child friendly; kids who come in are given a ball of dough to mash and shape as they please. The dough is then cooked in the oven and presented to them when it's done, a process that can keep even the most wriggly kid entertained long enough for parents to enjoy a nice meal.

See map p. 123. 7274 Melrose Ave. (near Alta Vista Blvd.). ☎ *323-936-9086.* www. angelicaffe.com. *Reservations highly recommended. Main courses: $8–$17. Open: lunch Tues–Fri 11:30 a.m.–2:30 p.m., dinner Tues–Sat 5 p.m.–11 p.m., closed Mon. AE, DISC, MC, V.*

Angelini Osteria
$$$ West Hollywood   HOME-STYLE ITALIAN

The operators of this instantly likable restaurant (everyone seems so darn pleased you came in) are longtime fixtures on the L.A. dining scene (chef Gino Angelini cooked for the now-defunct Rex in Downtown L.A.); consequently, their new establishment was an almost instant hit. Of course, that success is also due to the quality of the food — genuine Italian cooking, lovingly and thoughtfully prepared. Try the whole striped bass *(banzino)* roasted in sea salt, if only for the dramatic tableside ceremony, wherein the salt crust is cracked open, and the fish is carefully removed piece by piece. It just barely tops the drama of the carving of the veal shank when *stinco di vitello* is ordered. All the pastas are heavenly, but only at lunch can you find Nonna Elvira's (that's Gino's mom) green lasagna, which is light and airy and topped with flash-fried spinach, a favorite at Rex.

See map p. 123. 7313 Beverly Blvd. (near Martell Ave.). ☎ *323-297-0070.* www. angeliniosteria.com. *Reservations recommended. Lunch main courses: $7–$16.50. Dinner main courses: $7–$30. Open: lunch Tues–Fri noon–2:30 p.m.; dinner Tues–Sun 5:30 p.m.–10:30 p.m. AE, MC, V.*

A.O.C.
$$$ West Hollywood   MEDITERRANEAN/ TAPAS

The second restaurant from the people who brought L.A. Lucques (see below), this brick-lined place (a little too noisy to be as romantic as the deliberately Continental atmosphere would imply) specializes in "small plates." Think tapas, though not necessarily Spanish or just appetizers, except divine ones, or even just sampling the wares at the best French or Tuscan countryside grocer you can imagine. You can have a plate full of cheese samples, or slices of jambon or prosciutto ham, or stuffed figs, or

Santa Monica Dining and Beaches

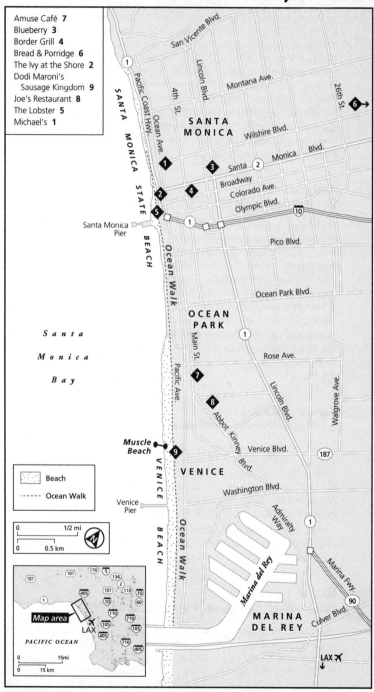

Amuse Café **7**
Blueberry **3**
Border Grill **4**
Bread & Porridge **6**
The Ivy at the Shore **2**
Dodi Maroni's
  Sausage Kingdom **9**
Joe's Restaurant **8**
The Lobster **5**
Michael's **1**

black squid rice, or fresh peas with tendrils. (The chef-owner spent two years in the kitchen at Chez Panisse, and her training shows.) Or all of them, and more, as we often find ourselves seduced by the seemingly low prices, and ordering so much that our bill comes out the same as it would have in a place with a traditional menu. The wine list (the restaurant's name is an abbreviation for the Appellation d'Origine Controlee laws of France, which governs all wine) is a finely tuned standout because this is really a wine bar that serves interesting food, and all these small plates are meant to enhance that experience.

See map p. 121. 8022 W. Third St. ☎ 323-653-6359. Reservations strongly suggested. Small plates under $15 (but adds up to around $30–$40 a person). Open: Mon–Fri 6 p.m.–11 p.m., Sat 5:30 p.m.–11 p.m., Sun 5:30 p.m.–10 p.m. AE, MC, V.

Authentic Cafe
$$ Hollywood   SOUTHWESTERN/CARIBBEAN

No longer the hot spot that had lines out the door nearly all the time (and created a desperate need for expansion), the Authentic Cafe is still a pleasant and affordable (if noisy) place to dine on Southwestern and Caribbean-influenced dishes. It's also vegetarian friendly, thanks to tamales and other blue-corn-emphasis items. Try the jerk chicken, or the Brie poblano-chile papaya quesadilla, or the seared albacore-tuna salad. And thanks to a brand-new bar that just opened as we wrote this, they may return to their former hot-spot popularity.

See map p. 123. 7605 Beverly Blvd. (at Curson Ave.). ☎ 323-939-4626. Reservations accepted only for parties of eight or more. Main courses: $12–$20. Open: Tues–Thurs 11:30 a.m.–2 a..m., Fri 11:30 a.m.–1 a.m., Sat 11:30 a.m.–1 a.m., Sun 11:30 a.m.–2 a..m. AE, MC, V.

Barney's Beanery
$ West Hollywood   AMERICAN

Anywhere else, this would be a down-and-dirty biker bar, but Barney's lies in the heart of West Hollywood, and boy, did they endear themselves to their gay neighbors with their "No Faggots Allowed" sign. (That's gone now.) Rockers love it: Jim Morrison would eat here, and we've sat next to Bono and the Edge. It's all about burgers, barbecue, fries, sawdust on the floor, much beer quaffed at the bar, and a very loud jukebox.

See map p. 121. 8447 Santa Monica Blvd. (east of La Cienega Blvd.). ☎ 323-654-2287. www.barneysbeanery.com. Main courses: $5–$13. Open: daily 11 a.m.–2 a.m. AE, DC, DISC, MC, V.

Bastide
$$$$$ West Hollywood   PROVINCIAL FRENCH

The only restaurant (as we write this) to hold the top rating (four stars) from the *Los Angeles Times,* naturally, this is a hot-ticket dining spot. We couldn't wait, of course, and went there as soon as we could find an occasion special enough to justify the financial outlay (since then, the prices

Dining in Westside and Beverly Hills

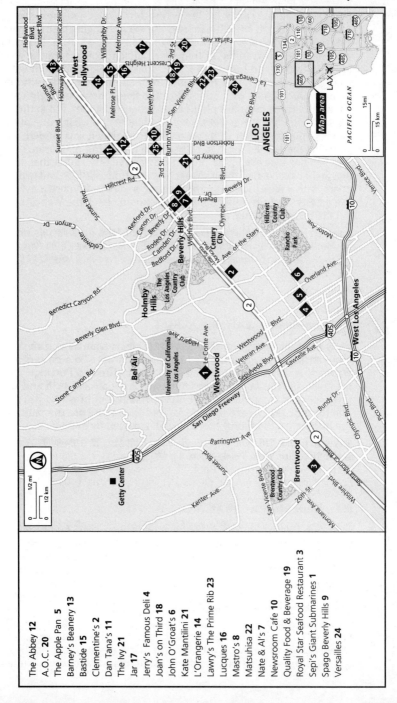

have gone even higher). The setting is stunning, one of the best-designed restaurants in the city, with Zen echos throughout a mature atmosphere. All ingredients are sumptuous, and the ever-changing menu reflects considerable invention and thought, especially in signature dishes like the crab and melon wrapped in thin slices of cantaloupe to make a "cannelloni," cold pea and nettle soup, and roasted veal tenderloin with sugar snap peas. It's entirely a set menu, from a four-course "traditional" that allows some choice with courses to the five-course and eight-course set menus (all three include a phenomenal cheese course). But in the end, can we say that while it was very, very good indeed, it wasn't one of the great meals of our life? That while we understood why it was lauded, we didn't see what made it a four-star, rather than three-star, restaurant? Judge for yourself because even if it's only utterly marvelous, rather than life-changing, is that such a bad thing? *Note:* At press time, Bastide had just changed chefs, with a plan to revamp the menu to something "more playful." While the quality ought to remain high, you should check the Web site for more details before booking.

See map p. 121. 8475 Melrose Place. ☎ *323-651-5950. Reservations strongly recommended. Four-course Traditional Menu $80, five-course Petits Pois Menu $90, eight-course Bastide Menu $100. (A vegetable menu is also available.) AE, DC, DISC, MC, V.*

Blueberry
$ Santa Monica CAFE/BREAKFAST

They bring blueberry muffins to your table as soon as you sit down, and you can keep 'em coming as long as you want. This cute cafe on the Westside is maybe not as strong food-wise as Bread & Porridge, its almost neighbor, but its service is well meaning, if not always swift and sure, and the pancakes are good (multigrain especially, but how can you resist the blueberry?), and so are the salads. And then there are the muffins. Bring the little ones; Blueberry has a casual, kid-friendly ambience.

See map p. 119. 510 Santa Monica Blvd. (at Fifth St.). ☎ *310-394-7766. Everything under $10. Open: Daily 7 a.m.–3 p.m. AE, MC, V.*

Border Grill
$$$ Santa Monica MEXICAN

Mary Sue Milliken and Susan Fenniger have been a serious presence on the L.A. food scene for a number of years, thanks to their first restaurants — the now defunct City on La Brea Avenue and the original Border Grill on Melrose. Now the nation knows them as "Two Hot Tamales," from their Food Network series and from several cookbooks. They made their rep by bringing real Mexican home cooking into the Southern California mainstream. Although purists may legitimately grumble that the Tamales have backed away from some of their more adventurous offerings (like pig's-foot tacos!), those who know Mexican food only from chains are in for some bemusement when faced with a Border Grill menu. Tacos are beautifully stuffed with fresh ingredients, from fish to marinated pork, with heaps of

Hollywood Dining

Angeli Caffe **16**
Angelini Osteria **22**
Authentic Cafe **24**
Campanile **21**
Canter's Deli **18**
Caroussel **3**
Cheebo **17**
El Cholo **20**
El Coyote **23**
The Fabiolus Café **9**
Farmer's Market **25**
Fred 62 **1**
The Kitchen **5**
Jerry's Famous Deli **12**

Musso & Frank Grill **10**
Off Vine **8**
101 Coffee Shop **6**
Patina Privé **11**
Pig 'N Whistle **13**
Pink's **15**
Pinot Hollywood **7**
Sanamluang Cafe **3**
Stir Crazy **14**
Swingers **26**
Taylor's Steak House **19**
Yuca's Hut **2**
Zankou Chicken **4**

herbs and veggies thrown in, all on homemade tortillas. *Ropa vieja* is a big, stewy mess that will have your eyes spinning, and the chicken *chilaquiles* (a casserole layered with tortillas, chicken, salsa, *cotija* cheese, and more) is worth trying, though we find the lauded fish dishes often rather bland. If creamy Mexican chocolate pie is available, be sure to get some. It's a loud, hectic, wildly colored place; you should make a reservation because it's justly popular.

See map p. 119. 1445 Fourth St. (between Broadway and Santa Monica Blvd.). ☎ *310-451-1655.* www.marysueandsusan.com. *Reservations recommended; online reservations (for four people and under) require 48-hour notice. Lunch main courses: $8–$14. Dinner main courses: $15–$26. Open: Sun–Thurs 11:30 a.m.–10:00 p.m., Fri–Sat 11:30 a.m.–11 p.m. AE, DC, MC, V.*

Bread & Porridge
$ Santa Monica   AMERICAN

This adorable little cafe is most notable for breakfast, though lunch is worthwhile as well. Omelets are huge affairs (the vegetarian has three eggs, spinach, mushroom, tomato, cheddar cheese, and onion, garnished with red potatoes and fruit), and the fluffy, well-constructed pancakes aren't much smaller. (We admit to having a great fondness for the choco-late-chip pancakes, oozing melted chocolatey goodness.) In short, all the meals are portioned to share. Hardcore bacon snobs say the applewood smoked version here is not quite up to snuff, but breakfast fans will revel in the aforementioned goodies plus gourmet sausages (try the chicken tequila or spicy Portuguese) and individual coffee pots ready for pressing. Lunch offerings include generously portioned fresh salads and sand-wiches. *Note:* It's a popular place (with plenty of kid-friendly dishes) and on the small side, so you might time your meal for off hours.

See map p. 119. 2315 Wilshire Blvd. (near 26th St.). ☎ *310-453-4941. Breakfast main courses: $4–$9. Lunch main courses: $7–$10. Open: daily 7 a.m.–2 p.m. AE, MC, V.*

Campanile
$$$$ West Hollywood   CALIFORNIA/MEDITERRANEAN

This is one of three restaurants most likely to be the answer to the question "What's the best restaurant in L.A.?" (the others are Patina and Bastide), and though we've never been quite as blown away as everyone else, we certainly understand why it's such a beloved institution. Certainly, appear-ance-wise, it's someplace special. Housed in an old building originally built by Charlie Chaplin as office space, it's all gracious, indoor courtyard, replete with Mexican tile and splashing fountains. Chef-owner Mark Peel is a great talent, and his wife, Nancy Silverton, is the genius behind La Brea Bakery (you've eaten their bread, no doubt, which is served all over the city), the original of which is next door. Come for dinner, where you can eat a beautifully simple bibb lettuce and herb salad with lemon vinaigrette and *fleur de sel* (one of the finest salads we've ever tasted), the likes of rose-mary-charred baby lamb, sautéed Copper River salmon, pulled-pork ravi-oli, ricotta gnocchi with squash blossoms, or grilled striped Trumpeter; or

Downtown Dining

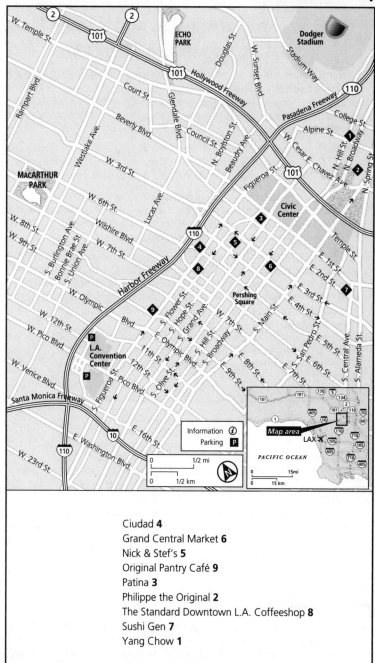

Ciudad **4**
Grand Central Market **6**
Nick & Stef's **5**
Original Pantry Café **9**
Patina **3**
Philippe the Original **2**
The Standard Downtown L.A. Coffeeshop **8**
Sushi Gen **7**
Yang Chow **1**

Doughnuts, diner pies, and James Dean: L.A.'s Farmers Market

A West Hollywood landmark since the Depression, the **Farmers Market** is not to be confused with those weekly farm stands all over town; instead, this is a series of buildings — a somewhat maze-like complex — nominally outdoors but with a roof over much of it, featuring everything from tacky souvenirs to pets to various dining options to, yes, even produce (and meat counters!).

Don't be tempted to ignore this unglitzy legend in favor of the sparkling new and entirely prefabricated Grove next door. The food here is much more interesting, with a number of fun places to grab anything from a nosh to a full meal.

Choose among **Kokomo's,** the trendy breakfast and lunch place (it used to have the best BLT in town); **Dupar's,** the classic old diner (noted for its pies); **Bob's Donuts;** the **Gumbo Pot,** serving the closest this area has to authentic Cajun cuisine; not to mention delis, soft-serve ice cream, Asian food, and more.

Look carefully, for this is a favorite hangout of up-and-coming, and already arrived, actors, writers (they are the grumpy ones with laptops), and other celebrated sorts, along with many plain old folks who've made this a gathering spot for decades. Legend has it that James Dean ate his final breakfast here. You may have to elbow your way through the market crowds (if you see tour buses in the parking lot, run), so it's a good idea to have breakfast or lunch during off hours. Prices vary, and most places prefer cash. Parking (for the first two or three hours) is free with validation (which usually requires at least a small purchase). (6333 W. Third St.; ☎ **323-933-9211.** See map p. 123. www.farmersmarketla.com. Open: Mon–Fri 9 a.m–9 p.m., Sat 9 a.m.–8 p.m., Sun 10 a.m.–7 p.m.).

for brunch, considered the best in town; or for Thursday night, when they try gourmet twists on the humble grilled-cheese sandwich. Or during our favorite time to visit, the month-long Persian mulberry season (it's around July), when these rare, delicate, and impossibly delicious berries are served with nothing but heavy cream. And always save room for dessert; the pastry chef (sometimes Silverton herself) is renowned.

See map p. 123. 624 S. La Brea Ave. (north of Wilshire Blvd.). ☎ ***323-938-1447.*** www. campanilerestaurant.com. *Reservations recommended. Main courses: $24–$38. Open: Mon–Fri 11:30 a.m.–2:30 p.m., Mon–Thurs 6 p.m.–10 p.m., Sat–Sun 9:30 a.m.–1:30 p.m., Fri–Sat 5:30 p.m.–11 p.m. AE, MC, V.*

Canter's Deli
$$ West Hollywood   DELICATESSEN

We just love Canter's. It's the whole package: classic old deli, open 24 hours, full of both elderly Jewish couples and young hipsters drawn to the large menu, and solidly good food. Okay, the musicians come because they can get soup at 3 a.m. and because two good clubs are across the street; plus, Canter's own **Kibbitz Room** still hosts its own music shows (for years, Jakob Dylan, before he was anyone other than his father's son, played there regularly). Local DJ legend Rodney Bigenhiemer eats here every day, so they put up a plaque at his booth. We've eaten more than our share of Canter's brisket (the Brooklyn: brisket, Russian dressing, slaw on a roll) when we aren't eating a bagel liberally covered with lox. Be nice to the waitresses, many of whom have been there since Hector's grandfather was a pup.

See map p. 123. 419 N. Fairfax Ave. (just north of Beverly Blvd.). ☎ *323-651-2030.* www.cantersdeli.com. *Sandwiches: $3.60–$10.25. Entrees: $8.50–$14.95. Open: daily 24 hours. AE, MC, V.*

Caroussel
$$ Hollywood ARMENIAN

Our hands-down favorite Armenian restaurant, which is not to say it's the hands-down best in town, but it's mighty darn close. Located in the eastern part of Hollywood, at the back corner of a dingy strip mall, it's actually a jumping joint, full of locals celebrating, well, life. If you have at least three in your party, we strongly urge that you get one of the sampler specials — about $20 each can produce an array of choices from the menu, blanketing the table with one of about every appetizer, from hummus, which you expect, to a walnut/red-bell-pepper paste, which you may not expect, plus stuffed grape leaves, beef tartare, and sausages, and on it goes. And then come the entrees, which you completely forgot about, at which point you may cry uncle. But carry on; we know you can.

See map p. 123. 5112 Hollywood Blvd. (near N. Normandie Ave.). ☎ *323-660-8060. Lunch entrees: $7–$12. Dinner entrees: $10–$15. Open: daily 11 a.m.–9 p.m. MC, V.*

Cheebo
$–$$ West Hollywood ITALIAN

This playful spot works for families and those on budgets but also attracts a decent number of Bright Young Things (or at least those wishing to become BYTs by scoring a series). It's best known for its long (up to a yard, for takeout only), narrow, sourdough bready pizzas, with a variety of toppings ranging from the traditional (maybe not pepperoni, but certainly homemade sausage with fennel, or pesto and mushrooms) to the sort of ingredients we here in California liberally throw on pizza dough (goat cheese, smoked salmon). Sandwiches, especially the popular pressed pork, are also a good choice, as are hearty pastas. The more expensive meat and seafood dishes are also good, but you'll get better value elsewhere.

See map p. 123. 7533 Sunset Blvd. (at Sierra Bonita). ☎ *323-850-7070.* www.cheebo. com. *Reservations suggested. Main course: breakfast under $10, lunch $7–$14, dinner $8–$24. Open: Mon–Sat 8 a.m.–11 p.m., Sun 8 a.m.–10 p.m. AE, MC, V.*

Ciudad
$$$ Downtown   LATIN

The "Two Hot Tamales," Mary Sue Milliken and Susan Fenniger, the hard-working chefs behind Border Grill, branched out a bit with this Downtown location. Instead of just focusing on regional Mexican cooking, here they get to flex their muscles by utilizing any and all Latin-influenced cuisines: a little Spanish tapas, a little Argentine steak, a little Cuban fried bananas, and so much more, all of it housed in a noisy, cheerful space that continues to show the Tamales' love for all things bright and wild. The menu changes regularly, but you can sample some tapas (goat-cheese-and-avocado-stuffed piquillo peppers, for example, or Morcilla sausage), try a couple different kinds of cerviche, order the butternut squash empanadas, and save room for dessert.

See map p. 125. 445 S. Figueroa St., Suite 100 (at Fifth St.). ☎ *213-486-5171.* www. marysueandsusan.com. *Reservations recommended; online reservations (for four people and under) require 48-hour notice. Lunch main courses: $7.75–$18.50. Dinner main courses: $16–$27. Open: Mon–Tues 11:30 a.m.–9:00 p.m., Wed–Thurs 11:30 a.m.–10 p.m., Fri 11:30 a.m.–10:00 p.m., Sat–Sun 5–10 p.m., Sun 5–9 p.m. AE, DC, DISC, MC, V.*

Clementine's
$ West Los Angeles   HOMEMADE SEASONAL

A small, charming cafe on a side street near Century City, Clementine's has quickly become a local favorite. The menu changes according to season, so only the most current, fresh ingredients are used in its sandwiches and salads. But here are some things we know that you can get at all times: tiny ham biscuits, hot chocolate with homemade marshmallows, perfect deviled eggs, bacon-and-cheddar flat bread, sweet cream-filled cupcakes, and many many cookies and tarts. We've had more marvelous sandwiches here than we can possibly list, especially during Grilled Cheese Month (that's April to you), when they have a different creation (from salami, fontina, and cherry tomatoes to cheddar, applewood-smoked bacon, and apples) every day, to the perpetually popular, but sadly seasonal (they take cooking with the seasons very seriously here) autumn chicken salad with apples, grapes, and celery root on pecan-raisin bread. It's lovely. Do come here. But know that everyone else in the surrounding neighborhoods does as well, which makes parking a pain and tables hard to find at the peak of lunch (12:30–1:30-ish) and weekend breakfast, so try to come at an off hour.

See map p. 121. 1751 Ensley Ave. (near Santa Monica Blvd.). ☎ *310-552-1080. Everything under $10. Open: Mon–Fri 7 a.m.–7 p.m., Sat 8 a.m.–5 p.m. AE, MC, V.*

Dan Tana's
$$$$ West Hollywood   ITALIAN/STEAKHOUSE

Everyone loves Dan Tana's, but we honestly don't know why. It's old-school Italian — gloppy, heavy cheese, and red sauce — and has steaks that many rave about (the "Dabney Coleman" is the favorite), but we find the food disappointingly mealy and bland. All of this is for prices that make our heart miss a beat every time we come here. Why do we keep coming? Because it's wonderful star-spotting (Rat Pack homage-payers, such as George Clooney, and of course, Phil Spector had his last meal here before going off to get involved in a murder case). Because it's old L.A. down to the waiters and the drawings on the walls. Because it's tradition. Also, it's right near the Troubador, and musicians love it.

See map p. 121. 9071 Santa Monica Blvd. ☎ *310-275-9444. Reservations suggested. Main courses: $18–$49. Open: daily 5 p.m.–1 a.m. AE, DC, DISC, MC, V.*

El Cholo

$$ Hollywood/Santa Monica   MEXICAN

If you want to try more-adventurous authentic Mexican cuisine, we'd take you to Border Grill (where the chef-owners learned everything from actual home cooks in Mexico) or to certain remote parts of East L.A. But if you want familiar Mexican fare such as burritos and tacos and you want them good, not gloppy and bland — well, maybe a little gloppy — and you like bean sauce, and cheese, and maybe even mole, we'd bring you over to El Cholo, an L.A. institution (the Hollywood location has been around since 1927) that serves Southern California Mexican food in all its glory. It's noisy, crowded, and entirely fun. Don't miss the guacamole.

See map p. 123. 1121 S. Western Ave. (south of Olympic Blvd.). ☎ *323-734-2773 (also: 1025 Wilshire Blvd.;* ☎ *310-899-1106). www.elcholo.com. Reservations recommended at dinner. Main courses: $8–$16. Open: Mon–Thurs 11 a.m.–10 p.m., Fri–Sat 11 a.m.–11 p.m., Sun 11 a.m.–9 p.m. AE, DC, DISC, MC, V.*

El Coyote

$ West Hollywood   MEXICAN

This very old-school Mexican restaurant has a hardcore loyal following who will be furious to find it in this box, but let's face it, gang, we've all had better Mexican food. Still, it's such a wacky place (and Sharon Tate ate her last meal here) — the waitress dresses up in frou-frou outfits, the margaritas are huge, the atmosphere is family friendly, plus, it's the Mexican food we remember from our childhood — that customers find it hard to care.

See map p. 123. 7312 Beverly Blvd. (near Martell Ave.). ☎ *323-939-2255. Everything under $10. Open: Sun–Thurs 11 a.m.–10 p.m., Fri–Sat 10 a.m.–11 p.m. AE, MC, V.*

The Fabiolus Cafe
$$ Hollywood   ITALIAN

Sure, this often overlooked Italian restaurant isn't as innovative as some, but it isn't just spaghetti and meatballs. Portions are generous (we've rarely finished one), prices are reasonable, everything is cooked fresh and well, the servers put bowls of olive oil dipping sauce on the table with the bread, it's got three locations, and each one is colorful and pleasant. What more can you want? (Well, avoid the Melrose location at lunchtime. It is located near Paramount and tends to fill up with studio folks, so it can get crowded.)

See map p. 123. 6270 W. Sunset Blvd. (near Argyle Ave.). ☎ *323-467-2882. (also: 5255 Melrose Ave.;* ☎ *323-464-5857). Reservations always recommended. Main courses: $5.75–$18.75. Open: daily 11:30 a.m.–10:00 p.m. AE, DC, DISC, MC, V.*

Fred 62
$$ Hollywood   DINER/ECLECTIC

Okay, it tries *waaaay* too hard to be hip, starting with its very loud shade of green. One may ask, legitimately, why wannabe hipsters come here, to a prefab old-fashioned diner, instead of to the House of Pies, a *real* diner, right across the street. But come they do, partly for the ambience (hip, remember; your waitperson probably has many tattoos and a hair color not found in nature) and partly for the food — big burgers, like the Juicy Lucy, or french fries delivered in cunning little boxes of twisted brown paper. Or maybe it's the toasters on the tables or a menu that lets you build your own sandwich (our current fave combines toasted rye bread with smoked salmon and avocado) and offers Asian noodle dishes in very large portions, just right for budget-minded folks.

See map p. 123. 1850 N. Vermont Ave. (in Los Feliz). ☎ *323-667-0062. Main courses: $3–$15. Open: daily 24 hours. AE, DC, DISC, MC, V.*

Grand Central Market
$ Downtown   VARIOUS

Operating since 1914, the Grand Central Market is precisely the sort of chaotic marketplace (open sides but with a roof overhead) you'd find in, say, Turkey or Asia, but not in Los Angeles. Stall after stall offers fresh produce, spices, meats (check out the cow tongues!), and junky toys and kitsch, and in between all that is stall after stall selling some of the best and most affordable Mexican food in town — when they aren't hawking Thai, Chinese, or deli fare. Try a monster burrito, a Mexican sandwich stuffed with pork and topped with fresh cilantro, or a bowl full of Chinese soup. Sample a little of this and some of that, grab some fruit from a nearby stall so that you can tell your mom you're eating a balanced meal, and then sit at a table and watch the Mariachis play amid the bustle while you try to figure out what to try next.

See map p. 125. 317 S. Broadway (near Third St.). ☎ *213-624-2378. www.grand centralsquare.com. Prices vary (but nothing over $10). Open: Mon–Sun 9 a.m.– 6 p.m. Cash only.*

Jar
$$$$ West Hollywood   STEAKHOUSE

The second restaurant from Mark Peel and Suzanne Tracht (he brought us Campanile, considered one of the best restaurants in town; she cooked with him there), this instantly likable space (modern, clean, just a step or two above cozy) is meant to be a more modest outing — food more familiar, prices less dear. Hence, a steakhouse, and one that is, though hardly burger-stand cheap, certainly more affordable than its peers around town. Even so, who could have predicted the single most popular dish would be pot roast? Braised with care, cooked for hours until it falls apart at a touch, it's what Mom would make if she were a gourmet cook. The steaks are just fine, but oh, that pot roast. If the savory pork belly appetizer is on the menu, get it; otherwise, indulge yourself in a lobster cocktail, the sweet meat still warm from the shell. Dinners are à la carte, but sides, such as creamed spinach, are big enough to share.

See map p. 121. 8225 Beverly Blvd. (corner of Harper Ave., between La Cienega and Fairfax blvds.). ☎ *323-655-6566.* www.thejar.com. *Reservations recommended. Main courses: $18–$29. Open: Tues–Sat 5:30 p.m.–10:30 p.m., Sun 10 a.m.–2 p.m. and 5:30–10 p.m. AE, DC, MC, V.*

Jerry's Famous Deli
$$ **Los Angeles**   **DELICATESSEN**

With its many locations and colossal menu, to say nothing of round-the-clock hours, Jerry's fits many a bill and budget. Although it is officially a deli and has all the usual suspects, its mile-long menu also features pastas, veggie dishes, Mexican entrees, oh, heck, we can't even keep up (14 kinds of chicken breast sandwich! Fajitas! Greek pasta salad! Meat loaf! Romanian skirt steak!). Plus, breakfast is served all day long. The odd thing is that they manage to do credible versions of it all, belying the conventional wisdom that trying to do too much means you do nothing well. Families with differing tastes (one dieter, one vegetarian, and one ravenous but unadventurous teenager) will find it a godsend. And for those on a budget, note that sandwiches are piled precariously high and can easily feed two.

See map p. 123. 8701 Beverly Blvd., West Hollywood. ☎ *310-289-1811 (also: 10925 Weyburn Blvd., Westwood,* ☎ *310-208-3354; 12655 Ventura Blvd., Studio City,* ☎ *818-980-4245; and several other locations).* www.epicure-market.com. *Main courses: $6–$17. Hours vary depending on location; some 24 hours. AE, MC, V.*

Joan's on Third
$ **West Hollywood**   **TUSCAN/MEDITERRANEAN**

It's just a tiny little cafe, better known for takeout, but it's an absolute treasure. From the lovely sandwiches (ham and brie with mustard-caper sauce or turkey meatloaf) on fresh, terrific bread (the baguettes, especially) to daily specials (pesto-crusted salmon or grilled maple-rosemary chicken breast), salads of all sorts, and finally, but most importantly, the desserts (coconut cupcakes; chocolate roulade — flourless chocolate cake rolled up with whipped cream; and the traditional and oh-so-sweet-and-frosting-heavy chocolate layer cake), everything is a delight. It also has a small but well-chosen cheese counter. Skip some fancy place for dinner and get Joan's for takeout to eat in your hotel room or in some nearby park.

See map p. 121. 8350 W. Third St. (near Beverly Blvd.). ☎ *323-655-2285. Everything under $10. Open: Mon–Sat 10 a.m.–8 p.m., Sun 11 a.m.–6 p.m. AE, MC, V.*

Joe's Restaurant
$$$$ Venice   CALIFORNIA

One expects funky beach cafes in this part of town, but this little gourmet spot is not only surprisingly elegant, it's also affordable ($40 or $51 for a high falutin' prix fixe with four courses!), with a most doable price for lunch (cost includes soup or salad). Portions for the latter are the right size for a midday meal (larger than spa size but not enough to destabilize your pants size), and it's all tasty and lovely. Butternut squash soup is astonishingly rich for having no cream. The most popular dish is California sand dabs (flatfish) with avocado and sweet shrimp, but we prefer the grilled sea scallops on tomato couscous with a veggie confit. Dessert includes an amazing chocolate crunch cake.

See map p. 119. 1023 Abbot Kinney Blvd. (in the Venice Place Building). ☎ *310-399-5811.* www.joesrestaurant.com. *Reservations highly recommended. Brunch main courses: $9–$14. Lunch main courses: $10–$13. Dinner main courses: $9–$24 or prix fixe $40 or $51. Open: Sat–Sun 11 a.m.–2:30 p.m.; Tues–Fri noon–2:30 p.m.; Sun, Tues–Thurs 6 p.m.–10 p.m.; Fri–Sat 6 p.m.–11 p.m.; closed Mon. AE, DC, MC, V.*

John O'Groats
$$ West Los Angeles   AMERICAN

You'd never believe that hidden behind this modest front is one of the hot breakfast spots for the movers and shakers of Hollywood, on weekdays at least, because of its proximity to Fox Studios. But it's also a very family-friendly place, so on weekends there's a line by 9 a.m. (when they put coffee out). Everyone is lured by the famous biscuits, tall and fluffy, but also by some of the best pancakes in town, as well as dishes like its version of huevos rancheros, which comes on biscuit dough instead of a tortilla. But the biscuits are served at night, too, along with tender pork entrees (smoked pork chop with apple-pecan sauce) and moist fish dishes, one of the best meatloafs in town, large salads, and fish and chips. Service is also solicitious; we know one Weight-Watcher who was served a quickly designed diet version of a club sandwich that tasted just about as good as the much-craved original.

See map p. 121. 10516 W. Pico Blvd. (near Overland Ave.). ☎ *310-204-0692. Breakfast main courses: $5–$12. Lunch main courses: $5–$13. Dinner main courses: $9–$16. Open: Mon–Fri 7 a.m.–3 p.m., Sat–Sun 7 a.m.–2 p.m., Sat–Wed 6 p.m.–9 p.m. AE, DC, MC, V.*

Kate Mantilini
$$$ Beverly Hills   AMERICAN

Kate Mantilini's is the place that made meatloaf chic. This upscale restaurant with dark wood, steel sculptures, and crisp white linens was featured briefly in the movie *Heat.* It's also where you can find agents, couples on dates, Beverly Hills families, wealthy senior citizens, actors, and success-ful writers — in other words, anyone willing to spend almost $15 for mac-aroni and cheese. The sand dabs are delightful, the steaks are tender, the icebox lemon pie is nicely tart, and the sourdough bread is (dare we say?) better than Musso & Frank's, to which Kate Mantilini's menu and decor owes a stylistic debt — it's a younger, modern version. The famous meat-loaf is not all beef (we suspect there's turkey rather than pork in the mix) and is made with carrots, herbs, and green onions. It comes with superla-tive garlicky kale and very mashed potatoes and okay gravy. We especially like that they don't seat women dining alone or in pairs out in Siberia by the kitchen; we've gotten booths every time.

See map p. 121. 9101 Wilshire Blvd. (at Doheny Dr.). ☎ *310-278-3699. Reservations accepted for six or more. $13.95–$30. Open: Mon–Thurs 7:30 a.m.–1:00 a.m., Fri 7:30 a.m.–2:00 a.m., Sat 11 a.m.–2 a.m., Sun 10 a.m. to midnight. AE, MC, V.*

The Kitchen
$–$$ Hollywood DINER/ECLECTIC

We list "Hollywood," but the location is really Silver Lake, and this diner/cafe is just the sort of place locals love — a little of this, a little of that on the menu, with décor that some call "dumpy" and others call "arty." They serve one of the best cheeseburgers in town, a thick, well-dressed ver-sion that comes with tasty fries. But they also have some of the best vege-tarian options in the city, like tofu sautée and a veggie "stack" (mushrooms, bell peppers and others, with pesto on foccacia bread). Those halfway between carnivore and green grazer might look to the salmon, and anyone craving comfort food will be pleased by the popular fried chicken and a meatloaf that one diner confessed was better than his mother's.

See map p. 123. 4348 Fountain (at Sunset). ☎ *323-664-3663. Everything under $15 except daily specials $15–$20. Open: Mon–Thurs 5 p.m.–midnight, Fri 5 p.m.–1 a.m., Sat noon–1 a.m., Sun noon–10 p.m. AE, MC, V.*

Lawry's The Prime Rib
$$$$$ Beverly Hills PRIME RIB

Okay, by rights, perhaps this should go in an "old school" section — it's been around long enough. But darn it, Lawry's is good — as long as you like prime rib. Otherwise, it's not so good. Time was when Lawry's had only the one dish — the prime rib — though now they've added chicken and fish. Don't bother. Come instead for a ritual shared by generations of Angelenos, one unchanged by time. A waitress comes up and asks if you want any side dishes (creamed corn, creamed spinach, baked potato) and then does the famous spinning salad bowl, a preparation production number to rival Busby Berkeley's. After that, she comes back with plates of Yorkshire pudding, and a man in a tall chef's hat wheels up a cow-sized steel cart and asks how big you want your cut of meat and at what degree of doneness you'd like it cooked. You tell him. Then you eat one heck of a good cut of prime rib, possibly as good as you've ever had. You may also want dessert. And that is all. And that is enough.

See map p. 121. 100 N. La Cienega Blvd. (just north of Wilshire Blvd.). ☎ *310-652-2827.*
www.lawrysonline.com. *Reservations recommended. Main courses: $24–$40.
Open: Mon–Thurs 5 p.m.–10 p.m., Fri 5 p.m.–11 p.m., Sat 4:30 p.m.–11:00 p.m., Sun
4 p.m.–10 p.m. AE, DC, DISC, MC, V.*

The Lobster
$$$$ Santa Monica   SEAFOOD

A former rundown fishermen's shack right smack at the start of the Santa
Monica Pier, The Lobster is now a gleaming restaurant thanks to a total
renovation. Thanks to high prices, but also undeniably stunning views
(floor-to-ceiling windows wrap nearly the entire exterior and look out on
beach, pier, and sea), this is definitely a special-occasion place (or a place
to impress your busty, blonde girlfriend, judging from a recent late-night
crowd). As you may guess, it serves lobster — good-sized steamed Maine
and smaller grilled Pacific spiny (the grilled helps the flavor of the latter,
but we prefer the classic perfection of the former) — but also other local
fresh fish dishes. Get the crab cakes, plump and dabbed with chili citrus
sour cream, as a smaller portioned appetizer (you have to ask), and do
also try the spicy snow crab soup. Enjoy the view and hold hands, and
remember that you are worth it.

See map p. 119. 1602 Ocean Ave. (at Colorado Blvd.). ☎ *310-458-9294.* www.the
lobster.com. *Reservations recommended. Main courses: $16–$32 (lobster priced
$25–$28 per pound). Open: Sun–Thurs 11:30 a.m.–10:00 p.m., Fri–Sat 11:30 a.m.–11 p.m.
AE, DC, DISC, MC, V.*

Lucques
$$$ West Hollywood   CALIFORNIA

One of the stars of the L.A. foodie firmament, Lucques (say "Luke" — it's a
kind of olive, and one that is placed on your table, along with salt, sweet
butter, and wonderful bread) features California cuisine with French and
Mediterranean influences. (And no wonder; one of the chef-owners trained
for two years in the kitchen at Alice Waters' Chez Panisse.) It's in a pretty
room, simple, with a fireplace that is often roaring away. The menu changes
seasonally; a recent lunch menu found short-rib sandwich with pickled red
onions and horseradish crème fraîche, wild-mushroom omelette with
chanterelle and duck confit. Dinner features items like rabbit crepinitte with
grilled loin, Tasmanian ocean trout with white asparagus, soft herbs and
truffled hollandaise, and Lucques's much-loved braised short ribs. Desserts
may feature bittersweet chocolate pot de crème. *Tip:* Those on a budget
can always come in for a drink at the bar, or in front of that fireplace, and
still enjoy the olives and bread. Note also the listing for A.O.C. (p. 118), from
the same chef-owners, which specializes in "small plates."

See map p. 121. 8474 Melrose Ave. (east of La Cienega Blvd.). ☎ *323-655-6277.*
www.lucques.com. *Reservations recommended. Main courses: $20–$35. Sun
three-course prix fixe dinner: $35. Open: Tues–Sat noon–2:30 p.m., Mon–Sat 6 p.m.–
11 p.m., Sun 5:30 p.m.–10:00 p.m. AE, DC, MC, V.*

Mastro's
$$$$ Beverly Hills STEAKHOUSE

Possibly the best of the steakhouses that cropped up during the Red Meat Revival a few years back, this is a very gentlemanly, clubby space, and the portions are man-sized indeed. All the steaks are large enough to split. We were pleased when they got an order for "black & blue" just right but bemused when they boasted of their hot plates that keep the steaks just so; they ruined the effect of whatever doneness we wanted. Sides are a broad selection of potatoes and vegetables and, of course, just one is enough for two people, but that never stopped us from ordering still more, even though we knew an order of fries would resemble a small mountain, and the creamed spinach could drown us if we somehow fell into it. You can only imagine the desserts, and the similar portion problems: Chocolate cake is rich and creamy, and the chocolate ice cream is made with Valhrona, so it's hard not to order both, even if both could feed a third grader's birthday party. Bring a hearty appetite and do your best.

See map p. 121. 246 N. Canon Dr. (between Clifton and Dayton ways). ☎ *310-888-8782. Reservations suggested. Main courses: Everything is à la carte, so appetizers start at $7.50 and steaks go up to $30. Open: daily 5 p.m.–midnight. AE, MC, V.*

Musso & Frank Grill
$$$$$ Hollywood AMERICAN

This is the oldest restaurant in Hollywood (1919, which means that everybody who was anybody has eaten here), all red leather booths and dark, wood-paneled walls and a menu that screams dated (red meat, and lots of it). Everything, but everything, here is à la carte — even your salad dressing costs an extra $3. People love the chops, the flannel cakes (thin, and slightly vanilla tasting), and the martinis at the bar.

See map p. 123. 6667 Hollywood Blvd. (at Cherokee Ave.). ☎ *323-467-5123. Reservations recommended. Main courses: $12–$30 (à la carte). Open: Tues–Sat 11 a.m.–11 p.m. AE, MC, V.*

Nate & Al's
$ Beverly Hills DELI

With its formica countertops and aging waitresses, it doesn't get more classic than this. Groucho used to eat here all the time; Larry King and Doris Day still do, sometimes every day. You can catch younger stars amidst the old-timers (Britney, an Olsen twin or two), but really, you want those wrinkly old men as your dining companions. Savvy diners know these guys are the last of a revered breed, the vaudevillians and others who made early Hollywood radio and TV what it was. Talk to them. They've got stories to tell. And then have a nosh yourself.

See map p. 121. 414 N. Beverly Dri. ☎ *310-274-0101. Main courses: everything under $15. Open: daily 7 a.m.– 9 p.m. AE, DISC, MC, V.*

Newsroom Cafe
$$ West Hollywood   ECLECTIC

So-called for its bank of TVs set to CNN and the rack of periodicals in the front, the Newsroom is a happening spot, both the West Hollywood location (where we have never yet gone and not seen a celebrity) and the Santa Monica location. It's also heaven sent for vegetarians and anyone trying to eat a bit healthy. With a focus on low-fat (if not low-carb, too) and meatless dishes (like vegan burgers, vegetarian Caesars, and lots of fun with tofu, including tofu scrambles), not to mention an array of juices and smoothies, it attracts the young and healthy crowd, which wants to stay that way. Fear not, however: There is meat to be found here, and all the portions are generous.

See map p. 121. 120 N. Robertson Blvd. (near Third St.). ☎ *310-652-4444 (also: 530 Wilshire Blvd,, Santa Monica;* ☎ *310-319-9100). Breakfast main courses: $5–$9. Lunch and dinner main courses: $5–$13. Open: Mon–Thurs 8 a.m.–9 p.m., Fri 8 a.m.–10 p.m., Sat 9 a.m.–10 p.m., Sun 9 a.m.–9 p.m. AE, MC, V.*

Nick & Stef's
$$$$ Downtown   STEAKHOUSE

Joachim Splichal (the man behind Patina and its numerous spinoffs) has created a lovely, modern steakhouse in Downtown L.A. Check out the windows full of beef, properly aging. Then order a slab. Share, we think, because too much beef, even this good, may not be good for you, and besides, that gives you more opportunity to order some of the incredible sides like Caesar salad made tableside, heavenly spinach, and 12 kinds of potatoes. (Vegetarians can get a fine meal off the sides.) Sadly, everything is à la carte. *Note:* They make one wonderful burger (using their own prime beef), which is served only at lunch and during happy hour (3 p.m. to 7 p.m. weekdays) in the sleek bar. The burger is pricey for lunch ($12!), but at happy hour it drops significantly — a good budget saver but also useful for a pretheater meal if you're going to the nearby Music Center.

See map p. 125. 330 S. Hope St. (near Fourth St.). ☎ *213-680-0330.* www.patina group.com. *Reservations recommended. Main courses: $19–$32. Mon–Fri 11:30 a.m.–2:30 p.m. and 5:00 p.m.–9:30 p.m., Fri–Sat 5 p.m.–10 p.m., Sun 5 p.m.–9 p.m. AE, MC, V.*

Off Vine
$$ Hollywood   AMERICAN

A charming restaurant in an old Craftsman house, Off Vine doesn't have the high profile it used to, and that's a shame for we always enjoy our meals here, both for taste and ambience. We've had lunches of veggie-intensive chopped salads and mango-avocado combos, and dinners of thick lamb chops, sweet crab cakes (with paprika-lime sauce), and penne with turkey sausage in a spicy marinara sauce. Nothing, truth be told, is shockingly innovative, but you aren't going to feel cheated for the food is interesting enough and done well and the prices are reasonable. The room

Help! My money is burning a hole in my pocket . . .

And I really want to spend some of it on expensive food! Okay. Start with **Matsuhisa** (129 N. La Cienega Blvd., Beverly Hills; ☎ **310-659-9639**; see map p. 121) and tell the master sushi chefs that you are putting yourself in their hands. They will place concoctions before you that will cause your eyes to spin with aesthetic delight, your mouth to buzz, and your heart to stop when you see the bill.

The Ivy (113 N. Robertson Blvd., West Hollywood, ☎ **310-274-8303;** see map p. 119) has a famous Cajun blackened prime rib, along with other high-priced entrees, but you may not notice the bill because you'll be too busy ogling the famous face sitting next to you. (**The Ivy at the Shore** is its Westside version: 1541 Ocean Ave., Santa Monica; ☎ **310-393-3113;** see map p. 119.)

L'Orangerie (903 N. La Cienega Blvd., West Hollywood; ☎ **310-652-9770;** see map p. 121) is staggeringly French and terrifyingly self-important. Many awards have been lavished upon its cuisine, but we worry that we don't dress well enough, nor speak with the right inflection, to eat here.

The chef at **Michael's** (1147 Third St., Santa Monica; ☎ **310-451-0843;** see map p. 119), along with Alice Waters at Berkeley's Chez Panisse, was one of the pioneers of California cuisine, and this has been a beloved restaurant since 1979. But anything that has been around a length of time runs the risk of ups and downs in quality, and Michael's has gone through its own. Currently, the food is marvelous (anything with fresh fish is a must), though service can be spotty. The room is romantic, and one can dine inside or out. But it will set you back a fair amount (entrees run close to $40 a pop) for this privilege.

And of course, don't forget **Bastide,** listed previously, where multicourse set menus start at $80, or the multicourse tasting menu at **Patina,** listed later in this chapter.

is pretty, as is the plant-filled courtyard. It's romantic but not intimidating and nicely situated for the Hollywood area.

See map p. 123. 6263 Leland Way (off Vine St.). ☎ *323-962-1900.* www.offvine. com. *Reservations accepted. Lunch main courses: $10–$15. Dinner main courses: $11–$24. Open: Mon–Thurs 11:30 a.m.–2:30 p.m., Fri 11:30 a.m.–3 p.m., Sat–Sun 10:30 a.m.–2:30 p.m., Mon–Thurs 5:30 p.m.–10:30 p.m., Fri 5:30 p.m.–11:30 p.m., Sat 5 p.m.–11:30 p.m., Sun 5 p.m.–10 p.m. AE, DC, DISC, MC, V.*

101 Coffee Shop
$$ Hollywood   DINER

A landmark restaurant, kinda, in that it is housed in the Best Western Hollywood Hills Hotel, the side of which carries a large sign informing the freeway-bound that it's the "Last Cappuccino Stop until the 101," a sign that has turned up in various movies, including *The Brady Bunch.* However, the coffee shop the sign used to signal has moved to Vermont and lost considerable gusto; the 101 took its place, and nicely. Check out the hours ("Why even close at all?" wonders one loyal patron), check out the patrons in the booth next to you (you've probably seen them in the latest movie or TV show), and check out the menu: the thick, hearty soups, the honest tuna melts, the more-exotic salmon and the grilled skirt steak, the wonderful banana shakes, and the honest-to-gosh breakfasts (served all day). It's an essential, you bet.

See map p. 123. 6145 Franklin Ave. (in the Best Western Hollywood Hills Hotel). ☎ *323-467-1175. Main courses: $6.25–$12.95. Open: Daily 7 a.m.–3 a.m. AE, MC, V.*

Original Pantry Cafe
$ Downtown   STEAKHOUSE

This 24-hour joint's rep is built largely on the fact that in decades of business it's never been closed. Never. Even when it switched locations; patrons just picked up their plates, walked down to the new place, and kept eating. The front door doesn't even have a lock on it. The waiters are all crusty and bad-tempered, but that's part of the fun (plus, they tell you if what you order isn't worthwhile), as is the sourdough bread and coleslaw they plunk down in front of you shortly after you're seated.

See map p. 125. 877 S. Figueroa St. (at E. Ninth St.). ☎ *213-972-9279. Dinner main courses: $5.75–$13.75; all other meals, everything under $10. Open: daily 24 hours. Cash only (ATM on-site).*

Patina
$$$$$ Downtown   FRENCH-CALIFORNIAN

A holy temple to gastronomy, Patina is justly considered by most to be L.A.'s finest restaurant (along with Campanile and Bastide), and it's the first by Joachim Splichal. Splichal's restaurant conglomerate, the Patina Group, had luck with restaurants at the Music Center and MOCA, so when the Disney Hall opened in 2003, they moved this chic Melrose-based restaurant into a corner of the complex. The result, visually, is the very model of a modern restaurant, an interior that is contemporary without feeling cold. We especially like the oak panels that ripple down the walls, just like the curtain that doesn't exist in the Disney Hall itself. Executive chef Theo Schoenegger has been accused of nouveau nonsense with accents like edible foam, but the food fills you well, and the menu reads like food pornography: hand-rolled pasta alla Chitarra, with wild mushrooms and porcini espuma (that's foam); a large piece of plump, superb, sautéed foie gras with black-pepper-rhubarb compote, green-pepper emulsion and pink-peppercorn ice cream; 1¼ pounds of lobster placed in a hollowed-out artichoke heart, lightly touched with butter and artichoke foam; plus a "Quartet of the Sea" nightly special. We sampled five cheeses from the superior cheese cart and still had room for the strawberry bombe (like a very sophisticated Heath ice-cream bar) and the Valhrona mousse on top of flourless chocolate fondant. We will be coming here regularly, to see what they are up to. *Note:* Patina Privé in Hollywood is for private parties and events only.

See map p. 125. 141 Grand Ave. (between First and Second sts.). ☎ *213-972-3331. (Also: 5955 Melrose Ave.;* ☎ *323-960-1762; see map p. 123.)* www.patinagroup. com. *Reservations strongly suggested. Lunch main courses: $12–$19. Dinner main courses: $31–$39 (tasting menus pricier). Open: Mon–Fri 11:30 a.m.–1:30 p.m., nightly 5 p.m.–10:45 p.m. AE, DC, DISC, MC, V.*

Philippe the Original
$ Downtown AMERICAN/SANDWICHES

Believe it or not, there are people in L.A. who have never heard of Philippe's, which completely bewilders those who consider it an essential component of life in this city. Founded in 1918 — right there, reason enough to come — Philippe's claims that one day its owner dropped part of a sandwich roll in the juices of a roast beef and gave it to a customer who raved. Voilà!, the French dip was invented. Curiously, Cole's P.E. Buffet, on the other side of Downtown, makes a similar claim. We don't care. We prefer the concoction here. Not only is it a heck of a fine sandwich, especially if you add the tangy mustard to it, but it's cheap (around $4), and coffee is but 9¢ a cup. The restaurant has many little side and upstairs rooms, all with sawdust on the floor and long tables for customers to share, customers who range from businesspeople at lunch and breakfast and formally dressed folks on the way to the theater to punk rockers on a break and skid-row types. All that, and mysterious purple pickled eggs in glass jars.

See map p. 125. 1001 N. Alameda St. (at Ord St.). ☎ *213-628-3781.* www.philippes. com. *Everything under $10. Open: daily 6 a.m.–10 p.m. Cash only.*

Pig 'N Whistle
$$$ Hollywood AMERICAN/ITALIAN

They don't make 'em like this anymore, and we are so grateful that the owners went to the loving care to resuscitate an old Hollywood establishment. It's conveniently located right on Hollywood Boulevard adjacent to all the new development. We just wish the food was an eensy bit better. Pastas are basic pestos and creams and roasted tomatoes; dinner entrees are grilled steaks and roasted chickens. Lunchtime offers solidly good sandwiches and salads. The french fries are heaven, and the scene at the bar is choice at night. You may even see some New Hollywood faces here.

See map p. 123. 6714 Hollywood Blvd. (near Highland Ave.). ☎ *323-463-0000. Lunch main courses: $8–$15. Dinner main courses: $12–$23. Open: daily 11:30 a.m.–11:00 p.m. AE, DISC, MC, V.*

Pink's
$ West Hollywood HOT DOG STAND

A dumpy little hot-dog stand, you might think, except there *is* that line of people standing outside at all hours of the day and night. Do they know something you don't? You bet — except, of course, we are letting you in on the secret. Pink's has divine hot dogs, juicy, with a casing that has the right amount of snap, available with chili or Chicago-dog style, or just plain. Or you can get a Polish dog, or chili fries. Or even, horrors, a hamburger, except nobody ever does. And you can sit down in what is basically a dumpy little shack, which has been around since the 1930s (Mr. Pink died not too long ago), and notice that you're sitting next to a face you saw on a magazine cover.

See map p. 123. 709 N. La Brea Ave. (at Melrose Ave.). ☎ 323-931-4223. Everything under $5. Open: Sun–Thurs 9:30 a.m.–2:00 a.m., Fri–Sat 9:30 a.m.–3:00 a.m. Cash only.

Pinot Hollywood
$$$ Hollywood   BISTRO

Although it would be a misnomer to think that coming here is a budget way of eating at Patina, the parent restaurant (sorta) of the Pinot chain, it is correct to think that it is a way to eat food created by the same originator of Patina. This is largely bistro food — one of the most popular dishes is a roast chicken with garlic fries — and it is less serious to eat here, though this particular Pinot hops with Hollywood heavyweights, drinking and noshing their way through deals. It's our choice for a midrange fancy, midpriced gourmet, with a number of vegetarian (like pumpkin crumble with honey-glazed cipollini onions) and diet-conscious (thyme-marinated swordfish or seared mahi mahi over parsley pearl-pasta risotto) options. Order the homemade Valhrona chocolate ice cream if it's on the menu.

See map p. 123. 1448 N. Gower St. (at Sunset Blvd.). ☎ 323-461-8800. www.patina group.com. *Reservations recommended. Lunch main courses: $8–$17. Dinner main courses: $14–$25. Open: Mon–Fri noon–3 p.m., Mon–Tues 5 p.m.–9 p.m., Wed–Thurs 5 p.m.–9:30 p.m., Fri–Sat 5 p.m.–10 p.m.; closed Sun. AE, DC, DISC, MC, V.*

Quality Food & Beverage
$ West Hollywood   DINER/ECLECTIC

This is a nice little cross between cafe and diner, featuring what some consider the best biscuits in L.A.. We won't quarrel with that. Breakfast is an excellent choice (and it's served all day), thanks to the various egg dishes and whatnot, and lunch is also worth a stop. Salads vary in quality — we thrill to the warm goat cheese and fresh white-peach combo (undoubtedly best when peaches are in season, which is the only thing preventing us from eating it every day), but the Cobb salad isn't an outstanding version of same. Sandwiches are thick but often could use a bit more oomph, and the seared tuna is good but not quite sushi grade by our standards. Sweet-potato chips are worth trying, and do save room for another biscuit, this one for dessert, topped with strawberries and whipped cream.

See map p. 121. 8030 W. Third St. ☎ 323-658-5959. Everything under $15. Mon–Fri 8 a.m.–3 p.m., Sat–Sun 8:30 a.m.–4 p.m. AE, MC, V.

Royal Star Seafood Restaurant
$$ West Los Angeles   CHINESE

Westside dim sum lovers no longer need despair over the long drive to Chinatown and points farther. Royal Star Seafood Restaurant, on the border of Santa Monica and Los Angeles, offers the cheap, filling, and tasty morsels 7 days a week, 365 days a year from 11:00 a.m. to 2:30 p.m., with regular — and excellent — traditional Chinese food served as well until closing. We like Royal Star as a relaxing alternative to holiday brunches! The baked honey pork bun (baked *bao*) is a decadent version of a Southern barbecue sandwich; steamed shrimp dumplings with cilantro are delicately flavored and satisfyingly shrimp-filled. As the carts of dim sum delicacies circle the room, brave souls can order chicken feet, while culinary chickens can just stick to the basics, like egg rolls or fried pork dumplings — or order off the menu. Dim sum brunch gets very crowded on weekends, so going on weekdays or getting there early on Saturday or Sunday is a good idea.

See map p. 121. 3001 Wilshire Blvd. (near Santa Monica Blvd.). ☎ *310-828-8812. Dim sum: $3 and up. Entrees: $6–$15. Open: Mon–Fri 11 a.m.–10 p.m., Sat–Sun 10 a.m.–10 p.m. AE, MC, V.*

Sanamluang Cafe
$ Hollywood   THAI

We call it "Samalangadingdong" because we can never remember how to pronounce it, but this carelessness does not reflect our real feelings for this utterly unprepossessing cafe situated in a tacky minimall. It's the first place we think of when we want to eat Thai food. Sanamluang is famous for its noodle dishes (General's Noodles, full of garlic, pork, duck, and spices; a bowlful feeds several and can cure the common cold), and you won't believe how good and cheap the food is. (We've brought a group of seven, ordered 11 dishes, and ended up paying about $7 each.) Some of the meat dishes (pork done several ways and barbecued duck) may be heavier on the rice accompanying it than the meat, but hey, that's filling. Skip the usual Pad Thai and go for noodle dishes you've never tried before (note that if you get them "wet" — in a broth — there is that much more to portion out), or get anything with garlic, especially the fried garlic and shrimp over rice.

See map p. 123. 5170 Hollywood Blvd. (near Winona Blvd.). ☎ *323-660-8006. Everything under $7. Open: daily 10:30 a.m.–4 a.m. MC, V.*

Sepi's Giant Submarines
$ Westwood   SANDWICHES

Right at the edge of the UCLA campus, Sepi's has been a local favorite since 1970, and deservedly so. Large subs are actually longer than a foot and come with the usual fillings plus shredded lettuce, tomato, onion, and oil-and-vinegar dressing; darn it, you can keep your famous name-brand sub chain — this is the real thing, and mighty good. Bring a sub to a UCLA basketball game (you won't be alone), order takeout for a picnic, or dine at this humble little store surrounded by Bruins boosterisms. **Note***: Sepi's recently did an extensive remodel that extended to their sub construction, rendering them not quite as sublime as before, but we are confident they will be back in good shape by the time you get there.*

See map p. 121. 10968 Le Conte Ave. (near the San Diego Fwy.). ☎ **310-208-7171.** *Everything under $7. Open: daily 10 a.m.–11 p.m. AE, MC, V.*

Spago Beverly Hills
$$$$$ Beverly Hills   CALIFORNIA

Time was, Spago was the symbol of all that was rich and fabulous, the most high-falutin' place you could go in L.A. It was the spot where the *papparazzi* hung around the entrance to get photos of a veritable who's who of Hollywood. But Spago has long since moved from its original location to this admittedly much larger and more user-friendly spot in Beverly Hills. And its owner-creator, Wolfgang Puck, has such a large empire (two dozen restaurants plus a frozen-food line) that he's no longer likely to be in the kitchen. And yet, the current executive chef is a master and has maintained Spago's reputation against all probability. The menu changes regularly, but recent creations include tempura softshell crab with pickled-ginger vinaigrette and marinated Japanese cucumbers; Austrian chicken bouillon with herb crepes and bone marrow; crispy roasted duck with wild huckleberries; and sesame-crusted tuna. (**Tip***:* The most popular pizza is sometimes not on the menu, the "Jewish" pizza of smoked salmon and crème fraîche. Ask for it, like everyone else.)

See map p. 121. 176 N. Canon Dr. (just north of Wilshire Blvd.). ☎ **310-385-0880.** www. wolfgangpuck.com. *Reservations a must. Lunch main courses: $15–$28. Dinner main courses: $29–$42. Open: Mon–Sat 11:30 a.m.–2:30 p.m., Sun–Thurs 6 p.m.– 10:30 p.m., Fri– Sat 5:30 p.m.–11:00 p.m. AE, DC, DISC, MC, V.*

The Standard Downtown L.A. Coffeeshop
$$–$$$ Downtown   DINER/ECLECTIC

Nearly a meta-take on the whole "hotel coffee shop" theme, with its bright-yellow retro Jetsons' décor overkill, which we would love if it didn't feel like it was trying too hard by half. Don't get us started on the waitresses in French maid/coffee-shop aprons and thigh-high stockings. You can escape the onslaught of yellow in the patio, where you will find chic business-people by day and even chicer folks at night. Despite somewhat higher prices than we would like, this is nonetheless probably your best bet for sassy downtown dining, and the hours make it even more attractive. The menu is haute coffee-shop fare — burgers, fries (tempura battered before frying, making them even more crispy), shakes — plus a bunch of wild cards like Moroccan lamb or prosciutto-topped pizza (all of which are flatbread — read: cracker-thin crust — style, so prone to some sogginess), or miso-glazed black cod, one of the most divine pieces of fish we've ever eaten, and prettily served with a ball of fragrant rice and nicely steamed asparagus. The signature chopped salad has too much creamy dressing for our taste, but the grilled shrimp on top are plump.

See map p. 125. 550 S. Flower St. (at Sixth St.). ☎ 213-439-3030. www.standard hotel.com. Main courses: breakfast $7–$10, lunch $8–$22, dinner $8–$25, late night menu $7–$15. Open 24 hours. AE, MC, V.

Sushi Gen
$$ Downtown   JAPANESE

There are those who say that you can only have really good sushi in pricey locales, such as Los Angeles' Matsuhisa, and perhaps they are right — but you can come darn close for considerably less money at Sushi Gen. When you've had Sushi Gen's lovely, ultrafresh cuts of yellowtail or toro (fatty tuna), it's hard to go back. And when you've sat back and let a skilled chef do what he wants with you, it's hard to settle for mere California rolls again. Sure, it may be a gimmick when the chefs all shout gleefully when you come in, sounding for all the world like a Japanese "Cheers," but we fall for it every time. Plus the appetizer menu features "original salted squid guts."

See map p. 125. 422 E. Second St. (near S. Central Ave.). ☎ 213-617-0552. Sushi: $4 and up. Open: Mon–Fri 11:15 a.m.–2:00 p.m. and 5:30–10:00 p.m.; Sat 5:30 p.m.– 10:00 p.m.; closed Sun. AE, MC, V.

Swingers
$ West Hollywood   COFFEE SHOP

It's a hip, modern — which means retro, somehow — coffee shop, so you can expect great burgers, plus fries, shakes, veggie burgers, and sandwiches. That sort of thing. But you don't come here for the food, you come for the scene, to see stars canoodling, way before the gossip pages report it. You come to see up-and-coming WB actors. You come to see what the fashion-savvy are wearing. You can do all that just about any time of day. You get the idea.

See map p. 123. Beverly Laurel Motor Hotel, 8020 Beverly Blvd. (between Fairfax Ave. and La Cienega Blvd.). ☎ 323-653-5858. Also: 802 Broadway, Santa Monica; ☎ 310-393-9793. Everything under $10. Open: Wed–Mon 6:30 a.m.–4:00 a.m., Tues 6:30 a.m.– 1:45 a.m. AE, DC, DISC, MC, V.

Taylor's Steak House
$$$ Hollywood   STEAKHOUSE

You may notice that the other steakhouses listed here have prices that suggest their steaks are dipped in gold. At Taylor's, you can dine very well indeed on cuts of beef such as the culotte steak, a baseball-shaped hunk of meat that is quite tender and, better still, affordable. This is an old-school steakhouse — red leather (or leatherette) booths, dark wood on the walls — with an old-school clientele. If you've got a hankering for meat and your budget is tight, you'll be quite happy here.

See map p. 123. 3361 W. Eighth St. (at Ardmore St.). ☎ 213-382-8449. www.taylors steakhouse.com. Main courses: $13.95–$23.95. Mon–Fri 11 a.m.–10:00 p.m., Sat 4 p.m.–10 p.m. AE, DC, MC, V.

Versailles
$$ Los Angeles CUBAN

Though it's not our hands-down favorite Cuban place (for that, you have to travel farther afield, to the east side of town), it's certainly a mighty good one with a loyal fan base — it's not uncommon to find a line at dinnertime at the Culver City location. Roast garlic chicken is the top menu item, but we are too fond of the garlicky roast pork to care. Most dishes come with sides of black beans and rice, and if they don't include plantains (bananas fried to lovely carmelization), be sure to get a side order of them.

See map p. 121. 1415 S. La Cienega Blvd. (near Pico Blvd.). ☎ *310-289-0392. Also: 10319 Venice Blvd., Culver City;* ☎ *310-558-3168. Main courses: $7.95–$18.95. Open: daily 11 a.m.–10 p.m. AE, MC, V.*

Yang Chow
$$ Downtown CHINESE

This Downtown Chinese is awfully good, and nowhere else can you eat Yang Chow's Slippery Shrimp, a dish that inspires devotion in countless customers and is not at all slippery; the dish features shrimp battered and deep-fried and then doused in a sweet, garlicky sauce of indefinite origin (but it came from somewhere good). They make platters and platters of this stuff daily; hardly a table is without one. After you get your own, try the moo shu pancakes, or the General Tseng's chicken, or the tofu with black bean sauce. And then have another plate of shrimp.

See map p. 125. 819 N. Broadway, Chinatown (at Alpine St.). ☎ *213-625-0811 (also: 3777 E. Colorado Blvd., Pasadena;* ☎ *626-432-6868).* www.yangchow.com. *Main courses: $5–$15. Open: Sun 11:30 a.m.–9:45 p.m., Fri–Sat 11:30 a.m.–10:45 p.m. AE, MC, V.*

Yuca's Hut
$ Hollywood MEXICAN

Just a little shack (so don't expect much in the way of a place to sit down) in one of the hippest neighborhoods in town (that would be Los Feliz, just east of Hollywood), Yuca's serves some of the best tacos in L.A. — well, apart from those found in certain roach coaches, but we aren't going to get into *that*. It's cheap, too. Be sure to try the *cochinita pibil,* Yucatan-style marinated pork in a soft taco, and finish off with some French pastries at La Conversation up the street.

See map p. 123. 2056 Hillhurst Ave., Los Feliz. ☎ *323-662-1214. Everything under $7. Open: Mon–Sat 11 a.m.–6 p.m. Cash only.*

Zankou Chicken
$ Los Angeles ARMENIAN/CHICKEN

The day we accidently stepped into this unprepossessing strip-mall hole-in-the-wall joint, with its dull Formica tables and utter lack of decor, is a day that will forever live in our hearts, for it is the day we discovered

Zankou chicken. It's not just because when you place an order, you barely have time to read one of the many glowing reviews on the wall before you get your food. It's not just because the roast chicken is perfect — juicy and flavorful, with a crispy seasoned skin that has you forgetting all the health warnings about fat and instead battling your loved ones for that last piece. It's all that, and then there's the garlic sauce. Trust us when we say that when we die, the food served to us in heaven will have Zankou garlic sauce accompanying it.

See map p. 123. 5065 W. Sunset Blvd. (near N. Mariposa Ave.). ☎ *323-665-7842. Also: 5658 Sepulveda Blvd # 103, Van Nuys,* ☎ *818-781-0615; 1296 E. Colorado Blvd, Pasadena,* ☎ *626-405-1502; and other locations. Everything under $9. Open: daily 10 a.m.–midnight. AE, MC, V.*

Dining and Snacking on the Go

Some of the best food in Los Angeles is often found in funky down-home dives or unprepossessing ethnic spots in less-than-swanky neighborhoods. For those of you who find yourselves busily racing from one L.A. attraction to another, have no fear: You can enjoy some deliciously fine snacks and meals on the run.

Great, cheap ethnic eats

We natter on about the delights of ethnic food in Los Angeles, so here's our chance to tip you off to a few more terrific choices. (Most of them missed the first cut because they are just a bit off to the left of "Centrally Located.")

At good, affordable, and reliable **Al Wazir** (6051 Hollywood Blvd.; ☎ **323-856-0660**), about $6 gets you a combo plate of juicy Armenian chicken kebobs (or lamb or beef kebobs), hummus, rice, salad, and pita. It even delivers within about a 2-mile radius (call and ask). Or try the Lebanese versions over at **Marouch** (4905 Santa Monica Blvd.; ☎ **323-662-9325**), a plusher (though still located in a strip mall) restaurant, where the happy owner will be thrilled to guide you through the choices — try the garlic *labneh* (tart sour-cream dip), some of the fat, dry, or spicy sausages, or the stuffed turnovers called *borek*. Note that it also offers many animal-free salads — happy news for vegetarians.

Vegetarians should also be pleased at **Electric Lotus** (1870 Vermont at the corner of Franklin Avenue; ☎ **323-953-0040**), a well-priced and quite pretty Indian restaurant that is full of come-with-me-to-the-kasbah ambience. It's fairly vegan friendly — it doesn't use ghee (the butter base that many Indian dishes are normally cooked in), and it's happy to make substitutions in other dishes that use cream and the like. Weekday lunch specials range from $6 to $10 and deliver a prodigious, and shareable, amount of food. To continue servicing the needs of vegetarians, we direct you to Fairfax Avenue, just south of Olympic Boulevard and north of Pico Boulevard, where a number of Ethiopian restaurants have propagated.

Each one has its fan base, especially **Nyala** (1076 S. Fairfax Ave.; ☎ 323-936-5918) and **Rosalind's** (1044 S. Fairfax Ave.; ☎ 323-936-2486).

Not the least bit vegetarian friendly but delicious nonetheless is the Hungarian **Czardas** (5820 Melrose Ave.; ☎ 323-962-6434). Here we order *porkolt* (stew with sour cream) and goulash and, if available, the multi-layered *dobos* torte cake.

Switching cultures again, we head to the **L.A. Food Court at Thailand Plaza** (5311 Hollywood Blvd.; ☎ 323-993-9000), where a strip mall has been blown up to department-store size with a grand palace of a Thai food court that once boasted eight different eateries. Although the kitchens have consolidated, and the food is no longer quite as magnificent (originally, you could find Thai food here that was as good as it was anywhere else in the Southland), it's still a hoot to visit. Thumb through the gaudy menu, with its photos of potential dishes (we direct you to the fried rice, the beef dish known as "crying tiger," and the pig-parts-intensive *nam sod kao tod*). Pray also that the phenomenon known as the "Thai Elvis" is performing while you are there.

If your Asian food tastes stray more toward Chinese, head Downtown (Broadway and Hill streets) and take your pick of the Chinese restaurants — just follow your nose. Our top choices include **Empress Pavilion** (988 N. Hill St., second floor; ☎ 213-617-9898) for dim sum or Dungeness crab covered in blankets of snowy garlic (it's crowded on weekends, so expect to take a number and wait a long time), and the **Hong Kong Low Deli** (408 Bamboo Lane; ☎ 213-680-9827). Located on an alley that cuts between the two main streets of Chinatown, the Hong Kong Low Deli is overseen by a despotic Asian woman, the Chinese equivalent of the "Soup Nazi" from the television show *Seinfeld.* You better have your order ready as she barks, "What you want? And what else? And what else?" or she is likely to pass you up and go on to the next customer. But she can be a softy in her own way; come late in the day, and she is likely to force something on you, "Six for $1!" Even without such discounts, you can feed a hungry family of four for about $10 as you load up on shrimp dumplings and flaky curry beef pies. In theory, this stuff ought to be taken home and heated for maximum effect; but we wouldn't know for we've always consumed it all right on the spot, in the car, or by the Wishing Well in the heart of Chinatown.

The earls (and kings) of sandwich

A sandwich is the perfect portable food, and oh so right for a picnic in Griffith or Will Rogers Park, or a beach lunch, or dinner at the Hollywood Bowl, or the "I'm tired and staying in tonight" munchies on the hotel bed.

 It's just as well that the following joints are takeout, for most are humble establishments and not the most attractive of dining spots; some are even situated in less than aesthetically pleasing locations.

We do so love our Italian groceries, especially in Italy, but we live near the Venice of the West Coast. Luckily, **Bay Cities Italian Deli & Bakery** (1517 Lincoln Blvd., Santa Monica; ☎ 310-395-8279) helps fill those Tuscan sun cravings. We've been eating dry salami on good Italian rolls (with just a touch of mustard, thank you) since we were bambinos. The bread is notable, but so is the array of cold cuts. You can stuff your bread with these cold cuts yourself, or you can let the employees fill it for you. Sandwiches cost under $10.

A claimant to the "inventor of the French dip sandwich" title, **Cole's PE Buffet** (118 E. Sixth St., Downtown; ☎ 213-622-4090) has been here since 1908. There are those who prefer Cole's to Philippe the Original (see p. 139). We are not among them, though we do note that the sandwiches are bigger, and the rolls are crustier. Cole's PE Buffet is a funky (and sometimes, truth be told, a tad too *Barfly*) bar and buffet, where you can find good mac and cheese, and nothing on the menu is priced over $10.

The usual winner of the "best pastrami in town" contest, which is sadly often overlooked by folks afraid to venture to this once fashionable but now rather seedy part of town is **Langer's Deli** (704 S. Alvarado St., Downtown; ☎ 213-483-8051). Here's the thing: It's right off a Metro Line stop, *and* you can call and place your order in advance, give them your ETA, let them know whether you're coming by car or on foot and what kind of cash you are bringing, and someone will meet you outside, at the curb, with a bag of food at the ready and exact change — no muss, no fuss, no parking, and no waiting. Just perfect pastrami (and other deli delights, but why bother?), and away you go.

Basturma is an Armenian cold cut that's sort of a cross between salami and pastrami (that's not really accurate, but it will do); it's dry, but it packs a wallop of spices. At **Sahag's Basturma** (5183 Sunset Blvd., Hollywood; ☎ 323-661-5311), basturma is served on toasted French bread, complete with some garlic sauce, tomatoes, and pickles. You can also try two kinds of Armenian sausage: one spicy and one milder. If in doubt, ask Sahag, the welcoming owner, who is usually behind the counter. He is always tickled when customers like you come by. He will happily offer samples and advice that only a fool, which you are not, would ignore.

Way on the outskirts of Hollywood, east of where you may well be spending most of your time, but right in the heart of Bohemian Central, is the **Tropical Cafe** (2900 W. Sunset Blvd., Silverlake; ☎ 323-661-8391). It's essentially a coffeehouse but with a Cuban twist, which means, in this case, marvelous Cuban sandwiches. You take ham, roast pork, cheese, pickles, and mustard, put them on French bread, and stick it in a grill that mashes the whole concoction down flat while heating it all the way through. The sandwiches are crusty, sticky, and good. You can get a version on a sweet roll, or you can substitute straight roast pork. Top it off with a guava pastry, and you have a true L.A. experience.

Hollywood has soul?

No one quite understands how such a soul food place as **Roscoe's Chicken and Waffles** (1514 N. Gower St, ☎ 323-466-7453) ended up in the heart of Hollywood, but judging from the lines outside at most hours of the day (and night?), no one questions it too hard. An institution beloved by many in L.A., primarily the African-American community, but not too far behind are bohemian hipsters, college students, and foodies. They all know that there is little better than the Sco #3, the excellent fried chicken topped with thick brown gravy on top of a superior waffle. Or do like we do and put the rather sweet waffle to the side and eat it with syrup for dessert. A scene not like any other in L.A.

All things sweet

Yes, even in a town where a size 6 can seem stocky, especially at a sample sale, there are desserts. Start by trying the West Coast boxed-candy favorite **See's** (various locations: www.sees.com), a longtime local tradition that devotees believe is superior even to Belgian chocolates like Godiva. See's most popular candy flavors are the slightly maple Bordeaux, the creamy chocolate butters, and all of the truffles. *Tip:* They liberally hand out a piece of candy as a "sample," even if you're just buying a single piece.

Next, we move on to baked goods, starting with the humble doughnut. Except the goodies found at Westwood's beloved **Stan's Corner Donut Shoppe** (10948 Weyburn Ave.; ☎ 310-208-8660) are anything but unassuming. For 35 years, UCLA students have feasted on the infamous Peanut Butter Pocket (creamy peanut butter stuffed in a raised dough and then coated in chocolate frosting and chocolate chips; sometimes they add bananas!) or the chocolate pretzel-shaped number that is larger than a softball and faintly flavored with cinnamon. There are many good reasons why this corner counter in a larger shop has outlasted dozens of others that have tried to take hold in the rest of the store — and most of the reasons feature glaze.

Just up the street from Stan's is **Diddy Reese Cookies** (926 Broxton Ave.; ☎ 310-208-0448), a more youthful institution that has been an instant hit since it showed up in the mid-'80s. All your favorite cookies, such as chocolate chip, peanut butter, and macadamia nut, are here, but each one costs a mere — *get this* — 35¢ each.

Okay, if pressed, we would have to grudgingly admit that the cookies at Diddy Reese Cookies are perhaps just a tad below Mrs. Field's (to name a comparable rival) as far as quality is concerned, but they are about one-fifth the price, so who cares? One dollar gets you two cookies and a container of milk, *or* two cookies with a blob of good ice cream smushed between. Just about the same dang prices they've had since they opened over 18 years ago. No wonder the lines are out the door.

Moving east, we come to the Jewish **Beverlywood Bakery** (9128 W. Pico Blvd.; ☎ 310-278-0122), where you can find black-and-white cookies gooey with frosting, sterling chocolate-chip Danish, *hamantaschen* (tri-cornered, filled cookies), and our favorite, checkerboard cake (yellow-and-chocolate cake in squares, happily mingling with chocolate frosting). The immigrant ladies who run it are brisk but thorough; closed on the Sabbath and High Holy Days.

The first, the original, and still champeen **La Brea Bakery** (624 S. La Brea Ave.; ☎ 323-939-6813; www.labreabakery.com) is a must-stop on any L.A. visitor's list. The owner, Nancy Silverton, is one of the world's great pastry chefs, and here you can find her creations. Cookies, tarts, pies, muffins, scones, and fruit crisps sound so simple, but if they were, could she have built such an empire? (Oh, they also have bread.)

Beware of the lines at La Brea Bakery on weekend mornings, when Los Angelenos get their brunch fixins.

The fluffy, glossy, multilayered treats at **Sweet Lady Jane** (8360 Melrose Ave.; ☎ 323-653-7145) have made many a fashion-conscious local say "to hell with it," which is why this tiny (and pricey) cafe is always crowded. Most notable are the cakes and cheesecakes; famous folk love getting their birthday cakes here.

But we cannot live by cake alone, and this brings us to the fabulously named **Mashti Malone's** (1525 N. La Brea Ave.; ☎ 323-874-6168), where homemade ice cream rules. The moniker comes from the Middle Eastern proprietor who took over the old-fashioned ice-cream parlor. And aren't we glad! Not only do they still make their flavors right on the spot, but they added (alongside superb cookies 'n cream and chocolate brownie) the less mainstream rosewater; it's like a flowery vanilla but better — smooth and creamy, an absolute must-have.

Speaking of cookies 'n cream, the first place we ever tasted this ice-cream flavor was at **Eiger Ice Cream** (124 S. Barrington Place; ☎ 310-471-6955). Although they have since switched locations and no longer use Double Stuf Oreos in their cookies 'n cream, they still have a loyal following, which includes us. Try their peanut butter fudge flavor — you can tell they use all-natural ingredients.

Coffee shops and tea rooms

Coffeehouses are no longer the rage they were in L.A. a few years ago, but they are still places to see, be seen, and, for poets and singer-song-writers, be heard. Sure, there are ample chain places — and we must admit, the **Coffee Bean and Tea Leaf** at Sunset Plaza (also at Larchmont Boulevard) are reliable star-sighting spots — but why would you go there when you can get far superior coffee and far superior visuals at independents around town?

The **Bourgeois Pig** (5931 Franklin Ave.; ☎ 323-464-6008) is so very, very dark that you may not be able to discern the red-cloth pool table through the gloom. It has its own fame as the longtime employer of the real-life Gunther on *Friends* — James Michael Tyler, the actor who plays Rachel's peroxided and unrequited swain who runs Central Perk, worked here for years, even after he got his regular sitcom gig.

Nova Express (426 N. Fairfax Ave.; ☎ 323-658-7533) is a sci-fi, rave-dazed themed spot open only at night, but it stays open until the wee, wee hours of the morning. **Highland Grounds** (742 N. Highland Ave.; ☎ 323-466-1507) is still the place for performers to strut their stuff. Smokers love it because it has an outdoor patio. You may like it because it serves a fine breakfast. Finally, relax after shopping or check out the late-night scene at **Stir Crazy** (6917 Melrose Ave.; ☎ 323-934-4656; see map p. 123). And for those of you who prefer tea for two instead of coffee for . . . oh, forget it, there is the **Chado Tea Room** (8422½ W. Third St.; ☎ 323-655-2056), where the varieties of tea are mind-boggling (and tend toward Eastern-style teas, rather than your basic English breakfast teas). The Chado Tea Room also has lovely sandwiches for lunch and afternoon tea.

Burger joints

We are working our way through all the burger joints in the city — it's our job, after all — and we anticipate that this extensive research project will take, oh, years. But here are our findings so far: The **101 Coffee Shop** (see p. 137) has a thick hamburger patty that spits juice at you. The **Apple Pan** (10801 W. Pico Blvd; ☎ 310-475-3585; see map p. 121) has been serving what is considered the best burger on the Westside for 55 years. **Original Tommy's** (several locations, but most notable at 5873 Hollywood Blvd., ☎ 323-467-3792, which has a drive-thru, and 2575 W. Beverly Blvd., ☎ 213-389-9060, www.originaltommys.com) is not to be confused with Tommie's, Tomy's, or even Tony's. These are all wannabe imitators who hope to sucker folks into thinking that they are Original Tommy's — the place where generations of Angeleno youths have wound up at 3 a.m., or even 3 p.m. (a 24-hour business, don't you know), inhaling drippy chili burgers, iridescent with sauce perfumes car interiors for days. The Beverly location is the original Original Tommy's. It's just a shack in a seedy neighborhood, so you may want to head to Hollywood Boulevard, where the location is more convenient, if less atmospheric and less of a scene, offering tidy indoor dining and, better still, a drive-thru.

Competing chili burgers can be found at the 50-plus-year-old shack **Jay's Jayburgers** (somewhat southeast, at 4481 Santa Monica Blvd.; ☎ 323-666-5204), which is not open 24 hours but so close as to make no difference. And **In-N-Out** (various locations; www.in-n-out.com) is the fast-food joint that devotees swear by. You should see those expat residents

L.A. street snacks: So wrong they have to be right

The latest junk food making inroads on L.A. waistlines is the **bacon-wrapped hot dog.** Judging by the vendors most likely to carry it, it seems to be a Hispanic-community contribution, and we thank them profusely. A strip of bacon is wrapped diagonally around a large (and well-chosen) hot dog, and then the whole shebang is fried up (which allows the hot dog to get warm and permeated with the grease from the bacon) and placed on a warmed bun along with all sorts of goodies (particularly onions and peppers, fried along with the dog). We recommend loading them with everything, especially mayo, which puts the whole concoction even more over the top of the fat scale. Bacon-wrapped dogs turn up at street festivals, but they can regularly be found at any number of curbside vendors outside Staples Center whenever there is an event therein. Skip the pricey food inside and take advantage of the outside vendors. Sure, these guys aren't health department regulated, but we doubt that there is much of a hygiene problem to worry about in the first place. Certainly, such fears have never stopped us from glorying in the results.

return to town, demanding their Double Double (double patty, double cheese) before their plane has touched the tarmac.

Bagel baby

The chain **Noah's Bagels** (various locations) can be found throughout the city, and it is good, we grudgingly admit — after all, it is from Brooklyn. But in our opinion, the best bagels in the city can be found at **Bagel Broker** (7825 Beverly Blvd.; ☎ 323-931-1258). We are not alone in loving the crusty, chewy jobs found here. We especially enjoy how it lavishly layers its lox.

Haut dog

From its humble beginnings as a stand along the Venice boardwalk, **Jodi Maroni's Sausage Kingdom** (2011 Ocean Front Walk, Venice; also look for them at Universal City Walk and Century City Shopping Plaza; ☎ 310-822-5639; see map p. 119), "Home of the Haut Dog," has indeed become a kingdom; everything is under $8, and you can get their inventive sausages (Moroccan lamb, apple maple pork, Toulouse garlic, or tequila chicken, just for starters), made with all-natural ingredients, in a number of Southland locales (and elsewhere in the country). They are served at Dodger Stadium and Staples Center, as well. But the original stand remains, still beckoning passersby with offers of sample bites. The buns are soft, the condiments a nice complement, and the sausages divine. Despite their increased prevalence around the city, we never leave the boardwalk without having one.

Index of Establishments by Neighborhood

Beverly Hills
Kate Mantilini (American, $$$)
Lawry's The Prime Rib (Steakhouse, $$$$$)
Mastro's (Steakhouse, $$$$)
Matsuhisa (Japanese/Sushi, $$$$$)
Nate & Al's (Deli, $)
Spago Beverly Hills (California, $$$$$)

Downtown
Ciudad (Latin, $$$)
Grand Central Market (Various, $)
Nick & Stef's (Steakhouse, $$$$)
Original Pantry Cafe (Steakhouse, $)
Philippe the Original (Sandwiches, $)
The Standard Downtown L.A. Coffeeshop (Diner/Eclectic, $$)
Sushi Gen (Japanese/Sushi, $$)
Yang Chow (Chinese, $$)

Hollywood
Authentic Cafe (Southwestern/Caribbean, $$)
Caroussel (Armenian, $$)
El Cholo (Hollywood/Santa Monica) (Mexican, $$)
The Fabiolus Café (Italian, $$)
Fred 62 (Diner/Eclectic, $$)
The Kitchen (Diner/Eclectic, $)
Musso & Frank Grill (American, $$$$$)
Off Vine (American, $$)
101 Coffee Shop (Diner, $$)
Patina (French-Californian, $$$$$)
Pig 'N Whistle (American, $$$)
Pinot Hollywood (Bistro, $$$)
Roscoe's Chicken and Waffles (Soul Food, $)
Sanamluang Cafe (Thai, $)
Taylor's Steak House (Steakhouse, $$$)
Yuca's Hut (Mexican, $)

Los Angeles
Jerry's Famous Deli (Delicatessen, $$)
Versailles (Cuban, $$)
Zankou Chicken (Armenian, $)

Santa Monica
Blueberry (Cafe/Breakfast, $)
Border Grill (Mexican, $$$)
Bread & Porridge (American, $)
El Cholo (Hollywood/Santa Monica) (Mexican, $$)
The Ivy at the Shore (American, $$$$$)
The Lobster (Seafood, $$$$)
Michael's (California, $$$$$)

Venice
Joe's Restaurant (California, $$$$)
Amuse Café (American, $)

West Hollywood
A.O.C. (Mediterranean, $$$)
The Abbey (American, $$)
Angeli Caffe (Italian, $$)
Angelini Osteria (Italian, $$$)
Barney's Beanery (American, $)
Bastide (French, $$$$$)
Campanile (California/Mediterranean, $$$$)
Canter's Deli (Delicatessen, $$)
Cheebo (Italian, $)
Dan Tana's (Italian/Steakhouse, $$$$)
El Coyote (Mexican, $)
Farmer's Market (Various, $)
The Ivy (American, $$$$$)
Jar (Steakhouse, $$$$)
Joan's on Third (Tuscan/Mediterranean, $)
L'Orangerie (French, $$$$$)
Lucques (California, $$$)
Newsroom Cafe (Eclectic, $$)
Pink's (Hot Dog Stand, $)
Quality Food & Beverage (Diner, $)
Swingers (Coffee Shop, $)

West Los Angeles
Clementine's (Homemade Seasonal, $)
John O'Groats (American, $$)
Royal Star Seafood Restaurant
(Chinese, $$)

Westwood
Sepi's Giant Submarines
(Sandwiches, $)

Index of Establishments by Cuisine

American
The Abbey (West Hollywood, $$)
Amuse Café (Venice Beach, $)
Barney's Beanery (West Hollywood, $)
Bread & Porridge (Santa Monica, $)
The Ivy (West Hollywood, $$$$$)
The Ivy at the Shore (Santa Monica, $$$$$)
John O'Groats (West Los Angeles, $$)
Kate Mantilini (Beverly Hills, $$$)
Musso & Frank Grill (Hollywood, $$$$$)
Off Vine (American, $$)
Philippe the Original (Downtown, $)
Pig 'N Whistle (Hollywood, $$$)

Armenian
Caroussel (Hollywood, $$)
Zankou Chicken (Los Angeles, $)

Bistro
Pinot Hollywood (Hollywood, $$$)

Cafe/Breakfast
Blueberry (Santa Monica, $)
Joe's Restaurant (Venice, $$$$)
Lucques (West Hollywood, $$$)
Michael's (Santa Monica, $$$$$)
Spago Beverly Hills (Beverly Hills, $$$$$)

California/Mediterranean
Campanile (West Hollywood, $$$$)

Chinese
Royal Star Seafood Restaurant
(West Los Angeles, $$)
Yang Chow (Downtown, $$)

Coffee Shop
Swingers (West Hollywood, $)

Cuban
Versailles (Los Angeles, $$)

Delicatessen
Canter's Deli (West Hollywood, $$)
Jerry's Famous Deli (Los Angeles, $$)
Nate & Al's (Beverly Hills, $)

Diner/Eclectic
Fred 62 (Hollywood, $$)
The Kitchen (Hollywood, $)
Newsroom Cafe (West Hollywood, $$)
101 Coffee Shop (Hollywood, $$)
Quality Food & Beverage (West Hollywood, $)
The Standard Downtown L.A. Coffeeshop (Downtown, $$)

French
Bastide (West Hollywood, $$$$$)
L'Orangerie (West Hollywood, $$$$$)

French-Californian
Patina (Hollywood, $$$$$)

Homemade Seasonal
Clementine's (West Los Angeles, $)

Hot Dog Stand
Pink's (West Hollywood, $)

Italian
Angeli Caffe (West Hollywood, $$)
Angelini Osteria (West Hollywood, $$$)
Cheebo (West Hollywood, $)
Dan Tana's (West Hollywood, $$$$)
The Fabiolus Café (Hollywood, $$)
Pig 'N Whistle (Hollywood, $$$)

Japanese/Sushi
Matsuhisa (Beverly Hills, $$$$$)
Sushi Gen (Downtown, $$)

Latin
Ciudad (Downtown, $$$)

Mediterranean
A.O.C. (West Hollywood, $$$)

Mexican
Border Grill (Santa Monica, $$$)
El Cholo (Hollywood, $$)
El Coyote (West Hollywood, $)
Yuca's Hut (Hollywood, $)

Sandwiches
Philippe the Original (Downtown, $)
Sepi's Giant Submarines (Westwood, $)

Seafood
The Lobster (Santa Monica, $$$$)

Soul Food
Roscoe's Chicken and Waffles
(Hollywood, $)

Southwestern/Caribbean
Authentic Cafe (Hollywood, $$)

Steakhouse
Dan Tana's (West Hollywood, $$$$)
Jar (West Hollywood, $$$$)
Lawry's The Prime Rib (Beverly Hills,
$$$$$)
Mastro's (Beverly Hills, $$$$)
Nick & Stef's (Downtown, $$$$)
Original Pantry Cafe (Downtown, $)
Taylor's Steak House (Hollywood, $$$)

Thai
Sanamluang Cafe (Hollywood, $)

Tuscan/Mediterranean
Joan's on Third (West Hollywood, $)

Various
Farmer's Market (West Hollywood, $)
Grand Central Market (Downtown, $)

Index of Establishments by Price

$$$$$
Bastide (French, West Hollywood)
The Ivy (American, West Hollywood)
The Ivy at the Shore (American,
Santa Monica)
Lawry's The Prime Rib (Steakhouse,
Beverly Hills)
L'Orangerie (French, West Hollywood)

Matsuhisa (Japanese/Sushi, Beverly
Hills)
Michael's (California, Santa Monica)
Musso & Frank Grill (American,
Hollywood)
Patina (French/Californian,
Hollywood)
Spago Beverly Hills (California,
Beverly Hills)

$$$$

Campanile (California/Mediterranean, West Hollywood)

Dan Tana's (Italian/Steakhouse, West Hollywood)

Jar (Steakhouse, West Hollywood)

Joe's Restaurant (California, Venice)

The Lobster (Seafood, Santa Monica)

Mastro's (Steakhouse, Beverly Hills)

Nick & Stef's (Steakhouse, Downtown)

$$$

A.O.C. (Mediterranean, West Hollywood)

Angelini Osteria (Italian, West Hollywood)

Border Grill (Mexican, Santa Monica)

Ciudad (Latin, Downtown)

Kate Mantilini (American, Beverly Hills)

Lucques (California, West Hollywood)

Pig 'N Whistle (American, Hollywood)

Pinot Hollywood (Bistro, Hollywood)

Taylor's Steak House (Steakhouse, Hollywood)

$$

The Abbey (American, West Hollywood)

Angeli Caffe (Italian, West Hollywood)

Authentic Cafe (Southwestern/ Caribbean, Hollywood)

Canter's Deli (Delicatessen, West Hollywood)

Caroussel (Armenian, Hollywood)

El Cholo (Mexican, Hollywood)

The Fabiolus Cafe (Italian, Hollywood)

Fred 62 (Diner/Eclectic, Hollywood)

Jerry's Famous Deli (Delicatessen, Los Angeles)

John O'Groats (American, West Los Angeles)

Newsroom Cafe (Eclectic, West Hollywood)

Off Vine (American, Hollywood)

101 Coffee Shop (Diner, Hollywood)

Royal Star Seafood Restaurant (Chinese, West Los Angeles)

The Standard Downtown L.A. Coffeeshop (Diner/Eclectic, Downtown)

Sushi Gen (Japanese/Sushi, Downtown)

Versailles (Cuban, Los Angeles)

Yang Chow (Chinese, Downtown)

$

Amuse Café (American, Venice Beach)

Barney's Beanery (American, West Hollywood)

Blueberry (Cafe/Breakfast, Santa Monica)

Bread & Porridge (American, Santa Monica)

Cheebo (Italian, West Hollywood)

Clementine's (Homemade Seasonal, West Los Angeles)

El Coyote (Mexican, West Hollywood)

Farmer's Market (Various, West Hollywood)

Grand Central Market (Various, Downtown)

Joan's on Third (Tuscan/ Mediterranean, West Hollywood)

Original Pantry Cafe (Steakhouse, Downtown)

The Kitchen (Diner/Eclectic, Hollywood)

Nate & Al's (Deli, Beverly Hills)

Philippe the Original (Sandwiches, Downtown)

Pink's (Hot Dog Stand, West Hollywood)

Roscoe's Chicken and Waffles (Soul Food, Hollywood)

Quality Food & Beverage (Diner/ Eclectic, West Hollywood)

Sanamluang Cafe (Thai, Hollywood)

Sepi's Giant Submarines (Sandwiches, Westwood)

Swingers (Coffee Shop, West Hollywood)

Yuca's Hut (Mexican, Hollywood)

Zankou Chicken (Armenian, Los Angeles)

Part IV
Exploring
Los Angeles

The 5th Wave   By Rich Tennant

In this part . . .

This part takes you straight to the top attractions the city has to offer. We give you the lowdown on the city's famed beaches, the wealth of museums, the theme parks and studio tours, and the strange and fascinating charms of Hollywood. Here, too, are the top shopping neighborhoods, and our favorite spots to shop, whether you're searching for antiques, books, music, or clothing. Finally, we include five fun-filled itineraries that are uniquely L.A, and four day-trips for adventures just outside of the city.

Chapter 11

Discovering Los Angeles' Best Attractions

. . . .

In This Chapter

▶ Finding the best beaches
▶ Touring Hollywood and "Hollywood"
▶ Cruising down Sunset Boulevard
▶ Exploring the best museums, buildings, and outdoor spots
▶ Scoring tickets to a sports game or TV taping

. . . .

*O*ne of the major frustrations that comes with guiding folks
around Los Angeles is that a great deal of what you point out
will be prefaced by "and that parking lot/strip mall/empty lot used to
be . . ." Alas, far too much of L.A.'s architectural history has been hit
with the wrecking ball, and the amount of time we take using the past
tense when showing folks around makes us sheepish.

Which isn't to say that there's not still plenty to see and do. Just come
for the beach or the all-around welcoming weather. We won't get too
worked up if all you do is sit and think, "Gee, it's pretty here. And
warm." Though that brings us to the second most common guiding-
people-around frustration: From the mountains to the sea, much of
the best of L.A. scenery may be obscured by smog or haze. The solution is simple — come in December, January, or February. It may be
cold (although you may not think so), but the sky will be clearer than
it is in the warmer months.

Of course, the average visitor wants to see Hollywood, by which they
mean "movies" or, better still, "movie stars," neither of which is often
found in Hollywood proper. In this chapter, we discuss how to tour
studios (not nearly as thrilling as it sounds) but also where to go to
see the *real* Hollywood (studios and scandals). You can find more
information on the latter in Ken Schessler's *This is Hollywood* (Ken
Schessler Publishing), which covers everything from landmarks to
murders and suicides.

Los Angeles' Top Sights

The following is a list of the more or less must-see attractions in the city, followed by a list of beaches. We give you many more options later in this chapter under "Finding More Cool Things to See and Do."

Hollywood area attractions

Grauman's Chinese Theatre
Hollywood

Normally, this is when we haul out phrases like "newly restored to its former glory." Although it is true that Sid Grauman's fabulous movie palace, which was built in 1927 and designed to look like a Chinese temple, has been given a massive facelift, the restoration removed some of the 1950s glitz — usually a good thing, but in this case, it turned what was a riot of Oriental stylings into a rather dull, gray concrete structure. Authentic is not always best, we note. Even the neon dragons are gone! But at least the Mann chain (which bought the theater some years ago) officially returned the name Grauman (locals never did cave in and call it *Mann's* Chinese Theatre), and the interior remains a classic example of glorious movie-theater pomp, with deep reds, gilt, fanciful curlicues, and one giant screen. And of course, there are the footprints immortalized in concrete outside the theater. It began as a publicity stunt — it's *still* a publicity stunt, but thank heavens for it because how else could we see that Mary Pickford had such itty bitty feet? How else could there have been one of the best *I Love Lucy* shows of all time, when Lucy "borrowed" John Wayne's bootprints as a souvenir? (The Duke's bootprints are still here.) Yes, the stars of yesteryear, and some of today, have enshrined their shoeprints and handprints, and in some cases noseprints (Jimmy Durante) and legprints (Betty Grable), in concrete to last beyond their ruin. Go ahead, compare your appendages to theirs; you know you want to. And when you're done, you can see a movie here (as long as it's on the big screen), even some cheap action piece of junk, because it's what the movie-going experience ought to be.

See map p. 161. 6925 Hollywood Blvd. ☎ *323-464-MANN or 323-461-3331.* http://mann.moviefone.com/services/graumanmain.adp. *Showtimes vary. Call for movie ticket prices.*

Hollywood Entertainment Museum
Hollywood

This museum isn't at all the schlock-fest you might think. It's a well-done tribute to the glory of movies and television and full of surprises. Visitors have to take a tour, which is tiresome, and sometimes docents/tour guides aren't ready to go. But you wait in a rotunda full of screens showing short Hollywood tributes such as Chuck Workman's *Precious Images,* which never fails to bring us to tears. On the tour, you can see various bits of Hollywood ephemera (including some bits and bobs from the late,

Hollywood Area Attractions

Capitol Records Building **5**
The Farmer's Market **14**
Former Charlie Chaplin Studios **12**
Grauman's Chinese Theatre **10**
Hollyhock House **2**
Hollywood Entertainment Museum **11**
Hollywood Erotic Museum **7**
Hollywood-Highland Complex **8**
Hollywood Sign **3**
Hollywood Walk of Fame **6**
Hollywood Wax Museum **9**
Los Angeles County Museum of Art **15**
Los Angeles Zoo & Musuem of the American West **1**
Paramount Pictures Studios **4**
Petersen Automotive Museum **16**
La Brea Tar Pits & George C. Page Museum **13**

Seeing the movies in style

If you, like us, prefer to see movies the way God, or at least Cecil B. DeMille, intended, not only should you catch a flick at Grauman's, but you should also try the nearby **El Capitan** (6838 Hollywood Blvd.; ☎ **323-467-7674**). Restored to full, gilded glory, thanks to Disney (consequently, only Disney movies are shown here), each summer's animation headliner gets its premiere at this location. The theater is complete with ushers in uniforms and the frequent prescreening of live shows (another touch from the early days of cinema).

The American Cinematheque restored the 1922 **Egyptian Theatre** (another Sid Grauman special). The theater's pharaoh-style decor is mostly confined to the outside areas; inside is what appears to be a state-of-the-art modern theater. Film buffs have made a number of complaints about the theater's updated design (sightlines, noise, you name it).

The **Cinematheque** does regular wonderful screenings (special programs, revivals, new works, and documentaries); be sure to check out its offerings during your visit (6712 Hollywood Blvd.; ☎ **323-466-3456**; www.egpytiantheatre.com).

And finally, the humbler but still noteworthy **Vista** (first-run movies) is another Egyptian-revival house that has gotten a facelift plus new seats that leave enough legroom between rows to allow for strolling elephants (4473 W. Sunset Blvd.; ☎ **323-660-6639**).

lamented Max Factor Museum, such as the "beauty calibrator" that looks like a futuristic torture device), which is pretty cool, but much cooler still are rooms where you learn how some of the art of moviemaking is done. We love the Foley room, where you are given the chance to supply the sound effects — footsteps, doorbell, paper crumbling — for a little detective short. You also go through a *Star Trek* set and watch yourself being "beamed up," admire Mulder's office from *X Files,* and end on the actual *Cheers* barroom set, Norm's stool and all perfectly intact. Kids may or may not love all of this, depending on their pop-culture references, but we bet you will find it all delightful.

See map p. 161. 7021 Hollywood Blvd. ☎ *323-465-7900.* www.hollywoodmuseum.com. *Admission: $10 adults, $4.50 students, children under 5 free. Open: Labor Day–Memorial Day, Thurs–Sun 11 a.m.–6 p.m. Memorial Day–Labor Day, daily 11 a.m.–6 p.m.*

Hollywood & Highland Complex
Hollywood

The Hollywood & Highland Complex is a little bit *nightlife,* a little bit *attraction,* and a whole lot *shopping* — but we're sticking it here because it's in Hollywood, right in the middle of everything else you're going to be seeing and doing. Plus, it is the spiffy new centerpiece of what the city still desperately hopes will be a major rejuvenation of Hollywood Boulevard. But basically, when you get right down to it, it's a shopping mall. A grand shopping mall, to be sure; we glory in the detailing that includes quotes in mosaic from anonymous actors and others about their epic struggles to "Make It," the way the staircase entrance is designed to frame the Hollywood sign, the courtyard full of stands and umbrellas and cafe tables, and, best of all, the **Babylon Court,** which pays homage to D. W. Griffith's fantastic Babylon set for his movie *Intolerance*. The **Kodak Theatre** was built specifically as a permanent home for the annual Academy Awards, although it also hosts concerts and theater road companies throughout the year. And there are **two nightclubs, a bowling alley, access to nearby movie theaters, restaurants**, and a **self-guided audio tour of the Walk of Fame.** They did a fine job with the design, we have to admit — for a shopping mall. *Note:* Ryan Seacrest's daily talk show, which taped in a studio in the complex, was cancelled in 2004

See map p. 161. Northwest corner of Hollywood and Highland. www.hollywood andhighland.com. *Hours: Mon–Sat 10 a.m.–10 p.m., Sun 10 a.m.–7 p.m.(some establishments may be open later).*

The Hollywood Sign
Hollywood

Icon. What else would you call those nine 50-foot-tall white letters perched high up in the Hollywood hills? They constitute one of the most instantly recognizable sights in the world. The sign dates back to 1923, and it originally read "Hollywoodland," the name of the development it was drawing attention to. (The last four letters came down in the '40s.) Struggling actors, despairing of ever getting their big break, were rumored to have made it a favorite suicide spot. But the only person confirmed to have actually done so was actress Peg Entwhistle, who jumped off the letter H in 1932. You can't drive up to the sign, nor can you walk right up to it, but you can hike up from Durand Avenue off of Beachwood Canyon. You can get a good picture of it from Sunset Boulevard at Gower and also at Bronson, but otherwise, you may have to drive up Beachwood until it gets closer and closer and you get the shot you want.

See map p. 161. At the top of Beachwood Canyon.

Hollywood Walk of Fame
Hollywood

Granite stars rimmed in brass are implanted in the sidewalk along Hollywood Boulevard (and down Vine Street towards Sunset Boulevard). They feature names of the Greats and the Once Greats (and those who had really good publicists and some pocket change) of film, radio, television, and the recording arts. We hate to shatter any illusions, but the stars *pay* for their stars — up to $15,000 — and pretty much anyone, with a rather minimal level of success, can get nominated. The Hollywood Chamber of Commerce makes sure that they can cough up the money, and then they give out a star. But so what? Walk along Hollywood Boulevard and see how many of those names you still recognize (to say nothing of seeing what strange accidental neighbors the juxtaposition of names creates). It's something you should do at least once.

Etiquette tips for celebrity encounters

"Oh, my God," you shriek (to yourself, we hope), "it's *him!*" Or her. Or them. Anyway, you've spotted one: There they are, a star, a celeb, a famous face, or whatever, sitting right next to you at In 'N Out Burger. What to do? Act like a local, we say, and ignore 'em. Although, you may want to take note of what they're wearing through a discreet glance out of the corner of your eye so that you can tell your friends. Remember, even if they do look better than we do, they're simply real people out having a burger or going to a movie.

You will not be the first, nor the tenth, person to run up to them and say, "I hate to bother you, but I just love your movies and can I have your autograph?" If you must, you must. But don't blame us if your target is less than polite, even if you're the soul of charm — especially if said celebrity is, at the very moment you make your request, chomping down on a greasy chili burger. Here are some tips on how to handle the encounter.

✔ **Don't** ask them why their album and/or movie didn't do as well as their last one, even if *you* thought it was great. Believe us, *they know.*

✔ **Don't** ask, "Hey, aren't you married?" if you happen to see them out with a giggling blonde or buxom redhead, or . . . you get the idea.

✔ **Don't** remind the celebrity of your previous encounters. ("We met at the book signing at Borders a couple of years ago, remember? I had on a navy sweater. . . .")

✔ **Don't** ask them if they ever think of "retiring" like Demi Moore did.

✔ **Don't** tell them you have an old yearbook of theirs, and "gosh, it says you graduated in 1980, not 1987 — what gives?"

✔ **Do** smile and keep it brief. Trust us, they aren't really listening to you.

✔ **Don't** think that because you won an MTV contest or a backstage pass from a radio station, they're thrilled to finally meet you, too! Sure they're pleased, but remember that they are working . . . do you like it when the intern or office temp gazes dreamily at you when you have a deadline?

✔ **Do** have a pen if you want an autograph and feel that it's an okay time to ask. "Oh, can I have your autograph, and oh, by the way, do you happen to have a pen with you, man?" is pushing the limit. Hey, the UPS guys offer a pen; why can't you?

(Special thanks to the studio tour guides at Universal Studios Hollywood who suggested this list.)

See map p. 161. Hollywood Blvd., between Gower St. and La Brea Ave., and Vine St. between Hollywood Blvd. and Sunset. ☎ **323-469-8311.** www.hollywoodcoc.org. *Call for information such as who is where and who may be getting a star while you are in town.*

J. Paul Getty Museum at the Getty Center
Brentwood

Once upon a time, there was an oilman named J. Paul Getty. He made a great deal of money. Buckets of it. He left it to his heirs, who then made tabloid history — but that's another story. He also amassed a great deal of art. He then created a trust to oversee and add to the collection after his death. This trust has to spend a certain sum every year, and that sum is more money than God has in His own checking account, which is why the Getty frequently outbids other institutions for great works of art. In the 1960s, J. Paul Getty built a re-creation of a first-century Roman villa on grounds located high above Pacific Coast Highway, specifically to house his collection of antiquities. It was opened to the public in 1974. The collection quickly outgrew the space, and the villa was closed to the public in 1997, when the new, billion-dollar Getty Center opened high above the 405 Freeway in Brentwood. This latter museum was designed by Richard Meier (and took 12 years to build) and houses scholarly facilities as well as the art galleries. (The villa is undergoing restoration and will be reopened to the public sometime in the future.) The museum specializes in Greek and Roman antiquities, European paintings, and photographs. It's an impressive collection, but can we say, without too many cries of heresy, that it's a little boring? That it's kind of underwhelming for all the hype? That it's more interesting that they paid $53.9 million to acquire Van Gogh's *Irises,* and that a couple of times they spent a ton of money acquiring art that proved to be forgeries? But all of that applies strictly to the collection.

The structure itself is extraordinary, a feat of modern design that dominates the hill it's perched on. The building offers a view of L.A. (to the sea) that's worth the visit alone. Come here in the early evening with a picnic and enjoy the views, the warm air, and the generally good-natured crowds. Some consider it a true, albeit uniquely L.A., urban experience (people! outside! mingling! doing cultural things!). Either way, the experience is a treat. Also, you can't beat the prices — admission is free! (You have to pay for parking, which often calls for reservations, or public transportation.) The tram ride up from the parking lot is a bonus hoot. The Getty has a special series of evening concerts, often musical gems that you simply can't see elsewhere. We strongly encourage you to find out what is playing and take advantage of these concerts.

See map p. 191. 1200 Getty Center Dr. ☎ **310-440-7330.** www.Getty.edu. *Admission: free. Parking: $5. (On-site parking restricted to availability.) Open: Tues–Thurs 10 a.m.–6 p.m., Fri–Sat 10 a.m.–9 p.m., Sun 10 a.m.–6 p.m. Closed major holidays. Parking reservations for RVs and other oversized vehicles required at all times. Parking on surrounding streets is restricted. Visitors to the Getty Center may now use a free parking and shuttle service available during public hours from a nearby lot on Sepulveda Blvd. and Constitution Ave. (located just north of Wilshire*

Blvd.). This shuttle is offered, in addition to on-site parking, as a service to Getty visitors and does not require reservations.The bus lines serving the Getty Center are the MTA Bus 561 and the Santa Monica Bus 14. Passenger drop-offs are permitted from vehicles of 15 passengers or fewer.

La Brea Tar Pits/George C. Page Museum
Los Angeles

It's goopy, it's smelly, it's oozing, and it's wonderful . . . it's the La Brea Tar Pits. It's a gruesome story, so let's repeat it. Millions of years ago (okay, 40,000; *whatever*), unsuspecting prehistoric critters (woolly mammoths, saber-toothed tigers, and so on) would wander over to an attractive pool of water and wade into it, only to discover that the water was floating on top of tar in which they would then be permanently stuck. Death would follow (through starvation or suffocation). Their bodies would sink down into the muck (sometimes additionally condemning a predator who had hopped on thinking it was getting an easy meal by preying on a trapped beastie — sucker!), and there they stayed, until the world discovered archaeologists. The archaeologists found that if you dredge those pits, you can find whole, beautifully preserved skeletons. And so they dig around in the tar pits and put what they find on display. And amazingly, all this is located right along Wilshire Boulevard, one of the busiest streets in L.A. In fact, all the buildings in this complex (including the Los Angeles County Museum of Art, the LACMA, next door) are built to float, more or less, on the tar, which remains in full forceful presence. (And it's still sticky, even if you are just picking up a little bit to give to someone as a souvenir — not that we know from personal experience or anything.) Kids love it, not the least for the pathos-ridden, life-size-critter sculptures that adorn some of the bubbling pools (the doomed pachyderm, with its sad baby calling from the banks is a perennial fave). During the late summer, the pits are open to the viewing public, so you can see the scientists at work as they try to excavate more bones. The museum is less enjoyable than the pits — the bones aren't quite as interesting after they are all cleaned up. *Fun fact:* La Brea means "the tar." So, yes, these are the The Tar Tar Pits.

See map p. 191. 5801 Wilshire Blvd. ☎ *323-934-7243.* www.tarpits.org. *Admission: $7 adults, $4.50 students and seniors, $2 children 5–10, under 5 free. Open: Mon–Fri 9:30 a.m.–5 p.m., Sat–Sun 10 a.m.–5 p.m.*

Los Angeles County Museum of Art
Los Angeles

Though for many years the Los Angeles County Museum of Art (LACMA) was *the* museum of the city, it is now much overlooked in favor of the splashy (and wealthy) Getty. But can we go out on a limb and say that, as local museums go, we prefer this to the Getty? And you might, too; there is something here for everybody, in part because this is the nation's largest, most comprehensive and encyclopedic collection next to New York's Metropolitan (and may offer a finer overall experience). The collections run the gamut from antiquities to masterpieces (Rembrandt,

Degas, and Cézanne) to contemporary art (including Magritte's *Ceci n'est pas une pipe*). It also has one of the finest collections of Asian art in the world, including the only building devoted soley to Japanese art outside of Japan, plus one of the world's most significant collections of Islamic art. The institution is housed in several buildings, so it is easy to focus a visit on sampling your particular interests. Further, it is shockingly uncrowded during the nonsummer months, when not even all that many groups of schoolchildren are running about. Having said all of that, certainly the complex and buildings pale compared to the Getty — or just about any other major American museum, which is why LACMA tried to do a major teardown top-to-bottom redo renovation. Plans for that had to be shelved after they lost their funding (to our quiet relief; the new complex plans were ugly, again). Currently, the plan is to use an enormous donation from a board member to build a new contemporary art building and then put up some other architectural doodahs to tie all the buildings in the complex (including LACMA West, down the street) together in one visual something-or-other. Since this was just announced as we were going to press, when this is going to happen hasn't quite been sorted out yet. But if you see construction, that's probably what's going on. Note that street parking is cheaper than the LACMA lots, but that the meter readers are notoriously vigilant.

See map p. 191. 5905 Wilshire Blvd. ☎ *323-857-6000 (for general information).* www. lacma.org. *Admission: $9 adults, $5 seniors and adult students with ID, children under 17 free. Open: Mon, Tues, Thurs noon–8 p.m., Fri noon–9 p.m., Sat–Sun 11 a.m.–8 p.m. Closed Wed.*

Museum of Contemporary Art/MOCA at the Geffen Contemporary
Downtown

First they decided to build L.A. a contemporary art museum, but they needed to start the museum before the real building was in place, so they used a warehouse-like building near Little Tokyo. It was dubbed the Temporary Contemporary. The real building (a geometric structure that promptly won architectural awards) opened on Grand Street near the Music Center, but by then, everyone loved the Temporary Contemporary so much (for one thing, it's fun to say!) that it was made permanent. Then David Geffen gave a great deal of money (as he is wont to do) to the institution, and the Temporary became the Geffen Contemporary, except many of us don't call it that for it's not as euphonious. Anyway, the upshot is one museum, two locations. All media are represented, from abstract to pop art to emerging new artists. Recent past special exhibits include the first major retrospective of Lucien Freud in years, the first Andy Warhol comprehensive showing since the artist debuted in Los Angeles 30 years before, and a very recent exhibition of minimalist art that was featured in *Time* magazine. The Geffen (Temporary, whatever) is more likely to have conceptual or installation art simply because the shape of the facility is conducive to such exhibits. Free gallery tours, offered by most-knowledgeable docents, are offered several times during most days — we highly encourage you to plan a visit around these tours as they are one of the best deals in L.A. (Having said that, take the latest tour you can; the museums tend to be the most busy until around 1:30 p.m.) Admission covers both buildings.

See map p. 191. 250 S. Grand Ave. and 152 N. Central Ave. ☎ *213-626-6222.* www. moca.org. *Admission: $8 adults, $5 seniors and students with ID, children under 12 free. Open: Mon 11 a.m.–5 p.m., Thurs 11 a.m.–8 p.m., Fri 11 a.m.– 5 p.m., Sat–Sun 11 a.m.–6 p.m., closed Tues–Wed.*

Olvera Street
Downtown

Olvera Street is the oldest remaining street in Los Angeles. It is made up of what may be the original cobblestones, or at least ones that date back to the 1930s, when this monument to old L.A. was erected. Its official name is El Pueblo de Los Angeles Historic Monument, but no one refers to it by this name. Several 19th-century adobe buildings remain standing alongside this street (one is the oldest existing building in L.A.). The rest of the structures are newer, but it feels like a bustling marketplace in Mexico. It's both a festive tourist trap and an utterly authentic South-of-the-Border experience; some wonderful Mexican food can be had here, and the stalls that clutter the streets are full of cheap trinkets and good clothing buys (to say nothing of Mexican sweets). You can easily run through here in well under an hour, unless you shop and snack.

Entrance is located near Alameda St. across from Union Station. ☎ *213-628-3562.*

Universal Studios Hollywood
Burbank

Out-of-town visitors put this attraction at the top of their must-see list, while the rest of us, quite frankly, tend to forget it exists. The magic of moviemaking is revealed — sort of — at this combination studio back lot/theme park. The latter features a dozen or so rides and attractions (a few of which have height restrictions and/or which may be too intense for young children; pregnant women are advised to avoid several rides, including, oddly, the incredibly popular Studio Tour, no doubt because there are bumps and jostles along the collapsing bridge). Universal offers visitors a chance to see and experience how movies are made. For the price of admission, you get a full day of things to do.

The real attraction at Universal Studios has always been the tram tour, which is guided by a real human, with help from videotaped comments by the likes of Ron Howard. In order to really see what's on the video screens, sit at least two rows back from the front of each car. It'll be tempting to want to rush for the first of the four cars in the tram, but you'll actually get a better sense of the action by taking a seat in the second or third one. A lot of the special effects on the tour take place on the left side of the bus, although the shark leaps up on the right. The tour (still just a touch creaky and dated) is in itself as artificial as the movie sets visitors get to peer at (real moviemaking will remain out of the sight of gawkers), but it does offer some interesting sights, such as the courthouse from the *Back to the Future* movies, a few leftover *Jurassic Park* vehicles, and Whoville from *The Grinch,* which looms oddly over the Bates Motel from *Psycho.* You can also travel

Universal City and Nearby Studios

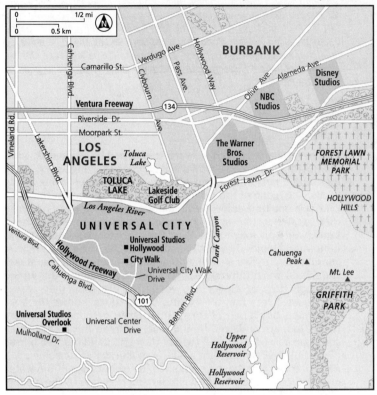

through effects-laden soundstages (which are really fun and exciting), find out how movie rain is made, experience a shark attack, and watch union crew members eat doughnuts. After the tour is done, kids will want to race off to the rides (see the "Rating the attractions at Universal" sidebar in this section). Aside from the tour, a big reason Universal is such a popular theme park is that it serves beer, and lots of it. There are also margaritas next to the Jurassic Park ride, so you can get soused after just getting drenched. Food is readily available, but it's of the costly junk-food sort. Your best bet may be to leave the park (ins-and-outs are allowed) and stroll over to the CityWalk (see Chapter 12 for details) for slightly more-nutritious, if not more reasonably priced, food options. Even without crowds, we spent five hours seeing shows and riding rides. With a summer crowd, expect to spend at least three hours longer because of lines. Get there when the park opens to maximize your time!

Note: At this writing, Universal is offering one of the best tour packages in Los Angeles; for $22 over regular admission, guests receive one-time-use tickets (good for 30 days) for **Starline Tours, the Hollywood Entertainment Museum, The Hollywood Museum,** and the **Kodak Theatre Guided Tour.**

See map p. 169. Universal Studios Hollywood, 100 Universal City Plaza, Universal City. ☎ *800-864-8377.* www.universalstudioshollywood.com. *Admission: adults $49.75, children under 48 inches tall $39.75, additional front-of-line passes and VIP packages also available. Open: Hours can vary, so call ahead. At times, special savings coupons are passed out upon admission to the park. Please check Universal's Web site for updates, changes, and additional specials, as well as changes in shows and attractions.*

Venice Ocean Front Walk
Venice

This several-mile stretch of beach is hemmed by a sidewalk, which is itself lined with shops, cafes, stalls selling clothes, sunglasses, and ear-piercings, street performers, and what used to be called bums. Every day is a scene — it's one of the best people-watching places in the city. Truth be told, this one-time epicenter of bohemia (you know, when it was new) and then hippiedom (Jim and Ray created The Doors on the beaches here!) got swallowed up a long time ago by the tourists who wanted to gawk at the bohos and hippies. Not that counterculture isn't still a major presence, but geez, kids in tie-dye and long dreads aren't new anymore. **Muscle Beach,** the famed weightlifters' spot, still features young "Ahnuld-wannabes," although they preen for the voyeurs more than they work on their physiques. Every first-time visitor needs to walk down the boardwalk at least once, buy a pair of cheap sunglasses, get a henna tattoo — unless those, too, are outlawed by the time you read this — have a sausage at Jodi Maroni's original stall (where they still hand out free bite-sized samples of all their wares), rent a bike or in-line skates for some speedy travel and exercise, and maybe even stick his or her toes in the water. It's less crowded on weekdays, although parking is always in short supply.

See map p. 173. Between Venice Ave. and Rose Ave. Parking in paid lots at Rose and Windward Aves.

Rating the attractions at Universal

Calling them "rides" is not exactly accurate — only a couple of the attractions at Universal Studios Hollywood qualify for that moniker. Instead what you mainly get are "immersive experiences" — fancy talk for movie-themed shows, special-effects extravaganzas, and stunt spectaculars. Here's a rundown on what to expect:

✔ At press time, Universal was preparing to open its first, true theme-park-worthy attraction: **Revenge of the Mummy: The Ride.** Part indoor roller-coaster, part special-effects thrill ride, the new attraction will take those with strong stomachs on a high-speed journey through the curse-ridden ancient Egypt depicted in the popular series of movies.

✔ Another new-as-of-2004 attraction is **Van Helsing: Fortress Dracula,** but we're going to save you some time here: You know those haunted houses your local

chambers of commerce set up around Halloween where you walk through dark-
ened hallways and lights flash and sometimes people in scary costumes jump out
you? It's like that, only not scary and with pictures of Hugh Jackman. Seriously,
you'll be more frightened by the prices in the gift shops.

✔ You will get very, very wet on **Jurassic Park,** a glorified log flume with a "small
world" full of robotic dinosaurs and one very steep drop. We paid $1 for a dis-
posable plastic poncho, and we suggest you buy two, one for your upper body
and one for your lower body.

✔ Expect the most jostling from **Back to the Future,** which left us longing for a mas-
sage, or at least a vibrating chair. The ride's conceit is that some evil guy in an
ugly Hawaiian shirt has stolen a time-traveling DeLorean (wasn't this funnier in
the 1980s?), and you're along for the ride.

✔ **Shrek 4-D** bridges the gap between the first and second movies with a fun 15-
minute animated 3D short featuring the original voice actors (Mike Myers, Eddie
Murphy, and so on). It's screened in a theater with motion-coordinated seats (they
move in time with stuff happening on screen) and water and wind special effects
that make the show entertaining without being too intense for people who usually
can't handle true motion-simulator rides.

✔ **Terminator 2 3-D** is a live-action show mixed with 3D filmmaking effects. It is based
on plot points of the first two *Terminator* movies that seem dated after the third
Terminator movie and that whole California gubernatorial thing.

✔ **Backdraft** and **The Special Effects Stages** take you behind the scenes to show how
fire effects, green screens, robotics, and sound engineering turn dull moments into
movie magic. Both are interesting, but if the line is long, come back later.

✔ **Animal Planet Live, Waterworld, The Blues Brothers,** and **Spider-Man Rocks** are
live-action shows featuring animals, stunts, music, and other assorted "entertainment." The only one really worth your time is the Animal Planet show, but it's too
short for the long lines getting in and out of the stadium. And the only reason you
should see the 20-minute musical version of "Spider-Man" is to giggle as they try to
work "Holding Out for a Hero," "She Bangs," and "Lady Marmalade" into the story.

The wait can be long (interminable actually) for these attractions, which brings us to
the Front of the Line Pass. With it, you get to cut to the head of the line on all attractions. Is this a good idea? Well, you pay $89 per person ($79 off season), including children, and you won't be the only person with one, but it does save you time, gives you
better seats in some cases, and offers a sense of entitlement over the plebes waiting
in the hot sun.

The top beaches

For a map of all of the following beaches, see "Los Angeles Beaches," on
p. 173.

If you don't care about anything other than warm water, nice sand, and
girls in bikinis or wiry surfer boys, just drive west and stop when you hit

water. Actually, you won't quite get that far; most of the L.A. beaches are separated from the road by A) another road, B) a grassy, park-like area, or C) a parking lot. Which brings us to the problem with going to the beach — you almost always have to pay. You can't park along the **Pacific Coast Highway,** which runs parallel to the ocean. The closer the parking lot (say, right next to the sand), the higher the price to park.

When you get to the sand, one beach is pretty much like another, except when it's not. The **Santa Monica** and **Venice** beaches are the most popular because they're closest to business areas. (For details on Venice Beach's famous boardwalk, check out "Venice Ocean Front Walk," p. 170.)

The farther up the coastline you go, into **Pacific Palisades** and **Malibu,** the "purer" the beach experience: fewer tourists, more locals, and more surfers. The waves get bigger, the beaches seem less touched by man (an illusion; this whole coastline is developed in one way or another), and the water quality is better. The Santa Monica Bay has struggled with bacteria and other contamination problems for some time, and the problem is often most acute at beaches beside piers or near storm drains. Heal the Bay, a nonprofit environmental group, has done a wonderful job helping to clean up the coastal waters, but beaches may still be closed for swimming from time to time. Signs will tell you when to avoid the water. As you get into Malibu, residences start popping up (full of really rich folks, by and large), and the beaches aren't precisely public. No one has fences all the way into the water, but residents do glare at you as you cruise along in front of their pricey property. *Note:* The high-tide line is where private property officially begins. Respect this property line, for you are essentially walking in someone's backyard. **Zuma,** the beach farthest north, is also by far the nicest, though the water is colder than at the southern beaches.

If you visit the beach in the winter, you probably won't be doing much swimming (unless you come equipped with a wetsuit or a really good constitution), although some splashing around can be done on all but the most inclement days. During the summer, as temperatures soar, so do the crowds; on the hottest weekend days you'll find nary an extra towel space on the sand.

Few experiences fuel the appetite like a day at the beach. Fortunately, many area beaches offer food and drink concessions. Concessions are available at **Dockweiler Beach, Manhattan Beach, Redondo Beach, Torrance County Beach, Zuma Beach County Park, Will Rogers State Park,** and **Hermosa Beach.** For full-blown restaurant dining, as well as shopping and entertainment options, you'll have plenty of choices at or near the **Santa Monica beaches, Venice Beach,** and **Redondo Beach.**

Many Los Angeles County beaches are well-equipped for travelers with disabilities, with ramps and boardwalks leading to the beach. Beach wheelchairs are available at **Zuma Beach County Park, Topanga County Beach, Venice, Will Rogers State Park, Dockweiler Beach, Manhattan**

Los Angeles Beaches

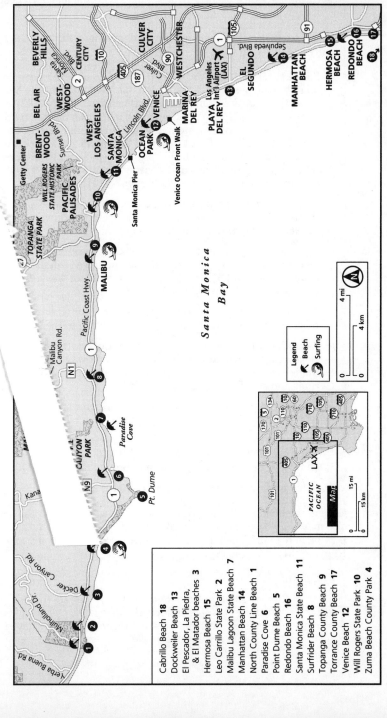

Cabrillo Beach **18**
Dockweiler Beach **13**
El Pescador, La Piedra,
 & El Matador beaches **3**
Hermosa Beach **15**
Leo Carrillo State Park **2**
Malibu Lagoon State Beach **7**
Manhattan Beach **14**
North County Line Beach **1**
Paradise Cove **6**
Point Dume Beach **5**
Redondo Beach **16**
Santa Monica State Beach **11**
Surfrider Beach **8**
Topanga County Beach **9**
Torrance County Beach **17**
Venice Beach **12**
Will Rogers State Park **10**
Zuma Beach County Park **4**

Beach, and **Torrance County Beach.** Check with the lifeguard headquarters at each beach.

Here are some tips to keep in mind when planning a day at a Los Angeles County beach:

✔ For **general information**, contact the Los Angeles County Department of Beaches & Harbors, which operates many of the beaches along the county's 72 miles of coastline (☎ **310-305-9503;** http://beaches.co.la.ca.us/). County beaches that are run by the California state parks system include **Dockweiler Beach, Leo Carrillo State Park, Point Dume, Will Rogers State Park,** and **Santa Monica State Beach** (http://cal-parks.ca.gov). For recorded surf conditions and weather forecasts up and down the Los Angeles area coast, call ☎ **310-457-9701.**

✔ Plan to **arrive early** during the summer, on most weekends, or if there is an unseasonably hot day the rest of the time; otherwise, expect to have trouble finding parking and a place to sit.

✔ Seniors can get a permit for **free weekday parking** at any county beach lot staffed by an attendant. All you have to do is show proof of age (62 and older). The permit is not valid for weekend or holiday parking.

✔ Keep in mind that **alcohol** and **pets** are prohibited on all county-run beaches. Notice how few people pay attention to this prohibition.

✔ **Campfires** are prohibited on every L.A. County beach *except* Dockweiler Beach (at the end of the 105 Freeway/Imperial Boulevard) and Cabrillo Beach (in San Pedro), which have fire rings and special hours for evening picnics.

✔ Most county and state beaches provide restrooms or chemical toilets. Many provide outdoor showers and picnic facilities.

✔ Be sure to **bring sunscreen** and reapply it frequently, especially when you come out of the water — you *will* sunburn otherwise, and it can ruin your trip (not to mention your complexion).

✔ **Bring and drink plenty of water** as well.

Gaze at the beach and leave, or take a nice long stroll along the shore. You may want to spend an entire day (even two!) basking in the sun and playing in the surf. The Pacific is happy to accommodate any and all. Here are the best beaches to

✔ Take the family:

• **Corona Del Mar State Beach:** Flat and broad, there is something for everyone, volleyball players, fire pits, kayakers, fishermen, sea lions, and even a little cove that may have been the lagoon for Gilligan's Island.

- **Dockweiler Beach:** It's the only L.A. beach with an RV park, plus you can light a campfire at night.

- **Leo Carrillo State Beach:** It has camping, good windsurfing, sea-lion sightings, and lots of neat coves and sea caves.

- **Redondo Beach:** It's got the beach, volleyball courts, and an arcade and shopping on the Redondo Beach Pier.

✔ Surf till you drop:

- **Malibu's Surfrider Beach:** It's the classic surfing beach, of Frankie and Annette fame.

- **Topanga County Beach:** The waves roll deep into the bay, giving surfers long, satisfying rides.

- **Torrance County Beach:** Longboarders love it, and so will you if you're looking for a quiet haven from the crowds.

- **Zuma Beach County Park:** The largest, nicest beach in Los Angeles offers big, strong waves.

- **Will Rogers State Beach:** The nouthern section, Sunset Point, is full of long-boarders and beginners, and is friendly and non-competitive.

✔ Pretend you're a Beach Boy:

- **Manhattan Beach:** Hang out with the surfers and boogie boarders at one of the gestation points for California beach music. Manhattan Beach is where surfer boy Dennis Wilson hit upon the theme that catapulted the Beach Boys to *Billboard* stardom.

Surfing etiquette 101

Rule number one: If you don't know what you are doing, at least do one thing; stay out of the way of those who do. The hardcore surf rats may have no qualms about mowing over some inept tourist. Not only is staying out of the way generally good manners — and safer all around — but there remain some vestiges of the fierce regionalism that characterized the surfing scene in the mid-'70s, when "Locals only" was the rallying cry, along with "Death to Vals" (referring to the kids from the Valley who dared to venture into the holy waters).

Besides, surfing is not something you can suddenly just up and do. Arrange for surfing lessons at **Malibu Ocean Sports** (22935 Pacific Coast Hwy., Malibu; ☎ 310-456-6302); hang with them, and you'll be much the wiser.

And finally, keep the following in mind for a happy, healthy dip in the ocean: If you are a boogie boarder, stay away from the surfers, and if you're body surfing, stay away from the boogie boarders *and* the surfers.

Finding More Cool Things to See and Do

Who says L.A. is a fine place to live but not visit? We give you more things to see and do while you're here: Sunset Boulevard attractions, museums, kid's stuff, outdoor options, sports, buildings, studio tours.

The Sensational, Star-studded, Scandalous Sunset Boulevard Tour

It's been called the most famous street in America. It inspired a TV show, and a movie, which in turn spawned a Broadway musical hit.

"Sunset *BOOO-LA-VAHD!*" bellows whoever is playing the musical Norma Desmond these days. It may be kitsch, it may be hokey, it may more often than not be seedy, but for better or worse, Sunset Boulevard is *the* artery for Los Angeles. It's not the fastest way to get around, but if you have only a few hours in which to try to get a sense of this sprawling, schizophrenic town, the legendary Sunset Boulevard is the place to do it.

Think about it. Sunset begins at Olvera Street, the oldest street in L.A., dating back to when the city was *El Pueblo de Nuestra Senora, La Reigna de Los Angeles* ("The Town of Our Lady, the Queen of the Angels"). From there it winds its way through a fabulous cross-section of everything Los Angeles has to offer, from the good, to the bad, to the ugly, to the glamorous, until it ends smack at the Pacific Ocean. Sunset Boulevard has it all: movie stars and moguls; immigrants, nouveau riche, and old money; sushi bars and strip joints; punks, parks, and prostitutes. And then some.

When you drive Sunset, you can get a taste of every flavor of L.A., from conventional tourist sights to a bit of the history of the city (both early and movie) to the sordid and sensational. You can see beautiful old buildings, garish homes, and decrepit structures. You can gawk at the spots where John Belushi and River Phoenix shuffled off their mortal coils. You get a spectacular view of the Hollywood sign and a glimpse of the stars on the sidewalks.

This tour is designed to be driven westward, beginning at Olvera Street, passing through such famous neighborhoods as Hollywood, the Sunset Strip, Beverly Hills, Bel Air, and Brentwood, and ending at the Pacific, but you can do it backward if you are more of a deconstructionist than a dreamer. Just reverse the directions where appropriate (east becomes west, right becomes left, and so forth). Plan on setting aside about three hours if you stick strictly to Sunset (this allows for some photo-op stops), though it will take longer, depending on the traffic or if you take in some of the suggested side trips. A whole day can easily be devoted to this tour, but it's a day well spent.

Naturally, the optimum mode of travel is a convertible, preferably a vintage T-bird. But your style-free rental car will get the job done, as long as it has a stereo — soundtrack suggestions are provided.

Note the sidebars that alert you to special side trips along the route. Side trips are those serendipitous little detours off Sunset Boulevard where we've found something truly delicious for you to see. Of course, for time's sake, you may choose to stay firmly on the route. See the "Sunset Boulevard Tour" map on p. 178 for the locations of all the tour stops.

Ready? Let's cruise. . . .

Get your kicks on old Route 66

We begin at ❶ **Olvera Street** (400–500 N. Main). Los Angeles was founded in 1781, and this is traditionally considered the oldest street. (If you need to fuel up before the tour, there are plenty of opportunities for Mexican food on this street and for Chinese a few blocks away in Chinatown.) Sunset originally began a block above at Spring Street. Over the last couple years, the first few blocks have been renamed Cesar Chavez Boulevard. Start at the original Spring Street beginning, anyway, for history's sake, though it's the 900 block where Sunset now officially begins.

Now crank up your stereo with "Route 66" by Bobby Troupe. Yes, this portion of Sunset was part of the late, lamented, and much-celebrated American Drive.

Now put on some mariachi music as you hit the Hispanic part of Sunset; it's a little rundown, a mix of sagging apartments and some older, funkier architecture, but it has a warm community feel. Or you can play "Take Me Out to the Ballgame" — you'll see the signs on the right directing you to the pride of the O'Malleys, Dodger Stadium, just to the east of Sunset.

Turn left at the corner of Glendale Boulevard and Sunset. On the left is the Deco/Moderne ❷ **Angelus Temple,** built by the evangelist Aimee Semple McPherson, whose ministry and good works were overshadowed by scandal; McPherson was at the height of her fame when she disappeared for a month in 1926. She was presumed drowned. When she turned up, she insisted that she had been kidnapped. Her fake story quickly fell apart, and the truth came out — she had rendezvoused with her married lover. McPherson's ministry never recovered from the scandal, and she eventually committed suicide (or took an accidental overdose of pills) in 1944.

A taste of Victorian L.A.

Turn left off of Sunset onto Marion Avenue, right on Edgeware Road, and then left on Carroll Drive to an area known as Angeleno Heights. This long block of perfectly restored **Victorian homes,** brave with much gingerbread trim, is all that remains of fashionable 1800s Los Angeles — proof that this city once had as much character as San Francisco, thank you very much. (There are more homes one block over on the less impressive Kellam Street.)

Sunset Boulevard Tour

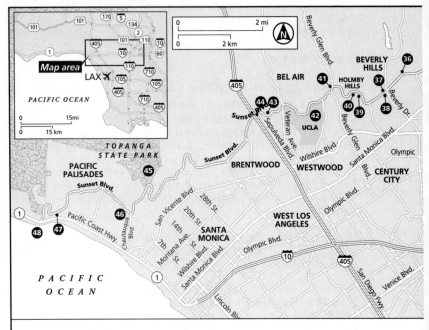

1 Olvera Street	**10** Original home of	**18** Ice cream shop
2 Angelus Temple	Columbia studios	**19** Charlie Chaplin's studio
3 1712 Glendale	**11** Hollywood Palladium	**20** Ralph's
4 KCET	**12** Earl Carroll Theater	**21** English Disco
5 Vista Theater	**13** Corner of Hollywood	**22** Virgin Megastore
6 Vons Market	and Vine	**23** Garden of Allah apartments
7 Scientology Center	**14** Cinerama Dome Theater	**24** Pandora's Box
8 William Fox's studio	**15** Hollywood Athletic Club	**25** Chateau Marmont
9 Original Warner	**16** Crossroads of the World	**26** Dudley Do-Right Emporium
Brothers studios	**17** Hollywood High	**27** Site of Source Restaurant

Cross back over Sunset to ❸ **1712 Glendale.** It's the former site of Mack Sennett's Keystone Studio, where Charlie Chaplin, Fatty Arbuckle, Gloria Swanson, and the Keystone Cops got their starts. Then return to Sunset Boulevard, traveling west.

Silver Lake and Los Feliz: Of bungalows and haciendas

As you cross Coronado Street, you enter Silver Lake, a remarkable multicultural, eclectic community of arty bohemians and homosexuals, young yuppies in love, budding Sammy Glick types burning to climb the Hollywood ladder by whatever means possible, immigrants, and older

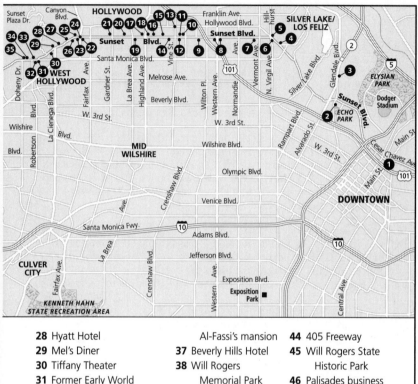

28	Hyatt Hotel		Al-Fassi's mansion	44	405 Freeway
29	Mel's Diner	37	Beverly Hills Hotel	45	Will Rogers State
30	Tiffany Theater	38	Will Rogers		Historic Park
31	Former Early World		Memorial Park	46	Palisades business
	restaurant	39	10000 Sunset		center
32	Viper Room	40	Former home of	47	Self-Realization
33	Whisky		Jayne Mansfield		Fellowship Lake
34	Roxy	41	Gates to Bel Air		Shrine and med-
35	Former Gazarri's	42	UCLA		itation garden
36	Site of Sheik	43	"Deadman's Curve"	48	Pacific Ocean

couples who have been residents for decades. Notice that the architecture, much left over from the early days of L.A., begins to improve — observe Hollywood bungalows (many built to house silent-screen actors) and Spanish haciendas.

If you're feeling hungry, stop at **Café Tropical** (2900 W. Sunset Blvd., corner of Parkman Avenue; ☎ **323-661-8391**), where many Silver Lake residents hang out, to load up on coffee, fruit shakes, guava pastries, and Cuban sandwiches.

As you keep driving, if the weather gods are kind, you should get a great view of the Hollywood hills straight ahead. As you cross the little bridge past the corner of Myra Avenue and Sunset, you can see the hills of Silver Lake on your right.

Just past Fountain Avenue on the right is ❹ **KCET,** the Los Angeles PBS affiliate. This lot was built as a movie studio in 1912 and has been in continuous use ever since, changing hands several times (the East Side Kids/Bowery Boys made their movies here). Next door is the **Tiki Ti Room** (☎ 323-669-9381), a bar shack that says it invented the tropical drink. Judge for yourself, if you can — the owner keeps his own hours.

You are now entering the Los Feliz neighborhood. On the northeast corner of the three-way intersection of Hillhurst Avenue (as it crosses Sunset going south, it changes names to Virgil Avenue), Sunset, and Hollywood boulevards is the ❺ **Vista Theater,** which was built in the early '20s and now boasts an interior facelift that shows off its Deco/Egyptian roots. It's a small but prime example of an early movie palace.

Diagonally across from the Vista to the left is a ❻ **Vons Market.** Big deal. But wait. In 1916, D. W. Griffith filmed his classic epic *Intolerance* at his **studio back lot,** which occupied the block on Virgil between Fountain and Sunset. He built the largest outdoor set ever for the "Babylon" segment of the movie. Afterward, the opulent set just sat there, decaying. It towered in the background over the increasingly growing skyline of Los Angeles. It was this sight that inspired Kenneth Anger's now-iconic phrase "Hollywood Babylon." So go stand in the parking lot of Vons Market; you are actually right smack dab in the middle of a metaphor for an era.

Sunset veers to the left at the three-way corner. If you continue straight, you end up on Hollywood Boulevard.

Keep going until you reach the intersection of Berendo Street and Sunset. On the left is the massive, blue ❼ **Scientology Center,** which actually takes up the whole block in all directions. The cult — oops, religion — owns most of the property around here. Right next door is a branch of the **Self Realization Fellowship** (the bigger version is in the Palisades — see "Pacific Palisades: sun, sand, and sea," p. 188).

Stan and Ollie's famous staircase

Just past Silver Lake Boulevard and Parkman Avenue, turn left on Vendome Street. Down on the right between 923 and 927 Vendome is a very steep, very long **staircase** (it's sometimes overgrown with vegetation, so it can look deceptively short). Imagine carrying a piano up it. Laurel and Hardy did, in their classic short *The Music Box,* and a nearby plaque honors the film.

Where Mickey Mouse was born

Make a right from Sunset onto Fountain Avenue and note the white triangle-shaped building a few yards down, on the right. It was built in 1916 for silent-film comedienne Mabel Normand, as her own studio. Normand, a gifted comic and film pioneer, was best known as Fatty Arbuckle's sidekick and was probably the first female star to direct her own movies.

Follow Fountain east as it curves to the left and becomes Hyperion Avenue. Go left on Griffith Park Boulevard (1.3 miles from the turn onto Fountain). At the corner is Gelson's market; it stands on the site of **Walt Disney's first official studio,** where he made the first Mickey Mouse cartoon and *Snow White and the Seven Dwarfs.*

A half-block up on the right are a **set of bungalows** that local legend swears were built by Disney or, at least, served as inspiration for the animators for his first movie classic. They certainly look like cottages for Sneezy, Dopey, Doc, and the gang.

Hollywood or bust

As you cross Vermont Avenue, you enter Hollywood proper, and it ain't pretty. A little dingy, with quite a few businesses, it's hardly the glamorous place of lore. But then, it never was. X's "Los Angeles" is the soundtrack for this stretch.

Both sides of the south corner of Sunset and Western Avenue used to be ⑧ **William Fox's studio** (he eventually merged and became Twentieth Century Fox). Not only did Western movie star Tom Mix shoot bad guys here, but this is also the place where John Wayne got his start.

On the left on Sunset Boulevard, ⑨ 5800 is local station KTLA, Channel 5, owned by Gene Autry. The station used to be the **original Warner Brothers studios,** where Al Jolson helped sink many of his silent-film colleagues' careers by making the first talking movie, *The Jazz Singer.* Pop on some Glen Miller or Artie Shaw for that nostalgic feel.

At the southeast corner of Sunset and Gower Street is the ⑩ **original home of Columbia Studios** (founded in 1921). Now mostly TV shows are filmed there. Across the street is "Gower Gulch," where Western players would wait, hoping for a shot in a cowboy picture. It was also the site of the movie studio where bit player Virginia Rappe was working when she achieved her own level of fame by dying — Fatty Arbuckle, then the most famous actor in Hollywood, was accused (and eventually acquitted) of her "murder" (it's not clear why she died of a ruptured spleen following a raucous Hollywood party).

Turn your head to the right at the Gower stoplight (and the next couple thereafter). Look up at the hills. There's the **Hollywood sign.** Built in 1923 and refurbished in the 1980s, it used to read "Hollywoodland," the name of the development below it.

Say farewell to Bela Lugosi

One block past Western Avenue turn right at St. Andrew's Place, and then turn left a block later onto Harold Way. Number **5620**, on the left, is where Bela Lugosi, one of filmdom's creepiest Count Draculas, died in 1956 at the age of 73. He was reportedly buried in his Dracula cape.

One block west, on the right, is the ⑪ **Hollywood Palladium.** It was the site of the studio that made the first feature-length movie (Cecil B. DeMille's *The Squaw Man*), and the spot where Rudolph Valentino made most of his movies. At one time it was the place to hear the big bands (Lawrence Welk played there for years), and it now hosts regular concerts. Across the street was the ⑫ **Earl Carroll Theater,** where the "most beautiful girls in the world" appeared. (A "gateway to Hollywood" at the corner of Hollywood and La Brea pays stylistic tribute to Carroll's girls.) It went through several incarnations after Carroll's plane-crash death in 1948, including a recent mortifying stint as the Chevy Chase Theater, when it was tarted up for Chase's short-lived talk show.

At the next signal is Vine Street. Look to the right on Vine, at the sidewalk. You should be seeing stars — for this is part of the famous **Walk of Fame.** Take a right turn at Vine. The ⑬ **corner of Hollywood and Vine** is one of the most famous places in the world. It's said that if you stand here long enough, you will see everyone pass by. (You may have to wait longer these days.) The **Brown Derby,** the legendary hat-shaped restaurant where all the stars dined and where Gable proposed to Lombard, was at the northwest corner (it's now a club/cafe). Farther north on Vine, on the right, is the round **Capitol Records building** (squint and it looks like a stack of records with a spindle on top).

Return to Sunset Boulevard. A block and a half to the corner of Ivar Avenue and Sunset, on the left, is the ⑭ **Cinerama Dome Theater,** the largest regular (not IMAX) movie screen in the nation. It's undergone a massive renovation and is part of the pricey **Arclight** movie-theater complex. (The newer screens offer plush leather seats and usher seating, and premovie introductions. It's the most expensive movie theater in town, and also the nicest.) Try to see a movie there. It's an experience.

At the northeast corner of Hudson Avenue and Sunset is the ⑮ **Hollywood Athletic Club,** which was recently nicely refurbished. It's the place where John Wayne and John Barrymore would drink, Valentino would hide from angry wives, and Roman Navarro would tryst. Tyrone Power, Sr., died there in the arms of Jr.

The ⑯ **Crossroads of the World,** the world's first planned outdoor shopping mall, is at 6671 Sunset (on the right). It opened in 1936, and yes, it looks like a ship.

At the northwest corner of Sunset and Highland Avenue is **⑰ Hollywood High,** where Lana Turner, Carol Burnett, and both David and Ricky Nelson went to school. Elvis Costello recorded a famous concert here in 1979. Across the street on Highland stood the **⑱ ice cream shop** where someone once asked then teenaged Turner if she wanted to be in movies. She said she had to ask her mother.

Keep driving until you reach the stoplight at La Brea Avenue. Just south of Sunset, on the left at 1418, is a series of Tudor-style buildings. This compound was **⑲ Charlie Chaplin's own studio** (1918). It's now the home of Jim Henson Productions, as you perhaps can tell from the giant Kermit (dressed like Chaplin's Little Tramp character) standing on the top of the building.

Welcome to Guitar Alley

Just past La Brea Avenue, Sunset starts to turn into Guitar Alley — note all the music stores (including Guitar Central and their "Rock Walk" of musicians' handprints). Crank up Guns N' Roses "Welcome to the Jungle" — or if you feel more goofball, some Van Halen.

The **⑳ Ralph's** on the right, at the corner of Poinsettia, is *the* place to see rock stars and wannabes buying red meat, sugar, and alcohol at 3 a.m. The **㉑** early 1970s home of local DJ and ancient scenester Rodney Bingenhiemer's **English Disco,** where sex and drugs and rock 'n' roll was a lifestyle, was at 7561 Sunset Boulevard.

If you were Hugh Grant, the corner of Sunset and Courtney Avenue would be a good place (or perhaps not so good) to pick up a prostitute.

James Dean's last meal, Oz's abode, and the Dahlia's roots

Turn right at Highland off of Sunset if you want to check out **Hollywood Boulevard.** Continue north on Highland to Yucca Street; then take a right. At 6735, on the left, stood the **Villa Capri restaurant** (it became Luther Vandross Studios), where James Dean had dinner the night before he headed down the highway and never came back.

Continue east on Yucca, turn right on Las Palmas, then left on Hollywood, and then left on Cherokee. L. Frank Baum used his earnings from his beloved *Wizard of Oz* books to build **Ozcot,** his dream house, here in 1909 (1749 on the left — it's now a vacant lot). And it was here that he "crossed the shifting sands" in 1919.

Elizabeth Short lived at 1842 Cherokee (on the right) four months before she achieved fame in 1946 as the **Black Dahlia.** Of course, she had to be murdered and dismembered to gain her fame.

At the southeast corner of Crescent Heights Boulevard and Sunset, you now have to resort to being discovered at the **㉒ Virgin Megastore** — the famous Schwab's Drugstore is no more. Oh sure, no one *really* got discovered there, but Harold Arlen stopped in to write down a melody that struck him while driving, and "Somewhere Over the Rainbow" was born. Across the street, on the southwest corner, was silent film star Alla Nazimova's fabulous **㉓ Garden of Allah apartments.** The apartments were home to dozens of celebrities and such Manhattan artistic refugees as Dorothy Parker, Robert Benchley, Harpo Marx, and a struggling-to-stay-sober F. Scott Fitzgerald. It was a wild and yet arty place, immortalized in songs written by musicians as diverse as Don Henley and L.A's own Ringling Sisters. (There is a cunning little scale model of the old building inside the bank in the strip mall.) Right in the middle of Crescent Heights (the triangular cement patch) is the former site of **㉔ Pandora's Box.** In the '60s, when the club was closed to make this part of Sunset wider, a hippie protest against the action turned into a riot. The Buffalo Springfield song "For What It's Worth" is about this event.

You can go north on Crescent Heights and into Laurel Canyon for a glimpse at the **golden landscape** that was home and nirvana to so many rock musicians and hippies of the late '60s/early '70s.

About half a block down, looming over Sunset on the right, is the **㉕ Chateau Marmont.** A magnificent, stately old hotel, which has been favored by celebrities (from Garbo to Keanu) for decades, it's now most famous for being the spot where John Belushi had one speedball too many in Bungalow #2. The grounds are striking, and the Art Deco rooms are straight out of *Barton Fink.* Next door is the Hollywood hangout Bar Marmont.

Across Sunset is the **㉖ Dudley Do-Right Emporium,** where cartoonist Jay Ward's widow still sells Bullwinkle and Natasha tchotchkes. (A Bullwinkle statue is a little farther west, in front of a psychic's shop.)

Get your kicks on Sunset Strip

Like Melrose Place, Sunset Strip became legendary thanks to a TV show, *77 Sunset Strip,* which showcased the Strip in all its early-'60s-cool (T-birds! Beatnik jive! Kooky sidekicks!) glory. Put on The Doors's "L.A. Woman" now — this is the beginning of the Sunset Strip, so the song fits. (Besides, the first billboard to advertise an album on the Strip was for the first Doors record.)

L.A.'s industry is entertainment, and every part of its cultural development has been reflected along these next couple miles. The street was once filled with glamorous nightclubs. Then, in the '60s and '70s, the sidewalks teamed with teenagers in bell bottoms and spandex, respectively. Now it's home to upscale rock 'n' roll clubs — and weekend evenings are likely to find the Strip jammed with cars — so you may want to avoid it during those times.

At the corner of Sweetzer Avenue and Sunset (on the right) is the site of the former ㉗ **Source Restaurant,** where Woody Allen and Diane Keaton had their last meal in *Annie Hall.*

The corner of King's Road brings you to the ㉘ **Hyatt Hotel** — also known as the "Riot House" because of the many rock bands that turned hotel staying into performance art (the TV-tossing capers of such guests as Led Zeppelin are rock-and-roll legend). This corner is also home to the modern-day club/restaurant the **House of Blues.** The corrugated tin on the outside of the House of Blues came from a building that stood at the famous crossroads where bluesman Robert Johnson supposedly made his mythical pact with the devil.

Just past La Cienega Boulevard, on the right, is ㉙ **Mel's Diner.** In the '60s, it was Ben Frank's 24-hour coffee shop and the hip place for rock-and-rollers to nosh (Arthur Lee and Bryan MacLean conceived of the band Love there, and when auditions were held to cast *The Monkees,* the notices asked for "Ben Frank's types"). It remains a good place for gawking.

On the other side of Sunset is the ㉚ **Tiffany Theater,** which is now surrounded by a mall. To its left was the site of **Dino's,** Dean Martin's night-club, used as the stand-in for *77 Sunset Strip.* To the right stood the **Trocadero** and the **Mocambo,** fabulous nightclubs of the Hollywood glamour years.

At the corner of Holloway, on the left, is a ㉛ **restaurant** (it keeps changing hands) that used to be called the Early World. It's where Diner's Club founder/Reagan kitchen-cabinet member Alfred Bloomingdale met Vicki Morgan and started a bizarre adulterous relationship that ended in pal-imony, allegations of S&M sex with powerful men, and murder.

The next light is Larabee Street. On the left-hand corner is ㉜ **The Viper Room.** It's gone through many incarnations as a rock club (the London Fog, Filthy McNasty's, the Central), but it's as Johnny Depp's prize that it became notorious. River Phoenix tossed away a beautiful life and career on the sidewalk outside the Larabee Street entrance.

The next light is Clark Street, and on the right is the ㉝ **Whisky a Go-Go,** where many a famous L.A. rock band, like The Doors, found fame. At the corner of Hammond, on the right, is ㉞ **The Roxy,** another landmark rock club. Next door is the **Rainbow Bar & Grill.** Under another name, it was where Vincente Minelli proposed to Judy Garland and where Marilyn Monroe met Joe DiMaggio on a blind date. Later, bands such as Led Zeppelin made the Rainbow their favorite place for debauched behavior. Big-haired rock dudes of varying degrees of fame still hang there. Two blocks down, also on the right, is the former ㉟ **Gazarri's** (now the Key Club), where such heavy-metal bands as Van Halen and Guns N' Roses got their starts. It's been a club since the '30s.

The big, the brassy: Beverly Hills

Beverly Hills begins at Doheny Drive and Sunset. Suddenly, the landscape becomes considerably more upscale (indeed, from here on out, no house you see will sell for much less than a million bucks). The transition is so abrupt that it almost causes a mental car crash. Beverly Hills is green and manicured within an inch of its life. And everything is big. Really big.

Drive one more block, and on the right you'll find a **36 huge vacant lot.** Sheik Al-Fassi bought this once-gorgeous mansion in 1978 and horrified his neighbors by painting the statues with anatomical correctness and adding other tacky elements. (For glimpses of the sheik's interior-decorating skills, rent Steve Martin's *The Jerk.* The mansion scenes later in the movie were shot at the sheik's home, which was untouched by set-decorator hands.) The house burned down in 1980 and was leveled a few years later. The lot is for sale, in case you have some loose change.

Drive two more blocks; on the right is the landmark **37 Beverly Hills Hotel.** The hotel just got a facelift, turning its famous hot-pink façade into more of a peach tone. Play the Eagles's "Hotel California" while admiring the song's inspiration; the top of the three towers is the shot on the cover of the album.

Across the street is the dainty and pretty **38 Will Rogers Memorial Park** (not to be confused with the Will Rogers State Historic Park). Apparently ascribing to Rogers's motto ("I never met a man I didn't like"), singer George Michael was arrested in the men's room here for committing a solo lewd act. (In an unrelated incident, Rod Stewart proposed to his last wife, Rachel Hunter, here.)

Check out **39 10000 Sunset,** on the left. Nope, that's not a crowd of people milling about on a stranger's lawn — they're statues. The almost certainly eccentric folks who live here have been adding figures to their lawn for some years.

Sunset now takes a long, hard curve (one of two referred to as the famous "Deadman's Curve" — put on the Jan and Dean song and try not to cut your trip short by wiping out), and on the left (corner of Carolwood Drive) is a **40 very large, very pink house.** It was Jayne Mansfield's — pink was her favorite color. Singer Englebert Humperdinck owns it now.

Old-money Bel Air

Bel Air, which starts at Beverly Glen Boulevard, feels somewhat older and warmer than Beverly Hills. Notice how the trees stand taller and wilder; everything is considerably less landscaped and ostentatious — symbolizing, perhaps, the difference between old money and nouveau riche. Notice the **41 gates to Bel Air** at Beverly Glen Boulevard (and later intersections) on the right. They have been closed only once — during the 1962 Bel Air fire (though closure was threatened again during the 1992 riots).

Looking up Lupe, Lana, Clara, and Bugsy

Go south on Rodeo Drive, which comes off Sunset at the same point as Benedict Canyon. One block down, **732** on the left, is the home where "Mexican Spitfire" Lupe Velez, despondent over a fading career and an unplanned pregnancy, took an overdose of pills. Scandal lore has it she dressed herself in all white, hoping to leave a gorgeous, picturesque corpse. Instead, nauseous from the pills, she stumbled to the toilet and drowned. It's too good not to be true.

Go back up to Lomitas Avenue; make a left. Two blocks down, on the corner of Bedford Drive, on the left **(730)** is the house where Lana Turner's daughter Cheryl stabbed her mother's mobster boyfriend to death.

Go left on Bedford, 2½ long blocks down, to **512** (on the left); that's where "It Girl" Clara Bow, according to legend, "entertained" the entire USC football team, including Marion "John Wayne" Morrison.

Go back up to Lomitas, turn left again, and then go right on Linden Drive. Number **810,** on the right, is the house where mobster Benjamin "Don't call me Bugsy" Siegel was murdered. (Shots went through the windows on the right.)

⓬ **UCLA** begins as Hilgard Avenue, and the left-hand side continues to be UCLA until Veteran Avenue. The next big curve you encounter is the other so-called ⓭ **Deadman's Curve.**

The freeway you cross is the legendary ⓮ San Diego **405 Freeway,** bane of all L.A. drivers. This is also the beginning of **Brentwood;** despite its Peyton Place reputation of the last couple years (courtesy of O.J. and company), it used to be a wealthy, low-profile, family-oriented community.

Side trip: Tragic Bel Air

This detour takes you off the Boulevard momentarily. Turn left at Kenter Canyon. It merges into Bundy Drive, which then doglegs first to the left across San Vincente Boulevard (admire the famous **coral trees** down the center), and then to the right. At one mile, on the right, on the corner of Bundy and Dorothy, is **Nicole Brown Simpson's condo.** Sneer at the rubberneckers taking pictures and then snap a few yourself. Why not? You're on vacation.

Return to Sunset. Turn left on Carmelita, the second street after Kenter Canyon (there is no light and it's a small street). The side streets on the left are all called Helena, starting with 18th Helena. Count down to 5th Helena. Marilyn Monroe died at **12305 5th Helena.**

Back on Sunset again. Go to Cliffwood, the seventh street after Kenter, and turn right. Take a left on Highwood (the next street) till it ends at Rockingham. Turn right. **O.J. Simpson's house** was two blocks up, at the corner of Ashford on the right (it was sold to pay legal fees, and the new owner razed it). For extra fun, time how long it takes you to drive from Nicole's to O.J.'s. Here's a hint; *not very.* The **house where Shirley Temple grew up** is also on Rockingham. And the **house where Joan Crawford became Mommy Dearest** is at 426 N. Bristol — keep going on Rockingham until it veers to the right and Bristol meets it, on the right. The other direction on Rockingham will take you back to Sunset. (Head downhill.)

Pacific Palisades: Sun, sand, and sea

Mandeville Canyon marks the beginning of **Pacific Palisades.** (Notice how the temperature has dropped as much as 20° since the beginning of the tour at Olvera Street. Thank the ocean breeze.) Put on the Beach Boys' "California Girls" and admire how open, sunny, and, well, California-y it all gets.

About a mile down the road on the right is the sprawling **45 Will Rogers State Historic Park,** which is built around the humorist's home. It's a fine place for a picnic and hiking, and polo matches are frequently held in the field.

A mile later, you hit the **46** business center of the Palisades.

About a mile and a half after that, you should have your **first ocean sighting.** Put on Randy Newman's "I Love L.A." (yes, it's more than a little sarcastic and ironic, but somehow it's also just right) as you round the home stretch. (Of course, you've now gone from the east side to the west side. The song sings about going in the opposite direction, so don't get confused.)

The final, and perhaps most unexpected, stop on the Sunset tour is the **47 Self-Realization Fellowship Lake Shrine and meditation garden** (watch carefully, or you may miss the entrance) at 17190 Sunset Blvd. It was dedicated in 1950 by the Fellowship's founder, guru Paramahansa Yogananda. (It's the bigger sibling of the one in East Hollywood.) This impossibly calm and lovely park-like shrine, complete with lake, is dedicated to meditation and harmony among all religions. It's a surprising find along busy Sunset and well worth taking a walk through. But the best part of the garden may be the marble sarcophagus containing the only entombed ashes of Mohandas Gandhi. The rest of Gandhi's ashes were scattered in India — but a portion was sent here as a gift, a most unlikely addition to Los Angeles.

And now, just keep driving. See the water? That's the **48 Pacific Ocean.** Don't forget to hit the brakes.

Fittingly, this is the literal end of Western Civilization — and don't think that we don't know it or aren't proud. From here out, it's the mysteries of the Far East.

Museums galore

L.A. may not have museums on the level, recognition-wise, of the Louvre, but that doesn't mean that the city lacks for museums of which it can be justly proud. Although we include the highlights earlier in this chapter (for example, the **Getty,** p. 165, and the **Los Angeles County Museum of Art/LACMA,** p. 166), the following all have their merits, be it the strength of their collections, the breadth of their vision, or simply their entertainment value.

California ScienCenter
Downtown

This highly enjoyable institution, a long-term staple of L.A. childhood formerly known as the Museum of Science and Industry, got a complete makeover, which helped bring it as up-to-date as a museum that focuses on the wonders of science and industry ought to be. Learn about the human body thanks to Tess, the 50-foot visible woman, build miniature structures and see how earthquake-proof they are, or ride a bike on a cable three stories above ground (it's safe, but there's an extra charge). There is plenty of hands-on, interactive fun — again, the sort of fun that probably thrills adults for its cleverness more than it does kids, who are often more interested in the bright lights and loud noises than they are in learning. But that's okay, you're both on vacation, and a little education is bound to sink in anyway, even by accident. It's hugely popular with school field trips, so take that into consideration when you plan your own visit. This is all state of the art (everything is done superbly), and even beyond; until January 2005 they have the first U.S. showing of the controversial and imperative Body Worlds exhibit (featuring real human beings preserved through a technique called "plastination"). If you are lucky enough to be in town while it's still up, the exhibit is worth a trip on its own.

See map p. 199. 700 State Dr. (Exposition Park). ☎ *323-724-3623.* www.cascience ctr.org. *Admission: free. Open: Daily 10 a.m.–5 p.m. Parking: $6 per vehicle (lot at 39th and Figueroa).*

The Erotic Museum
Hollywood

There are those of you who we won't have to convince to see this museum; it's the rest of you who we are going to work on. You might think you should avoid a museum about . . . furtive glance . . . *sex* . . . because it's probably crass and crude and a tourist trap or you are easily embarrassed or you don't want your parents to know you've ever heard of such a thing. We can't help the latter problem, but as for the other two, we can assure you; this is a dignified place. (Though we can't vouch for the attitudes of all attendees, who may well giggle their way through.) The owners took a venerable old Hollywood building (former site of the beloved Pickwick Books), restored the gorgeous 1911 exterior as best they could and beautifully refurbished the interior (down to the gleaming vintage hardwood floors), creating a space that could stand beside any New York art gallery with pride. The exhibits are done with equal professionalism; the curator has taste and wit. Permanent exhibits include a time line of great moments in the history of modern sex; a display on Picasso's latter-day erotic works; and most intriguing, a "blue movie" that may or may not star Marilyn Monroe. (We think not, but judge for yourself.) Graphics for exhibits both temporary (at press time, plans were in the works for a look at sex in Los Angeles) and permanent strike just the right balance of tone between mischief and serious sociological contemplation. In other words, and here we address the second of your potential concerns, you may begin downstairs snickering and blushing over John Holmes' first stag reel (make no mistakes; the nature of this museum is adult and graphic), but you may well end upstairs seriously musing over the role the world's most favorite activity has played in shaping that very world.

See map p. 161. 6741 Hollywood Blvd. ☎ *323-GO-EROTIC (323-463-7684).* www. theroticmuseum.com. *Admission: $12.95 adults over 18 (no one under 18 will be admitted), $9.95 seniors over 55 and students with valid ID. Sun–Thurs noon–9 p.m., Fri–Sat noon–midnight.*

Huntington Library and Gardens
Pasadena

This is a true treasure of L.A., though one a bit off the beaten path, located as it is in one of the oldest and richest sections of old-money Pasadena. Huntington was a turn-of-the-20th-Century railroad baron, and this was his home — yes, that mansion over there, with the art, was his house, and that lawn lined with classical statues (surely we've seen many an early rock video shot there?) was his side lawn. This place has something for nearly everyone. Art lovers will thrill to the famous portraits fondly known as *Pinkie* and *Blue Boy,* which had no connection to each other until they were displayed here in the '20s — *Pinkie* was painted by Thomas Lawrence 25 years after Thomas Gainsborough painted *Blue Boy.* By the way, Sarah Barrett Moulton, the real-life Pinkie, who died a few months after being the subject of the painting, was the paternal great-aunt of poet Elizabeth Barrett Browning. The library collection here is one of the finest in the world and includes a Gutenberg Bible and a Chaucer manuscript.

Horticulturists will thrill to the expansive gardens (200 acres' worth), from rolling English lawns to a Japanese fantasy tea garden to an otherworldly 12-acre section of succulents (which recently got a lot of attention when a rare "corpse flower" bloomed — one of the few times a corpse flower has bloomed in the United States — putting forth the putrid smell that gives it its name).

See map p. 191. 1151 Oxford Rd., San Marino. ☎ *626-405-2100.* www.huntington. org. *Admission: $12.50 adults, $10 seniors, $8.50 students with ID and children 12–18, $5 children 5–11, children under 5 free. Open: Sept–May Tues–Fri noon–4:30 p.m., Sat–Sun 10:30 a.m.–4:30 p.m., closed Mon; June–Aug Tues–Sat 10:30 a.m.–4:30 p.m.*

Los Angeles Museums

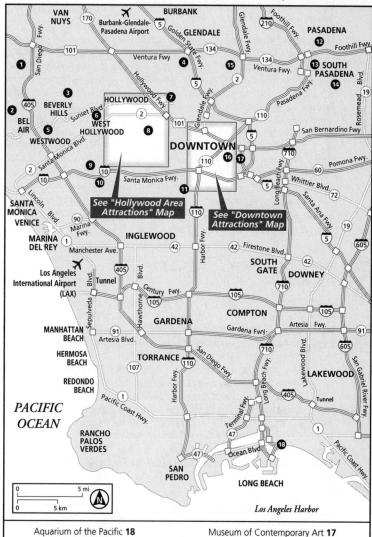

Aquarium of the Pacific **18**
Exposition Park Museums **11**
  California ScienCenter
  Natural History Musuem
Gamble House **12**
Getty Center & Art Museum **2**
Griffith Park Observatory **7**
Huntington Library & Gardens **14**
Japanese American National Museum **21**
La Brea Tar Pits /
  George C. Page Museum **8**
Los Angeles County Museum of Art **8**
Los Angeles Zoo **4**

Museum of Contemporary Art **17**
Museum of Jurassic Technology **10**
Museum of Television & Radio **3**
Museum of the American West **4**
Museum of Tolerance **9**
Norton Simon Museum of Art **13**
Petersen Automotive Museum **8**
Ronald Reagan Presidential Library
  & Museum **16**
Schindler House **6**
Skirball Cultural Center **1**
Southwest Museum **15**
UCLA Hammer Museum **5**

Japanese American National Museum
Downtown

This small and often neglected gem is easy to visit if you're already Downtown checking out the Geffen Contemporary for it's virtually right next door. In addition to art exhibits and a moving reconstruction of an actual building from a relocation camp (that term is never used; here, they are rightly called concentration camps), this museum explores the Japanese-immigrant experience in America, which, of course, began primarily on the West Coast. Displays show artifacts such as a set of typical belongings brought over by an immigrant and the schoolbooks children once used here in America. They all lead up to a heartbreaking display about the camps and the Japanese-American war experience. (Our favorite exhibit is the display that features 100 small birds, all carved and painted by hand as a way of passing the time in the camps.)

See map p. 191. 369 E. First St. (at Central Ave.). ☎ *213-625-0414.* www.janm.org. *Admission: $6 adults, $5 seniors, $3 students and children 6–17, children under 5 free. Open: Tues–Wed and Fri–Sun 10 a.m.–5 p.m., Thurs 10 a.m.–8 p.m. Closed Mon.*

Museum of Jurassic Technology
Culver City

You may spot this little storefront along a nondescript street in an unremarkable part of town and wonder why we sent you here. You will probably be greeted at the door by a slightly distracted, amiable, elfish man, who happens to be the proprietor. You will begin to wander through the deliberately arcane exhibits, all of which seem dusty, even if they actually aren't. You will learn about bats, and stink ants, and how one man can carve images into a single strand of hair. You may or may not realize that some of what you see is entirely made up. This wholly remarkable museum — there is nothing else like it in the world — is one giant art project, all of it springing from the incredibly fertile mind of its owner, David Wilson, who is already the subject of a book (*Mr. Wilson's Cabinet of Wonder,* by Lawrence Weschler, published by Vintage Books) and the recipient of a 2002 MacArthur Genius Grant. And this is his homage to wonder, to creativity, and to the imagination.

See map p. 191. 9341 Venice Blvd. (four blocks west of Robertston Blvd.). ☎ *310-836-6131.* www.mjt.org. *Admission: adults $5; children 12–21, students with ID, seniors, and unemployed $3; disabled or active military in uniform $1.50; children under 12 free. Open: Thurs 2 p.m.–8 p.m., Fri–Sun noon–6 p.m.*

Museum of the American West
Los Angeles

Gene Autry was the "Singing Cowboy"; he loved the Wild West and the money it made him. This museum was his gift to Southern California. It's mostly a romanticized view of the Old West, with an emphasis on the romance of the cowboy. The uninformed could easily come away from a visit to the museum believing that nothing really bad happened during the country's relentless pursuit of Manifest Destiny, and that what did take place in the Old West was all for the good of America. (You know, as in, it's kind of too bad we killed the buffalo, but wasn't it fun to shoot them from trains?) Still, even though it's more or less Hollywood pop culture, the museum is most entertaining, and popular with the kids, who love the part where they get to dress up in period clothes and enter dioramas depicting L.A. and Chinatown in the 1930s. A terrific gift shop features everything from cornbread mix to videotapes.

See map p. 191. 7400 Western Heritage Way (at Curson Ave.). ☎ *323-667-2000.* www.museumoftheAmericanwest.org. *Admission: $7.50 adults, $5 students and seniors over 60, $3 children 2–12. Open: Tues–Sun 10 a.m.–5 p.m., Thurs 10 a.m.–8 p.m. Free parking.*

Museum of Television & Radio
Beverly Hills

Ah, the timeless family vacation dilemma: Junior is whining about having to visit some dusty old art exhibit because he feels that it would really be a lot more fun to watch TV. Voilà — the solution: a contemporary museum (a branch of the institution located in New York City) where the idiot box is enshrined and treated like the cultural touchstone it really is. From Muhammad Ali to the Muppets, Ed Sullivan to Ed Norton, Walter Cronkite to Bill Cosby, it's all viewable here (in private cubicles). Request a favorite program, re-experience a special TV moment, or rediscover the glories of radio. Finally, you won't have to justify your Three Stooges habit; you're watching in a museum! It's educational! *Note:* The Museum's William S. Paley Television Festival is an annual event of great local popularity, and nearly every event sells out, and fast, so start checking the museum Web site around January (events generally start toward the end of February and run into March) for info on tickets.

See map p. 191. 465 N. Beverly Dr. (at Santa Monica Blvd.). ☎ *310-786-1000.* www.mtr.org. *Admission: $10 adults, $8 students and seniors, $5 children under 14. Open: Wed–Sun noon–5 p.m.*

Museum of Tolerance
West Los Angeles

One can make the argument that tolerance, or rather, a lack thereof, is at the base of many of the most pressing issues of our day. This isn't to say that everyone has to like each other; they just have to *tolerate* each other by learning to understand each other and allowing for differences in appearance, religious worship, and cultural mores. We ignore this to our peril. The Holocaust is the most obvious example of the tragedies and horrors that occur when this sort of understanding fails to manifest. This excellent facility naturally focuses much attention on that event. Located in the Simon Weisenthal Center, the museum covers many more related areas — in other words, this isn't just a Holocaust museum. It's designed to topple many of your preconceived notions at the very beginning of your visit, when you have a choice of starting your tour through one of two doors — "prejudiced" and "not prejudiced." Guess which one simply doesn't open at all? Note that the museum is laid out so that you follow a mandatory route, which can take upwards of three hours to complete. Note, too, that kids who have been convicted of hate crimes are often sentenced to do community service here. Pay careful attention to hours of operation and consider calling in advance regardless as they can change. The Museum often stops taking visitors two hours before official closing (especially on Fridays, when sunset will determine the hour of closing as well, to allow the staff time to get home to prepare for Sabbath) and often shuts down some of the interactive exhibits around then as well. Earlier attendance, though more crowded, is consequently advised. The visually impaired should note that the Holocaust exhibit is dark, which can make it difficult to view, so you have to rely on the mandatory (and sometimes not very audible, so hearing impaired should be similarly cautioned) tour guides.

See map p. 191. 9786 W. Pico Blvd. (at Roxbury Dr.). ☎ *310-553-8403.* www.wiesenthal.com/mot. *Admission: $10 adults, $8 seniors, $7 children 2–18 and students with ID. Open: Mon–Thurs 11:30 a.m.–6 p.m., Fri 11:30 a.m.–3 p.m. Nov–Mar and 11:30 a.m.–5 p.m. Apr–Oct, Sun 11 a.m.–7:30 p.m. Closed Sat.*

Natural History Museum of Los Angeles County
Los Angeles

We are most fond of this place, although we have to admit that a great deal of that fondness is attributable to nostalgia. Many a local child, ourselves included, has passed through these Beaux Arts halls (so beautiful they're often booked for fancy parties), admiring the dioramas of taxidermied animals (likely the same dusty critters throughout the generations), exclaiming over the gem collection (one of the finest in the country), and cooing over the dinosaur skeletons (especially the *Tyrannosaurus rex* and *Triceratops,* locked in mortal combat). That said, we have to admit that this is not the most up-to-the-minute museum (though it does often host important traveling exhibits, such as *T. rex* Sue, the largest and most complete *Tyrannosaurus rex* skeleton ever found). The hands-on explorer room, featuring all kinds of touchy-feely stuff, is such low-tech fun that kids won't even know that they are getting an education.

See map p. 199. 900 Exposition Blvd. (Exposition Park). ☎ *213-763-DINO.* www.nhm.org. *Admission: $9 adults, $6.50 seniors and students, $2 children 5–12, children under 5 free. Open: Mon–Fri 9:30 a.m.–5 p.m., Sat–Sun 10 a.m.–5 p.m.*

Norton Simon Museum of Art
Pasadena

This is one of the world's foremost art collections, with an emphasis on old masters and Impressionists. We put it here instead of in the "must sees" partly because it's not in L.A. proper, and so it's a bit of a distance from where you may expect to find the average tourist. For art lovers, it certainly can't be missed. Here's just a sample of what you can expect — Picasso *(Girl with Guitar),* Rembrandt, Degas, Monet, Manet, Cézanne, Kandinsky, and Rodin. The museum houses a copy of Rodin's iconic *The*

Thinker, plus one of the world's great collections of South Asian sculpture. But despite an architectural facelift by the ever-amusing Frank Gehry, this museum always struck us as the kind you go to because it's good for you, and because it's important. Our view of the musuem is doubtless doing it a disservice, and with the patient help of art students and scholars, we could come to see the error of our ways.

See map p. 191. 411 W. Colorado Blvd., Pasadena. ☎ 626-449-6840. www.norton simon.org. *Admission: $6 adults, $3 seniors, children under 18 and students with valid ID free. Open: Wed–Thurs and Sat–Mon noon–6 p.m., Fri noon–9 p.m.*

Petersen Automotive Museum
Los Angeles

The Miracle Mile, as the strip along Wilshire Boulevard between Fairfax and La Brea is known, was built in the 1920s as the world's first linear shopping district (that's architectural lingo for "strip mall") designed specifically for drive-by viewing. So it's fitting that the Petersen Automotive Museum — with a changing display of over 150 cars, motorcycles, and trucks — sits at the corner of Wilshire and Fairfax in what was once Orhbach's department store. Even people who aren't obsessed with cars (like us) enjoy the super-friendly layout and displays. The first-floor dioramas allow visitors to move through and around the displays, which include a re-creation of a highway crash, a pretty effective reminder to stay at the speed limit. On the second floor, theme exhibits — featuring celebrity-owned cars, movie cars, custom cars, hot rods, and motorcycles — demonstrate automobiles as objects of art and desire. Occasionally we find ourselves lusting for a flame-painted woody or the Batmobile, both of which have been on display. The third-floor Discovery Center provides interactive fun geared toward kids, including the opportunity to dress up in vintage clothes and pose on a Model T.

See map p. 191. 6060 Wilshire Blvd. (at Fairfax Ave.). ☎ 323-930-2277. www. petersen.org. *Admission: $10 adults, $5 seniors and students with valid ID, $3 children 5–12, children under 5 free. Open: Tues–Sun 10 a.m.–6p.m. Closed Mon and some major holidays.*

Ronald Reagan Presidential Library & Museum
Simi Valley

It's possible that you may have missed that Ronald Reagan died on June 5, 2004. It's not like it was in the news, or anything. The 40th president of the United States was laid to rest at his Presidential Library in Simi Valley, a 40-minute or so (depending on traffic) drive from the center of Los Angeles, instantly transforming the overlooked establishment into a highly popular tourist site. It is a lovely setting, perched above the valleys and hills of Southern California, with a view all the way out to the sea if the air is clear. The library itself is, like most presidential libraries, full of interesting, if naturally deeply biased, exhibits. In addition, there is a full section of the Berlin Wall (colorful and surprisingly moving) on display, along with a rotating selection of gifts (ranging from the valuable to the goofy) given to the president from dignitaries and just plain old folk.

See map p. 191. 40 Presidential Drive, Simi Valley. ☎ *800-410-8354.* www.reagan
library.com. *Admission: adults $7, seniors $5, children 11–17 $2, under 10 free.
Open: daily (except Thanksgiving, Christmas Day, and New Year's Day) 10 a.m.–5 p.m.
Take the 405 north or 210 west or I-5 north to the 118 (Ronald Reagan Freeway) West.
Exit Madera Rd. South. Turn right onto View Line Dr. Turn right onto N. Madera Rd.
Turn right onto Presidential Dr. Pass through one roundabout.*

Skirball Cultural Center
Los Angeles

This institution is devoted to all aspects of Jewish life and history, both in
Europe and in America, from historical beginnings to immigration to political involvement to artistic achievements. Obviously, the Holocaust figures prominently, but it does not overshadow the rest of the exhibits; there
is so much more to a people than even the greatest catastrophe. It's a
lovely facility (with both permanent and traveling exhibits; examples of
the latter include an exhibit on a Colonial-era Jewish silversmith), noted
for its frequent cultural offerings. It features everything from the obvious
(klezmer concerts, lectures on religious archaeology) to the not so (a conversation between sex columnist Dan Savage and actor Andy Dick). It's
easy to miss because it's located in the shadow of the great big Getty.

See map p. 191. 2701 N. Sepulveda Blvd. (at Mulholland Dr.). ☎ *310-440-4500.* www.
skirball.org. *Admission: $8 adults, $6 seniors and students, children under 12
free. Open: Tues–Sat noon–5 p.m., Sun 11 a.m.–5 p.m. Closed Mon.*

Southwest Museum
Highland Park

Opened in 1907, this was the first museum in Southern California. Exhibits
focus on the grim flip side of the Old West myth presented by the Museum
of the American West (see earlier). This very serious and very well done
museum outlines different aspects of American Indian life by covering the
Western tribes. There are three ways to enter this Mission-style building;
you can journey through a tunnel lined with very good dioramas of
American Indians, you can walk up the "Hopi Trail," which is very steep
and landscaped, or you can bypass it all and drive up to the tippy-top.
Local educators prefer the Southwest Museum (politically correct, sensi-
tive, and enlightened, not to mention educational) to the Museum of the
American West (rip-roaring, cowboy fun). We don't disagree with their
preference. Of course, all of this got quite a shake-up when the Autry
people essentially bought the always finanically struggling Southwest
Museum. Both are now under one blanket foundation umbrella. It's too
early in the relationship to judge how this will affect either — more flash
for this one? More cred for the other? Stay tuned. In the meantime, if you
have to pick only one, do you want to learn or do you want to have a really
good, goofy time?

See map p. 191. 234 Museum Dr. (in the Highland Park District). ☎ *323-221-2164.*
www.southwestmuseum.org. *Admission: $7.50 adults, $5 students and seniors, $3
youths 2–12. Open: Tues–Sun 10 a.m.–5 p.m.*

Jonesing for the jacarandas

Jacarandas are gnarled trees that once a year seem to replace their leaves entirely with bright purple flowers. It's a spectacular sight, even as they shed, because the ground beneath looks covered in lavender snow. It's one of the best sights of Los Angeles, the sort of thing that, for about a month, reconciles natives to living, and even driving, here. You can spot the trees all over town, but note that Alta and Oakhurst drives in Beverly Hills, between Sunset and Santa Monica, are both lined with mature (and thus, very tall and arching) jacarandas. If you find yourself in town during jacaranda time (varies according to the weather and temprature of that particular spring: usually it's a few weeks on either side of Mother's Day), be sure to drive down one or both. But be careful; with a such a canopy above, it's hard to keep your eyes on the road.

UCLA Hammer Museum
Westwood

So much has been written about billionaire (except he really wasn't a billionaire) art lover (except he really wasn't an art lover) Armand Hammer (much of it by his own self), that it's hard to separate the publicity, scandals, and whatnot from the true value of this institution. There is too much history to go into here (darn the luck because it's a hoot). Suffice it to say that UCLA had to take over the art museum. Although the true significance or value of its permanent collection is debatable (it focuses primarily on collections with such recognizable names as van Gogh, Monet, and Cassett), the frequent special exhibitions are truly noteworthy. Check and see what will be exhibited during your stay.

See map p. 191. 10899 Wilshire Blvd. (at Westwood Blvd.). ☎ *310-443-7000.* www. hammer.ucla.edu. *Admission: $5 adults, $3 seniors and UCLA alumni with ID, children 17 and under free (accompanied by an adult). Thurs is free for all visitors. Open: Tues–Wed and Fri–Sat 11 a.m.–7 p.m., Thurs 11 a.m.–9 p.m., Sun 11 a.m.–5 p.m.*

Especially for kids
The following sights are for kids. This, by no means, implies that you, the more grownup reader, will not have a blast at any of these attractions.

Aquarium of the Pacific
Long Beach

Our only complaint about this state-of-the-art facility is that it is in Long Beach instead of Los Angeles, and so a (doable, certainly) drive is required whenever we need a fish fix. It is so worth it. The aquarium features 12,000 (give or take) critters from the planet's largest body of water, which is mere yards away. Because the Pacific covers icy northern waters and tropical reefs, the range of finny bodies is remarkable. Some of the aquarium's recent highlights included, in terms of science, the first successful breeding in captivity of weedy sea dragons. In terms of sheer delight, you can't beat the Lorikeet exhibit, a walk-in aviary full of colorful birdies who enjoy sitting on visitors, especially if the visitor has thoughtfully prepurchased a cup of nectar for a feathered friend to drink. (Purchase the nectar or just wear something sparkling — and sturdy because it will get pecked at — and you may well end up covered in birds; don't forget the camera to prove it later.) Kids, needless to say, love the place — especially the younger, unjaded ones. Be sure to pick up a "fish spotting" map on the way in (see if you can find an Oriental Sweetlips or, our personal favorite, a Sarcastic Fringehead). Ask about the "sleep with the fishes" kids' slumber parties and the behind-the-scenes tours (they cost extra). *Note:* Consider taking a combo Metro Rail Blue Line and bus, which is a not unreasonable alternative to driving, to the aquarium.

See map p. 191. 100 Aquarium Way, Long Beach. ☎ *562-590-3100.* www.aquarium ofpacific.org. *Admission: $18.95 adults, $14.95 seniors, $10.95 children 3–11. Open: daily 9 a.m.–6 p.m.*

Los Angeles Zoo
Los Angeles

The L.A. Zoo has always suffered from an inferiority complex, thanks to the huge recognition factor enjoyed by its compatriot down in San Diego. The inferiority complex is a bit unjustified, for sure. Certainly, the L.A. Zoo has had its share of ups and downs over the years, experiencing a high in the late 1980s after it not only hosted a panda exhibition during the 1984 Olympics but opened a permanent koala exhibit (well designed in that it exhibits these nocturnal animals in twilight during zoo hours, so visitors have better odds catching the rather sluggish, if entirely adorable, creatures doing something other than snoozing) and a fabulous children's zoo area, including a new play park opening approximately fall 2004), full of interactive playful exhibits. At present, the L.A. Zoo is not in the top echelon of zoos (following various management and fiscal scandals in the '90s), but it does continue to boast attractive natural habitats, including a new chimp exhibit. Kids don't care about that sort of thing and so they love it. Adults need to remember that it gets very hot here during the summer — the phrase "dumb animal" is a canard, as most animals will rest during the heat of the day. So come early or late, or figure on spotting only snoozing beasts. *Note:* The single busiest day at the zoo is Thanksgiving Day; apparently, it's a way to get kids and noncooking adults out from underfoot while the feast is being prepared.

See map p. 191. 5333 Zoo Dr. (Griffith Park). ☎ *323-644-4200.* www.lazoo.org. *Admission: $9 adults, $6 seniors, $4 children 2–12, children under 2 free. Open: daily 10 a.m.–5 p.m.*

The great outdoors
It doesn't matter whether you're an exercise fiend who is determined to work up a sweat or a confirmed couch potato who just wants to partake

Downtown Attractions

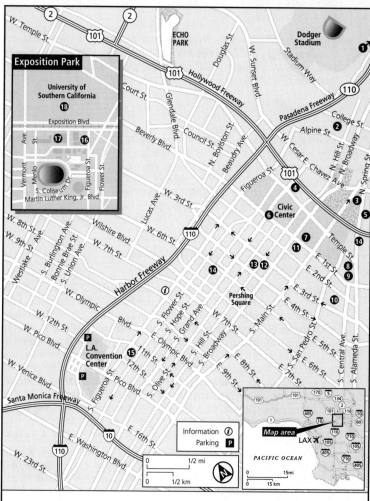

Bradbury Building **12**

California ScienCenter **16**

Central Library **14**

Chinatown **2**

City Hall **10**

El Pueblo de Los Angeles
Historic District **3**

Geffen Contemporary at MOCA **7**

Grand Central Market **13**

Japanese American National
Museum **8**

The Los Angeles Times Building **11**

Little Tokyo **9**

Natural History Museum
of Los Angeles County **17**

Our Lady of Angels Cathedral **4**

The Southwest Museum **1**

Staples Center **15**

Union Station **5**

University of
Southern California (USC) **18**

Walt Disney Concert Hall **6**

of the city's fresh-air attractions; everyone can enjoy L.A.'s many out-door pleasures.

Regardless of what you do and where you do it, remember that even in the cloudy days of "June gloom" or the overcast moments during the rest of the year, the sun shines strongly in SoCal, so apply a sunblock with a minimum SPF of 15 accordingly.

No sweat

Certainly, the very image of L.A. is one of healthy people jogging, in-line skating, hiking, and generally sweating up a storm. Good for them. But if you just want to stroll around and enjoy the warm California sun without intentionally exercising, you have a number of options; you can stroll around the neighborhoods best suited for walking, stopping to shop if you want (particularly at the Third Street Promenade and Venice Main Street, both listed in Chapter 12, or the Venice Boardwalk, discussed on p. 170), or you can make a trip to one of the following outdoor attractions.

UCLA Botanical and Sculpture Gardens
Westwood

A trip to this outdoor museum operated by the UCLA Hammer Museum is also a good opportunity to explore the lovely UCLA campus. The **Franklin D. Murphy Sculpture Garden** is 5 acres of some of the finest outdoor sculptures in the country, including works by Matisse, Moore, Rodin, and Calder. It's only enhanced by the many good-looking college students studying beneath and against the statues — what a pleasure to see art out in the open, incorporated into daily life! If you prefer life in your inanimate objects, you can walk over to the **Botanical Gardens,** 7 acres' worth of highly significant plant life. And then you can skip around the campus, which is so attractive that it ends up standing in for many a typical gorgeous college in various TV and movie sets.

405 Hilgard Ave; UCLA is bordered by Sunset and Le Conte to the south and north, and Hilgard and Veteran to the east and west. The sculpture garden is in the northeast part of the campus, whereas the botanical garden is in the southeast area of campus. ☎ *310-825-1260. Open: Sculpture Garden is always open, Botanical Gardens is open Mon–Fri 8 a.m.–5 p.m. (8 a.m.–4 p.m. during winter months), Sat–Sun 8 a.m.–4 p.m. Closed university holidays. Free admission.* **Note:** *The Gardens may close without notice because of bad weather or hazardous conditions.*

The Farmer's Market
Hollywood

A collection of buildings dating back to the Great Depression (and surrounding an adobe house, one of the older buildings in L.A.), the Farmer's Market is a local favorite, but tourists may wonder what all the hype is about. Many stalls and shops sell tacky souvenirs, as well as all kinds of food (doughnuts to deli, sushi to sweets), but the produce tends to get overwhelmed in the bustle. Still, it's a regular hangout for many a

Hollywood writer wannabe and already-is, retired folks, and lots and lots of tourists. The locals' fondness for the place is probably due to sentiment more than anything else, but it's well-placed sentiment. These same locals worried when the fancy-pants Grove complex opened up next door, providing a sanitized, manufactured urban experience instead of the authentic one that was here all along. The Grove (connected to the Farmer's Market via a cute little trolley) has better shopping (if of the generic mall shop sort), we admit, and it certainly sparkles more, but the Farmer's Market *is* L.A. Plus, it has better food.

See map p. 161. 6333 W. Third St. (corner of Fairfax Ave.). ☎ *323-933-9211.* www.farmersmarketla.com. *Open: Mon–Fri 9 a.m.–9 p.m., Sat 9 a.m.–8 p.m., Sun 10 a.m.–7 p.m.*

Santa Monica Pier
Santa Monica

Part tourist cheesiness, part genuine pleasure, this longtime L.A. institution (it's been around since 1909!) is worth at least one stroll. It's free, so you can walk down and look at the motley collection of souvenir shops, people gamely fishing, the Pacific Park's carnival rides (including one scary roller coaster), various undistinguished restaurants, and best of all, a genuine all-wood, 1930s-era merry-go-round, which may seem familiar to you — it played a large role in the movie *The Sting*. It costs something like a quarter for a turn, and we've seen even nihilistic punk rockers burst into grins riding it, so what are you waiting for?

See map p. 173. Ocean Ave. (at the end of Colorado Blvd.). ☎ *310-458-8900.* www.santamonicapier.org.

Hiking

If you like to hike, the Los Angeles area offers some lovely trails. You might want to bring a nice big bottle of water and wear sunblock when hiking, even in the city. **Will Rogers State Historic Park** (1501 Will Rogers State Park Rd.; ☎ 310-454-8212), off of Sunset Boulevard in Pacific Palisades, is the former home of the man who never met a man he didn't like. It's a sweet little spot, with convenient trails through the Santa Monica Mountains. Covering 4,000 acres in Los Feliz, **Griffith Park** (4730 Crystal Springs Dr.; ☎ 323-913-4688) is America's largest park in a municipal area. The park was a donation from the double-barreled-named Colonel Griffith J. Griffith, who was trying to get on the city's good side after a messy courtroom drama involving the attempted murder of his wife, not to mention to seek tax relief and remove a curse put upon him by his first wife (bad luck with women), a Spanish heiress, after he stole much of the property from her. Located in the hills above Los Feliz, it is home to the Griffith Observatory, the Greek Theater, the L.A. Zoo, the Gene Autry Museum, a fine golf course, a merry-go-round, and Travel Town. Thus, it's popular with a strong cross-section of L.A., from families at play to picnicking bohos to the healthy and health-seeking, who march up and down trails that range from easy to challenging. The Bronson

Canyon Trail goes past the Bat Cave entrance from the old *Batman* TV series. **Runyon Canyon** (Franklin Avenue at Fuller Boulevard) is part of the old Errol Flynn estate, and the trails are easy, with astounding views. But they can be crowded. If you don't like dogs (many of which are off leash), you may want to avoid this place, especially daily after 4 p.m. and on weekends. You may be missing out, however: Anytime you go, you run the chance of passing actors and other famous faces catching fresh air alone, with their dogs, or with their trainers.

 When hiking in the spring and summer, please be aware that there are snakes, specifically rattlesnakes, in the brush, and that they can be very cranky if disturbed. Wear light-colored clothes and appropriate shoes, stay on the trails, and don't try to pick up anything that looks like a stick.

Golf

Los Angeles boasts acres and acres of golf courses; many of the city's courses are municipal, open-to-the-public courses. **Rancho Park** (10460 W. Pico Blvd.; ☎ 310-838-7373) is gorgeous and challenging — Arnold Palmer once took 12 strokes to finish the 18th hole. The **Armand Hammer Pitch-n-Putt** (601 Club View Dr.; ☎ 310-276-1604) is located in Tony Holmby Hills. **Griffith Park**'s courses include the 9-hole Roosevelt (2650 N. Vermont Ave.; ☎ 323-665-2011) and the 18-hole Wilson and Harding courses (4730 Crystal Springs Dr.; ☎ 323-663-2555). The courses were built in the 1920s. All are tournament quality, and all provide golf-club rental. For a complete listing of municipal courses, go to www.la parks.org/dos/golf/golf.htm.

Running

Of course you'll find runners and in-line skaters all over the city, but one of the most popular spots for jogging is along the coral trees that run down the meridian of San Vicente in Brentwood (not to be confused with the San Vicente in West Hollywood). If you prefer a jog on the sand, see the beach listings on p. 173.

Tennis

In Los Angeles, you can find convenient courts in Westwood (1350 Sepulveda Blvd.; ☎ 310-575-8299), West Los Angeles (2551 Motor Ave.; ☎ 310-836-8879), and Los Feliz (2715 Vermont Canyon; ☎ 323-664-3521). For more information, go to www.laparks.com/dos/tennis/tennis. htm#pay. West Hollywood and Beverly Hills also offer public courts at La Cienega Park (325 S. La Cienega Blvd., Beverly Hills; ☎ 310-550-4765) and Roxbury Park (471 S. Roxbury Dr., Beverly Hills; ☎ 310-550-4979).

West Hollywood's courts at Plummer Park (1200 N. Vista St.; ☎ 323-876-8180; www.weho.org/hsd/recreation/index.cfm) are popular and packed.

Yoga

"Bend me, twist me, anyway you want me" is the mantra of Los Angeles fitness fans who have embraced yoga wholeheartedly with every chakra of their being. And you know you want to join them. There are several types of popular yoga offered at studios and gyms: Power or ashtanga yoga combines yoga moves and aerobics into a grueling working out, Iyengar teaches stretching using belts and wood blocks in an overheated room to increase one's flexibility, and the vigorous kundalini and milder hatha are designed to raise energy and awareness through poses, stretching, and breath; some classes are "flow," which technically means one pose flows into the next, but in practical terms means there's not a whole lot of verbal instruction going on — everyone seems to know the pose and strikes it at the instructor's shout-out. Call the studios and ask for schedule and types as classes vary daily. In Santa Monica, **Strike A Balance** (1131 Montana Ave.; ☎ 310-260-1177) and **Yoga Works** (1426 Montana Ave. and 2215 Main St.; ☎ 310-393-5150) offer all levels of classes, as does the Beverly Hills branch of **Yoga Works** (324 S. Beverly Dr.; ☎ 310-553-4223). In the Hollywood/West Hollywood area, **Justinsight Yoga** (6541 Hollywood Blvd.; ☎ 323-871-9642) offers single classes, as do **Divine Motion** (8368 Beverly Blvd.; ☎ 323-651-2804) and **City Yoga** (1067 Fairfax Ave.; ☎ 323-654-2125) and the kundalini-based (and celeb fave) **Golden Bridge** (5901 W. Third St., at Fuller Ave.; ☎ 323-936-4127), which also has a gift shop and snack bar attached.

Spectator sports

If you're a sports fan, you can have a very good time, indeed, in L.A. The five major professional sports teams, the **Lakers** (NBA basketball), the **Clippers** (NBA basketball), the **Sparks** (WNBA basketball), the **Dodgers** (MLB baseball), and the **Kings** (NHL hockey), are big draws and receive national coverage.

For some time, L.A. has been without a **professional football team** (down from a high of two!); this is something that only occasionally seems to bother anyone. But there is **college football**, in the form of a decades-long fierce rivalry between **UCLA** and **USC.** The University of California Los Angeles (UCLA) plays at the Rose Bowl in Pasadena; the University of Southern California (USC) uses the Coliseum near Downtown (see map p. 199). Football tickets, with very few exceptions, are easy to get for both UCLA and USC home games. Occasionally, one of these teams plays a top-name team, and then it's harder to find tickets (even these games rarely sell out).

Tickets are difficult to get for **college basketball games** at UCLA because season ticket holders have held all the prime locations for about 37 years now. Some individual games don't sell out (all the big ones do), so you may be able to walk up and buy one for one-third to one-half of the games, perhaps more. But that wasn't the case until recent years. The USC basketball ticket is the easiest to get because they've been trying to build their own arena for over 30 years. During the time the Trojans have left to play in the 40-year-old Sports Arena (pending construction of a new arena), they will have thousands of tickets available for almost every game (the only one you may have difficulty getting a ticket for is the UCLA-USC game).

For ticket information for **UCLA** football and basketball games, contact the UCLA General Ticket Office at ☎ **310-825-2101**, or go online (http:// uclabruins.collegesports.com/tickets/ucla-tickets.html). For ticket information for **USC** football and basketball games, contact the USC ticket office at ☎ **213-740-4672**, or go online (http://usctrojans. collegesports.com/marketplace/tickets/tickets-body.html).

World champs: Los Angeles Lakers

With back-to-back-to-back world championships (2000, 2001, and 2002) as well as two of the most well-known players in basketball — Shaquille O'Neal and Kobe Bryant — the Lakers are one of the most dominating franchises in basketball. Mere mortals can't really get tickets, thanks to the popularity of this powerhouse team and the buckets of money spent on the Lakers' still relatively new home, the **Staples Center** (see map p. 199; ☎ **877-305-1111**; www.staplescenter.com), a state-of-the-art arena in Downtown L.A. In other words, you can give up dreams of just strolling in and buying tickets to sit courtside next to Jack Nicholson and Dyan Cannon. But don't despair: Although season ticket holders have snatched up all the seats by the time you read this for, well, just about every season until the end of time, you may still be able to buy tickets either through local ticket brokers (expect to pay a premium) or on eBay (because season ticket holders do unload single-game tickets there). Otherwise, tickets are officially only available through Ticketmaster or at Ticketmaster outlets around the city (Tower Records and Robinsons-May stores). Hey, you never know — some of those limited cheap seats ($14, the least expensive) *waaaay* up in the rafters may still be available (check the team's Web site at www.nba.com/lakers/ or www.staplescenter.com). For ticket info only, write to: **Los Angeles Lakers**, 555 N. Nash St., El Segundo, CA 90245. Note that parking is fiendishly expensive, and traffic is nasty on game nights. You may want to use the Metro Rail subway, which has an outlet right near the Staples Center.

Up-and-comers: Los Angeles Clippers

Not so long ago, it was considered acceptable, if not expected, to roll your eyes and snicker whenever the Clippers came up in conversation. Such was the lowly opinion held by sports-loving Angelenos of their second-tier NBA team. Sure, the Clippers remain a young, frisky bunch, but they've become a team to be reckoned with of late, with the addition of wise-beyond-his-years Elton Brand and a handful of talented guys who have the legs to play all night. This may be the time to see them for yourself. The Clippers also play in the Staples Center in Downtown L.A. (see the previous blurb on the Lakers for the location and ticket information). For Clippers information, call ☎ **213-745-0400** or go to www.nba.com/ clippers.

Belles of the basketball: Los Angeles Sparks

While the NBA men hibernate through the summer, the women come out to play. The WNBA Sparks play at the Staples Center from May through August (see the preceding section on the Lakers for the location and ticket information). For Sparks information, call ☎ 310-330-2434 or go to www.wnba.com/sparks.

Former Bums of Brooklyn: Los Angeles Dodgers

The Dodgers were once the "Bums of Brooklyn," where an entire borough's hopes and dreams rested on their rise and fall. They broke the hearts of countless fans by moving to L.A. in 1958. (By then, they had already made history by signing Jackie Robinson, the first African-American major-league ballplayer.) Overall, Dodger Stadium is one the most attractive parks in the country thanks to a graceful shape and a picturesque setting (the audience gazes out over the field to foothills with palm trees dotting the horizon). Naturally, there are frequent rumblings that it needs to be torn down and made more fancy.

Season ticket holders have snapped up the good seats, but you can still get tickets for these prime spots. Not only do season ticket holders dump their seats through eBay and ticket brokers, they also hand them off to scalpers who can be found waving extra tickets on the roads leading up to the ballpark. Or you can get really sneaky by buying the cheap seats, which generally do remain available up to game time for many dates (so just getting inside isn't that hard, and it's rather cost-effective if you sit in the upper levels), and moving closer (from the foul lines inward to home plate) during the game when you see that a number of those season ticket snots haven't shown up and their seats are empty and begging for someone to sit in them. Just be discreet, and move if the rightful owner does show. And if you really want to do like the natives, show up around the third inning and leave right after the seventh-inning stretch, regardless of the score. Maybe L.A. doesn't deserve a team like the Brooklyn Dodgers.

Tickets can be purchased at the box office (1000 Elysian Park Ave.; Monday through Saturday 9 a.m.–5 p.m., and during games), online (www.dodgers.mlb.com), or over the phone (☎ 323-224-1-HIT). Tickets are $6 to $37. There is ample parking at the stadium, but it does get slow and crowded, so consider arriving early. Also, unless you arrange for handicapped parking, there is a very long walk from the parking lot to the stadium, and there are many, many stairs to climb inside the stadium (there are elevators, but they're small and limited to those who really need them).

L.A. on ice: The Los Angeles Kings

The Los Angeles Kings play hockey in the Staples Center (see the preceding section on the Lakers), thanks to Jack Kent Cooke, who founded the team in the late 1960s on the premise that many Canadians had moved to Southern California. Unfortunately, Mr. Cooke discovered that the reason they had moved was because they hated hockey. Nonetheless, the team has at times been exciting enough to draw a solid following, although they've never won the championship. Thus, tickets, which are priced from $25 to over $300, are scarce but not as pricey as those for the Lakers. You can order tickets online (www.lakings.com) or over the phone (☎ **888-KINGS-LA**).

And speaking of hockey, the Los Angeles area is also home to the **Mighty Ducks.** They're located in Anaheim and owned by Disney. And they're called "The Mighty Ducks," for cryin' out loud. Oh, all right, for ticket information, check out the team's Web site (www.mightyducks.com) or call ☎ **877-WILDWING.**

Structural L.A.

Okay, L.A. is not, we admit, the most impressive-looking of cities, at least to the naked eye. It lacks the *fin de siècle* romance of Rome, Paris, and London. It lacks the impressive skyline of Manhattan. It lacks the Victorian aesthetic of San Francisco.

But L.A. used to have some of those impressive features — well, the Victoriana, at least — in fact, it had more than its share of gingerbread Victorian buildings back in the day (see "A taste of Victorian L.A." on p. 177). But earthquakes and fires took their toll, and, more to the point, so did development and lack of hind- or foresight. (After all, this is the city where your humble travel-book writer keeps pointing out parking lots and strip malls, mumbling things like, "and that used to be the Brown Derby.")

However, L.A. still has its architectural landmarks: Some are significant, some are historical, and some are just plain wacky. From Frank Lloyd Wright, Rudolph Schindler, and Richard Neutra to hot-dog stands shaped like hot dogs to, yes, a sprinkling of Victorians, we've got a list of L.A. landmarks well worth checking out. Don't want to do it for yourself? **Architecture Tours L.A.** (P.O. Box 93134, Los Angeles, CA 90093; ☎ **323-464-7868;** www.architecturetoursla.com) offers several two-hour tours, ranging from overviews and highlights of L.A. architecture to specific programs designed around various neighborhoods and their own special look (the Pasadena tour might specialize in Greene & Greene, for example, while the Silver Lake tour gives you plenty of Neutra and Schindler). Customized tours are also available. The owner has a master's in architecture history, and she conducts most of the tours herself in a 1962 vintage Caddie.

Capitol Records Building
Hollywood

It looks like a stack of records, it does, complete with stylus (remember those?) on top. They claim that's a coincidence. We doubt it. Elvis once said his great ambition was to play on the roof.

See map p. 161. 1750 Vine St.

Freeman House
Hollywood

Frank Lloyd Wright build the Freeman House as an experiment in afford-able mass-produced housing. The textile block structure is what sets it apart from any tract house you may have seen (1962 Glencoe Way; ☎ 323-851-0671). Having said that, the **Ennis-Brown House** really has to be seen to be believed. The house, patterned after a Mayan temple, was built in 1924. It is located in the Los Feliz hills near Griffith Park. It's a breathtak-ing piece of work, perhaps the most extraordinary private residence in the United States. Trust us when we say that this is one of the (alas, not too well-known) highlights of L.A., and think of us as you gasp when you step into the living room. Regular tours and special packages are offered.

2655 Glendower Ave. ☎ *323-660-0607.* www.ennisbrownhouse.org.

Griffith Observatory
Los Angeles

This gleaming white jewel crowning a Griffith Park hillside will be closed during the lifetime of this book, but it's worth noting nonetheless. It will open again (probably in 2005) with a brand-new facelift, a fine new theater, and updated exhibits to aid visitors in better understanding what they see as they gaze toward the heavens. (A fundraiser for the renovation included a hefty donation by Leonard Nimoy, who seems to have accepted that he is indeed Spock.) This glorious Art Deco structure (you can see it in the cli-matic scene in *Rebel Without A Cause* — there is even a bust of James Dean at the observatory) has one of the best views in all of L.A. See if you can drive up fairly close to take advantage of the view (which, of course, can vary depending on the weather and smog level).

See map p. 191. 2800 E. Observatory Rd. (in Griffith Park at the end of Vermont Ave.). ☎ *323-664-1191.*

Former Charlie Chaplin Studios
Hollywood

It's a bird, it's a plane, it's a . . . frog? Dressed like . . . Charlie Chaplin? What gives? It's simple enough; in 1918, Charlie Chaplin built his own studio (back when the road was just dirt) in this charming English Tudor style. It later became the longtime home of A&M Records. In 2000, the studio was bought by the Jim Henson Company. The new owners understood the importance of acknowledging one's roots, so they put a giant statue of Kermit, dressed as the Little Tramp tipping his hat to Charlie, on the roof. Go by and wave hi.

See map p. 161. 1416 La Brea Ave. (at Sunset Blvd.).

Hollyhock House
Hollywood

Hollyhock House was Frank Lloyd Wright's first Los Angeles project. Built between 1919 and 1921 for an oil baroness who, a few years later, donated it and the 60-plus-acre hillside it rested on to the city of L.A. It is now part of **Barnsdall Art Park** (where affordable art classes are offered for adults and children, along with rotating exhibitions), an oasis of calm and trees in a surprising urban setting (a decidedly unglamorous stretch of Hollywood Boulevard). The house is undergoing extensive renovations (to repair the ravages of time plus damage from the Northridge earthquake) and was closed as this book was going to press, but the plans (and hope) were that it would reopen by late 2005. Tours of the outside of the three Wright structures on the property (including photos of the interior and the history of Aline Barnsdall, for whom the house was built) plus the park are offered by appointment during the week, and on Saturday and Sunday at 12: 30 p.m., 1:30 p.m., 2:30 p.m., and 3:30 p.m.

See map p. 161. 4800 Hollywood Blvd.. ☎ *323-644-6269.* www.hollyhock house.com.

Tail O' the Pup
West Hollywood

It's a hot-dog stand shaped like a hot dog in a bun. So simple. So sublime. So utterly ridiculous. (We miss representational architecture. We really do.)

San Vincente Blvd. (between Beverly Blvd. and Melrose Ave.). ☎ *310-652-4517.*

Bradbury Building
Downtown

The Bradbury Building is an unbelievably fabulous bit of turn-of-the-20th-century architecture. Don't think of it as Victorian for this office building (which still has commercial tenants) was way ahead of its time. (You can argue that the results are noir in a Raymond Chandler kind of way, but even that doesn't do it justice.) Five floors surround an indoor courtyard. The courtyard is an airy atrium that combines tile, brick, wrought iron, marble, oak, and glass and bedazzles as a result. Tour this one.

See map p. 199. 304 N. Broadway (at Third St.). ☎ *213-626-1893.*

Gamble House
Pasadena

Arts and Crafts fans should not miss this building, which is perhaps the high point of the career of the famous architect team of Greene & Greene. The two-story home, built in 1908, has Mission detailing (everything from windows to light switches to wood grooves) done to a fair-thee-well, and all is lovingly maintained. You can see it by tour only (which lasts an hour). Don't miss the bookshop, which has helped many a preservationist, or just enthusiast, re-create period touches for their own homes; it's run by knowledgeable clerks, eager to help you find that piece of Batchelder-inspired tile.

See map p. 191. 4 Westmoreland Pl. ☎ *626-793-3334.* wwwgamblehouse.org. *Admission: $8 general admission, $5 seniors and students, children under 12 free. Hours: Thurs–Sun noon–3 p.m. (Arrive early because they sometimes sell out.)*

Our Lady of the Angels Cathedral
Downtown

When the Archdiocese of Los Angeles announced plans to abandon its original cathedral, St. Vibiana's (built in 1876), because of the extraordinary costs it would take to repair damage from the 1994 Northridge earthquake, and instead build a new cathedral from scratch (for considerably more), there were a number of voices raised in protest. But when the new Our Lady of the Angels cathedral was dedicated, many of those voices were silenced, dumbstruck by this very model of a modern cathedral. Except for ours, of course, because we think the thing looks like a giant yellow armadillo. Every element that every art and architecture critic everywhere has praised — the Robert Graham sculpture of Mary that combines ethnic features in a way that reflects the melting pot of Los Angeles, the opaque sheets of thin alabaster used instead of traditional stained glass windows — we hate. We think the place is just ugly, cold, and a deeply troubling waste of money. (Even though we do admire the considerable thought and care that went into every aspect of its design.) You may disagree, and you should see and judge for yourself. There's a gift shop (with the cathedral's private line of wine, among other surprising items) and even a good cafe. (Don't forget to say hello to Gregory Peck, who is buried in the mausoleum.) Maybe this really is the kind of cathedral needed for the new millennium. But we still don't understand what was wrong with the ones from the last millennium.

See map p. 199. 555 W. Temple St. ☎ *213-680-5200.* www.olacathedral.org. *Open: Mon–Fri 6:30 a.m.–7 p.m., Sat 9 a.m.–7 p.m., Sun 7 a.m.–7 p.m. Self-guided tours possible by purchasing a guidebook. Guided tours: Mon–Fri 1 p.m. Free.*

Schindler House
West Hollywood

Rudolf M. Schindler's own home and studio served as what was perhaps one of the first New Age hippie communes; it was an experiment in artistic and healthy living, full of nuts, berries, natural fibers, and few rules for kids. It's also a highly influential structure, known for its simplicity and integration of both outdoor and indoor space. It currently houses the MAK center for Art and Architecture in Los Angeles.

See map p. 191. 835 N. King's Rd. ☎ *323-651-1510.* www.makcenter.com/ schindler.html. *Admission: $5, free Fri 4 p.m.–6 p.m. and on Sept 10, Schindler's birthday. Open: Wed–Sun 11 a.m.–6 p.m.*

Legacies of the giants of architecture

Some of the giants of architecture, particularly within the area of residence design, worked in Los Angeles, and each left a lasting legacy. Although Spanish-influenced homes (thanks in large part to **Wallace Neff,** who favored old-world styles) and Arts and Crafts–style housing (in large part drawn from the inspired work of architects **Greene & Greene,** whose "ultimate bungalows" are still found around Southern California) immediately evoke quintessential early Los Angeles, it was arguably the advent of the great **Frank Lloyd Wright** that changed California forever. Not only did he leave behind a number of extraordinary buildings, but it was thanks to him that **Rudolph Schindler** came to town. Schindler started working with the master in 1920 and eventually became the first to design buildings that took true advantage of California's unique climate. From 1922 to his death in 1953, he designed houses and commercial buildings that are considered landmarks in the modern architectural movement. Then came **Richard Neutra,** a former schoolmate of Schindler's, who worked with him for a few years and became, in his own right, one of the most important modern architects in Los Angeles. Schindler and Neutra were essentially responsible for creating the California look; indeed, it was Schindler who designed the "California House" — a one-story dwelling with an open floor plan and a flat roof, which opened to the garden through sliding doors while turning its back to the street — which became a staple of postwar housing.

Walt Disney Concert Hall
Downtown

At last, Los Angeles has a landmark piece of architecture. Skeptics abounded when famed, and sometimes controversial, architect Frank Gehry's plans for the new home of the Los Angeles Philharmonic were unveiled, and even more eyebrows were lifted during the lengthy construction process. But since then, only the most stodgy and churlish are anything other than delighted. It looks like, well, nothing, other than maybe aspects of other Gehry structures. It's a gleaming, rolling, rippling mass that puts one in mind of a galleon ship with full, billowing sails. It's so sensuous and sinuous that you want to run your hand along it. (Go ahead. We've done it.) Walk all the way around, and then do it again, from the other side of the street. It looks different from every angle, and by gosh, by the time you get to where you started, it looks different yet again. It seems to change while you watch it. The inside, featuring acoustics unmatched in the world, is pretty extraordinary, too. This is a can't miss sight, even if you don't take the tour.

See map p. 199. 111 S. Grand Ave. ☎ *323-850-2000. www.musiccenter. org/wdch. Audio tours: $10 adults, $8 seniors and students, 9 a.m.–3 p.m. except on matinee days when they stop at 10:30 a.m. Calling in advance for reservations is suggested.*

Applause, please: Touring studios and going to a TV taping

This is Tinseltown, so of course you want to see Hollywood in action. Note that, as of this writing, in reaction to September 11, many of the television and movie studios have cut or at least severely curtailed their tour offerings. The tour schedules are likely to have changed by the time you read this, but we urge you to call in advance.

Studio tours

NBC Studios
Burbank

This 70-minute behind-the-scenes walking tour lets you check out the sets of *The Tonight Show with Jay Leno,* wardrobe, makeup, special effects and sound effects sets, and set construction demonstrations. You should call at least two weeks in advance for tickets.

See map p. 169. 3000 W. Alameda, Burbank. ☎ *818-840-3538. Admission: $7.50 adults, $6.50 seniors, $4.50 children 5–12, children under 5 free. Open: Mon–Fri 9 a.m.–3 p.m. on first-come basis.*

Sony Pictures Studios
Culver City

This two-hour walking tour guides visitors through the facets of a real working studio (home to Columbia Pictures and Columbia TriStar Television). Visit the archival museum, watch movie clips in a private screening room, sneak a peek at artists painting scenic backdrops, and visit the stage sets of current television shows.

10202 W. Washington Blvd., Culver City. ☎ *323-520-TOUR. Admission: $24 adults and children 12 and over, no one under 12 admitted. Open: Mon–Fri (call for hours).*

Universal Studios Hollywood
Universal City

This is really part of the larger theme-park day at Universal, but many guests still enjoy the behind-the-scenes tour of the world's biggest motion picture and TV studio. See how special effects were made before the era of CGI, and get a look at the Bates House and other classic sets. Attractions — that's "rides" (kinda) to the rest of us — beyond the tour include the new The Mummy Returns: Chamber of Doom, as well as Terminator 2 3-D, Back to the Future, and Jurassic Park: The Ride. Nickelodeon Blast Zone and Animal Planet Live! are geared toward families.

See map p. 169. 100 Universal City Plaza, Universal City. ☎ *818-508-9600. Admission: $49.75 adults and children over 48 inches tall, $39.75 children under 48 inches tall. Call for hours.*

Warner Bros. Studio Tour
Burbank

Visitors to this working movie and TV studio observe filming whenever possible. The two-hour tour includes a film collage (Errol Flynn to Denzel Washington), the Warner Bros. Museum, historic back lots, cavernous soundstages, and what they bill as "the world's most extensive costume department."

See map p. 169. Gate 4, Hollywood Way and Olive Ave., Burbank. ☎ *818-972-TOUR. Admission: $32. Open: Mon–Fri 9 a.m.–3 p.m.*

TV tapings

For tickets to live tapings of TV shows, contact **Audiences Unlimited** at ☎ 818-753-3470, or go to the Web site (www.tvtickets.com). They provide audiences for over two dozen shows, and their schedule is updated daily, listing available shows up to 30 days in advance. Your best chance of getting tickets is to request shows that are new or aren't big hits. The highest-rated comedies sell out months in advance, so don't plan a special trip on the off chance that you'll get tickets to your favorite show.

Audiences Unlimited also has a booth inside Universal Studios, near the tour departure area, that provides tickets for shows taping that day. They often provide bus transportation from Universal Studios to the set of the show.

Note: **Paramount Studios** (see map p. 161) offers the opportunity to be an audience member at shows taped on the Paramount lot. Call ☎ 323-956-1777 for tickets and information. Tickets are released five business days prior to a taping; you can call and ask what shows have seats available. A show that tapes on a Thursday will release tickets the previous Wednesday.

Some general rules and tips for attending a TV taping:

- ✔ All TV shows begin taping in the early evening, and audience members are requested to line up an hour in advance.

- ✔ You must be over 18 to attend. Photo ID is a must.

- ✔ No backpacks or large bags are permitted. Security is very tight at studios in the aftermath of 9/11.

- ✔ No photos can be taken during the taping.

- ✔ There are bathroom breaks for the audience because tapings usually take four hours, but audience members will not be fed. If the studio allows discreet snacking, bring non-noisy foods.

TV tapings can be a thrill and an economical way to have a real show-biz experience to tell the folks back home. What they don't tell you is that you will be sitting for a very long time. For most shows, seating begins in the late afternoon. A warm-up act will tell some jokes to get you relaxed, and then the taping begins. TV-show scenes are often shot out of sequence, and some scenes are shot multiple times to allow for different camera angles — and yes, they think it would be nice if you laugh every single time the stars offer up the same joke.

You should probably attend a TV taping at least once. Although, after having done it, you may understand why natives get jaded and rarely go themselves.

The art of the card

As you wander L.A., you will often be approached by someone offering tickets to a free movie test screening, an early cut of an upcoming feature. At the end of the movie screening, you will be asked to fill out a card rating the movie. It's no small deal — important and lasting decisions are often made based on these cards. A famous example is *The Big Chill,* which originally ended with a shot of the whole gang, including the character who committed suicide, alive and well, back during their college hey-days. The audience hated it, and that's why the only visible parts of Kevin Costner, who played the character who committed suicide, are his wrists in the opening scene.

The practice is derided by moviemakers and critics alike, but it's also here to stay. Art's loss is your gain; you can see some high-profile flicks way in advance. Lie like crazy if you have any connection at all to the entertainment business; they won't want you at the screening if you do. Tickets are free, but screenings are sometimes held at inconvenient times. They always tell you the title and stars of the movie so that you can decide whether it's worth your time or not.

Tip: More often than not, there seems to be a ticket person during the weekdays out-side the **Bally Total Fitness** health club in Hollywood, 1628 N. El Centro Ave., between Hollywood and Sunset boulevards, west of Gower.

Chapter 12

Shopping the Local Stores

● ●

In This Chapter

▶ Getting your bearings before you shop
▶ Hitting the ritzy shops and retail markets
▶ Shopping by neighborhood
▶ Hanging out at the malls
▶ Finding the best specialty stores

● ●

*T*he City of Disposable Income offers much in the way of fine shopping, from the very best of designer clothing to some of the most curious and wacky stores anywhere. Shopping is a major activity in this city, and though we admit that it may not be as mentally stimulating as a couple of hours in, say, the Getty Museum, browsing is a perfectly legitimate cultural pastime. Plus, think of the people-watching possibilities.

Surveying the Scene

You can buy just about anything you want in L.A., in a variety of price ranges. If you're looking for ultra-high-end stores, head to legendary **Rodeo Drive** (where we, frankly, can't even afford the oxygen). For all things trendy, try **Melrose Avenue** (where punk rock first went mainstream). For the cheap stuff, keep reading.

Where the sales are

The major department stores and malls tend to have sales during most holiday weekends (Labor Day, Presidents' Day, Memorial Day, and so on), to say nothing of their half-price, let's-get-rid-of-stuff sales right after Christmas and their back-to-school events beginning around mid-August. Right before these events begin, the *Los Angeles Times* is crammed with full-page ads, which often have coupons that promise still more discounts.

Shopping hours

In the greater Los Angeles area, most stores open at 10 a.m., Monday through Saturday, and close between 6 p.m .and 7 p.m. On Sunday, most stores open at 11 a.m. *Exceptions:* Some bookstores and record stores stay open late every night, some mall shops stay open until 8 p.m. or 9 p.m., and some stores in Beverly Hills decline to open at all on Sundays. It's always best to call ahead.

A divine week in December

The biggest shopping event of the year is probably the **Divine Design sale,** held the first week in December. Hundreds of clothing, housewares, and accessory designers donate extra goods and samples, which are then offered to the public at steep discounts that decline sharply each day. Nervy shoppers try to stick it out as long as they can, watching the prices plummet to 75 percent off by the last day. Crowds are big, bargains are bigger, and every penny goes to Project Angel Food, which supplies hot meals to the ill and otherwise housebound. In other words, you can do good while indulging yourself — what a deal! The most recent event was held at the Barker Hangar of the Santa Monica Air Center, and it's likely to be held there again; call ☎ 323-845-1800 or go to www.angelfood.org for more information.

Checking Out the Big Names

You won't want for basic department stores in Los Angeles. The nicest of the mainstream ones are **Bloomingdale's** (Beverly Center: 8500 Beverly Blvd.; ☎ 310-360-2700; Century City, 10250 Santa Monica Blvd.; ☎ 310-772-2100) and **Macy's** (Downtown: 750 W. Seventh St.; ☎ 213-628-9311; Beverly Center: 8500 Beverly Blvd.; ☎ 310-854-6655), **Robinsons-May** (Downtown: 725 S. Figueroa.; ☎ 213-683-1144; Beverly Hills: 9900 Wilshire Blvd.; ☎ 310-275-5464), and **Nordstrom** (The Grove at Farmers Market: 6301 W. Third St.; ☎ 323-930-2230; Westside Pavilion: 10830 W. Pico Blvd.; ☎ 310-470-6155; Howard Hughes Center: 6081 Center Dr.; ☎ 310-641-4046). **JCPenney** and **Mervyn's** (various locations) are a little more, oh, let's try not to be snobbish and say, um, *economical.* These are the spots to do basic shopping, where you can expect to find typical brand-name goods.

Then you have those stores with real star-spotting potential. If you have the figure and the financial wherewithal, head over to **Barneys New York** (9570 Wilshire Blvd., Beverly Hills; ☎ 310-276-4400), the only local branch of the fabled fashionista New York department store. It helps to be well heeled and well shaped as you'll find little here that costs under three digits and comes larger than a size 6 — but oh, the filmy lingerie, the Vera Wang dresses, and *the shoes.* It also has some of the best makeup selections in town, including one of the few places to find Kiehl's products. The store is five levels of chic heaven. The **Saks Fifth Avenue** made famous by Winona Ryder's video-taped adventures in shopping is located just half a block away (9600 Wilshire Blvd.; ☎ 310-275-4211), and unlike some stores, they have a department which stock sizes 14–24.

You may also want to visit **Fred Segal** (8100 Melrose Ave.; ☎ 323-651-4129 and 500 Broadway, Santa Monica; ☎ 310-458-8100). If Carrie Bradshaw from *Sex and the City* lived in L.A., she would be here every single day. As it is, Gwyneth Paltrow makes up for her. Actually, to heck with the clothes (hip), the shoes (flimsy and gorgeous), and the accessories (trendy), the children's wear (pricey) — the star-spotting is so good here that one wag quipped that celeb hounds may just as well set up a lawn chair and a cooler in the parking lot and make a day of it. Although it looks like a bunch of different stores or stalls cobbled together under one roof, it's really just one store, but for everyone's sanity, pay for your purchases in the area in which you found them. The salespeople appear terrifying (perhaps they are), but they seem to care about their jobs, so don't be intimidated.

Taking It to the Street

Vintage and resale

In a glamour capital like Los Angeles, it makes sense that people would recycle their clothes with more regularity than they recycle their bottles and cans. And, in a town where dressing to impress can mean sporting a pair of 40-year-old Levi's with a $4,000 leather jacket, it's important to know where to go to get your goods for less.

Vintage designer clothes have been made popular by actresses like Winona Ryder, Chloe Sevigny, and Julia Roberts. **Paper Bag Princess** (8700 Santa Monica Blvd., West Hollywood; ☎ 310-358-1985) and **Decades** (8214½ Melrose Ave., West Hollywood; ☎ 323-655-0223) both offer vintage wear from the likes of Halston, Chanel, and Pucci. Be prepared to drop some heavy cash for highly collectible names. You can find basic vintage clothes at dozens of outlets. **Aardvark's** (7579 Melrose Ave.; ☎ 323-655-6769), **Squaresville** (1800 N. Vermont Ave.; ☎ 323-669-8464), and **Jet Rag** (825 N. La Brea Ave.; ☎ 323-939-0528) are some of the best, with wide selections and price ranges. **American Rag** (150 S. La Brea Ave.; ☎ 323-935-3154) and **Wasteland** (7428 Melrose Ave.; ☎ 323-653-3028) charge more for vintage designer pieces than they do for the racks of plain vintage clothes lining their stores. You may find that certain types of used jeans and tennis shoes are worth hundreds of dollars!

When women (and some men) tire of their pricey designer duds, they often resell them to **consignment shops,** such as the **Address Boutique** (1116 Wilshire Blvd., Santa Monica; ☎ 310-394-1406), **Ravishing Retail** (8127 W. Thirrd St.; ☎ 323-655-8480), or **P.J. London** (11661 San Vincente Blvd.; ☎ 310-826-4649). With consignment shops, prices are 20 percent or more below retail, the clothes are usually only a season or so old, and you can find a wide array of sizes.

Thrift shops can often be a source of cool clothes, but the previously listed vintage stores regularly raid them to flesh out their own stock. **Out**

Not your local thrift shop

When film, television, and video productions need to dump wardrobes after they've served their purpose, **It's A Wrap** (3315 W. Magnolia Blvd., Burbank; ☎ **818-567-7366**) is happy to provide an outlet. This is a great place to pick up a soap-opera-fan souvenir, such as a T-shirt worn by a favorite hero or villain. Clothes, shoes, and accessories are labeled with the name of the show or film they are from and the name of the actor who wore them. Prices range from $10 to thousands of dollars, with the latter being the price for a specific costume worn by, say, Arnold Schwarzenegger in a major film. Keep in mind that many actresses are teeny-tiny (size 4 or under), so you may not find the dress of your dreams to fit, but you'll certainly find some bargains and unique gifts. Or, as in our case, a once-worn Pierre Cardin tux and tails for $60!

of the Closet, a store that benefits the AIDS Healthcare Foundation, has a dozen locations in the greater Los Angeles area. The Fairfax (360 N. Fairfax Blvd.; ☎ **323 934-1956**) and Hollywood (6120 Hollywood Blvd., Hollywood; ☎ **323-467-6811**) locations are home to two of the largest Out of the Closet stores. The Santa Monica branch of the **Salvation Army** (1658 11th St., Santa Monica; ☎ **310-450-7235**) is huge, and so is the Hollywood-area **Goodwill** (4575 Hollywood Blvd.; ☎ **323-644-1517**).

Flea markets

Flea markets are major scenes in L.A.; many locals attend them religiously. Flea market addicts know to arrive as soon as the doors open; otherwise, you can kiss the true bargains and finds goodbye. Still, these are the places to pick up one-of-a-kind souvenirs, articles of clothing, and unique furniture, household goods, and accessories. Wear sunblock and comfy shoes, bring cash in small bills, and prepare to haggle. Buy only what you love, and leave the rest for someone else.

Churches and schools hold **swap meets** as fundraisers; these giant rummage/tag sales are often not worth the time unless you get there the second they open and are able to battle the hardcore shoppers.

 Those big buildings you see with "Swap Meet" painted on the side are simply minimalls stocked with cheap T-shirts, off-brand tennis shoes, and strange plastic utensils.

The **Melrose Trading Post** (Fairfax High School, 7859 Melrose Ave.), held every Sunday from 9 a.m. to 5 p.m., is packed with vendors selling all types of clothes, antiques, and knickknacks — it's a huge garage sale/ party with plenty of bargains and a $2 admission fee.

Plan to get to the second-Sunday-of-the-month **Pasadena Rose Bowl Flea Market** (1001 Rose Bowl Dr., Pasadena; ☎ **323-560-7469**; Admission: $7 from 9 a.m. to 3 p.m., $10 from 8 a.m. to 9:00 a.m., $15 from 7:00 a.m. to

8 a.m., and free for children age 12 and under) early, by say 8 a.m. Although, in the latter part of the day, vendors are willing to make a deal on whatever dregs are left at their stands. You'll find more than 2,000 stalls, which hold everything from old lunchboxes and LPs to ashtrays and fur coats. The **Pasadena City College Flea Market** (1570 E. Colorado Blvd., Pasadena; ☎ 626-585-7906) is held on the first Sunday of each month. It's not as overwhelmingly large, but it's still full of cool stuff. The flea market is open from 8 a.m. to 3 p.m., and admission is free.

Farmers markets

Not to be confused with the permanent buildings on Fairfax known as the Farmer's Market (although produce is naturally in abundance there on a daily basis), L.A.'s farmers markets are weekly neighborhood events where vendors from various parts of the Southland gather to hawk their wares. Local chefs, both professional and home-based, shop at the markets because they know that the best cooking is dictated by the season. Naturally, the joints jump more during spring and summer, when produce productivity is at its highest and choices run amok. Organic produce has a high profile — this is L.A., after all — but the offerings are not exclusively organic. Many of the stands feature wonderful fresh breads, prepared foods, and even clothing.

The two largest and most popular farmers markets are **Santa Monica** (Arizona Avenue between Second Street and Third Street; ☎ 310-458-8712; Open: Wednesday from 9 a.m. to 2 p.m. and Saturday from 8:30 a.m. to 1:00 p.m.) and **Hollywood** (Ivar Street and Selma Street between Sunset and Hollywood boulevards; ☎ 323-463-3171; Open: Sunday from 8 a.m. to 1 p.m.). Both are early-morning destinations for young stars who leave clutching organic veggies and large bouquets of flowers.

The Best Shopping Neighborhoods

Melrose Avenue: The ultimate scene

The ultimate scene is to be found on **Melrose Avenue** between Fairfax and La Brea boulevards, especially on weekends, when music blasts from every storefront. Youth culture propels the street. The neighborhood also has a few retirement homes, from which senior citizens can watch punk rockers, with unnaturally bright-colored hair, and tourists, who meander from shop to shop, loaded with purchases.

Melrose may no longer be the true cutting-edge mecca it was in the '80s, but it's still the place to come for clothes and style. **Retail Slut** (7308 Melrose Ave.; ☎ 323-934-1339) is one of the original retailers on Melrose, stocking shocking garb and glittery goods. **Shrine** (7574 Melrose Ave; ☎ 323-655-1485) and **Necromance** (7220 Melrose Ave.; ☎ 323-934-8684) have ghoulish gear for the Goth set, though the latter is more of a natural history museum cum gift shop than a clothing store. It has a number of death- and morbid-themed one-of-a-kind items (from mourning jewelry

and other Victorian mementoes of death to jewelry made from bone).
Trendy styles and retro wear line both sides of the street. You can find
Doc Marten shoes (half a dozen stores stock them) and vintage clothes
at such stores as **Wasteland** (7428 Melrose Ave.; ☎ **323-653-3028**) and
Aardvark's (7579 Melrose Ave.; ☎ **323-655-6769**). You can buy silver jewelry (they may have the largest stock of earrings in a single store ever) at
Maya (7452 Melrose Ave.; ☎ **323-655-2708**) and expensive antique jewelry at **Wanna Buy a Watch** (7366 Melrose Ave.; ☎ **323-653-0467**). Along
with these longtime residents, there is a constantly shifting array of shops
selling shoes and other accessories.

The west end of Melrose, from Fairfax to Doheny, is the more grownup
section of this busy retail district. Lined with antiques shops and clothing boutiques, this portion of Melrose offers a soothing respite from the
frantic trendiness of the eastern section. Revive and relax your senses
at **Spirituali** (7928 Melrose Ave.; ☎ **323-653-3471**), a candle and aromatherapy boutique that provides gift baskets for celebrities and regular
folks, before blowing your mind over the expensive and d.d. (as longtime
London devotee Bridget Jones would call it) sexy lingerie at **Agent
Provocateur** (7961 Melrose Ave.; ☎ **323-653-0229**) or blowing your souvenir budget on Disney collectibles at **Fantasies Come True** (8012 Melrose
Ave.; ☎ **323-655-2636**). **Xin** (8064 Melrose Ave.; ☎ **323-653-2188**) delivers
clean, minimalist designs for women. **Miu Miu** (8025 Melrose Ave.; ☎ **323-
651-0072**), showcasing Prada's secondary line, and **Costume National**
(8001 Melrose Ave.; ☎ **323-655-8160**), the Gap for the very rich, are
across the street from the high-fashion haven **Fred Segal** (8118 Melrose
Ave., Los Angeles; ☎ **323-651-1800;** see "Checking Out the Big Names,"
p. 215). And for the vintage shopper, **Decades** (8214 Melrose Ave., West
Hollywood; ☎ **323-655-0223**) has plenty of high-end collectible and wear-
able designer clothes, many of which were once owned by celebrities.

Refreshments can be had at **Sweet Lady Jane** (8360 Melrose Ave., West
Hollywood; ☎ **323-653-7145**), where luscious cakes and pastries beckon
from the cases. **Urth Café** (8565 Melrose Ave., West Hollywood; ☎ **310-
659-0628**) is a favorite with models, actors, agents, and others who are
drawn as much to the outdoor see-and-be-seen patio as they are to the
organically grown coffees and vegetarian snacks, including an egg-and-
butter-free chocolate cake that, despite its lack of "normal" ingredients,
is actually good. Keanu Reeves and Red Hot Chili Pepper Anthony Kiedis
know that, across the street, the Zen-style garden at **Elixir** (8612 Melrose
Ave., West Hollywood; ☎ **310-657-9300**) is the perfect place to relax with
a sparkling tonic made in accordance with Chinese herbal principles.

Melrose West also features a fine selection of bookstores and antiques
stores, as well as art galleries. **Dailey Rare Books** (8216 Melrose Ave.,
West Hollywood; ☎ **323-658-8515**) and **Heritage Books** (8540 Melrose
Ave., West Hollywood; ☎ **310-659-3674**) have provided rare and first editions to the likes of Johnny Depp and U2. Visit the world-famous **Bodhi
Tree** (8585 Melrose Ave., West Hollywood; ☎ **310-659-1733**), where
actress Shirley MacLaine and other less famous folk have received enlight-
enment (and lightened wallets) amongst the spiritual and pop-religious

books, feng shui mirrors, and statues of Egyptian gods. **Open Door** (8257 Melrose Ave., West Hollywood; ☎ 323-653-5296) and **Grumps** (7965½ Melrose Ave.; ☎ 323-655-3564) are just two of the antiques shops on Melrose emphasizing American and European furnishings.

From Robertson Boulevard to Doheny Drive, Melrose is lined with design studios for interior decorators and art galleries that have exhibited such familiar artists as Picasso and Maxfield Parrish, as well as rising local painters such as Mark Ryden and Sandow Jones.

Melrose has street parking with meters, so bring plenty of quarters. If you decide to park on side streets, read the signs carefully; some areas are permit-parking only; other streets only allow two-hour parking.

Rodeo Drive and Sunset Plaza: Where the stars are

The heart of the Beverly Hills shopping experience is **Rodeo Drive.** It's loaded with jewels, dripping with furs, and swathed in silk and leather. Do yourself a favor and go on a weekday, and please don't dress like a tourist. In other words, black jeans and a white T-shirt will help you blend in (you will never look as chic and thin as the regulars here, but go ahead and try if you dare), but a pair of shorts and a backpack are no-gos. Check out **Gucci** (347 N. Rodeo Dr.; ☎ 310-278-3451), the store that features the latest in stratospheric fashions, including $300 dog collars, and **Harry Winston** (371 N. Rodeo Dr.; ☎ 310-271-8554), where the stars get their award-show gems. **Tiffany & Company** (210 N. Rodeo Dr.; ☎ 310-273-8880) is located in a mall called **Paseo Rodeo,** which is designed to look like a medieval European street. To the east and west of Rodeo Drive are other Beverly Hills standards, such as **Eidelweiss Chocolates** (444 N. Canon Dr.; ☎ 310-275-0341) and **Fred Hayman** (190 N. Canon Dr.; ☎ 310-271-3100). To the south is Wilshire Boulevard, with big department stores such as **Barneys** (9570 Wilshire Blvd.; ☎ 310-276-4400), **Neiman Marcus** (9700 Wilshire Blvd.; ☎ 310-550-5900), and **Saks Fifth Avenue** (9600 Wilshire Blvd.; ☎ 310-275-4211).

The city of Beverly Hills provides two hours of free parking in the city lots, which are clearly marked, and then charges $1 for each additional hour. Those with lost tickets pay the maximum charge. If you don't park in the Beverly Hills lots, expect to pay at least $5 to park in private lots. You can also search for a parking meter.

Sunset Plaza is one of the oldest and poshest shopping districts in Los Angeles. It lines both sides of Sunset Boulevard, from 8720 Sunset to 8589 Sunset, and is anchored by the celebrity dining spot **Le Dome** (8720 Sunset Blvd.; ☎ 310-659-6919) on the southwest (James Coburn, Elton John) and the celebrity "caffeination" spot **Coffee Bean & Tea Leaf** (8591 Sunset Blvd.; ☎ 310-659-1890) on the northeast (Britney Spears, Mark Wahlburg). Sunset Plaza is also home to superstar retailer **Tracey Ross** (8595 Sunset Blvd., West Hollywood; ☎ 310-854-1996), whose clients include some of the brightest stars in Hollywood, and jeweler **Philip Press** (8601 Sunset Blvd., West Hollywood; ☎ 310-360-1180), which offers fine platinum, gemstones, and diamonds. **Armani Exchange** (8700 W. Sunset Blvd., West Hollywood; ☎ 310-659-0171), **H. Lorenzo** (8660 Sunset Blvd.; Los Angeles; ☎ 310-659-1432), **Calypso** (8635 Sunset Blvd., West Hollywood; ☎ 310-652-4454), and other boutiques beckon. And the spawn of the rich and famous are not forgotten either; **Sunset Kids** (8669 Sunset Blvd.; ☎ 310-659-4411) offers a selection of cute but expensive children's clothes. With over a half-dozen restaurants offering sidewalk brunching, lunching, and dining, (expect smokers on the patios), Sunset Plaza provides a wealth of people-watching and a cosmopolitan flair.

Free parking is offered in the Sunset Plaza lots only for people who are eating and shopping at Sunset Plaza. Under no circumstances should you leave your car and go off the boundaries of Sunset Plaza. If you do so, you could be ticketed and/or towed; Sunset Plaza employs under-cover security to both safeguard its clientele and ensure that the free parking is not abused. Once again, park at the Sunset Plaza lots *only while you're at Sunset Plaza.*

Third Street: Eclectic energy

Third Street in West Hollywood is very different from Santa Monica's Third Street Promenade. The latter features one chain store and fast-food outlet after another, while the former is an eclectic blend of unique boutiques, antiques shops, bookstores, and restaurants strung along a three-block section of the city.

Located next door to each other, **Free Hand** (8413 W. Third St.; ☎ 323-655-2607) and **New Stone Age** (8407 W. Third St.; ☎ 323-658-5969) are high-end shops with handcrafted giftware and objets d'art, including glass, clothing, pottery, and jewelry. **Plastica** (8405 W. Third St.; ☎ 323-655-1051), which is located on the same block, celebrates plastic furniture, toys, and household goods.

Antiques at **Memory Lane** (8387 W. Third St.; ☎ 323-655-4571), and **Sophie's Stuff** (8377 W. Third St.; ☎ 323-651-4325) lean toward vintage collectibles and cool retro housewares. Vintage clothes can be found at **Julian's** (8366½ W. Third St. ☎ 323-655-3011) and **Polka Dots & Moonbeams** (8381 W. Third St.; ☎ 323-651-1746). The latter also has a shop featuring modern clothes on the same —while new styles, including handbags and Robert Clergerie shoes, are featured at **Noodle Stories** (8323 W. Third St.; ☎ 323-651-1782). **Paul Frank Store** (8101 W. Third St.; 323-653-6471) stocks the designer's signature monkey-faced tees, pajamas, and other cute things favored by Britney Spears and Drew Barrymore.

Room Service (8115 W. Third St.; ☎ 323-653-4242) has expensive haute moderne toys, such as metal address books for adults. **Cook's Library** (8373 W. Third St.; ☎ 323-655-3141) and **Traveler's Bookcase** (8375 W. Third St.; ☎ 323-655-0575) are excellent examples of niche marketing, both well stocked with specialty books on cooking and travel, respectively. If all this shopping has worn you out, indulge yourself with a huge assortment of luxurious bath and beauty supplies at **Palmetto** (8321 W. Third St.; ☎ 323-653-2470).

Food fanatics love **Joan's on Third** (8350 W. Third St.; ☎ 323-655-2285), a small cafe with sandwiches, desserts, and salads (see p. 131). Others find respite from their busy shopping at **Chado Tea House** (8422½ W. Third St.; ☎ 323-655-2056). After the sun goes down, hipsters fill up on tacos and tequila at campy chic **El Carmen** (8138 W. Third St.; ☎ 323-852-1552).

All of Third Street, except the food, has been distilled into one shop, **Zipper** (8316 W. Third St.; ☎ 323-951-0620), whose motto, "Art Form + Function," is demonstrated by the pillows, incense, bathware, toys, books, and gift items attractively displayed and lovingly collected for your viewing and buying pleasure.

Montana Avenue: Upscale boutiques

This Santa Monica beachside community was once a sleepy enclave with little more than a couple of markets, a couple of pharmacies, and some dry cleaners. Then the upscaling began, as the ritzy boutiques and decaf-nonfat-lattes unleashed their relentless assault on Montana Avenue. Even the local funeral parlor was recently torn down; a retail-residential complex will be put up in its place. Thank goodness actor Robert Redford bought the Aero Theatre so that it could not be turned into an overpriced antiques store.

Be careful driving along Montana Avenue — oblivious locals love to jay-walk as they juggle their packages, lattes, baby strollers, and golden retrievers, and drivers have trouble managing their SUVs while chatting nonstop on cell phones.

Fine silk and velvet dresses with exotic prints beckon at **Harari** (1406 Montana Ave.; ☎ 310-260-1204) and **Citron** (1615 Montana Ave.; ☎ 310-458-6089), while antiques gleam from the windows at **Rosemarie McCaffrey** (1203 Montana Ave.; ☎ 310-395-7711) and **Room with a View** (1600 Montana Ave.; ☎ 310-998-5858). There's plenty of stuff for the wealthy here, including funky one-of-a-kind furnishings at **Raw Style** (1511 Montana Ave.; ☎ 310-458-7662), and soul-soothing bath and body-care products at **Palmetto** (1034 Montana Ave.; ☎ 310-395-6687). Guys can find high fashion at **Weathervane for Men** (1132 Montana Ave.; ☎ 310-395-0397) and **Trek & Travel** (1412 Montana Ave.; ☎ 310-260-2500). Kids and pets get pampered at **Babystyle** (1324 Montana Ave.; ☎ 310-434-9590) and **The Wagging Tail** (1123 Montana Ave.. ☎ 310-656-9663).

Montana Avenue provides street parking with meters; bring quarters. Some parking is available on side streets. Be sure to read signs carefully for time limits.

Vermont Avenue and Sunset Boulevard: Boho L.A.

Vermont Avenue is the hip shopping spot for the bohemians of the Los Feliz and Silver Lake areas of Los Angeles, also known as the Eastside. From peculiar knickknacks, such as the rubber skulls and tiki statues and vintage '60s pop-culture doodads, at **Y-Que** (1770 N. Vermont Ave.; ☎ 323-664-0021; pronounced ee-*kay*) to the fine selection of reading material at **Skylight Books** (1818 N. Vermont Ave.; ☎ 323-660-1175) and the interesting clothing boutiques, such as the vintage and designer resale shop **Squaresville** (1800 N. Vermont Ave.; ☎ 323-669-8464), Vermont provides a quirky view of L.A. life.

Follow Vermont Avenue south to Hollywood Boulevard and turn left to find the irrepressible **Soap Plant/Wacko** (4633 Hollywood Blvd.; ☎ 323-663-0122). It's really three stores in one (including the La Luz de Jesus Gallery), all originally located on Melrose. If you can't find a gift among the oddball books, candles, specialty soaps, goofy toys, and modern art here, you aren't trying. While there, comb the musty but well-priced volumes at the used book store **Aldine Books** (4663 Hollywood Blvd.; ☎ 323-666-2690).

If you keep going on Hollywood Boulevard, you will come to the three-way intersection of Hollywood, Virgil, and Sunset. Go east on Sunset about 1/4 mile to the intersection of Sunset and Santa Monica (look for **Circus of Books** on the left, though don't let the happy name fool you — it's for big boys, not little ones). The big burnt-umber building is Sunset Junction, the apex of Silver Lake, and holds **The Cheese Store of Silver Lake,** a temple to our favorite dairy product (over 150 different kinds; 3926 W. Sunset Blvd; ☎ 323-644-7511). Try a couple strange items, get a few wedges for a picnic (they also sell excellent baguettes), and then take a stroll down the next two blocks, both sides of the street, popping into the various (and oft-changing) gift, trendy clothing, and imported-furniture stores that dot this stretch of L.A's most happening neighborhood.

Vermont Avenue offers street parking with meters; parking is available on side streets, as well. Read signs carefully for time limits and street-cleaning information.

Third Street Promenade: Street shops

The Third Street Promenade, which runs between Wilshire Boulevard and Broadway Street in Santa Monica, is a pedestrian mall that gamely attempts to emulate the street scenes that have popped up organically in big European cities. Day or night, it's always packed with people. It's one of the most pleasant things to do in Los Angeles; even we, who are deeply cynical about this sort of packaged urban experience, the only way you can get Los Angelenos to participate in city life, succumb to its charms whenever we are there. On Thursday and Saturday mornings, there's a farmers market on Arizona Street with fresh fruits, vegetables, and tasty snacks. The mall has three multi-screen movie theaters, a police station (at 1400 Third St., in the Market Pavilion kiosk), and plenty to take in, including street vendors and musicians, who must be licensed and pay a fee to be there, and grungy street people, who exhibit their charms free from city regulations. It's both charming and kind of creepy in that it is so carefully tended.

The promenade is grounded by Santa Monica Place Mall on the south, with **Barnes & Noble** (1201 Third Street Promenade; ☎ 310-260-9110) and **Banana Republic** (1202 Third Street Promenade; ☎ 310-394-7740) to the north. The flagship Banana Republic will even recharge your cell phone for you while you shop — so *very* L.A. Upscale chains like **Anthropologie** (1402 Third Street Promenade; ☎ 310-393-4763) and **Urban Outfitters** (1440 Third Street Promenade; ☎ 310-394-1404) line both sides of the walkway, but there are also gems, such as sexy soap shop **Lush** (1404 Third Street Promenade; ☎ 310-255-0030) and **Puzzle Zoo** (1413 Third Street Promenade; ☎ 310-393-9201), with its unique stock of puzzles and toys.

The promenade has street parking and city lot parking; bring quarters and read the meters carefully — some street meters are only 36 minutes! City lots on Fourth and Second streets offer meters on the bottom floors and longer-term parking on the top levels, with hourly rates. If you lose your ticket, you will pay the maximum charge at lots that use the ticket method. You can park in the Santa Monica Place Mall on Broadway for three hours for free, but any longer will get you a ticket.

Universal CityWalk: Family fun

Look, ma — it's like all of Los Angeles in one place, only smaller, louder, cleaner, more crowded, and *waaaaay* more contrived. Universal CityWalk mimics the urban experience with sanitized, safe shopping and people-watching. You won't find a single local here except for the teen and teen gangsta sets. We only come here when we are paid to do so, like when writing this book. Still, we grudgingly admit that it's good for families. Spots of humor do appear (the entrance to the **Hard Rock Cafe** is a 78-foot, neon-green Fender Stratocaster); the movie theaters are great (we applaud their policy of banning small children in movies rated R and PG-13), plus there's an IMAX theater; and there are plenty of ways to spend your money, whether it's surfwear from **Billabong,** mass-produced punk-rock garb from **Hot Topic,** or really cool bobble heads, tops, and candy from the retro-toy shop **Sparkey's.**

But the coolest store by far is **Them,** which sells horror and sci-fi gift items and is the only place in the entire CityWalk/Universal Studio area where you can buy reproductions of vintage movie posters. Sadly, they aren't posters from classic Universal films; these veer more to the B-movie genre, but it's nice to find one CityWalk shop that appreciates the cinematic past, even if it's on the cheesy side.

Along with plenty of shops selling schlock, including a place where you can have your face digitized onto a magazine cover for $34.95 plus tax, there are two sportsgear/memorabilia shops, **UCLA Spirit** and **All Star**

Collectibles (NBA Barbies, who knew?), and food — plenty of it. Really, what self-respecting mall would be complete without a food court? CityWalk provides a sumptuous bounty reflecting the finest in local fast food — and you don't have to drive all over town to get it. **Tommy's Burgers** and **Versailles** (great garlicky Cuban chicken and pork plates) are the premier examples of the food you'll find. And the balcony provides an awesome view of the giant-screen TV monitor that plays videos from Vivendi-Universal Music acts. Along with fast food — such as **Jodi Maroni's** exotically flavored sausages and our vote for best on-site food buy, **Tropic Nut**'s peanut-butter-and-jelly sandwich, cookie, and soda combo for $5 — you'll find stuff to do, most of which costs money.

There's the testosterone-fueled **NASCAR** racing experience, where drivers sit in bouncing replica cars and try not to wipe out at video-induced "speeds" of up to 195 miles per hour. *A word to the wise:* If you are prone to motion sickness, avoid this ride! **Jillian's Hi-Lite** has a black-light bowling alley with a Jetsons vibe. The more sedentary types will be relieved to discover **Upstart Crow,** a fairly decent bookstore with a cafe and a children's bookshop named **Crow's Nest.** People-watching is free, and so is running through the fountain in front of **Sam Goody's** music store.

Parking is available in the Universal City lot off Universal City Drive at a cost of $8. Make sure that you write down your location within the lot; it's easy to get confused by "Curious George Yellow Level 7" and "Curious George Blue Level 5." Or do what the locals do: Park at the meters on Cahuenga West and walk up the very steep, long hill; this area is fine if you only plan to spend a couple of hours at Universal City. A trip to see a movie there will get you a $2 parking rebate. You can also take the Metro Rail from Hollywood Boulevard to Universal City and walk up to CityWalk.

Main Street: From hippie to hipster

This low-profile Westside street blends Santa Monica chic with Venice funkiness. The result? A stimulating seven-block mix of hippie (check out **One Life Market,** at 3001 Main St.; ☎ 310-392-4501) and hip (head for **Blonde,** at 2430 Main St.; ☎ 310-396-9113). The street even has its own Web site (www.mainstreetsm.com).

Vintage-fashion aficionados flock to **Paris 1900** (2703 Main St.; ☎ 310-396-0405) for lace and frills that make us want to get married again and again, just to wear the dresses it sells. **Sumiko** (3007 Main St.; ☎ 310-399-2803) — located in what was once the Vixen adult theater — has romantic modern dresses.

Aromatherapy addicts drift languidly through the doors of **Bey's Garden** (2919 Main St.; ☎ 310-399-5420) for a scent fix. Pets are not neglected at **Nature's Grooming Boutique** (3110 Main St.; ☎ 310-392-8758), with its treats, toys, themed collars, leashes, and accessories (such as sweaters and hats) for all sizes of canines.

Angel City Books (218 Pier Ave.; ☎ 310-399-8767) specializes in new and used volumes about Los Angeles, while next door the **Novel Cafe** (212 Pier St.; ☎ 310-396-8566) serves up snacks, coffee drinks, and used books for reading or buying.

For food, there's always the neighborhood taco stand, **Holy Guacamole** (2906 Main St.; ☎ 310-392-6373). Along with tacos, the stand also sells a large selection of bottles of searing hot sauces. **The Galley,** Santa Monica's oldest restaurant and bar (2442 Main St.; ☎ 310-452-1934), is open from 5 p.m. to closing, seven days a week.

The **California Heritage Museum** (2612 Main St.; ☎ 310-392-8537), located in a Craftsman-style house, lives up to its name with exhibits that have included tiles, pottery, and textiles. The heritage of designer Charles Eames is preserved at **Eames Office Gallery** (2665 Main St; ☎ 310-396-5991), which features originals and licensed reproductions from this seminal modernist.

Metered parking is available on Main Street and in city lots west of Main Street. All the lots have extended hours, so read signs carefully.

Hitting the Shopping Malls

The Beverly Center
Westside

Known colloquially as the Bev Center, this mall was built on the site that once held an amusement park called Kiddie Land, and it's the only mall in the world to have a working oil well on its property (it's hidden behind a wall on the San Vincente Boulevard side of the building). The Bev Center is anchored by **Macy's** and **Bloomingdale's**, with restaurants, including the country's first **Hard Rock Cafe,** on the ground floor, a food court and movie theaters at the top, and parking and plenty of shops sandwiched in between. Most of the stores at The Beverly Center are chains such as **Victoria's Secret, Restoration Hardware,** and **The Gap,** but there are high-end retailers such as **Traffic** that feature designers such as Helmut Lang and Gaultier. **Louis Vitton, Betsy Johnson,** and **Mont Blanc** also have stores at the Bev. These high-end retailers are among the reasons the Beautiful People haunt this place, but frankly, we tend to avoid it. The multistory parking garage is a locally known horror — it gets really crowded, and it's constructed in such a way that it takes a long time to get in, find a place to park, and find your way to the mall. Then you have to do the reverse when you leave. Shudder. A **California Welcome Center** (☎ 310-854-7616) is located on the ground floor, with the entrance on the Beverly Boulevard side of the building. The Welcome Center provides fax and Internet services, free maps, tour information, and tickets for attractions, along with free coffee and free shuttle service.

8500 Beverly Blvd., Los Angeles, with entrances on Beverly, La Cienega, and San Vicenteboulevards. ☎ *310-854-0071.* www.beverlycenter.com. *Parking: First three hours or portion thereof $1, with each additional hour $1; parking validation not required; lost ticket pays maximum.*

Century City Shopping Mall
Century City

The Century City Shopping Mall was once part of Twentieth Century Fox Studios (the high cost of making the Elizabeth Taylor/Richard Burton movie *Cleopatra* forced the studio to sell off land to developers). This outdoor mall was also featured in the movie *Battle for the Planet of the Apes.* It holds a **Macy's** and a **Bloomingdale's** (larger than the one at the Bev Center), a food court with a good selection of ethnic and American food, small kiosk carts selling T-shirts, jewelry, and hair gewgaws, and ubiquitous chains such as **The Gap, Ann Taylor, Origins**, and **Crabtree & Evelyn**. Recently bought by megamall developers Westfield, the Century City Mall is undergoing a major remodel which will mean a bigger multiscreen theatre and who knows what all else.

10250 Santa Monica Blvd. ☎ *310-277-3898. Parking: First three hours free with validation; make sure you take your ticket with you for validation; lost ticket pays maximum.*

The Glendale Galleria
Glendale

The Glendale Galleria is a huge shopping mall anchored by **Nordstrom, JCPenney, Robinsons-May,** and **Macy's.** Add in almost any conceivable chain store — plus a food court with Hawaiian barbecue, Indian, and Thai snacks, and a **Hot Dog on a Stick** with servers dressed in fetishistic striped costumes, along with the **Zone,** "a one-of-a-kind multimedia and shopping experience customized for teens," on the second floor — and you have a whole downtown shopping arena under one roof. But despite its size and ambition, The Glendale Galleria is comfortable and almost cozy. Maybe that's because of the giant plastic palm trees or the carpeting, or the lack of movie theaters. No matter; this is a mall on steroids, complete with more than 50 stores devoted to women's wear (including **Bebe** and **Frederick's of Hollywood**), a **Thomas Cook Foreign Exchange** and postal center, a police substation, and, thankfully, plenty of places to sit and rest as you shop.

100 W. Colorado Blvd. ☎ *818-246-6737.* www.glendalegalleria.com. *Free parking. From Santa Monica, Beverly Hills, and Hollywood, take the I-10 east to the I-5 north and exit at Colorado, and then drive east to the Galleria.*

The Grove
West Hollywood

Great was the local dismay when this shopping mall was built right up against the venerable Farmer's Market. Presevationists and sentimentalists worried that an influx of the usual retail suspects (**Crate & Barrel, the Gap, Anthropologie, Barnes & Noble, L'Occitane, J. Crew, Victoria's Secret**) would lure the unimaginative away from the little shopping area that could, and it would spell the death of yet another unique L.A. landmark. Jury's still out on that one. Though crowds are flocking to this rather Disney-esque, fake Euro-village complex, a nifty free trolley shuttle takes them over to the previously overlooked Farmer's Market, which might just be getting an economic kick as a result. As much as we hate that L.A. needs to manufacture adorable neighborhoods for strolling and drinking coffee, we can't help but be won by the (entirely planned) whimsy of this place, complete with a miniature dancing water fountain. Also, the likes of Quentin Tarantino and Janeane Garofalo come here, and who are we to quibble with such authorities on cool? So we will make you a deal: You can come here, especially if it's to take in a movie at the excellent **Pacific Theaters** (expensive, but with stadium seating and other plush amenities), but then hop on that trolley and go eat at the Farmer's Market; the food is cheaper and better, and the selection greater. And see if you don't have the reaction of one tourist we brought to both; she was smitten with the Grove, but when she arrived at the Farmer's Market, she said, "Oh, I see. This is where the soul is." Well, yes.

198 The Grove Drive (between Third St.t and Beverly Blvd.). ☎ **888-315-8883** *or 323-900-8080.* www.thegrovela.com.

Hollywood & Highland Complex
Hollywood

At the heart of the oft-promised revitalization of Hollywood is this already troubled — and yet, very fine — entertainment complex, a multilevel outdoor mall. It's frustrating because on one hand, so much was done right, in terms of clever design. In a perhaps over-the-top attempt to integrate and pay homage to local legend, not to mention make sure you never ever forget that the **Kodak Theatre,** home to the Oscars and little else, is part of the complex, there are all kinds of cute and witty bits of business: a stairway with a "red carpet" made out of tile; various quotes from anonymous Hollywood professionals about the cool and cruel nature of the industry, spelled out in the pavement; a building arrangement that forms a sort of frame around the Hollywood sign; and, best of all, a courtyard with giant elephant statues in homage to the Babylon set of D. W. Griffith's landmark spectacle, *Intolerance.* But on the other hand, almost all the stores are the same predictable brand names you can find anywhere else (**Banana Republic, The Gap, Express, Hot Topic, Victoria's Secret** — though there is also a **Sephora** which stays open on the late side). Consequently, it's rarely all that crowded here, and word has it the place (which has already changed ownership once in its short existence) is in financial trouble. We figure, if you are going to shop at the usual stores, why not do it here? Bonuses include a Metro stop right on the corner, parking for $2 for four hours, and a short walk to Grauman's Chinese Theatre down the street, along with the rest of Hollywood sightseeing. For dining, you can try **Vert,** yet another Wolfgang Puck restaurant, or **California Pizza Kitchen,** along with some Asian and other food options, plus a **Tollhouse Cookie Café.**

The complex stays open as late as 10 p.m. every night except Sunday, though many stores close earlier than that.

6801 Hollywood Blvd. (at Highland). ☎ **323-467-6412.** www.hollywoodand highland.com.

Westside Pavilion
Beverly Hills/Santa Monica

Located between Beverly Hills and Santa Monica, this mall right off the 10 Freeway has the most confusing, though thankfully free, parking we've ever experienced; sections are named Quail, Poppy, and Cactus in the insanely laid-out garages. But they do have a **Nordstrom,** plus all the usual mall suspects (**The Gap, BCBG, Bebe, Victoria's Secret,** and so on). The movie theater shows primarily art-house, independent, and foreign films, which is unusual for most mall theaters, and it's the mall where Alicia Silverstone shops in the movie Clueless.

10800 W. Pico Blvd. (between Westwood and Overland blvds). ☎ **310-474-6255.** www. westsidepavilion.com. *Free parking. From Santa Monica, take the I-10 east to the National/Overland exit, turn right onto National Place, which becomes Westwood Boulevard leading you to the mall; or take Pico Boulevard east. From points east either take the I-10 West, exit Overland, go straight, turn right on Westwood and proceed to mall; or take Pico Boulevard west to the mall.*

Specialty Shopping

Antiques
Antiques and retro furnishings abound in Los Angeles. A number of stores on Santa Monica's Montana Avenue provide vintage furnishings and accessories, including **Rosemarie McCaffrey** (1203 Montana Ave.; ☎ **310-395-7711**) and **Room with a View** (1600 Montana Ave.; ☎ **310-998-5858**). There are a lot of stores along Robertson Boulevard that offer vintage furnishings and accessories, as well, including **Anna Hauck's Art Deco** (8738 Melrose, West Hollywood; ☎ **310-659-3606**). **Sonrisa** (7609 Beverly Blvd., Los Angeles; ☎ **323-935-8438**) and **Modernica** (7366 Beverly Blvd., Los Angeles; ☎ **323-933-0383**) fulfill minimalist urges with sleek mid-20th Century styles.

Books
General independent bookstores such as **Vromans** (695 E. Colorado Blvd., Pasadena; ☎ **626-449-5320**), **Duttons** (11975 San Vicente Blvd., Los Angeles; ☎ **310-476-6263**), and **Book Soup** (8818 Sunset Blvd., West Hollywood; ☎ **310-659-3110**) — all are top-flight shops with knowledgeable, helpful staff and a marvelous variety of books, and we urge you to patronize them — vie for business with the big chains, such as **Borders** (1360 Westwood Blvd., Los Angeles; ☎ **310-475-3444** and 1415 Third Street Promenade, Santa Monica; ☎ **310-393-9290**), while other independent booksellers have carved out niches in specialty markets.

The **Bodhi Tree** (8585 Melrose Ave., West Hollywood; ☎ 310-659-1733) stocks tomes on Eastern, Western, and pop philosophies, along with incense, gifts, and candles. **Storyopolis** (116 N. Robertson Blvd., West Hollywood; ☎ 310-358-2500) entertains the youngster in all of us with a huge range of children's books. **Wacko** (4633 Hollywood Blvd.; ☎ 323-663-0122) blends art and pop-culture books with toys and collectibles and throws free art openings on the first Friday night of the month. **Hennessy & Ingalls** Promenade (214 Wilshire Blvd., Santa Monica; ☎ 310-458-9074) focuses purely on art and architecture books. **Dailey Rare Books** (8216 Melrose Ave.; ☎ 323-658-8515) and **Heritage Books** (8540 Melrose Ave., West Hollywood; ☎ 310-659-3674) sell fine first editions and other rarities. **Mystery Pier** (8826 W. Sunset Blvd.; ☎ 310-657-5557) solves readers' desire for crime fact and fiction. **Cook's Library** (8373 W. Third St., Los Angeles; ☎ 323-655-3141) is dedicated to the culinary arts (you will not believe how many cookbooks have been written throughout the years) and is a paradise for chefs. Cinema fans browse the movie posters, books, photos, and other cinema memorabilia at **Larry Edmunds Bookshop** (6644 Hollywood Blvd., Hollywood; ☎ 323-463-3273). For new and used books about Los Angeles, drop into **Angel City** (218 Pier St., Santa Monica; ☎ 310-399-8767). A vast selection of used books can be found at **Iliad** (4820 Vineland Ave., North Hollywood; ☎ 818-509-2665) and **Cosmopolitan** (7017 Melrose Ave., Los Angeles; ☎ 323-938-7119), whereas tiny, dusty **Aldine Books** (4663 Hollywood Blvd.; ☎ 323-666-2690) often has books (of which it has a curious selection) for sale by the pound.

Nerd alert: **HiDeHo** (525 Santa Monica Blvd., Santa Monica; ☎ 310-394-2820), **Golden Apple** (7711 Melrose Ave., Los Angeles; ☎ 323-658-6047), and **Meltdown** (7522 Sunset Blvd., Los Angeles; ☎ 323-851-7283) are premier comic-book shops.

Kid stuff

Sure, you can find kids' clothes at **Old Navy** (8487 Third St., Los Angeles; ☎ 323-658-5292 and 1232 Third Street Promenade, Santa Monica; ☎ 310-576-7787) and **Gap Kids** (1931 Wilshire Blvd., Santa Monica; ☎ 310-453-4551), as well as in department stores and malls, but why go generic when you can pick up way-out, cool, funky stuff, such as at rock-and-roll-themed toddler wear at **Meltdown/Baby Melt** (7522 Sunset Blvd., Los Angeles; ☎ 323-851-7283), a combination comic-book and kids' clothing store?

Sophie Fox (1308 Montana Ave.; ☎ 310-656-0238) and **Babystyle** (1324 Montana Ave.; ☎ 310-434-9590) dress Westside wunderkinds, whereas movie-industry offspring romp in clothes from **Sunset Kids** (8669 Sunset Blvd.; ☎ 310-659-4411). **Storyopolis** (116 N. Robertson Blvd.; ☎ 310-358-2500) has an amazing range of children's books, and **Puzzle Zoo** (1413 Third Street Promenade, Santa Monica; ☎ 310-393-9201) has smart, fun toys for kids of all ages.

Pet paraphernalia

Three Dog Bakery (24 Smith Alley, Pasadena; ☎ 626-440-0443) has tasty snacks for dogs, such as Pet-It Fours, Ciao Wow Cheese Pizzas, Beastro Biscotti, and Snickerpoodles made with ingredients such as whole-wheat flour, carob, and lots of love. It also sells pet accessories. **Fifi & Romeo** (7282 Beverly Blvd., Los Angeles; ☎ 323-857-7215) is a special store for special pets; check out the vintage cashmere sweaters ingeniously repurposed for Rover-wear, along with pet-and-person matching outfits (go ahead; we dare you) and precious pooch carriers. **Nature's Grooming & Boutique** (3110 Main St., # 104, Santa Monica; ☎ 310-392-8758) has everything from Halloween to Hanukkah and Christmas accessories for dogs and cats. It also has collars, leashes, and tasty treats, as does **The Wagging Tail** (1123 Montana Ave.; ☎ 310-656-9663).

Records and music

If you are one of the people who saw *Hi Fidelity* and wondered if those record-obsessed geeks really exist, come to super-sized **Amoeba Records** (6400 Sunset Blvd., Hollywood; ☎ 323-245-6400), and you'll realize that the movie was actually a documentary. People lined up four hours in advance for the grand opening of this used-music-hound's paradise (a highly anticipated branch of the Northern California–based store). The record store features tens of thousands of used (and new) CDs and LPs at bargain prices, along with rarities, oddities, and cool stuff. Just two blocks north, **Vinyl Fetish** (1614 Cahuenga Blvd.; ☎ 323-957-2290) is another stop for collectors and fans of Goth music. And if the geeks aren't in that two-block vicinity, you can bet that it's because they are pouring over the bins at **Rhino** (yes, the label was spawned from the store, 2028 Westwood Blvd., Los Angeles; ☎ 310-474-8685) and **Aron's** (1150 N. Highland Ave., Hollywood; ☎ 323-469-4700) — both of which offer good deals on used records and stock a wide range of new products. If new items are more your bag, **Tower Records** (8801 W. Sunset Blvd.; ☎ 310-657-7300 and 8844 W. Sunset Blvd.; ☎ 310-657-3344) and **Virgin Megastore** (8000 W. Sunset Blvd.; ☎ 323-650-8666) are giant superstores selling hot-off-the-assembly-line records, CDs, videos, and DVDs.

Sam Ash Music (☎ 323-654-4922), located next door to the Virgin Megastore in the same West Hollywood mall at 8000 W. Sunset Blvd., stocks musical equipment from amps to zithers, as does **Guitar Center** (7425 W. Sunset Blvd.; ☎ 323-874-1060), which also boasts the Rock Walk of Fame in front of the store.

Chapter 13

Following an Itinerary: Five Great Options

*W*e wish, oh how we do, that we all were European and therefore could enjoy weeks-long vacations. But the reality is that many of us are not European and only travel for up to a few days at a time. So here is how you can make the most of a brief visit and get the most bang for your buck.

Still, if you want to just plunk yourself down on the beach and never move, we won't say a word.

Los Angeles in Three Days

This itinerary provides a general tour of the city's highlights, giving you a taste of the beach, touching down at a museum or two, and delivering you to some of our favorite restaurants and snack spots.

Day one

Start by driving the **Sunset Boulevard Tour** (with or without the designated side trips) listed in Chapter 11, beginning on p. 176. It gives you the opportunity to see a little bit of everything, from the city to the sea, with a little cinema, a little music, a little Hollywood, a little Beverly Hills, a few scandals, a few stars, and the rich and the not-so-rich thrown in for good measure.

You can modify the tour to take up an entire day, or maybe even two, depending on how often you get out of your car to look more closely at the sights listed and how long you spend looking. Because the tour ends (or begins, depending on your whims) at the ocean, you can spend part of a day at the **beach.** In truth, between Sunset and the beach, you cover some of the very best of L.A., soaking up the history and the kitsch, and getting a glimpse of the timeless and a sense of what has passed.

Or you can take a more ambitious tack. Turn off Sunset on to Sepulveda Boulevard near the 405 Freeway and see the **Getty Museum** (see p. 165). But that would make for a pretty crowded day, so if you have just the one day, stick to Sunset and the water.

Do stop for lunch at **Zankou Chicken** (p. 144) on Sunset Boulevard, probably our hands-down favorite place to eat in L.A. (and now semifamous thanks to a song by Beck), and have some of its roast chicken with divine garlic-paste sauce. At the end of the day, have drinks at **Shutters on the Beach** (p. 235) (1 Pico Blvd.; ☎ **800-334-9000;** www.shutterson thebeach.com), the poshly casual Santa Monica hotel so loved by the beautiful people. Or continue those drinks over dinner at **Spago** (p. 142) in Beverly Hills, even if you can't precisely afford it — because perhaps you can't precisely afford *not* to if you want to claim that you "did" Beverly Hills.

Day two

Hit the beach, if you haven't already. Stroll the **Venice Ocean Front Walk** (p. 170), stopping to have a sausage at **Jodi Maroni's Sausage Kingdom** (p. 151; their original stand is here on the boardwalk, and they hand out samples of some of their gourmet sausages), or to buy a beach wrap or a pair of sunglasses or three. Maybe even wander the **Santa Monica Pier** (p. 201), being sure to take a ride on the 1920s wooden carousel. Sit on the sand and admire the water. Drive up Pacific Coast Highway and admire the ocean some more.

After you're done with the beach — if you ever are — go do the **Getty Museum** properly. Try to time it so that you're there at sunset, which is dramatic, of course, and tends to lead into a fragrant, balmy evening, especially in summertime.

As for food, eat whatever strikes your fancy — yesterday you had some of the best ethnic and nouveau food that L.A. has to offer, so you've covered, in just two meals (how efficient of you!), the most typical L.A. dining. If your budget is holding up, tonight you may want to head to Hollywood to try **Campanile** (p. 124) or West Hollywood to **Bastide** (p. 120) or Downtown for **Patina** (p. 138), considered by many to be the city's three best restaurants. (Though don't leave it to chance; call in advance for reservations for all of them.) **Jar** (p. 130), in West Hollywood, the newer restaurant from Campanile's owner, is somewhat more affordable.

This evening, try one of our **star-spotting** suggestions (check out Chapter 20); there are a number of bars ranging from cozy to trendy to classy, and even if a famous face fails to materialize, you will pass the time well. Or just admire the spread of twinkling lights, like jewels on black velvet, as Steve Martin said in his book *Shopgirl*. Take a vantage point such as **Yamashiro** (p. 279), a gorgeous Japanese restaurant situated in the Hollywood Hills, featuring average food, solid drinks, and some of the best views of L.A. around.

Day three

Today you have to make some choices. If you have kids and you aren't going to **Disneyland** (see Chapters 17 through 19), this is the time to visit **Universal Studios** (p. 168). Otherwise, head to the **Los Angeles County Museum of Art (LACMA)** (p. 166), perhaps the nation's finest comprehensive museum. While you're there, stroll around the **La Brea Tar Pits** (p. 166) and try to think of another city that has something so absurd and yet so wonderful right in the very center of it.

These choices will leave you nicely situated for some noshing on Melrose Avenue or Beverly Boulevard, where you have a number of choices, such as delightful cafes (perhaps takeout sandwiches from **Joan's on Third,** p. 131, for a picnic on the LACMA or Getty grounds?) or dinner at **Lucques** (p. 134) or the "small plates" restaurant by the same owners, **A.O.C.** (p. 118).

If your art tastes are more toward the modern, head downtown to the **Museum of Contemporary Art (MOCA)** (see p. 167). While there, you can also stroll **Olvera Street** (p. 168), L.A.'s oldest street and home to a rollicking Mexican-style market area. You can also experience the delightful chaos of the **Grand Central Market** (p. 130), where you can grab cheap, wonderful ethnic food. MOCA is also right by Little Tokyo, so you can dine on fresh sushi at **Sushi Gen** (p. 143). If it's a summer night, grab some of those cheap seats in the **Hollywood Bowl** (p. 268) for a perfect L.A. evening. (And don't forget to carry a box dinner to eat up there! Many of the aforementioned places will be happy to put one together for you, but you may have to order in advance.)

Los Angeles for Surfers and Beach Bums

It's awesome, dude. Unless, of course, it's righteous. Totally.

This is a day in which you spend your time seeing the sights and doing the activities that can only be described as quintessentially L.A. Be sure to wake up very early because right where Sunset Boulevard meets the Pacific Coast Highway (call it the "PCH," and you'll fit right in), there's a swell of tasty waves forming, and you won't be the only surfer waiting to ride a few of them. Want to be sure? Double-check the best spot for waves by calling the hotline, better known as **L.A. surf and weather** (☎ 310-578-0478), to get the current surf and beach conditions. As you head toward the beach on the bike you rented from **Spokes n' Stuff**

(1700 Ocean Way, Santa Monica; ☎ **310-395-4748**), don't forget to stop at **ZJ's Boarding House** (2619 Main St.; ☎ **310-392-5646**) to rent that wetsuit (which you'll need from October through May) and, preferably, a *long* surfboard. (The wider and longer the board, the easier the ride, and thus the better chance for you to actually stand up.) Think of it as renting a colorful canoe for a few hours. Make sure to pack a few power bars in your backpack to get you up and running.

Conveniently, one of the best surf spots is next to **Gladstone's 4 Fish** (17300 Pacific Coast Hwy.; ☎ **310-454-3474**), all the better to rinse the sand off your teeth with a few Coronas on its outdoor patio.

Whoa, dude, forgot you don't know how to surf? Bummer. You can always arrange for lessons at **Malibu Ocean Sports** (22935 Pacific Coast Hwy., Malibu; ☎ **310-456-6302**; prices vary), where they happily take on beginners (perhaps only so they can enjoy a few laughs).

After the morning batch of tasty waves, you'll be in the right frame of mind to do some power yoga, but not before you have your shot of wheat-grass juice, which can be found at **Jamba Juice,** a chain that makes smoothies with fresh-squeezed juices. There's a Jamba Juice on Santa Monica Boulevard and La Cienega, which is perfect, because you won't be late for yoga class at **Body and Soul** (8599 Santa Monica Blvd., West Hollywood; ☎ **310-659-2211**), where the Asian-inspired decor and non-gym-like setting mellow you out long before you realize that the Downward Dog pose you're holding is starting to burn.

Because you've, like, *totally* expended plenty of calories already, head south in your new Zen state until you hit the greasy love shack in West Hollywood — **Tail O' the Pup** (see p. 208). This classic California hot-dog stand is shaped like — you guessed it — a hot dog. You've seen this colorful building in a million movies; now go and enjoy the Mexican Ole chili dog at the "Tail," as the locals call it.

As your sports watch can tell you, it's almost sundown. So cruise back toward the beach for a relaxing hour to watch the dolphins and catch the sunset. Why not do it from the best seat in the house? Malibu Ocean Sports (yes, them again; see earlier in this section) rents a single kayak for around $15 an hour. While you're at it, paddle over to **Shutters on the Beach** (see "Los Angeles in Three Days," earlier in this chapter). It's the only hotel in Santa Monica that is actually *on* the beach — well, it and its hottie lil' sister spot, the **Hotel Casa Del Mar** (1910 Ocean Way, Santa Monica; ☎ **310-581-5533;** www.hotelcasadelmar.com). Stop in for a coffee or drink by the fire. Those ocean breezes can get chilly, you know.

End your day at **Chez Jay's** (1657 Ocean Ave.; ☎ **310-395-1741**), an old beachfront roadhouse in Santa Monica that was established in 1959. You can freely embellish your morning surf session up at the bar with the other surfers and dream about your awesome SoCal day.

Downtown in a Day

No really, L.A. *does* have a downtown, and although residents of certain other major metropolises might snicker at ours, it is getting better, and more urban-user friendly, all the time. Of course, urban friendly doesn't necessarily mean transportation friendly, especially in Los Angeles. If you can, try taking the Metro Rail Red line subway from Hollywood or Burbank. Exit at Union Station and return via either the Civic Center or the Pershing Square Metro stations (depending on how late you plan to stay in Downtown; check to make sure the trains are still running). If you are driving, you could begin up at Hope Street, near the **Music Center,** and pick an open-air lot that offers $10 all-day parking charges, but that's usually for parkers arriving before 10 a.m. Then you can take the DASH downtown bus (25¢ one way, including one transfer) if the following becomes too much to walk. Your only other option is to keep moving your car and possibly accrue large parking fees along the way.

However you do it, begin at either Chinatown or Olvera Street (the latter is directly across from Union Station). If you are starting at breakfast time, be bold and eat the way many Chinese people do — have some dim sum. You can get takeout at the **Hong Kong Low Deli** (408 Bamboo Lane; ☎ 213-680-9827) or go to **Empress Pavilion** (988 N. Hill St., Second Floor; ☎ 213-617-9898), sit down and have an adventure choosing from the passing little steam-carts. If you are getting a later start, begin with an early lunch at the flavorful **La Luz del Dia** (1 W. Olvera Street; ☎ 213-628-7495). Or if neither Chinese nor Mexican strikes your fancy, and you don't see any of the bacon-wrappedhotdog street carts around, pop into **Philippe's** (1001 N. Alameda, across from Union Station, between Olvera Street and the start of Chinatown; ☎ 213-628-3781), where they claim to have invented the French dip sandwich in 1918. Since you are already on Olvera Street — or in Chinatown, depending — spend a half hour browsing for some inexpensive souvenirs and gifts to take back home.

Now walk or drive to the **Geffen Contemporary** (152 N. Central Ave.; ☎ 213-626-6222), the first of the two branches of the **Museum of Contemporary Art.** One ticket gets you into both branches. Consider also viewing the excellent (and fairly small) **Japanese American National Museum** (369 E. First St, at Central Ave.; ☎ 213-625-0414), which explores the not-as-well-known Japanese immigrant experience in California, including the shameful internment camps of WWII. For lunch, walk down Central to Second Street, to the excellent **Sushi Gen,** or turn right on Second for a dozen Japanese options. Pick one, and try a bowl of noodles, some teriyaki, or better yet, whatever the servers recommend.

From here, either walk up Second Street or take the DASH up First Street to Grand Street, and go about two blocks south to **MOCA.** Too much art? You have several options: Keep walking down Grand to Fifth Street. At the corner is the **Biltmore Hotel,** a Beaux Arts and Deco delight that serves an afternoon tea under a soaring ornate ceiling. Next door, farther up Fifth, is **Central Library,** another old masterpiece that often has interesting programs. Either building is worth poking through. Or stay in the MOCA California Plaza and see if the little old funicular, **Angel's Flight,** is back up and running. (We hope so. We miss it.) It's a rattling thrill ride down a steep hillside that puts you on Hill Street (or you can just take the steps). Turn to the left and walk about a block to the **Grand Central Market,** a crowded, noisy hall of ethnic gastronomy, where you can have a strolling lunch of everything from burritos to pastrami.

Exiting back at MOCA, turn right on Grand, and walk down the block towards Second Street; across the street is L.A.'s first major landmark piece of architecture, the **Walt Disney Concert Hall.** Walk around it on Grand and First and see how many synonyms for "Wow" you can generate. Tours are offered daily if you want to see the interior. Keep going down Grand for one more long block and cross the street to visit **Our Lady of the Angels Cathedral,** the Archdiocese's multi-million-dollar, state-of-the-art house of worship. We think it's hideous; others think it's superlative. You decide. Head back up one block and across the street to the **Music Center,** and if you planned things right (that is, bought tickets already or picked a relatively unpopular production), you can enjoy a theater performance at the **Ahmanson** or **Taper** theater, or a music performance at either the Disney or the **Dorothy Chandler.** Have dinner before at **Kendall's Brasserie,** part of the Patina Group, or at **Patina** itself. If you're full, figure on eating after the theater, either a light snack in some of Kendall's cushy leather chairs by the windows where you may see actual urban dwellers walking by, or have a multicourse chef's tasting menu, deep in Patina's booths.

Los Angeles for Rock Stars

So you want to be a rock-and-roll star? Here's how to live like one for a rock-and-roll L.A. day. Read on.

Start your day late by rolling out of bed, preferably one in a fleabag crash pad (or, at the very least, the **Alta Cienega Motel,** where Jim Morrison regularly slept it off). Don't wash your hair. Get your motor up and running at the **Rock N' Roll Denny's** (Sunset Boulevard and Gardner Avenue). A Grand Slam breakfast is economical, which is good because you need to save your money for later. Of course, it may be lunchtime by now, in which case you may opt for a bacon-cheddar burger.

Head over to Melrose for some rock duds; your first stop should be the **SERIOUS store,** but if you have a bigger budget, try **Blest Boutique** (featuring many local designers). Or you can get a pair of nicely worn-in, strategically torn jeans at **Aadvark's Odd Ark** (7579 Melrose Ave.; ☎ 213-655-6769) or **Wasteland** (7428 Melrose Ave.; ☎ 323-653-3028). Head to the nearest **Rite-Aid,** or other large pharmacy, to stock up on **Wet 'n' Wild** cheap makeup (as little as 99¢); girls and boys both need their black eyeliner and mascara. Grab some serious eyeshadow, red lipstick, and a can of hairspray while you're at it. Check out the stores on Hollywood Boulevard between Cahuenga Boulevard and Highland Avenue, such as **LaLa** (6440 Hollywood Blvd.; ☎ **323-957-3170**), for footwear. Think excellent spike heels and platforms.

Head back to Sunset Boulevard and over to the **Guitar Center** (see p. 231), where metal and hard rock never, ever go out of style. You may wish you had a model girlfriend who would help you pay for that Marshall amp. Admire the handprints of famous rock stars, such as Aerosmith, and know that one day, your prints will reside alongside them.

After all that shopping, you will need some fuel to help keep up your energy. Dine on burgers and barbecue at **Barney's Beanery** (p. 120), located right near the **Alta Cienega Motel** (p. 82), or order the breakfast you slept through this morning at **Duke's** coffee shop (8909 Sunset Blvd.; ☎ **310-652-3100**), near the main rock clubs.

After dinner, it's time to hit the club circuit. Start with — and heck, end with — drinks at the **Rainbow** (p. 185), which is conveniently located right next to **The Roxy** (p. 272) and down the street from the **Whisky a Go-Go** (p. 185). Gazarri's, where Van Halen and so many hair bands got their start, is now the **Key Club** (p. 272). Finish up at **The Troubadour** (p. 273), where, if you don't like the band, you may just want to have a drink in the bar. Speaking of drinks, it's probably been a quarter of an hour since your last one, so it's time to go barhopping; **Boardner's** (1652 N. Cherokee Ave.; ☎ **323-462-9621**) and **Bob's Frolic Room** (6245 Hollywood Blvd.; ☎ **323-462-5890**) are waiting for you. After you are finished, you can roll your way home to bed (perhaps you should have someone drive you) — if you can find it.

Los Angeles for the Morbidly Curious

We have many suggestions for star-spotting scattered throughout this book, but we know of one tried-and-true method of getting within 6 feet of your favorite celeb. There is, however, just one catch; said celeb has to be dead. Even celebrities have to shuffle off their mortal coils some day, and when that day comes, they gotta go somewhere unless they opt for cremation (spoilsports). And that brings us to cemeteries. Morbid, perhaps, but more efficient and reliable than those Maps of the Stars' Homes hawked on every street corner, many of which are seriously out of date.

A number of books give thorough details as to who's buried where, including *Hollywood: Remains to Be Seen,* by Mark Masek (Cumberland House); *This is Hollywood,* by Ken Schessler (self-published); and the out-of-print but findable *Permanent Californians* (Chelsea Publishing Co.), by Judi Culbertson and Tom Randall.

For precise directions and photos of celebrity gravesites, go to www. findagrave.com. For now, here is a brief sampling. But please, wherever you go, be respectful, especially if there is a funeral going on or if there are people visibly mourning. Cemetery workers will probably help you, but not if they're busy for these are, after all, places of business.

The cemeteries

Hollywood Forever (6000 Santa Monica Blvd.; ☎ 323-469-1181), formerly Hollywood Memorial Park, is L.A.'s most user-friendly cemetery, thanks to new owners who understand the tourist appeal of their property. Maps and guidebooks, plus little ad hoc memorials here and there, help you find the graves of **Rudolph Valentino, Alfalfa** from the *Little Rascals,* **Cecil B. DeMille, John Huston, Marion Davies, Virginia Rappe** (the woman whose death ruined silent-film star Fatty Arbuckle's career), several **Chaplin family members** (but not **Charlie,** who is eternally resting in Switzerland), **Douglas Fairbanks (Sr., and Jr.),** and **Tyrone Power.** It's aesthetically appealing, culturally and historically significant, and right near the heart of Hollywood. It offers a gift shop full of the precise kinds of tchotchkes you want as mementoes.

Pierce Brothers Westwood Village Memorial Park (1218 Glendon Ave.; ☎ 310-474-1579) is small and tucked behind a movie theater in the very heart of Westwood. It's so crammed full of famous people that we don't know where to begin. Oh, wait, it's obvious: **Marilyn Monroe.** But here, too, are the gravesites of **Natalie Wood, Jack Lemmon** and **Walter Matthau, Truman Capote, Frank Zappa** and **Roy Orbison** (both are unmarked), **John Cassavetes, Bob "Hogan's Heroes" Crane, Will and Ariel Durant, Eva Gabor, Joseph Heller** (author of *Catch 22*), **Dean Martin, Carroll O'Connor, Donna Reed,** and **Dorothy Stratten.** The cemetery is visitor friendly, and if workers aren't busy, they're often happy to point out the park's famous residents.

Forest Lawn, whose founder, Hubert Eaton, more or less invented the concept of the modern-day cemetery — whoops, excuse us, *memorial park* (you know, flat, park-like, grave markers flush to the ground, boring) — has for years marketed itself as a nice place to visit, with worthy burial locations and self-proclaimed "great works of art" (the Last Supper in stained glass, most notably). So you would think that they would encourage respectful visitation of their more notable residents. Wrong. They try to pretend that they have no celebrities, and asking will get you turned away. Fear not; the aforementioned books and Web site will help you find your way to the gravesites of the likes of **Buster Keaton, Bette Davis, Liberace, Andy Gibb, Lucille Ball, Freddie Prinze, Stan Laurel,** and **Ozzie, Harriet, and Rick Nelson,** in their Hollywood Hills location — which is really in **Burbank** (6300 Forest Lawn Dr.; ☎ 800-204-3131). Over in the **Glendale** location (1712 S. Glendale Ave.; ☎ 800-204-3131), which is right next to Silver Lake, you can find **Jimmy Stewart, Mary Pickford, Walt Disney, Clara Bow, George Burns and Gracie Allen, Dorothy Dandridge, Nat King Cole, Chico and Gummo Marx, Spencer Tracy,** and **Sammy Davis, Jr.** In a mausoleum accessible only if you have a relative buried there (or can sneak in behind another visitor) are the remains of **Jean Harlow**, as well as **Clark Gable** and **Carole Lombard**.

Holy Cross Cemetery (5835 W. Slauson Ave., Culver City; ☎ 323-776-1855) is a little bit farther afield, but it's well worth the extra effort, with a hilly landscape that holds the mortal remains of **Sharon Tate, Bing Crosby, Bela Lugosi, Rita Hayworth, Jimmy Durante, John Candy,** and **Lawrence Welk,** among others. The office can give you a map.

Dens of iniquity

Having seen many of Hollywood's final resting places, you may, if you are of a morbid, or simply curious, turn of mind, want to visit the spots where certain luminaries became candidates for cemeteries. **John Belushi** took, perhaps wittingly, perhaps not, a speedball in Bungalow #2 at the **Chateau Marmont** (8221 W. Sunset Blvd.). You probably can't see the precise bungalow unless you rent it (and you can, if you have money enough), but you can go have a drink in the hotel's lobby and then slip into the pool area behind a guest. From there, you can peer into the foliage at the back of the bungalow. Please don't disturb the occupants, however.

Just down the street is **The Viper Room** (8852 W. Sunset Blvd.; ☎ 310-358-1880), the club owned partly by actor Johnny Depp. On the sidewalk in front of the door on Larabee Street is where River Phoenix succumbed to a drug overdose.

Where would a tour of morbid sights be without a couple of good murder scenes? L.A.'s most notorious in recent years is, of course, the **Nicole Brown Simpson and Ron Goldman murders.** Their bodies were found at 875 S. Bundy Dr. (the address has been changed to avoid looky-loos like you, but it's on the west side of the street, near the corner of Dorothy Street), while the bloody glove was found at the home of Nicole's ex-husband, football player **O. J. Simpson** (360 Rockingham, corner of Ashford). O. J.'s house was sold to pay his debts and has since been razed. Since his acquittal, O. J. himself has spent his time tirelessly searching for the real killers, down near his new home in Florida.

Prior to the Simpson case, the "Most Famed Murder Case" title was held by the **Manson murders.** Actress Sharon Tate and five others were found gruesomely slain at her rented home at 10050 Cielo Dr. in Benedict Canyon north of Sunset. After years of fruitlessly trying to sell the place, and enduring Nine Inch Nails' leader Trent Reznor recording an album there (he says he didn't know of the connection; we say we weren't born yesterday), the owners finally tore it down, and a new home stands on the property. The night after Tate and friends met Charlie Manson's girls, **Leno and Rosemary LaBianca** became victims in their home at 3301 Waverly Dr. in Silver Lake/Los Feliz (the number was changed to this to avoid sightseers, but the house remains the same). If you find yourself growing faint at this point, have something to eat at **El Coyote** (7312 Beverly Blvd.; ☎ **323-939-2255**), as did Sharon and friends the night before they died.

The house at 722 N. Elm in Beverly Hills is where **Lyle and Eric Menendez** shot their parents and then begged for the mercy of the court because they were now orphans. (Perhaps we twist their defense, but not by much.)

Morbid souvenirs

If you need souvenirs of your special day for the folks back home, you can support those wacky folks at the L.A. County Coroner's office and visit **Skeletons in the Closet** (1104 N. Mission Rd.; ☎ **323-343-0760**) — the Coroner's office . . . *gift shop*. Yes, you can pick up beach towels with body outlines, T-shirts, and more, all of it raising proceeds for a program wherein they scare the heck out of drunken teens by taking them to see the tragic results of mixing drinking and driving. A worthy cause and, of course, good conversation pieces.

Or stop in at **Necromance** (7220 Melrose Ave.; ☎ **323-934-8684**), where you can choose from a wide selection of animal and human bones (legally obtained, usually from kaput medical schools that have teaching skeletons for sale), jewelry and other ornaments, plus critters in formaldehyde, books about funeral customs, antique mourning jewelry, and other items appealing to the Goth and ghoulish crowd.

Chapter 14

Going Beyond Los Angeles: Five Daytrips

● ●

In This Chapter

▶ Oceanfront-dining in Orange County

▶ Lounging on Laguna Beach

▶ Lingering in Little India's shops

▶ Casino-hopping on Catalina Island

▶ Sportfishing in Santa Barbara

● ●

*I*f you get the urge to skip town and explore the areas surrounding Los Angeles, you have many fine options for great beaches, art festivals, and shopping centers. We've even included a few destinations that *don't* have their own television series.

Orange County

The popularity of the prime-time teen soap opera *The O.C.* has perked up interest in this once-ignored section of Southern California. It puzzles us, since we grew up feeling superior to those culturally deprived kids living "behind the Orange Curtain." Still, we have to admit the beach is *quite* nice down here, and there are a few towns that, although in some instances reeking to high heaven of Beverly-Hills-by-the-Beach attitude, nonetheless are worth paying a visit to. Our advice: Stick to the coast unless you're going to Disneyland (see p. 287).

Getting there

Coastal Route 1 South to Newport Beach. Or take I-405 south to the Jamboree exit west. Go about 5 miles on Jamboree, cross Pacific Coast Highway (PCH), and drive onto the island. Mild thrill seekers might want to try the ferry (take Balboa Boulevard off of PCH). It departs from the end of Palm Street north of Balboa Boulevard every few minutes, lasts four minutes, and costs 50¢. You can also take your car on the ferry, but that line can last an hour. Travel time from Los Angeles: approximately one hour.

Getting to the Fun Zone by freeway, take I-405 south to I-55 west; stay on the 55 as it becomes Newport Beach Boulevard, dropping you right at the Fun Zone. You can then ferry across to Balboa Island.

Seeing the sights

Newport Beach, where you can't afford to live, but don't feel bad, neither can we, has more than just the ritzy **Fashion Island** shopping center (401 Newport Center Dr., at Pacific Coast Hwy.; ☎ 800-495-4753 or 949-721-2000) with its over-200 stores including department stores, specialty boutiques, and high-end retailers. Well, okay, maybe it doesn't. No, really, it does; it's one of the largest small-boat harbors in the world. And that means seafarin' adventures. Start with the old-time carnival atmosphere of **Balboa Fun Zone** (600 E. Bay Ave.; ☎ 949-673-0408) with games, arcades, a Ferris wheel, and bumper cars. There's no entrance fee, though each ride costs a certain number of prepaid tickets. Check www.thebalboafunzone.com for details, prices, and hours (which vary). Within these six blocks is pretty much the center of Newport water fun, from the Pier to the Balboa Island ferry. At the **Pavilion Paddy,** part of the Fun Zone, you can take a 45-minute boat tour of the harbor ($6). You can also rent waverunners from **Marina Water Sports,** located in the heart of the Fun Zone (☎ 949-673-3372). Small watercraft are available for a leisurely tour of the bay, as are fishing boats and paragliding rides. The **Newport Harbor Nautical Museum** (151 E. Pacific Coast Hwy. ☎ 949-675-8915; www.nhnm.org. Open: Tues–Sun 10 a.m.– 5 p.m.) doesn't afford us enough opportunities to talk like a pirate, but it does have beautiful model ships, exhibitions of maritime paintings, and other exhibits around oceanic activities, and they support some of Newport's stunning regattas.

You must take a visit to Balboa Island (man-made, by the way), which has the feel of a small town, albeit a very expensive small town with yachts docked all about. (In the past, some owners of those very yachts included Shirley Temple, John Wayne, Errol Flynn, and Humphrey Bogart.) However, rental homes cost less per week than hotel rooms in L.A., if you can find one. Explore the quaint shops strung along the main drag, Marine Avenue, such as **Balboa Candy** (303 Marine Ave., ☎ 949-723-6099) and **Dad's Donut Shop and Bakery** (318 Marine Ave., ☎ 949-673-8686), which claims to be the home of the "original" Balboa Bar, a groovy kind of chocolate-dipped ice cream on a stick. Along with snack shops and forgettable restaurants, you'll find cute shops stuffed with great items to bring home. The **Barkery** (322 Marine Ave., ☎ 949-675-0364) has treats and toys for Fido, while art lovers can explore the many galleries. Little girls and their moms may like to bond over high tea or light shopping at **Teddy Bears and Tea Cups** (225 Marine Ave., ☎ 949-673-7204). A quick stroll to the **Balboa Island Museum and Historical Society** (502 S. Bayfront Ave. upstairs, next to the ferry; ☎ 949-675-3952) is worth taking, though it is only open Wednesdays and Saturdays. The whole island can be done in about two hours. Visit www.balboanewportbeach.com for schedules of events.

Dining locally

Dozens of seafood restaurants are in Newport, and they are all probably more or less the same. Consider having lunch at a local institution, the **Crab Cooker** (2200 Newport Blvd.; ☎ 949-673-0100), and giggle at the silly signage on the walls. **21 Oceanfront** is one of the most expensive choices, but boy do they have stunning views of the sunset (2100 W. Oceanfront; ☎ 949-673-2100).

Laguna Beach

Just ten minutes south of Newport, Laguna Beach has long been a favorite getaway for Southern Californians, and for many a good reason. Number one, with its clean beaches, beautiful homes, and terrific landscape, it is simply gorgeous. Number two, although it could be considered a sleepy little town — oh, all right, that's exactly what it is — the artist community here ensures that you're never at a loss for things to do. And finally, it's just a short road trip from Los Angeles.

The height of tourist season is between Memorial Day and Labor Day. Keep in mind, however, that Southern California usually gets hit with what we call June Gloom — overcast mornings that tend to burn off by mid- to late afternoon.

Getting there

From Los Angeles: Take the 405 (San Diego) Freeway South. Veer onto the 133 South toward Laguna Beach. This highway will become Laguna Canyon, which will then become Broadway and take you directly to Coast Highway. Or take the Coast Hwy 1 south to Laguna Beach. Travel time is between an hour and an hour and a half (though the coast route can take longer.)

As is true in much of California, relying solely on your feet may not be in your best interest. If you're staying in the village, you'll be fine, but if you like to explore, you'll need your car.

Seeing the sights

Laguna is best known for the **Festival of the Arts,** California's oldest art show (held annually since 1932), featuring over 140 local, award-winning artists and the **Pageant of the Masters,** in which real live people replicate classical and contemporary paintings. It sounds cheesy until you actually see it, at which point you think, "Wait, those people are alive? Those are people? This is so cool!" Tickets to the pageant sell out months in advance, so a good deal of preplanning is involved in attending, but tickets can be purchased at the gate for the Festival of the Arts exhibit. These events run concurrently for six weeks, July through August. Details can be found at www.foapom.com or call ☎ 949-494-1145. You can reach the box office at ☎ 800-487-3378 or 949-497-6582.

The summer **Sawdust Festival** is also on during this time, while the winter version of this arts and crafts fair arrives in November, just in time for holiday shopping. Expect to pay a minor admission fee (less than the cost of a movie, per person). For details, go to www.sawdust artfestival.org or call ☎ **949-494-3030.** On the first Thursday of every month, locals and visitors alike converge upon the eclectic group of galleries that line Laguna's Pacific Coast Highway for the **Laguna Beach Art Walk.** Some proprietorships rely solely on the merit of the art work to bring in a crowd, but others resort to bribery in the form a light snack and beverages. Adding to the festival feel is music, sometimes live and sometimes canned. Admission is free. Free trolley service from approximately 6 p.m. to 9:00 p.m. starts at the Laguna Art Museum. For more information, call ☎ **949-497-0716** or go to www.firstthursdays artwalk.com. Oh and then there's the **Laguna Art Museum** (307 Cliff Dr.; ☎ **949-494-8971**). You can see there isn't that much to say about that.

Whether you're a mountain biker, a couple in search of the perfect sunset, a walking enthusiast trying to burn off what you've been indulging in, or a family with children, the **Alta Laguna Park** will intrigue you. Begin by heading east on Park Avenue (the first light south of Forest at Coast Highway). You'll drive up a steep hill and pass many architectural delights until you can no longer drive forward at Alta Laguna; at that point, make a left. Continue over two speed bumps and then pull into the parking lot on your right-hand side. After parking, exit the lot the way you came in, only this time by foot and make a right. On a clear day, as you reach the picnic tables, you'll be able to see the coastline extending all the way from Palos Verdes to the north down to southernmost San Diego. Offshore, Catalina Island will seem much, much closer than 26 miles across the sea.

Or just walk around town and buy stuff. It won't be hard for you to find souvenirs. **Aero** (207 Ocean Ave.; ☎ **949-376-0535**) stocks crafts, candles, and soaps, some made by local artisans, while **Fawn Memories** (384 Forest Ave., Suite 7, ☎ **949-494-2071**) and its neighbors in the same shopping complex offer a variety of sea shells, antiques, and accessories for the home. **Peppertree Lane** (448 S. Coast Hwy.) is another shopping complex with a variety of small boutiques. And then there's **Shelby's Foot Jewelry** (577 S. Coast Hwy.; ☎ **949-494-7992**), where you can buy that toe ring and other fetching foot accessories you always wanted.

For more information about Laguna Beach, contact the **Laguna Beach Visitors Bureau** (252 Broadway, just east of Coast Highway; ☎ **800-877-1115** or 949-497-9229; www.lagunabeachinfo.org).

Dining locally

If staring at all that art makes you hungry, Laguna Beach has dozens and dozens of restaurants of all types, so feeding yourself won't be a problem. **The Sundried Tomato** offers delicious California cuisine, complete with a dog-friendly patio (361 Forest Ave., two blocks east of Coast Highway; ☎ **949-494-3312**). **Dizz As Is** has such generous portions that it remains a local favorite, even though it's a few miles south of the village (2794 S. Coast Hwy., at Nyes Place; ☎ 949-494-5250). **La Sirena Grill** has the freshest Mexican food in the village (347 Mermaid St.; ☎ 949-497-8226). Grab a burger at **Ruby's Auto Diner** (30622 Coast Hwy.; ☎ 949-497-7829 or 949-497-RUBY) or relax at a sidewalk cafe with a full bar at **230 Forest Ave;** (230 Forest Ave.; ☎ 949-494-2545).

Spending the night

Hotel Laguna
$$–$$$$ Laguna Beach

Slightly south of Main Beach, in the heart of the village, this Laguna Beach classic boasts the best rates for an oceanfront hotel. The view and food from the Terrace and Claes restaurants attract diners from all over, and The Lounge is a great spot to enjoy a cocktail or two.

425 S. Coast Hwy. ☎ *800-524-2927 or 949-494-1151. Fax: 949-497-2163.* www.hotel laguna.com. *Rack rates: $90–$300. AE, DC, DISC, MC, V.*

Inn at Laguna Beach
$$–$$$$$ Laguna Beach

On the ocean side of Coast Highway stands this family-friendly, comfortably appointed hotel. CD players and VCRs are standard in each room, and the hotel has an extensive VHS library. Adjacent to Main Beach and overlooking the town's infamous volleyball and basketball courts (where, if you're lucky, you may very well see a Clipper or Laker on his day off), it features a heated pool, a spa, and a sun terrace. Complimentary continental breakfast is served in your room.

211 N. Pacific Coast Hwy. ☎ *800-544-4479 or 949-497-9722. Fax: 949-497-9972.* www. innatlagunabeach.com. *Rack rates: $99–$599. AE, DC, DISC, MC, V.*

Little India

Artesia, a small suburb southeast of Los Angeles almost in Orange County, is home to Little India, one of the most vibrant communities in Southern California. Restaurants, textiles shops, jewelry stores, and groceries line the blocks of Pioneer Boulevard, providing visitors with plenty to do, see, taste, and buy. This is really just a half-day trip, but if you've fallen in love with movies like *Bend It Like Beckham,* and want to see what a real Indian immigrant community is like (or just want to buy some of the heavenly clothes the women wear), this is a most curious and interesting outing.

Getting there

Take I-405 south to I-105 east (toward Norwalk) and then merge onto I-605 south. Stay on the 605 for approximately 1½ miles and then merge onto I-91 east. Exit the 91 at Pioneer Boulevard. Turn right on Pioneer; Little India is less than a mile from the freeway exit.

Seeing the sights

Again, all you can do is wander the few blocks, glancing at anything that catches your eye — or nose. **Cottage Arts** (18505 Pioneer Blvd.; ☎ 562-860-1076) has a huge selection of beautiful tablecloths, bedspreads, and hangings made of sari material, silks, and patchwork, along with clothing, furnishing, and statues. More saris can be found at **Loveleen Sari Palace** (18507 Pioneer Blvd.; ☎ 562-809-2603), which also stocks clothes for men and boys, plus embroidered dresses and shirts, and **India Sari Palace** (18640 Pioneer Blvd.; ☎ 562-402-7939). **Ravissant** (1850 Pioneer Blvd.; ☎ 562-402-4005) has a large array of bangle bracelets, whereas serious jewels can be found at **Lord's Jewelers** (18608 Pioneer Blvd.; ☎ 562-809-9378) and **Shreeji Jewelers** (18628 Pioneer Blvd.; ☎ 562-402-1061). If you're daring, you can get your eyebrows shaped by "threading," a traditional method of plucking using a length of string carefully and swiftly manipulated by a board-certified cosmetologist at **Ziba** (17826 Pioneer Blvd.; ☎ 562-402-4131). The more squeamish may opt for *mehndi* temporary designs drawn on hands or feet using henna paste, also offered at Ziba.

Dining locally

Of course, you won't lack for opportunities to try Indian food here. Sweets and chai tea can be found at little snack shops up and down the boulevard (our favorite is **Ambala,** 18433 Pioneer Blvd, ☎ 562-402-0006 — look at the pretty colors on the walls and in the sweets case!), but for more serious meals try the vegetarian buffet at **Annapurna** (17631 Pioneer Blvd.; ☎ 562-403-2200) or **Udupi Palace** (18635 Pioneer Blvd.; ☎ 562-860-1950), where we recommend *rava dosa,* a type of Indian crepe. Or just ask someone in a shop where they take their relatives when they come for a visit (for Indian food, that is, not for American food). If you'd like to try your hand at cooking Indian food at home, **House of Spices** (18550 Pioneer Blvd.; ☎ 562-860-9919) has the supplies, including spices, aprons, and incense.

Santa Catalina Island

"Twenty-six miles across the sea, Santa Catalina is a-waitin' for me," goes the old song (though it's really more like 22 miles), and many a resident of Los Angeles has found this pretty little island a wonderful respite from hectic city life _ well worth the trouble it can take to get here. The island has been inhabited for 7,000 years, though its modern history begins with the Spaniards, who "discovered" it in 1602 and named it after St. Catherine. From there, it's the usual story of smugglers, miners, and squabbles over provenance, until one owner finally kicked everyone out in the mid-1800s and left the sheep in charge for the next 20 years. The island was developed as a resort by William Wrigley in 1919 (his hilltop mansion, a local landmark, was turned into a pricey B&B and can no longer be toured) and became a popular destination for the early stars of Hollywood before turning into a play area for the mainstream. There are full-time residents in the tiny (about a mile long) and only town of Avalon. Virtually the entire island is a nature preserve. Keep your eyes peeled for buffalo, descendants of ones brought over to perform in a Western filmed decades ago on the island. The Web site www.Catalina. com has a variety of useful information in an intermittently useful layout.

Getting there

It's an island. You've got two ways to go. Okay, three if you swim, but few people do that without intense preparation. You can either take a boat or a helicopter. The **Catalina Express** full-size catamaran (☎ 800-481-3470; www.catalinaexpress.com) leaves from San Pedro and Long Beach harbors (Long Beach has covered parking lots; parking is an additional charge per day, and the Web site has a link to a number of public parking options) and takes about an hour. They have several trips daily which cost around $44 for an adult, $34 for children. You should make reservations ahead of time. **Catalina-Marina del Rey Flyer** (☎ 310-305-7250; www.catalinaferries.com) just started running boats out of Marina Del Rey, a trip that takes about 90 minutes. They charge more for the boat ride (about $52 round trip), but parking costs less. Boats have their drawbacks; that's a couple hours out of your day, not including drive time down to the harbor of your choice. And though the tourism office brags that the ride during the summer is usually smooth (notice they say nothing about the ride during the rest of the year), every time we or anyone else we've known has gone, someone suffers from mal de mer. But take your seasick medication (those patches do work wonders), and you should be fine. The trip does give you the chance to watch the island loom into view, and often dolphins lead the way.

To Catalina Express: **Downtown at Catalina Landing:** Take the Long Beach Freeway (710) south into Long Beach. Stay to the left, follow signs to downtown, and exit Golden Shore. Turn right at the stop sign, follow around to Terminal on the right. Park in parking structure on the left.

To Catalina-Marina del Rey Flyer: From 405 Freeway, take CA-90 west toward Marina Del Rey. Turn left onto Lincoln Boulevard. Turn right onto Fiji Way. Ferry departs from the El Torito Dock directly in front of the restaurant.

You can also fly in a helicopter, but it's considerably more expensive, if more dramatic and certainly faster. **Island Express** (☎ 800-2AVALON; www.islandexpress.com) has 15-minute flights all day long for $132 plus tax round trip. They also leave from San Pedro and Long Beach. Take the 710 Freeway to the *Queen Mary* (follow the signs that say Port of Long Beach or Queen Mary; the freeway ends there) and enter the Queen Mary parking-lot entrance. Keep to the right and follow the signs saying "Heliport." They will take you to the last parking lot. Park on the right side, and the offices are about 200 feet from the parking area. You will have to walk across a service road, so be careful of the traffic. You can also take the service road on the right side of the Queen Mary parking-lot ticket entrance to the location for pick up and drop off.

Seeing the sights

There is a great deal to see and do in Catalina, though how long that will take entirely depends on your feelings about ocean activities, shopping, and beach-going. With just one day, you probably want to walk around the little town of Avalon — the chamber of commerce recommends you either rent a golf cart (but it's only a mile total) or take a tour to hear more local history, but we think you should just explore on your own. It's *small* for pity's sake! Save the formal tour for other options, like **an inland tour;** because the island is essentially a nature preserve, you aren't allowed to go into the interior unless you are with a tour or hiking. It's worth doing if you have an interest in native plants and rapidly vanishing, well-conserved ecological areas. And it's additionally cool because of the buffalo sightings. A **glass-bottom boat tour** is goofy fun, though the water isn't really clear enough to see all that much, so even better (though more expensive) is **a semi-submersible submarine tour.** There are two main tour companies on Catalina, both of which offer all these options and more, including help with other activities: **Discovery Tours (☎ 310-510-TOUR)** and **Catalina Adventure Tours (☎ 310-510-2888** or 310-510-0409). You can call in advance to make reservations, or just show up and ask them what they have going. Both companies also offer **casino tours;** Catalina's landmark building is that gorgeous round confection out on the point. It's not really a casino. When it was built in 1929, they used the word in an Italian sense meaning, roughly, "place of entertainment." It was originally a ballroom and a theater, and it was where all the glamorous people of the era came. You can take an over-priced tour, or go see a movie in the theater, or simply see if you can sneak in and take a peek. Once a month, an organist plays the historic organ before the shows, and sometimes they have other special screenings.

For the more outdoorsy types, Catalina does not lack for options. **Kayaks** are a great way to explore the bay as the island is stunning from the ocean vantage point. They can be rented from several locations: near the dock where the ferries dock, the Pleasure Pier, and Descanso Beach (behind the casino). They are the same kayaks wherever you go, and they rent by the hour. Lover's Cove, west of the main beaches, is a nature preserve and a must-see for people who love to **snorkel and scuba.** Catalina is a popular place for that sort of underwater sightseeing as the water is clearer here than in other nearby parts of the Pacific, but it will disappoint anyone who has snorkeled in Hawaii or the Caribbean. Also, the water here can be cold even in the summertime. You can rent equipment by the hour at Lover's Cove, the Pier, and other locations. **Parasailing** always looks like fun, even though we are too chicken to try it. Tours run through the day, from the dock where the ferry boats come in. You can also rent **jet skis.** For the more sedate among us, **paddle boats** can be rented by the Pleasure Pier. Just about all of the above can also be arranged through the tour companies.

Or you can just wander around Avalon, browsing in shops like **High Tide Traders** (☎ 310- 510-1612). It's a clothing store, it's a bait and tackle shop . . . it's both! A pretty cool store with cute clothes and access to fishing licenses, accoutrements, and local gossip — what more could you ask for? Many visitors want to just soak up the sun, but you better get there early; overnight guests come out around dawn to lay towels down in order to claim space on the small and easily filled beach. And no trip to Catalina would be complete without a visit to **Lloyd's** (315 Crescent Ave.; ☎ 310-510-7266), a local institution since 1934, where you can try to guess what flavor of salt water taffy this famous candy shop is spinning in the window that day.

Dining locally

Truth be told, Catalina is not a gourmand's paradise, but when we have the famous Pier Burger from **Eric's on the Pier** (on the green Pleasure Pier (☎ 310-510-0894), a hot dog and hamburger combo of wonder, we don't much care. For fine fish and chips, try **Rosie's on the Pier** (same place, no telephone), and it's not their fault Thomas Kinkade turned them into a sentimental piece of kitsch art. Some feel the island's best burgers are at the outdoor stand **Coney Island West** (215 Crescent Ave.; ☎ 310-510-0763). If you would rather not go the fast-food route, there's **Lori's Good Stuff** (501 Crescent Ave.; ☎ 310-510-2489) for healthy sandwiches and smoothies. Avoid the famous **Busy Bee** restaurant, where poor service, crowds, and lousy food have ruined a landmark. If you've taken the early boat, be sure to have breakfast (large portions of waffles and the infamous "Chef's Mess" omelet that can feed a hungry nation) at the **Pancake House** (118 Catalina Ave.; ☎ 310-510-0726), but not unless you are going to be early as they don't take reservations and it fills up. Try, if you can, to sit in Dorothy's section; she's been a waitress there for 30 years and is a treasure. **Antonio's** is the longtime local favorite pizza place; the original location (114 Summer Ave.; ☎ 310-510-0060) is small and amusing, with a "Sorry, We're Open" sign, while the newer one (230 Crescent Ave.; ☎ 310-510-0008) is larger and noisier, though diners do like to staple dollar bills to the walls. **Mi Casita** (111 Claressa Ave.; ☎ 310-510-1772) is a gem, with the best Mexican food on the island. **Channel House** (205 Crescent Ave.; ☎ 310-510-1617) has an elegant dining room and a more casual patio overlooking the bay, a good choice if you want a more expensive, but romantic and grownup, meal.

Spending the night

Please note that the addresses listed below are the physical addresses of the hotels. Please call directly for P.O. Box mailing addresses.

Hotel Metropole

This is a very popular hotel, with a pretty view, but it's also on a busy corner with a lot of shops. We wish it still looked like the original Hotel Metropole that occupied this same site, a Victorian pile that was *the* place to stay on Avalon. Rooms are mostly large (and some have ocean views, fireplaces, or balconies), with DVD players in most (and a whole library to choose from), plus Frette linens and other luxuries.

205 Crescent Ave., Avalon, CA 90704. ☎ *310-510-1884. Calif: 800-300-8528, Other: 800-541-8528.* www.hotel-metropole.com. *Rack rates: $125–$300 (includes continental breakfast). AE, MC, V.*

Pavillion Lodge

Fresh from a costly remodeling, they've done a nice job with bringing this funky old place into the modern world of competitive hotelery. Just steps from the beach, you can't beat the location. The newly done rooms are spiffy, clean-lined versions of classic mid-20th Century rooms, not precisely our style, but we do love the Frette bedding. It's a two-story structure with a grassy courtyard so you can lounge or play shuffleboard. A nice touch: They will store your gear, such as boogie boards and inner tubes, after your busy day at the beach, so no taking sandy playthings back to your tidy room.

513 Crescent Ave., Avalon, Catalina Island, CA 90704. ☎ *800-626-1496 or 310-510-2239. Rack rates: $94–$279. AE, DISC, MC, V.*

Snug Harbor

Each room in this cute little place is nicely done up in its own (vague) theme, and each is full of the sort of comforts that please us most (Frette sheets, down comforters, VCR, CD players, hot tubs). All have at least some ocean view. There is a continental breakfast, plus wine and cheese in the evening.

108 Sumner Ave., Avalon, CA 90704. ☎ *888-394-7684 or 310-510-8400.* www.snugharbor-inn.com. *Rack rates: $140–$350. AE, DISC, MC, V.*

Zane Grey

This pueblo-style building was the former home of the ultimate Western author, Zane Grey, back in the 1920s. Local folklore has it that the nearby Chime Tower, which rings every 15 minutes, was built by Mrs. Wrigley because she couldn't stand Grey's "oat opera" novels and wanted to disturb him at his work. The accommodations are nice, if funky, and lack clocks, TV, phones, and anything else that might "disrupt the serenity" of a guest's stay. Given said chime tower, this is very funny. It's also out of the way, perched up on the mountain side, so the views are fantastic, but it might be more remote (relatively speaking) than you would like, though that makes for very affordable rates. Plus the history is unparalleled. They do offer a courtesy taxi to town several times a day. There is a nice pool, a good continental breakfast, and, of course, most of Grey's books in the library.

199 Chimes Tower Rd., Avalon, CA 90704. ☎ *310-510-0966.* www.zanegreypueblo hotel.com. *Rack rates: $85–$175 (off season midweek $59.) AE, MC, V.*

Santa Barbara

Getting there

Santa Barbara is 134 miles southeast of Hearst Castle, 35 miles southeast of Solvang, and 102 miles northwest of Los Angeles. U.S. 101 is the fastest and most direct route to Santa Barbara from points north or south. The highway runs right through town.

Attention, southbound travelers: For a scenic detour that will add no more than a few minutes to your drive, pick up the **San Marcos Pass (Highway 154)** near Los Olivos, about 35 miles northwest of Santa Barbara. Highway 154 offers a gorgeous peek at ranch lands and forests before depositing you back onto U.S. 101 just north of Santa Barbara.

Seeing the sights

Downtown Santa Barbara is laid out in a grid and is easily navigable — though keep in mind that the coastline here generally faces south. When you're taking in a romantic ocean view, you're likely gazing in the direction of Santa Monica, not Hawaii as you might think, which can make directions confusing. Restaurant- and boutique-lined State Street is the main drag. It runs perpendicular to the coastline — which means it goes north-south — and serves as the east-west dividing line: Ortega Street, for example, is East Ortega to the east of State Street, West Ortega to the west. Cabrillo Boulevard runs along the ocean and separates the city's beaches from the rest of the town.

Even if you drive into town, you may want to leave your car parked for the duration of your stay because parking can be tough to find downtown, and weekend traffic can be a nightmare.

Santa Barbara is a joy for strollers, and most attractions are easily reachable on foot.

Another option is to hop aboard the **Downtown-Waterfront Shuttle**. These electric shuttles run along State Street every ten minutes and Cabrillo Boulevard every half-hour daily from 10:15 a.m. to 6:00 p.m. The visitor-friendly shuttles are foolproof; you can pick them up at designated stops every block or two along each route. The fare is 25¢ (free for kids under 5); if you'd like to transfer to the other line at the junction of State and Cabrillo, ask the driver for a free transfer. For more information, call the **Metropolitan Transit District (MTD)** at ☎ 805-MTD-3702 or the **visitor center** at ☎ 805-965-3021, or go online at www.sbmtd.gov.

For the best and most efficient overview, catch a ride on the **Santa Barbara Old Town Trolley** (☎ 805-965-0353; www.sbtrolley.com). These motorized red trolleys offer narrated 90-minute tours of SB's main sightseeing areas, including State Street, the beachfront, and Santa Barbara's mission. It's a particularly good bet if you're short on time and long on curiosity. The fee is $16 for adults, $8 for kids 12 and under. The trolley runs daily, and you can pick it up anywhere along the route. Your ticket allows for on and off privileges all day long. Call for the stop nearest you or check the Web site. **Santa Barbara Car Free** (www.santabarbara carfree.org) has information about a number of tour companies offering tours around town, sea and shore nature excursions (whale-watching, kayaking, scuba, hiking, and more),and trips into the wine country and beyond.

Hitting the beaches

Santa Barbara has a terrific collection of beaches. Most are flat and wide, with calm waters, gorgeous white sands, and lots of blanket space, even on busy summer days.

East Beach/West Beach: These sister beaches run as an unbroken strip along Cabrillo Boulevard for about 2 miles. **Stearns Wharf,** at the end of State Street, serves as the dividing line: The wide white sands to the east of the pier are **East Beach,** and those to the west are (you guessed it) **West Beach.** West Beach is fine, but East Beach is the real beaut. A grassy median and a palm-lined bike path separate it from the busy boulevard. On Sundays, a local artists' mart pops up along here. On the sand you'll find volleyball courts, a picnic area with barbecue grills, good facilities, and a landmark bathhouse from the 1920s. An excellent choice, and the best one for families.

Rent bikes, in-line skates, tandems for couples, and four-wheeled surreys to accommodate the whole family at **Wheelfun Rentals,** just up from the beach at 22 State St. (☎ 805-966-2282). Rates are $7 to $35 for the first hour ($12 to $60 for three to five hours), depending on the kind of wheels you want. Beach toys are available for rental, too.

Leadbetter Beach: On Cabrillo Boulevard just west of the harbor (turn left past La Playa School), this very pretty beach runs to Santa Barbara Point. Less protected than other local beaches, Leadbetter is popular with the local surfers when the waves kick up; fortunately, the waters generally stay calm for swimmers in summer. This is a great vantage point for watching boats cruise in and out of the harbor. The nice facilities include a sit-down cafe and limited, free, 90-minute parking. Otherwise, parking is $6 and up for the day.

Shoreline Park: Long, grassy Shoreline Park sits atop the cliffs just past Leadbetter Beach. Spectacular panoramic ocean views make it a marvelous spot for a picnic. A lovely, bench-lined strolling path leads to neatly kept facilities and a small playground. Parking is free.

Arroyo Burro Beach County Park (Hendry's Beach): Arroyo Burro Beach County Park is well worth the 2-mile drive from downtown. This narrow but long crescent-shaped beach nestled below the cliffs feels secluded thanks to its distance from the main road — and its status as a wetlands sanctuary for shorebirds adds an appealing natural element. The sands are dark but still lovely, and locals love 'em for sunbathing, shelling, and swimming. This beach makes a great choice for sunset strolling, too. The Brown Pelican restaurant is here, plus restrooms, showers, and free parking. To get there, follow Cabrillo Boulevard west as it turns into Shoreline Drive. Turn right on Meigs Road, then left onto Cliff Drive; go 1¼ miles and turn left into the signed lot.

Seeing the county courthouse and other cultural highlights

The county courthouse serves as a great starting point for the **Red Tile Tour,** a self-guided walk covering a 12-square-block area of historic downtown. Pick up the map and brochure at the visitor center (see "Gathering more information," p. 256). Allow 1½ to 3 hours to see everything along the route.

County Courthouse

In a city of stunning Spanish Colonial Revival architecture, the courthouse serves as the finest example of the vernacular. Completed in 1929 and taking up an entire downtown block, the building is utterly magnificent, and well worth a look. You can explore on your own. If the clock tower is open, you'll be rewarded for the climb to the observation deck with great views of the surrounding red-tile roofs and the ocean and mountains beyond. Don't miss the courtyard garden. Free guided tours are offered Monday, Tuesday, and Friday at 10:30 a.m. and Monday through Saturday at 2 p.m. — but times can vary, so call ahead.

1100 Anacapa St., between Anapamu and Figueroa Sts. (enter midblock from the Anacapa St. entrance to reach the information desk). ☎ **805-962-6464.** www. sbcourts.com/ *Admission: free! Open: Mon–Fri 8:30 a.m.–4:30 p.m., Sat–Sun 10 a.m.–4:30 p.m.*

Old Mission, Santa Barbara

Founded in 1786, this majestic hilltop complex is considered the queen of the California mission chain. Even if you're not interested in the Spanish Colonial and/or Native American history of California, it's well worth a look. The mission sets the architectural tone for the rest of Santa Barbara and offers spectacular views all the way out to the Channel Islands. The self-guided tour includes a very cool cemetery.

2201 Laguna St. (at Los Olivos St., at the north end of town). ☎ **805-682-4149.** www. sbmission.org. *Admission: $4, free for kids under 11. Open: daily 9 a.m.–5 p.m.*

Santa Barbara Museum of Art

This little gem feels like a private gallery — one with works by Monet, Picasso, Braque, Chagall, Rodin, and other masters. It contains some good 20th-century Californian and Asian art, too, and is well worth an hour. Even if you don't go inside, stop by to examine the mural recently mounted in a special display along State Street and read the thrilling story of its discovery (the artist, David Alfaro Siquieros, was a very important Mexican muralist) as part of a Pacific Palisades pool house, and the absurdly cautious and executed journey to get it to its current display position. (Here's a preview: They had to move the entire pool house to get it here.)

1130 State St. (at Anapamu St.). ☎ *805-963-4364.* www.sbmuseart.org. *Admission: $6 adults, $3 seniors, $3 students and kids 6–17, free for the under-6 set; free every Thurs and the first Sun of the month. Open: Tues–Thurs and Sat 11 a.m.– 5 p.m., Fri 11 a.m.–9 p.m., Sun noon–5 p.m.*

Experiencing the harbor life

At the end of State Street is **Stearns Wharf,** a 19th-century vintage pier that offers great views but is otherwise pretty touristy. Head instead to **Santa Barbara Harbor** for a genuine look at local maritime life. To get there, follow Cabrillo Boulevard west, past Castillo Street, and turn left on Harbor Way. While you're there, **Brophy Bros. Clam Bar & Restaurant** makes a great place to soak in the atmosphere, not to mention some divine chowder and oysters on the half shell (see "Where to dine," earlier in this chapter).

If you want to hit the water, **Stardust Sportfishing** (☎ 805-963-3564) offers half-day and full-day sport-fishing trips. **The Santa Barbara Sailing Center** (☎ 800-350-9090 or 805-962-2826; www.sbsail.com) has a wide array of excursions, including dinner cruises, afternoon sailing, and whale-watching (February through May).

If you'd like to cruise over to **Channel Islands National Park,** check out the offerings from the fleet at **Truth Aquatics** (☎ 805-962-1127; www. truthaquatics.com), which offers hiking, camping, and natural-history trips as well as fishing, diving, and whale-watching.

Shop 'til you drop

The main shopping area is the Paseo Nuevo, the new mall that was nicely built to copy the classic State Street Spanish architecture. You won't find many non-chain stores within this meandering landmark, but it's so pretty (splashing fountains, carts with jewelry and such), even usual mall haters don't mind. State Street between Canon Perdido and Ortega streets.

Boutiques abound along State Street and in the offshoot blocks, where you'll find such local treats as the **Book Den** (11 East Anapamu St.; ☎ 805-962-3321; www.bookden.com), a used bookstore.

Antiques hounds should seek out **Brinkerhoff Avenue,** a block-long passage 1½ blocks west of State between Cota and Haley streets that brims with vintage goodies. Most shops along Brinkerhoff are closed Monday and close as early as 5 p.m. or 6 p.m. on weekdays.

Also worth seeking out is **El Paseo,** at 814 State St. (between Cañon Perdido and de la Guerra Street), a charming arcade lined with boutiques and galleries that's reminiscent of an old Spanish street. It also happens to be the oldest shopping street in Southern California — and is across the street from the Paseo Nuevo (hence the name).

Touring the local wine country

In the past few years, Santa Barbara's wine country has really come into its own, with local labels achieving national prominence and wineries attracting visitors from the far reaches of the globe. If you'd like to explore the local tasting rooms — which include such familiar labels as Cambria, Firestone, Meridian, and Au Bon Climat — stop into the local visitor center here or in nearby Solvang and pick up the brochure and map called **Santa Barbara County Wineries.** You can also order a copy in advance by contacting the Santa Barbara County Vintners Association at ☎ **800-218-0881** or 805-688-0881. You can even download a version online at www.sbcountywines.com.

Gathering more information

The **Santa Barbara Conference and Visitors Bureau** (☎ **800-549-5133** or 805-966-9222) has a wealth of information, much of it in easily print-able form, at www.santabarbaraca.com. The **Santa Barbara Tourist Information Center** is just across from the beach at 1 Garden St., at Cabrillo Boulevard (☎ **805-965-3021**). This center offers good maps and other literature, and the friendly staff can answer specific questions. Open Monday through Saturday from 9 a.m. to 5 p.m. and Sunday from 10 a.m. to 5 p.m.

Dining locally

Baccio
$$ Santa Barbara   MEDITERRANEAN

Often, after we've tried to find a nice place to eat lunch in Santa Barbara and settled for something less, we recall Baccio and smack our heads. It's a most pleasant, reliable place, with fresh pastas, salads, and seafood dishes, all with a Mediterranean angle (read: predominantly Italian, but feta cheese creeps in, and either way, expect olive oil), all of it tasty, and all of it appearing at least vaguely healthy.

905 State St. ☎ *805-564-8280. Reservations accepted. Main courses: lunch $7–$8, dinner $11–$15. Open: Mon–Thurs 11:30 a.m.–11 p.m., Fri–Sun 11:30 a.m.– 10 p.m. AE, MC, V.*

The Habit
$ Santa Barbara   HAMBURGERS

Part of a family-owned business that goes back 30 years, don't miss this walk-up window, where you can get a fat, juicy, well-dressed char-broiled burger of such perfection that, well, let's just say the last one we ate was during a day that included a dinner at one of the nicest restaurants in town. And you know which meal we most want to repeat? They also have thick shakes, real fries, and even an ahi tuna burger if you are of that sort of mind. A great deal on sometimes a bit pricey State Street.

628 State St. ☎ 805-892-5400. Main courses: Everything under $6. Open: Mon–Fri 10:30 a.m.–8 p.m., Sat–Sun 10:30 a.m.–10 p.m. MC, V.

La Super-Rica Taqueria
$ Santa Barbara   MEXICAN

A legend that reaches well beyond the confines of this small beach town. People drive just to eat here, which explains why this unassuming taco shack has earned a whopping 25 (out of a possible 30) rating from the restaurant bible Zagat — no mean feat for a place where nothing costs over $6.95. Portions are small, so order generously — but at these prices, you can afford to. The prices also make this a good family-friendly choice. The soft tacos are divine, and the weekend brings freshly made tamales. A few casual tables allow for instant satisfaction. Expect lines.

622 Milpas St. (just north of Cota St.). ☎ 805-963-4940. Reservations not taken. Main courses: $1.30–$6.95. Open: Mon–Sun 11 a.m.–9 p.m. No credit cards.

The Palace Grill
$$$ Santa Barbara   CAJUN-CREOLE

This rollicking Creole-Cajun restaurant is a nice antidote to Santa Barbara's wealth of romantic bistros and one of our perennial favorites in town. Come for big portions of bold and fiery N'awlins favorites like jambalaya, étouffée, house-smoked andouille sausage, our favorite chicken Tchoupitoulas (a Cajun hollandaise sauce), and even Bananas Foster for dessert (though we prefer the pastry swan filled with ice cream, floating on a lake of warm chocolate). Saturdays bring a sax player and a singalong rendition, complete with toasting, of Louis Armstrong's "What a Wonderful World." Free valet parking is a nice plus, as are their baskets of warm muffins. The lunch menu offers significantly lower prices on some items such as the blackened filet.

8 E. Cota St. (between State and Anacapa sts.). ☎ 805-963-5000. www.palace grill.com. Reservations accepted Sun–Thurs (Fri–Sat for 5:30 p.m. seating only). Main courses: lunch: $5.50–$25, dinner $12–$25. Open: daily 11:30 a.m.–3 p.m. lunch; Sun–Thurs 5:30 p.m.–10 p.m. dinner; Fri–Sat 5:30 p.m.–11 p.m. dinner. Note: They also own the Palace Express, which offers a simpler, cheaper version of the menu, in the Paseo Nuevo. AE, MC, V.

Sage & Onion
$$$$ Santa Barbara   CALIFORNIA

A lovely, utterly marvelous establishment, perhaps the best restaurant in town, so good even the most snooty of foodie cities would be glad to have it. The menu changes seasonally (check out past menus on its Web site), but among the entrees from the past that have thrilled us are an English cheddar soufflé, silky Hudson Valley foie gras, venison with maple-glazed garnet yams, and roast pork with potato-apple-onion purée. It's a natty place but not stuffy, and it would be a mistake to miss it.

34 East Ortega St. ☎ *805-963-1012.* www.sageandonion.com. *Reservations suggested. Main courses: $24–$34. Open: Mon–Thurs 5:30 p.m.–10 p.m., Fri–Sat 5:30 p.m.–10:30 p.m., Sun 5:30 p.m.–9:30 p.m. AE, MC, V.*

Tupelo Junction
$$$ Santa Barbara   SOUTHERN

A delightful addition to the Santa Barbara dining scene, with whimsical dishes rooted in the South. It's moved from its previous location to a much more readily convenient one right on State Street. Try the messy barbecue pulled pork, with a splash of Jack Daniels in the sauce, and Gouda sloppy Joe; the hush puppies, with shrimp and more Gouda; the fried green tomatoes; or the lobster-and-sweet-corn chowder. Or anything, really, as long as you save room for dessert. Breakfast is served at lunchtime, so you can still get the biscuits, with traditional cream gravy. The place is small, so you may want to book ahead. Maybe the best restaurant in the price range in town.

1212 State St. ☎ *805-899-3100. Reservations recommended. Main courses: $9–$15 breakfast and lunch; $16–$28 dinner. Open: daily breakfast and lunch 8 a.m.–2 p.m.; dinner Wed–Sat 5 p.m.–9 p.m. MC, V.*

Spending the night

El Prado Inn
$$ Santa Barbara

Full disclosure: Author Herczog is married to the family who owns this hotel. Nepotism aside, there is much to recommend the El Prado. Start with a basic hotel (one regularly upgraded and renovated for additional guest comfort, earning a AAA three-diamond rating), albeit one that is family owned and operated — which translates to friendly and personal service — and add nice touches like a good continental breakfast, afternoon cookies, and even lobby mascots (one cat, one dog). The location is hard to beat for downtown accessibility: three blocks from the Arlington Theater and the start of the main State Street action, eight blocks from the bustling Paseo Nuevo, and 15 blocks from the beach. Ask for manager specials for even lower prices.

1601 State St. ☎ *800-669-8979 or 805-966-0807.* www.elprado.com. *Rack rates: $85–$180. AE, DC, DISC, MC, V.*

Glenborough Inn
$$–$$$$ Santa Barbara

This is precisely what you want in a B&B (well, maybe you would want lower prices, and we can't blame you): sweet rooms (each with its own personality — and they vary in size), with perhaps a fireplace or Jacuzzi or patio; a full breakfast (brought right to your room for breakfast in bed!); a welcoming atmosphere (including evening snacks such as homemade cookies); and a hot tub in the garden, for private use if you wish. It's a real romantic getaway.

1327 Bath St. ☎ ***805-966-0589*** *or 888-966-0589 (reservations). Fax: 805-564-8610.* www. glenboroughinn.com. *Rack rates: $125–$287 (some suites/cottages higher); rates include breakfast. AE, DC, DISC, MC, V.*

Harbor House Inn
$$–$$$ **Santa Barbara**

By far the best option on the hotel-heavy blocks of Bath Street. This hotel has only ten rooms, but the new owners stripped the rooms of icky wallpaper, repainted in soft colors, and then filled the rooms with all sorts of refurbished and gorgeous antiques (many of which belonged to their grandmother). The results are striking, such a change from the cookie-cutter hotel rooms around town and in very good taste. We absolutely love room 4. Rooms 1 and 10 are the smallest, and most have small kitchens. There is free wireless Internet access throughout the property, which does not have a pool. Add in a welcome breakfast basket full of unusual goodies, and the best prices in the nearby couple of blocks, and no wonder locals who put up their own families here begged us not to reveal their secret. We're sorry.

104 Bath St. ☎ ***805-962-9745*** *or 888-474-6789.* www.harborhouseinn.com. *Rack rates: $109–$255. AE, MC, V.*

Simpson House Inn
$$$$ **Santa Barbara**

AAA's only five-diamond B&B (in all of North America!) is simply spectacular. Hidden behind towering hedges on dazzlingly manicured grounds, this 1874 Victorian oasis feels like a world unto itself. Rooms are decorated to perfection and overflowing with luxuries, including the homemade cake that greets your arrival. Some of the main-house rooms have space issues (what with being converted maids' quarters complete with closets turned into bathrooms). We adore the Greenwich, Abbywood, and Plumstead Cottages (the latter, two stories) with their river stone, wood-burning fireplaces, soft beds, and big, oval Jacuzzi tubs — utterly romantic. The staff provides concierge-style service, and an evening hors d'oeuvres spread makes dinner redundant. Spa services are available, and they provide complimentary bikes for tooling around town. Very expensive, but it's money well spent if you're celebrating — and we'd stay here over posh resorts anytime.

121 E. Arrellaga St. (between Santa Barbara and Anacapa sts.). ☎ ***800-676-1280*** *or 805-963-7067. Fax: 805-564-4811.* www.simpsonhouseinn.com. *Parking: free! Rack rates: $225–$550 double, $525–$575 suites and cottages. Rates include full gourmet breakfast, evening hors d'oeuvres, and wine. AE, DISC, MC, V.*

Part V

Living It Up After Dark: Los Angeles Nightlife

The 5th Wave   By Rich Tennant

"That's what I love about Los Angeles. It's so creative and diversified. Where else could you see Macaulay Culkin in a performance of 'La Bohème?'"

In this part . . .

The Los Angeles nightlife scene is a thriving one. The city has first-class theater and music offerings, big-name sports events, and some of the most seductive bars and nightclubs in the world. If you want to dance, you can find any number of places to wiggle your toes; if you want to rock, you can discover those seminal venues where many famous bands began. If you want to sip a cold drink with the city laid out in front of you like a scattering of diamonds, you can find that, too.

Chapter 15

Applauding the Cultural Scene

● ●

In This Chapter

▶ Looking for the news on the latest shows and events

▶ Finding tips on hot tickets

▶ Relaxing at the theater, symphony, and opera

▶ Choosing a show at the big music venues

● ●

*L*os Angeles has plenty of culture, thank you.

The Inside Scoop

It has serious, major theater, often featuring highly recognizable names. (There are a whole bunch of actors out here, for some reason — oh, right, they work in TV and movies — and they often enjoy doing a theater stint between films or during TV-season hiatus; the work keeps their acting chops up, and it's a nice change of pace.) L.A. boasts a dazzlingly staged opera and a major symphony so significant that a whole new hall is being built just for it.

Where can you find these hotbeds of cultural activity? Like the sprawling city landscape, you find them all over L.A. Los Angeles has no theater district. The Music Center downtown is host to four of the most prominent venues in town, whereas the rest of the arenas, clubs, and music halls are scattered willy-nilly around the city. Most small- and mid-sized theaters and performance spaces can be found in the Hollywood/West Hollywood neighborhoods, but they certainly aren't restricted to these areas.

Finding Out What's Playing and How to Get Tickets

Although there aren't as many hot tickets in L.A. as there are in, say, New York City, you will need to do a little research ahead of time to procure tickets in advance for that certain something wonderful. We would hate for you to hit town and discover some great performance is playing only to learn that everyone else in L.A. gobbled up the tickets before you arrived.

Using the Internet

The Internet is your friend when it comes to finding information and deals on live performances in Los Angeles. Just about every venue we list has a Web site, enabling you to check out their schedules as much as a year in advance. For a more comprehensive look, try www.citysearch.com, which helps you find things to do, places to eat, and more. Or better still, type in www.lastagealliance.com, which lists all the productions on 210 stages, plus listings for whatever is closing and opening each week on L.A. stages, and links to half-price tickets. The highly perusable **L.A. County Arts Commission** Web site (www.lacountryarts.org) has a number of contacts and information about performances (including free music) around Los Angeles. A week or so before your arrival, check the L.A. Weekly Web site (www.laweekly.com) for its comprehensive calendar.

Reading the news

Take a look at the Calendar section of the Thursday and Sunday *Los Angeles Times;* the former gives listings for the upcoming weekend's events, and the latter some events months in advance. *Los Angeles* **magazine** may also be of help.

After you hit town, get a copy of the *L.A. Weekly,* a free weekly newspaper with extensive listings and trustworthy picks on what is going on that week. Although the Sunday *Los Angeles Times* is valuable, it's only available from Saturday night through Sunday night, while the *L.A. Weekly* can be found at many locations (including online) all week long. Right up there with the *Weekly* is the other free paper, *L.A. CityBeat,* which offers a "Seven Days in L.A." weekly calendar of suggestions for the best local events (though some of these can be daytime activities).

Buying your tickets

Nearly all events sell tickets through their box offices (call for hours), and just about every venue sells them online. Some venues sell tickets over the phone. Keep in mind that when you purchase by phone or over the Internet you often have to go through the dreaded ticket conglomerate **Ticketmaster** (☎ 877-870-4929 or 213/480-3232; www.ticketmaster.com). It's convenient, certainly (you can buy over the phone or at one of several Ticketmaster locations in the city, such as Tower Records, Wherehouse Music, and Robinsons-May department stores), but it also charges a per-ticket handling fee that can add anywhere from a couple of dollars to some outrageous sum ($15 or more) to the price of each ticket. If you want to save some dollars, buy directly at the venue's box office whenever possible.

You can almost always guarantee that about 10 percent of an audience won't show up, so you might take your chances on last-minute seats (unused house seats also get released just before show time), but we advise that you arrive at least an hour before the show begins so if others have the same idea, you'll be ahead of them on the wait list.

The Performing Arts in Los Angeles

Theater in L.A. gets a bad rap, and unjustly. Yes, it's true that the city can't compete with New York City on the level of Broadway shows (for one thing, L.A. doesn't have a theater district like the one on and around Broadway), or even on the level of theater found off-Broadway. But L.A. does have a plethora of small, 99-seat-and-under theaters that do some fine work for a modest cost to the audience member. There are too many of these theaters to mention — that's where the extensive theater listings in *L.A. Weekly* and the *Los Angeles Times* come in handy (see the previous section). Just browse and see what grabs you.

Theater: The big boys

Of course, Los Angeles has theater on a larger level, and that brings us to Downtown's venerable **Music Center** (the Performing Arts Center of Los Angeles County; www.musiccenter.org). Actually, it's four separate theaters: the spanking new **Walt Disney Concert Hall** (111 S. Grand; ☎ 323-850-2000) (see later in this chapter for description); the **Dorothy Chandler Pavilion,** which usually hosts classical music and opera (135 N. Grand Ave.; ☎ 213-972-0711); the **Ahmanson,** the midsize theater that runs about four plays a year; and the smaller **Mark Taper Forum,** with nearly in-the-round seating (both the Ahmanson and Mark Taper Forum: 135 N. Grand Ave.; ☎ 213-628-2772; www.taperahmanson.com). Together, they are known as the Center Theater Group.

Audio tours of the Disney Concert Hall are offered on nonmatinee days from 9 a.m. to 3 p.m. and on matinee days from 9 a.m. to 10:30 a.m. Prices are $10 for adults and $8 for students and seniors. Tickets can be arranged by calling ☎ 323-850-2000 or in person at the box office. We encourage you to take advantage of this, because the Frank Gehry–designed building really is one of the wonders of Los Angeles, inside and out. There's also a complimentary tour of the overall Music Center facility from **The Symphonians,** the volunteer docent organization. Tour times and schedule vary, so call ☎ 213-972-7483 for more information.

Some fine touring productions are likely to end up performing at the Center Theater Group. But original works, some of great significance, have also been developed and debuted on these stages. The Pulitzer Prize–winning *Angels in America* was developed through the Taper, which also recently helped David Henry Hwang rework Rodgers and Hammerstein's *Flower Drum Song,* currently headed to Broadway. Add to these August Wilson's *Piano Lessons, QED* (the one-man show about physicist Richard Feynman), the upcoming revival of the reworked *Into the Woods,* and how Kushner's *Homebody/Kabul* warmed up its cast at the Taper before heading off-Broadway, and you can see that New York theater owes a debt to L.A., whether it likes it or not.

One complaint of L.A. theater is that casting often takes the form of a beauty pageant. Not literally, but it does seem to favor beauty over talent; Hollywood, and Los Angeles by extension, values looks perhaps to the neglect of greater talent, while New York theater (to pick on the most obvious theater city) tends toward more regular-folks-type performers. The Taper seems to really enjoy having recognizable names (with good-looking faces attached) in casts, whether those actors are best suited to the role or not. Which is not to say that the acting is lacking, but sometimes you can't help but muse that there might well be some lesser-knowns or even outright unknowns who would be better suited for the parts. Still, it can be fun to see TV or film actors working on their live-theater skills.

Note that you can park at the Music Center parking garage for 30 minutes (free with validation) if you choose to buy directly from the box office rather than over the phone or online. At all other times, the rate for self-parking in the garage is $8, available starting at 5 p.m. for evening performances and between noon and 2 p.m. for matinees; if you park before noon, you're charged $16. See p. 269 for information on the free shuttle service to the Music Center from participating restaurants. At the heart of the ongoing Hollywood revitalization project is the **Pantages Theater** (6233 Hollywood Blvd; general information only: ☎ 323-468-1770; www. nederlander.com), a grand old movie palace (circa 1930) turned live venue. Tickets are only sold at the box office or through Ticketmaster (☎ 213-480-3232 or 714-740-2000) or Ticketmaster outlets throughout the city. It was recently lovingly restored by the folks at Disney, who made it the L.A. residence of their smash production *The Lion King* for quite some time before turning it over to road-company shows like *Mamma Mia!, The Producers,* and *Hairspray.*

Speaking of (as it seems we often do) the Hollywood revitalization project, the **Kodak Theatre** (located in the new Hollywood & Highland Complex; general information only: ☎ 323-308-6300; www.kodaktheatre.com) was built primarily as a permanent home for the Oscars. The theater is also intended to serve as a live-performance venue, taking the place of the Shubert Theater. For many years, the Shubert was the only other theatrical house of any size, apart from the Pantages. It was recently shuttered to make way for office buildings. The Kodak still doesn't do enough to say anything specific about it, apart from the fact that it looks real purty. You can check out the schedule for the theater at www.kodaktheatre.com. Tickets can be purchased at the box office or through Ticketmaster (see contact information in the previous paragraph) or Ticketmaster outlets throughout the city.

Theater: The little big guys

For smaller productions, the **Colony Theatre Company** (555 N. Third St., Burbank; ☎ **818-558-7000;** www.colonytheatre.org) is hard to beat. Established in 1975, it presents half a dozen or so plays (ranging from reliable classics to world premieres to revivals of overlooked and happily rediscovered gems of any vintage) annually of consistent and frequently award-winning quality. A couple years ago, it finally left its longtime, and admittedly time-worn, small facility in Silver Lake and moved to a new (and nearly 300-seat) venue in Burbank.

Ah, but let's not forget **The Actors' Gang** (6209 Santa Monica Blvd.; ☎ **323-465-0566;** www.theactorsgang.com), not that they would ever let us. A collection of theater-major friends at UCLA founded their own theater group back in the early '80s and they just kept going. It didn't hurt that one of them was actor-director Tim Robbins, who never forgot his friends or his roots and who helped support the Gang in their quest for renegade, bold, original productions and rethinkings of classics (Shakespeare and Chekhov may never recover; but then again, even the greats can use a little shaking up from time to time). This always raucous, always bold bunch may miss as often as it hits, but the Gang reaches high — and isn't that what art and theater are all about?

Highways Performance Space (1651 18th St.; ☎ **310-319-1459;** www.highwaysperformance.org) consistently offers challenging, intriguing, controversial, or just plain good, fun performances (performance art, spoken word, dance, world music, small theater, you name it) nearly every night.

Symphony

We won't say that there is but one game in town when it comes to classical music, but it's sort of true (certainly it's hard to get anyone other than the critics to recall any other options). Its name is the **Los Angeles Philharmonic** (135 N. Grand Ave.; ☎ **213-850-2000;** www.laphil.com), led by Finnish poster-boy Esa-Pekka Salonen. Despite a storied history, stretching back to the early 1900s, it's only been in the last generation under Solonen's baton that the Los Angeles Philharmonic has risen to true world-class status, ranking among the most accomplished and trailblazing orchestras. Now it has a house worthy of it, the **Walt Disney Concert Hall**. (See later in this chapter for description.) The Philharmonic's programs include a slate of classics, from the expected to the not-so, as well as pieces commissioned especially for the new hall, along with its annual slate of regular performances, celebrity artist recitals, chamber music, and visiting artists-in-residence. Prices vary according to the kind of performance. The tickets can be as cheap as $12 (up in the heavens) and as expensive as $80.

Opera

It may not be La Scala (but then, what is?), but the **Los Angeles Opera** (135 N. Grand Ave.; ☎ 213-972-8001; www.losangelesopera.com) regularly stages some extraordinary shows, generally earning across-the-board raves. No wonder; besides the depth of musical talent, the company has regular access to superb visual artists who are always creating sets and staging that sparks serious talk. One complaint might be that the company relies too heavily on tried-and-true classics; but then again, it also stages and performs the classics magnificently. Placido Domingo is the opera's Artistic Director, and he has been known to turn up as guest conductor. Hollywood director Billy Friedkin (yes, *The Exorcist* guy) recently directed Bartok's *Bluebeard's Castle,* so you can see that the company does have a curious range. Perhaps this is why opera has quietly become quite a little scene in L.A.; along with the expected older crowd, you can spot a few young punks (among other nonstereotypical opera-going types) with their Doc Marten boots sticking out under their velvet gowns. (This is also one of the few true dress-up places in L.A.; half the fun is going for the fashion show.)

Another reason for the opera's increased following may be that nosebleed seats are surprisingly inexpensive: Seats go for as little as $20 to $35, but that's for seating way up in the sky. The seats down front can go for up to $165 (suddenly distance seems like a nice thing). The theater also has a large screen showing translations above the proscenium, so don't worry about not understanding what's happening. The majority of the performances sell out, so check as far in advance as you can.

The Venues

For performances of all stripes, from rock to jazz to country to comedy, L.A. has a smart selection of classic venues. Plus, you can find more rock/pop/world music/whatever at different-sized venues around town.

The Hollywood Bowl
Hollywood

One of the absolute treasures of Los Angeles, the Hollywood Bowl, inaugurated in 1922, is one of the largest natural outdoor amphitheaters in the world (seating about 18,000). The Beatles played here. Leopold Stokowski conducted the Philharmonic here in the 1930s. The L.A. Philharmonic still holds regular concerts here. Barbra Streisand, Rudolf Nureyev, Elton John, Radiohead, Abbott and Costello, Monty Python, Billie Holiday, Judy Garland, Isaac Stern, and Leonard Bernstein have also played, danced, or yukked it up here. Summer nights at the Bowl (a distinctive shell-shaped bandbox backdrop facing out into a tiered seating level that begins with "boxes" and heads up into bleacher-type seats) is one of the best places to find entertainment in L.A., as the Summer Series (Playboy Jazz Festival, plus a wealth of shows ranging from Pops to pop, world music to movie music, classical to classics) kicks in. Tickets for regular performances, for seats way up high, can be ridiculously cheap (like $2!). Plus, dining is encouraged, making it a whole scene, as audience members bring picnics and boxed suppers (a number of restaurants around town offer special boxed meals just for Bowl-goers), with some going full-out elaborate (candles and wine) and others wolfing down burgers and the like from fast-food joints. And then everyone hangs out in the warm, fragrant night and wonders, "Why on earth don't I do this more often?"

Note: Parking for the Bowl is abysmal; there is parking, but it is limited and expensive. Nearby lots (run by the Bowl) offer shuttles to and from lots around the city where you park and ride, but these shuttles often don't leave until after the performance has ended. So if you want to sneak out early, you may get stuck. We strongly recommend taking the Metro Rail, which operates a free regular shuttle to and from Hollywood and Argyle, right next to the Hollywood and Vine stop. Unfortunately, the Metro Rail shuttles have the same problem as the Bowl parking shuttles — the shuttle stops during the performance. Regardless, we encourage you to visit the Bowl's Web site for parking instructions and tips — to say nothing of dining suggestions!

2301 N. Highland Ave. ☎ *323-850-2000.* www.hollywoodbowl.com.

The Staples Center
Downtown

The Staples Center is a brand-new, 20,000-seat stadium that was built for the Los Angeles Lakers NBA team. This state-of-the-art arena is also the home of the L.A. Clippers (NBA), the L.A. Kings (NHL), and the L.A. Sparks (WNBA). It's a premier venue for concerts, as well, showcasing such performers as Madonna and U2. The stadium is surrounded by parking lots and offers both preferred seating and general public. Costs for parking start at $20; see the stadium Web site for information on the prepaid parking service and directions to each lot.

1111 S. Figueroa St. ☎ *877-305-1111.* www.staplescenter.com.

Universal Amphiteatre and the Greek Theatre
Universal City and Griffith Park

If you can't sell out a venue the size of the Staples Center, you're likely to be found playing the Universal Amphitheatre or the Greek Theatre. The difference between the two, more or less, is that the former is indoors, and the latter is outdoors. Given our druthers, we like the Greek Theatre; built in the 1920s, the graceful and pretty theater is set in the middle of Griffith Park. It's a delight, but the parking lot is a nightmare. (We park in or around Los Feliz Boulevard and walk the 3/4 mile up to the theater. You will have company, so it's safe enough.) Bring a sweater in case it gets chilly. The Universal is fine, but it's located in the middle of Universal Studios, which means you have to park a considerable distance away — so you may want to forgo high heels.

Greek Theatre: 2700 N. Vermont Ave., Griffith Park. ☎ *323-665-1927.* www.greek theatrela.com. *Universal Amphitheatre: 100 Universal City Plaza, Universal City.* ☎ *818-622-4440.* www.hob.com/venues/concerts/universal.

Walt Disney Concert Hall
Downtown

As we said above, the Philharmonic finally has a venue worthy of it — and that's just the outside, with the waves of reflective silver sculpted by architect Frank Gehry, seemingly as a physical representation of serpentine melody and as homage to the namesake Disney aesthetic. Inside, it's no less a wonder, the main concert hall done up in billows of dirty-blond wood, a veritable cathedral to music. The acoustics make the term "state of the art" seem obsolete, to the point that in the inaugural year musicians have been feeling their way through the superior sonics. There shouldn't be a bad seat in the house, acoustically speaking, though the closer you are, the more likely it is you can hear the musicians fiddling about, as they clean their instruments between their parts. Yes, the sound is that good. (And having said that, note that whispers and coughs do seem to carry embarrassingly.) In addition to classical performances (including some works commissioned specially for the new facility), the Disney Hall has hosted such artists as folk-bluegrass star Alison Krauss and jazz piano master Keith Jarrett. (The acoustics have been criticized as being almost too good for nonclassical acts, though fine-tuning has been done to correct that.) The Disney complex also houses other, smaller rooms, including the Red Cat, meant for smaller avant-garde and cabaret performances (its first New Year's Eve featured neolounge ensemble Pink Martini).

111 S. Grand; ☎ *323-850-2000.* www.musiccenter.org.

Chapter 16

Bars, Stars, and Gee-Tars: L.A. at Night

● ●

In This Chapter

▶ Rocking in L.A.

▶ Seeking out the star bars

▶ Putting on your dance shoes

▶ Uncovering L.A.'s gay scene

▶ Finding the popular hangouts

● ●

*I*t's no secret that L.A.'s nightlife is *hot, hot, hot,* and you may find that getting past the velvet ropes is easier said than done. Don't worry, we have you covered. Whether you're just in town for the night or you have a few days to kick it, a trip to any of the following hot spots should give you bragging rights back home.

Before you venture out into the night, you may want to stop by such hipster clothing stores as **Blest Boutique** (1634 Cahuenga Blvd., Hollywood; ☎ 323-467-0202; appointment only), **Hot Topic** (6801 Hollywood Blvd. #345, Hollywood; ☎ 323-462-2590; www.hottopic. com), or the **SERIOUS store** (7569 Melrose Ave., Hollywood; ☎ 323-655-0589; www.seriousstore.com) for the latest in lounge pants, platforms, and rock-star duds. A studded belt and Led Zeppelin T-shirt will get you more play than pleated Dockers. And, in spring, if you're angling to look like Paris Hilton, try the pinky, fresh boutique **Dari** (1284 Ventura Blvd., Studio City; ☎ 818-762-3274). Dari is owned by Melanie Shatner (daughter of William), and she's got a very keen eye for rock-star chic.

Note that the parking rates get steeper as the week progresses (expect to pay up to $30 to park on the Sunset Strip Fridays and Saturdays). And it goes without saying that you should splurge on a taxi if you're partying without a designated driver.

For Those About to Rock

The rock scene in L.A. is thriving, with both new and veteran rock clubs. The area with the highest concentration of good rock clubs is the Sunset Strip in West Hollywood. It's well lit at night, and most venues have valet parking. The clubs listed below are open to all ages unless noted.

The Roxy
West Hollywood

Since the early '70s, this Sunset Strip club has been part of the celebrated Hollywood rock triumvirate that includes the Whisky a Go-Go and the Troubadour. Although its history includes storied superstar shows by Neil Young, Bruce Springsteen, David Bowie, and others, these days it tends to be the home of unknown local acts trying to break into the business. Check the *L.A. Weekly* and *New Times* concert ads to see what's playing here. Tickets will be scarce for big-name shows — and if you do get in, it will be crowded.

9009 W. Sunset Blvd. ☎ *310-278-9457.* www.theroxyonsunset.com. *Cover varies.*

Key Club
West Hollywood

At the west end of the Sunset Strip is the ultrasnappy Key Club. This post-modern rock club was built at the site of a legendary L.A. rock club called

Getting past the velvet ropes

Be prepared to encounter velvet ropes during your foray into club land. Here are some tips for getting past them:

✔ **Call each venue in advance.** Ask specific questions about gaining entrance. Sometimes, if a club serves food, the surest way to get in is to make dinner reservations.

✔ **Get there early.** The biggest key to lassoing yourself in is early arrival.

✔ **Forget about attitude.** Everyone's someone in Hollywood, and seasoned doormen have heard all the lines. What almost never fails is a smile and a bit of patience.

A word to any underage readers: **Forget about using a fake ID** at L.A. bars and clubs. You will get busted, and you will be publicly humiliated. L.A. is very strict about its entrance policies. Some dance clubs do have special nights for all ages or 18 and over, so you may want to call and check on age limits. And hey, there's always Bang! at **The Ruby** (7070 Hollywood Blvd., Hollywood; ☎ 323-462-7442), L.A.'s hottest and hippest youth dance party on Saturday nights for anyone 18 and over.

Gazzarri's, where bands such as The Doors and Buffalo Springfield started out. It's become a very popular destination for live music and late-night dancing, which is understandable. Compared with its neighboring warhorses, the bare-bones Roxy and the Whisky a Go-Go, the Key Club offers first-class comfort.

9039 Sunset Blvd., West Hollywood. ☎ *310-274-5800.* www.keyclub.com. *Cover varies.*

The Viper Room
West Hollywood

The music legacy of the Viper Room is unparalleled. Since its '93 debut, this black-hot nightclub has featured world-class talent on a weekly basis. You never know who's going to show up on stage; the club often schedules unannounced shows by big-name acts. You may find yourself taking a chance on a $10 cover only to find that the L.A. foursome Weezer is headlining. Hey, stranger things have happened. If you're in town on a Monday, check out the Viper Room's Metal Shop. Think fast bands, loose women, big hair, and loads of cocktails. It can get crowded, so you may lose sight of the stage even in such a small club.

8852 Sunset Blvd. ☎ *310-358-1881.* www.viperroom.com. *Cover $10–$15.*

House of Blues
West Hollywood

Fans of Southern kitsch and jambalaya will want to check out the original House of Blues, the first in the nightclub's ever-expanding chain (there's also one in Downtown Disney in Anaheim). It showcases a wide variety of live music, and the venue itself is worth taking a look at. It attracts top-flight acts from all pop and rock genres — including blues. Eric Clapton gave a special acoustic show here in the mid-'90s. Today, all kinds of not-just-blues-affiliated names pop up here. Sightlines from anywhere except the main floor can be iffy, and the chatter of Hollywood wannabes can compete with even the loudest bands, but the general quality of sound and production is high. The upstairs restaurant features a decent, Southern-derived menu, and the Sunday gospel brunch, though not cheap, is a great time, both for the food and the exuberant performances. From its colorful selection of folk art to the fanciful stage, the House of Blues offers a unique way to spend an evening.

8430 Sunset Blvd. ☎ *323-848-5100.* www.hob.com/venues/clubvenues/ sunsetstrip/.com. *Cover varies (there's no fee if you're dining, but you have to pay an additional charge to see any scheduled concerts).*

The Troubadour
West Hollywood

Just down the hill from the Sunset Strip is this veteran nightclub offering cutting-edge live music. The wood-grained interior is a relic from the days when this cozy Hollywood club showcased the Byrds and Eagles in the '60s and '70s. It was also a key stop for such quintessential L.A. acts as Van Halen in the '70s. In recent years, the booking has been something of a hodgepodge. There are a few rows of bleacher-like seats in the small balcony, but they get taken early most nights. Otherwise, it's mostly standing room on the crowded floor. The bar in front is often teaming with midlevel music-business staffers who should probably be inside watching the show instead. The all-ages venue books a wide variety of rock, punk, and alternative music.

9081 Santa Monica Blvd. ☎ **310-276-6168.** www.troubadour.com. *Cover varies.*

Knitting Factory
Hollywood

The Knitting Factory, the western outpost of the New York club known for challenging, avant-garde presentations, is a high-tech, if a little aesthetically cold, complex of bar-restaurant, main performance room, and small "AlterKnit Lounge." It doesn't go as far outside the mainstream as its eastern sibling, but it still offers an impressively eclectic array of top rock, jazz, and experimental acts. Macy Gray, P.J. Harvey, and Beck are among those who choose it for special intimate performances. Lately, though, it's been trimming its regular concert gig bookings in favor of more hip-hop and other dance music parties, pushing the live music off to the tiny AlterKnit Lounge space.

7021 Hollywood Blvd., Suite 209. ☎ **323-463-0204.** www.knitmedia.com. *Cover varies.*

Avalon
Hollywood

This Art Deco, ex-vaudeville theater on Vine across from the famed Capitol Tower recently underwent a multi-million-dollar renovation transforming it into a state-of-the-art facility. It offers weekly rock events, weekend dance clubs, and a private club-within-a-club called the Spider Room.

1735 N. Vine St. ☎ **323-462-8900.** www.avalonhollywood.com. *Cover varies.*

The Hollywood Palladium
Hollywood

From '40s swing ballroom glory to '90s mosh-pit mayhem, the Palladium, with its chandeliers and sculpted balconies, has long been a landmark venue. Lately, though, it's been used only sporadically for rock shows. So watch listings in the *L.A. Weekly* and *New Times,* or check the Web site for primary rock promoter **Goldenvoice** (www.goldenvoice.com, worth checking for other area concerts, as well), and be prepared to stand — or mosh!

6215 W. Sunset Blvd. ☎ **323-962-7600.** www.hollywoodpalladium.com. *Cover varies.*

Spaceland
Silver Lake

The Silver Lake nightclub that started it all still rocks. The live-music venue born out of an old discothèque is permanently art-damaged and not terribly fancy, but that's part of its charm. Surprise guests show up often during the week. Beck, Daniel Lanois, and Fiona Apple are among the name artists who have performed spontaneous sets.

1717 Silver Lake Blvd. ☎ *323-661-4380.* www.clubspaceland.com. *Cover varies. 21 and older only.*

Dragonfly
Hollywood

This way-happening rock venue in mid-Hollywood is at the heart of L.A.'s rock-and-roll hurricane. On Wednesdays, the Pretty Ugly Club takes over, cranking up the volume to 11. Its cohost, Taime Downe, singer for Faster Pussycat and the Newlydeads, brings in stellar rock acts from around the country. On Fridays, it's Rawk House, another hot spot for new music and cute rock-and-rollers.

6510 Santa Monica Blvd. ☎ *323-466-6111. Cover varies. 21 and older only.*

Largo
Hollywood

People are so devoted to this live music-and-comedy supper club that if you duck out of the show early, you may get the stink-eye. It's understandable — musical mad-hatter Jon Brion, composer and producer for such artists as Fiona Apple, did a regular residency, as did spouses Michael Penn and Aimee Mann, fast-rising singer-songwriting star Joe Henry, and Grant Lee Buffalo. (All are likely to return for further month-or-longer residencies). A variety of musical and comedy acts fills out the rest of the week.

432 N. Fairfax Ave. ☎ *323-852-1073. Cover varies.*

Thunderbird Saloon
North Hollywood

The hottest thing to hit the San Fernando Valley is the Thunderbird Saloon, a rockin' NoHo hang that's ripe with rock, alternative country, and rockabilly sounds. Its laid-back attitude and hip style make it worth the trip over the hill from H-town (about ten minutes from central Hollywood).

4657 Lankershim Blvd., North Hollywood. ☎ *818-766-4644. Cover varies. Open nightly.*

Temple Bar
Santa Monica

Those who want to get a taste of postmodern world beats can sample from the Temple Bar, a candlelit lounge with a friendly vibe. Its multi-culti bookings make it a sweet stop any night of the week. Note that its sister location, the Little Temple, has taken over the former location of lamented Silver Lake club the Garage, though the commitment to alterna-acts remains.

1026 Wilshire Blvd., Santa Monica. ☎ *310-393-6611. Cover varies. Open nightly.*

Malibu Inn
Malibu

Just a stone's throw from the Pacific Ocean, the Malibu Inn is a seaside joint with a fabulous weekly lineup of talent. From punk to mod to bilingual rock, this funky nightclub and restaurant has just about everything. We recommend its afternoon outdoor reggae fest, which takes place on Saturdays, rain or shine.

22969 Pacific Coast Hwy., Malibu; ☎ *310-456-6060.* www.malibu-inn.com. *Cover varies. Open nightly.*

Snazzy Bars

There's nothing like a night on the town at one of Hollywood's gorgeous bars. We handpicked some of our favorites based on style, comfort, and easy access.

Hot, sharp, and cool

One of Hollywood's hottest bars is **Beauty Bar** (1638 Cahuenga Blvd., Hollywood; ☎ 323-464-7676; www.beautybar.com), a luscious, pink confection with deejays nightly. The bar, which is designed to look like an old-school beauty parlor (the original in New York *was* an actual beauty parlor), serves martinis and manicures by appointment on weekends. No cover.

We love **Daddy's** (1610 Vine St., Hollywood; ☎ 323-463-7777) because it's a sharp-looking cocktail lounge with no attitude, comfortable seating, and super-nice servers. Although it's only been around for a couple of years, it feels like it's been here forever. It's a gem. No cover. Open nightly.

If you like the idea of chilling like a genie in a bottle, you'll probably enjoy **Belly** (7929 Santa Monica Blvd., Los Angeles; ☎ 323-692-1068; www.bellylounge.com). The artfully designed tapas bar and lounge is a favorite spot for singles on the prowl, and the soulful deejay's music adds to the mix. Every food item is priced at appetizer rates, but the portions are plentiful. Cover varies. Open nightly.

Sapphire (11938 Ventura Blvd., Studio City; ☎ 818-506-0777) is a gem of a bar a stone's throw from the studios. With its cushy booths, well-stocked jukebox, and the odds-on chance George Clooney might pop in, Sapphire really shimmers. No cover. Open nightly.

If you're looking to fall hopelessly in love, try **Falcon** (7213 Sunset Blvd., Hollywood; ☎ 323-850-5350). With its zebra walls and sweet-smelling herb garden, this classically designed restaurant and lounge hearkens back to the days when women wore white gloves and men sported fedoras. Falcon even has a private VIP area called the Valentino Room, and we hear the ghost of Rudolf makes random (and belligerent) appearances. Reservations required on weekends. Open nightly.

Dive bars and hipster hangs

The **Burgundy Room** (1621½ Cahuenga Blvd., Hollywood; ☎ 323-465-7530) is a dive bar in the heart of Hollywood, just down the street from the Beauty Bar. The deejays spin rock and punk. We advise you to arrive early on weekends or you may have to wait in line (the small bar hits capacity early). No cover; open nightly.

One of our favorite hipster hangs is the **Bigfoot Lodge** (3172 Los Feliz Blvd., Los Angeles; ☎ 323-662-9227). The bar is cleverly designed to look like a folk-art ski lodge, down to its hydraulic Smokey the Bear. But don't let the Sasquatch National Forest sign fool you: The only wildlife you'll find here are the hot chicks dancing on the bar top. Although the Bigfoot Lodge is located in Atwater Village, a quiet community about 10 or 15 minutes from Hollywood (and right next to Los Feliz) by surface streets, it's worth the drive. Cover varies; open nightly.

Swingers actor Alex Desert is an investor in **Vine** (1235 N. Vine St., Hollywood; ☎ 323-960-0800), one of the new breed of hipster Hollywood bars. It's located up the street from Three Clubs (see the next listing). Vine is a late-night fondue spot that also serves beer and wine. This low-key nightclub has a small dance floor and an upstairs lounge, and it is the only place we know of that serves a fondue recipe from Bo Derek. 21 and older; no cover.

At 10 years old, the **Three Clubs** (1123 N. Vine St., Hollywood; ☎ 323-462-6441) was among the first of the new wave of hipster bars that took Hollywood by storm in the late '80s and '90s. It still has that sizzle, with its dark interior, friendly bartenders, and casual-cool clientele. Some nights you may find a deejay lurking in the back room, where it's *really* fun to lurk. 21 and older; no cover.

The legendary **Lava Lounge** (1533 N. La Brea Ave., Hollywood; ☎ 323-876-6612; www.lavahollywood.com) opened its doors a month before the great quake of January 1994, and it's still shaking. The tiki-themed bar serves up exotic drinks adorned with plastic monkeys and mermaids, and you can't beat that with a swizzle stick. 21 and older; open nightly.

Martinis and stilettos

What if you could shop for shoes while sipping on a cocktail? Well, **Star Shoes** (6364 Hollywood Blvd., Hollywood; ☎ 323-462-STAR/7827) can grant you your wish. The beautiful bar doubles as a shoe store, with eye-popping displays of vintage shoes enticing customers in off the street. There's a dance floor for late-night frolicking and an easy, breezy, attitudeless atmosphere. No cover; open nightly.

One of the grooviest bars is the **Little Cave** (5922 N. Figueroa Ave., Highland Park; ☎ 323-255-6871). Located in L.A.'s outer limits (about ten minutes from Downtown L.A.) in an area known as Highland Park, the Little Cave is a favorite hangout of Eastside hipsters, rockabilly girls, and rock stars trying to drink under the radar. Cover varies. Open nightly.

Swingers' hall of fame

The hidden gem the **Room** (1626 N. Cahuenga Blvd., Hollywood; ☎ 323-462-7196) is located at the epicenter of the Cahuenga Corridor, but you need to pay attention to find it. Forget the address and walk south from Beauty Bar on Cahuenga Boulevard, cut through the parking lot on your left, and make another left when you hit the alley. You'll see a door and a stool and, depending on the night, a few people hanging out. As this particular area of Hollywood has gotten more popular, the Room has become a more treasured bar because it's still a quasi-secret despite its place in the Swingers' hall of fame. 21 and older; no cover.

Speaking of Swingers' hall of fame, don't forget to stop by the **Dresden Lounge** (1760 Vermont Ave., Los Feliz; ☎ 323-665-4294; www.the dresden.com) and give a thumb's up to Marty and Elayne, the jazz combo popularized in *Swingers*. We have known that lovely couple for a long time, and frankly, they're tired of being asked to play "Stayin' Alive." Do us a favor: Ask Elayne to play "Autumn in New York"; she'll blow you a kiss. Marty and Elayne perform Monday through Saturday. 21 and older in lounge; no cover.

Hot Hotel Bars

Hotel bars are more popular than ever in L.A. Maybe it's the proximity to all those crispy rooms. And hey, if you decide to check yourself in, you eliminate the drinking-and-driving equation all together. Not bad.

There is nothing standard about the lobby bar in the **Standard** (Standard Hotel, 8300 Sunset Blvd., West Hollywood; ☎ 323-650-9090), a whimsical hotel bar that's a big favorite among Hollywood scenesters. There's lots of outdoor seating. A general party ambience takes over on weekends. No cover; open nightly.

The Grafton Hotel boasts the very popular bar and restaurant **Balboa** (8462 Sunset Blvd., West Hollywood; ☎ 323-650-8383). Balboa is divided into two separate areas — a lovely modern restaurant to the left of the lobby, and a cocktail lounge to the right. To hang in the lounge, guests must enter from outside the hotel. No cover; open nightly.

Adjacent to the great Chateau Marmont lies **Bar Marmont** (8171 Sunset Blvd., West Hollywood; ☎ 323-650-0575), a picturesque restaurant and bar that attracts entertainment royalty on a nightly basis. On weekends, Bar Marmont is hosted by the famous bald drag diva Constance, who is liable to burst into song on a whim. No cover.

The famed Hyatt Hotel is sizzling with its new Asian-inspired bar/restaurant **Chi** (8401 Sunset Blvd., West Hollywood; ☎ 323-848-3884). Co-owned by Justin Timberlake, Chi specializes in dim sum and then some. With its '30s Shanghai-meets-*Bladerunner* motif and celebrity clientele, Chi is worth the trip. See if you can get on the elevator for a trip to the Roof, the hotel's private penthouse nightclub. Reservations required. Open nightly.

Drinks with a View

The Japanese restaurant **Yamashiro** (1999 Sycamore Ave., Hollywood; ☎ 323-466-5125; www.yamashirorestaurant.com), one of the city's legendary haunts, still has our favorite view, overlooking Hollywood in all its glory. It's terribly romantic, especially at sunset, and worth the long, winding drive up the hill. No cover; open nightly.

Cindy Crawford's hubby, Rande Gerber, knew what he was doing when he created **Skybar** (8440 Sunset Blvd., West Hollywood; ☎ 323-848-6025), a sexy indoor/outdoor bar with a poolside view of stars of both varieties. If you're not a hotel guest, you need to call in advance to make a reservation. It's worth the hassle. No cover.

Located in the Hollywood & Highland complex, the **Highlands** (6801 Hollywood Blvd., Fourth Floor, Hollywood; ☎ 323-461-9800) is a nightclub with a stellar view of Hollywood Boulevard in all its gritty, neon glory. Book yourself a reservation in the restaurant's Loggia area, which offers drinking and dining outside under the stars, and you can follow the action below.

The **Downtown Standard** (550 S. Flower St.; ☎ 213-892-8080) has a most sublime rooftop view. Conjuring up visions of '60s L.A., the poolside roof deck looks out over Downtown's skyscrapers, making you feel as if you're in a real city. Cover varies. Open nightly.

Latin Flava

The **Conga Room** (5364 Wilshire Blvd., Los Angeles; ☎ 323-938-1696; www.congaroom.com) is a wildly colorful nightclub, featuring bands from all over the globe. You can wine, dine, and unwind on its spacious dance floor, which stays cooking all the way to closing. If you want to splurge, the club offers VIP packages, which give guests first-class treatment in special seating areas. Hey, with such investors as J. Lo and Jimmy Smits, you never know who may be shimmying next to you. Cover varies.

The **Rumba Room** (1000 Universal CityWalk, Universal City; ☎ 818-622-1226; www.rumbaroom.com) is a crown jewel of the capitalistic mecca known as CityWalk — a shopping and clubbing area adjacent to Universal Studios. The upscale Latin dance club has live music on weekends and a hot roster of deejays. Cover varies.

One of L.A.'s best-kept secrets is **El Floridita** (1253 N. Vine St., Hollywood; ☎ 323-871-8612; www.elfloridita.com), a small Cuban hot spot. Despite its hole-in-the-wall status, big-time actors like Sandra Bullock and Jack Nicholson are regulars, both on and off the dance floor. Cover is $10; entrance is free with dinner. Open nightly.

Saturday Night Fever

If you find yourself in town on a Saturday night and you're feeling frisky, the following dance clubs offer memorable ways to sample L.A.

Saturday Night Finger at **Goldfingers** (6423 Yucca St., Hollywood; ☎ 323-962-2913; www.goldfingershollywood.com) is one sweet dance scene. Deejay and local rock legend Coyote Shivers spins '80s glam, rock, new wave, and punk, much to the crowd's delight. Goldfingers, a trashy nightclub with a rock-and-roll heart, is located in a section of Hollywood

---

Burlesque anyone?

Former actor Ivan Kane has a dirrrrty mind and that's just fine with Hollywood. Kane's two burlesque nightclubs, **Deep** (1707 N. Vine St., Hollywood; ☎ 323-462-1144; www.deeptheclub.com) and **Forty Deuce** (5574 Melrose Ave., Hollywood; ☎ 323-465-4242) put the cheese in cheesecake. At Deep, it's erotic city every night as women and men gyrate behind glass windows and on top of the see-through ceiling above the dance floor. The style is red-light district; the effect is red-hot. At Forty Deuce, Kane's created an old-style burlesque show, where all the dancers work it out with a live jazz combo. Everything's done with a wink and a nod, and it's a real treat for both women and men. Cover varies. Open Wed through Sat.

that's a bit divey, but there's parking to the right of the club's entrance, and everything is cheap, including the $5 cover.

The **Sunset Room** (1430 N. Cahuenga Blvd., Hollywood; ☎ 323-463-0004) is a super supper club for the well-heeled set that features hot deejays and a celebrity clientele. The cover is usually $20, but call in advance for guest-list inquiries. Dinner reservations are recommended.

Xes (1716 N. Cahuenga Blvd., Hollywood; ☎ 323-461-8191) is part of the next wave of L.A. nightlife and the most likely spot to trip over Christina Aguilera and/or Jessica Simpson on a Saturday night. The supersexy dance club, which features go-go gals in teensy-weensy bikinis, is aimed to get your love buzz flowing. The club's name is SEX spelled backwards, and it's pronounced EX-CESS. You don't need to be Einstein to get the equation: SEX + EXCESS = Good time. To get in on a Saturday night, call Bolthouse Productions at ☎ 323-848-9300. It's a handy number to have on speed dial because the company runs all of Hollywood's exclusive, star-studded dance parties. $20 cover.

Ivar (6356 Hollywood Blvd., Hollywood; ☎ 323-465-4827; www.ivar.cc). The owners of such tony Hollywood hot spots as the upscale dance club Nacional and the Cuban-themed restaurant Paladar came together to open Ivar, an '80-style discothèque with an industrial edge. Saturday's dance party is must-see boogieing, as the best members in L.A.'s dance community converge under one roof to get their groove on. Known to bust a move at Ivar on Saturdays are Britney Spears, Chris Judd, and Wade Robson.

One of the sweetest-smelling clubs on a Saturday happens at **White Lotus** (1743 N. Cahuenga Blvd., Hollywood; ☎ 323-463-0060; www.whitelotus hollywood.com), an ambitious venue with a spacious dance floor, famed sushi menu, and plenty of private nooks and crannies for star-sighting. White Lotus owners also operate the sharp Sunset Room and Pig 'n Whistle (both high on Hollywood's hot list).

Gay Faves

Just a couple of blocks from the hard-rocking hetero nightlife of the Sunset Strip lies the heart of gay Los Angeles, Santa Monica Boulevard, and what is affectionately (most of the time) known as Boys' Town. Most of West Hollywood is gay friendly, but the area near San Vicente Boulevard boasts the hottest of the hot meeting places, stores, restaurants, and, of course, nightclubs.

Every day of every week of every year, **Rage** (8911 Santa Monica Blvd., West Hollywood; ☎ 310-652-7055; www.ragewesthollywood.com) rages. The long-running gay dance club is a scorcher of a scene — aggressively young, pretty, and trendy — so you may want to stop at the gym and do a few thousand ab crunches before you go. Rage books a wide variety of deejays, who spin everything from progressive house to alternative rock. 21 and older. Cover varies.

Micky's (8857 Santa Monica Blvd., West Hollywood; ☎ 310-657-1176; www.mickys.com) is sort of "Rage Lite," with big crowds, a packed dance floor, and pretty men, but a little less stand-and-pose attitude. 21 and older most nights. Cover varies.

Other notable Boys' Town bars include **The Abbey** (692 N. Robertson Blvd., West Hollywood; ☎ 310-289-8410; www.abbeyfoodandbar.com), a trendy java joint and restaurant by day and a busy indoor/outdoor cruise bar at night; **Revolver** (8851 Santa Monica Blvd., West Hollywood; ☎ 310-659-8851), a video bar that hosts very popular karaoke events several nights a week; and — just to prove it's not all about the boys — **Girl Bar** at the **Factory** (652 La Peer Dr., West Hollywood; ☎ 310-659-4551) is L.A.'s hottest lesbian nightclub. The spacious dance party boasts women deejays, go-go dancers, and promoters. It's a weekly girl-power powwow. Fridays only. $10 cover. Also for the girls, **Club 7969** has a mix of gay and lesbian clubgoers and on Tuesdays has a female stripper revue (7969 Santa Monica Blvd., West Hollywood; ☎ 323-654-0280).

One of the most popular West Hollywood bars is located a couple of miles up the street from the Boys' Town epicenter but is worth the trek. **Fubar** (7994 Santa Monica Blvd., West Hollywood; ☎ 323-654-0396; www.fubarla.com) somehow managed to turn a narrow, hole-in-the-wall neighborhood bar into a hip, happening lounge with hot deejays (despite the lack of dance floor), a fun crowd of all types, and wild entertainment that verges on performance art. We once saw a drag queen attack a Christmas tree — you had to be there.

If the West Hollywood "What gym do you go to?" ethos is too much for you, you may be more comfortable in the Silver Lake area of Los Angeles, just east of Hollywood. Here's where you'll find the "rougher" trade frequenting bars like **Faultline** (4216 Melrose, Silver Lake; ☎ 323-660-0889; www.faultlinebar.com), L.A.'s premiere leather/cruise bar, and **The Gauntlet II** (4219 Santa Monica Blvd., Silver Lake; ☎ 323-669-9472; www.gauntletii.com), a hard-rocking leather/Levi's/fetish bar that draws a diverse crowd. Be warned, however, that although both are friendly, neighborhood-style bars, neither of these places is for the faint of heart or pretenders to the scene, so save your crisply pressed Versace jeans for West Hollywood.

If you're looking for something in between the extremes, you could try the newer **MJ's** (2810 Hyperion Ave., Silver Lake; ☎ 323-660-1503; www.mjsbar.com), a high-energy West Hollywood–style dance and cruise bar with a Silver Lake address. It draws an eclectic crowd with a little something for everyone. 21 and over. Cover varies.

Tourist Traps

The **Saddle Ranch Chop House** (8371 Sunset Blvd., West Hollywood; ☎ 323-656-2007; and at Universal CityWalk, 666 Universal Terrace Pkwy., Universal City; ☎ 818-760-9680; www.saddleranchsunset.com) has something for everyone. The country-themed restaurant serves whopping steaks, and its desserts need their own zip code. Good thing you can work it off on the mechanical bull. This place gets loud and rambunctious, just like a good spaghetti western. No cover; open nightly.

The geniuses behind the Saddle Ranch also created **Miyagi's** (8225 Sunset Blvd., West Hollywood; ☎ 323-650-3524; www.saddleranch sunset.com), a Sunset Strip sushi restaurant that's actually a three-level nightclub. Karaoke heats things up on weekends, and don't be surprised to find guests doing the "wasabi" on bar tops. Blame it on the sake. No cover; open nightly.

Te amo, **Morel's** (189 The Grove Dr., Unit H10; ☎ 323-965-9595). This French bistro and steakhouse is located smack in the middle of the Grove. Morel's offers live jazz on weekends, and its outdoor seating is not only prime people-watching terrain, it's perfectly in view of the Grove's center-piece — a dazzling fountain, which spews water every half hour to the tune of Dean Martin singing "That's Amore." Bravo.

Part VI
A Trip to Disneyland

The 5th Wave
By Rich Tennant

In this part . . .

*W*e give you the lowdown on the park that started it all — and no, you shouldn't miss it. We tell you how to find your way around the Disneyland Resort — which includes both Disneyland and California Adventure — and offer tips on the best times to go, how to avoid crowds, which rides are best for the little ones, and how to save money on the resort's offerings. We advise you on the best places to stay and dine, and give our oh-so-humble opinion on which rides will rock you — and which ones may just rock you to sleep.

Chapter 17

Finding Your Way to Disneyland Drive

- -

In This Chapter

▶ Gazing at the map

▶ Choosing the best time to visit

▶ Deciding how long to stay

▶ Buying tickets and special passes

▶ Getting there and parking

- -

*T*hey laughed when Walt Disney said he was going to build an amusement park. "Walt's Folly," they called it, just an expensive playground doomed to failure. Really. This happened. They said this. But Walt became rich, and they did not.

Disneyland opened in 1955. Although the park wasn't quite what it is now, either in content or in terms of the scary efficiency with which it runs, it was an instant hit, naysayers be darned. The bugs that plagued it in the beginning were quickly worked out, and the modern-day Disneyland is a well-oiled machine of legendary proportions, one that calls visitors "guests" and employees "cast members" and refers to off-limit areas as "backstage." See if you can catch a Disney employee — oops, we meant "cast member" — not smiling. And if you do catch one wearing a grimace, see if he or she is still working there a day later. Hey, we can mock it all day long, but we can't argue with the success of the place in terms of the lucrative dividends it has generated, the copies it has spawned (hello, Euro-Disney!), and, yes, the overall delightful experience to be had there on all but the hottest, most crowded days.

We can, however, complain about the constant evolution of Disneyland, as many locals do. Uncle Walt's original vision remains largely intact — a microcosm of the best of America, from small-town iconic images to the wonders of futuristic utopia to the best of mythology, all by way of Disney treatment, of course. The park was fairly simple to begin with; some of the most beloved rides (Pirates of the Caribbean, It's a Small World) didn't turn up until the mid-1960s, after they were entries in the 1964 World's Fair in New York.

Disneyland Resort

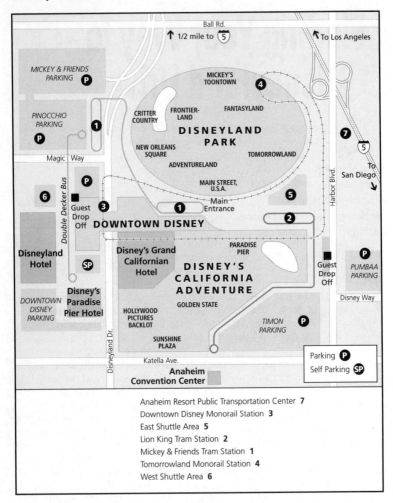

Ball Rd.

↑ 1/2 mile to ⑤   ↖ To Los Angeles

MICKEY & FRIENDS
PARKING Ⓟ

PINOCCHIO
PARKING
Ⓟ

❶

Magic Way

MICKEY'S
TOONTOWN ④

CRITTER   FRONTIER-   FANTASYLAND
COUNTRY   LAND

**DISNEYLAND
PARK**

NEW ORLEANS
SQUARE   TOMORROWLAND

ADVENTURELAND

MAIN STREET,
U.S.A.

Double Decker Bus

Ⓟ

⑥   ❸

Guest
Drop
Off   **DOWNTOWN DISNEY**

Main
❶   Entrance

⑤

②

**Disneyland
Hotel**   ⓈⓅ

DOWNTOWN
DISNEY
PARKING

**Disney's
Paradise
Pier Hotel**

**Disney's Grand
Californian
Hotel**

PARADISE
PIER

**DISNEY'S
CALIFORNIA
ADVENTURE**

GOLDEN STATE

HOLLYWOOD
PICTURES
BACKLOT

SUNSHINE
PLAZA

Disneyland Dr.

Harbor Blvd.

⑦

⑤

To
San Diego
↓

Guest
Drop
Off   Ⓟ
PUMBAA
PARKING

Disney Way

TIMON
PARKING   Ⓟ

Katella Ave.

**Anaheim
Convention Center**

Parking Ⓟ
Self Parking ⓈⓅ

Anaheim Resort Public Transportation Center **7**
Downtown Disney Monorail Station **3**
East Shuttle Area **5**
Lion King Tram Station **2**
Mickey & Friends Tram Station **1**
Tomorrowland Monorail Station **4**
West Shuttle Area **6**

Over time, rides have come and gone — one of the favorite games of longtime attendees is "What is your favorite Disney ride from the past?" You can always tell boomer attendees because they can still sing the theme from the House of the Future, which became history — as in completely demolished — in 1967. It is with no small measure of regret that they recall the house's space-age picture telephones, plastic chairs, and ultrasonic dishwashers.

There is even some concern among boomers, who grew up at the park and now bring their own children, about the changing face of Disneyland.

It's not just nostalgia for lost rides, it's also complaints about how fast-paced it's become and how it caters more, it seems, to the short-attention-span generation, with rides that do all the work for you rather than appeal to the imagination. This may be why, when describing the park, we tend to point out the small details, the simple pleasures that can get overlooked in the rush towards megaeffects.

 In honor of Disneyland's 50th Anniversary, the park's "Happiest Home-coming on Earth" celebration kicks off May 5, 2005. Expect some major parades, new attractions, retrospective exhibits, a souped-up castle exterior, and probably some special promotions. And, of course, even more crowds.

Introducing the Disneyland Resort

Disneyland has come a long way since its inception, from "Walt's Folly" to something so huge it spawned parks in Florida, France, and Japan. Here in California, it even expanded into a new park, the California Adventure, which, along with the original Disneyland, three hotels, and one big shopping center, comprises the sprawling complex known as the Disneyland Resort. To lure big kids, there are clubs and late-night offerings; to lure their parents, there are fancy restaurants and shopping. It would be too easy to dismiss the park as commerce over fantasy for Disneyland has always been about product tie-ins; it's just real slick about it. (A spoonful of sugar helps the medicine go down, don't you know.)

But to every inch of the place there is still given a tremendous amount of thought, detail, research, and, yes, imagination. No matter how it evolves, Disneyland (we still say that, even though it's Disneyland Resort) remains a place of delight where, even in the midst of souvenir stands and over-priced snacks, a kid bursts into pure giggles of joy because a mouse waved at him. And every time we go, we still play the game of "who can spot the Matterhorn first," and then shiver with pleasure when it appears for it means that we are almost there.

Deciding When to Visit

The best time to visit may be when you are able take a vacation from your job and the kids are off from school. If you're flexible with your schedule, though, a number of factors can influence your decision because Disneyland has seasons of its very own.

✔ **Busiest times:** Disneyland is busiest in summer (between Memorial Day and Labor Day), but it can also be crowded on holidays (Thanksgiving week, Christmas week, Presidents' Day weekend, Easter week, and Japan's "Golden Week" in early May) and week-ends year-round. All other times make up the off-season. During the busy summertime, Tuesday through Thursday is the best time to come; Friday and Saturday are the most crowded days.

✔ **Fireworks, shows, and parades:** If you want to see all the shows, parades, and fireworks, you'll have to come during the high season because scheduling is sporadic on off-season weekdays. Christmas brings its own special magic to Disneyland. The park is dressed up for the holidays, complete with giant decorated trees, wreathes everywhere, visits with Santa, and the Candelight Parade, wherein carolers from all over Southern California lead visitors in a special recital of the Christmas story.

✔ **Summer scorchers:** Consider the summer heat when deciding when to go. Scorching days in July, August, and September can make waiting to board a ride feel like a death march, with everyone crowding into available shady spots to find some protection from the heat, or lining up to buy cold drinks. Visiting during these months can be fine; just plan to take advantage of the indoor attractions during the midday heat. Your reward later on will be a pleasantly balmy evening, when being outdoors becomes a delight — though there can still be big crowds, with a heavy emphasis on slightly rowdy high-school and college kids.

✔ **Crowd-free days:** If you want to avoid crowds, visit on a weekday, preferably in November, December, or January (excluding Thanksgiving and Christmas weeks). You run the risk that some rides may be closed for maintenance (never more than three or four at a time), but visiting during this low season is the best way to maximize a single day.

✔ **First-quarter rains:** Southern California gets most of its precipitation between January and April, but only a sustained downpour should affect your Disney plans (some rides can, however, be closed on account of weather). If the forecast predicts rain, bring both a collapsible umbrella and waterproof rain poncho (or splurge on the cute Mickey Mouse ponchos that suddenly appear when the first raindrop falls). Even if you get wet, you'll enjoy the lightest crowds of the year!

The locals know the truth; the very best day to come to Disneyland is a midweek winter day with a slight drizzle. The amateurs tend to stay away — and you may find that you have the park virtually all to yourself.

Since 1998, the last Sunday in August is "Bats Day in the Fun Park," also known as Goth Day at Disneyland, which draws attendees from all over the United States and Europe. Over the years the Disney "cast members" have gotten used to the sight of fashionable Ggoths (some with baby Gothlings in strollers) flittering about the park in corsets, high heels, and sinister-looking makeup. For the unsuspecting, it can be a bit of a shock.

Deciding How Long to Stay

You'll want to devote at least one (very) full day to Disneyland alone. If you're planning to visit during one of the peak periods, crowds and wait times will limit the attractions you're able to enjoy in a single day, so plan to spend the night and re-enter Disneyland fresh the following morning. Depending on how you feel about California Adventure, you may want to set aside two days to experience both parks.

 Park Hopper Passes (see the following section) are a great deal for the money and don't require you to visit on consecutive days (if you want to break up your Disney stay with a day at the beach, for example). Families with small children will especially want a multiday option, regardless of the season. While surviving a marathon Disney day is a badge of honor for older kids, you all know that your toddler's naptime crankiness will eventually rear its ugly head.

All in all, we suggest allotting two or three full days for the Disney attractions, which gives you enough time to immerse yourself in the fantasy before moving on to the next leg of your California visit. (If you're staying elsewhere in Southern California and would like two days to experience the park, plan on spending the night at the park rather than driving back again the next day. Trust us, you'll be glad you did.)

Getting the Lowdown on Admission

At press time, admission to Disneyland or California Adventure — including unlimited rides and all festivities and entertainment — was $49.75 for adults and kids ages 10 and over, and $39.75 for kids ages 3 to 9 (kids under 3 enter free). These figures are given only as guidelines because new prices can pop up at any time. This price allows you admission to one park of your choice.

Disney currently offers the aforementioned multiday **Park Hopper Pass,** which allows the holder unlimited access to both Disneyland and California Adventure. A three-day pass is $124 for adults, and $94 for kids ages 3 to 9. Five-day admission costs $129 and $99, respectively. Though the passes must be used within a two-week period, the days spent at the park need not be consecutive, so this is a most practical way to go. We go into further detail in the following chapters, but there are good reasons to have access to both parks, provided you don't pay full price for California Adventure.

 Disney offers regular deals on ticket prices, especially during the slow winter months (when those three-day Park Hopper Passes go for less money). However, at press time, the Park Hopper Passes for use during the summer months were going for $90 each when purchased online (www.disneyland.com). So it's well worth your time to do some check-ing around, especially on the Internet.

Expect to pay a parking charge of between $7 to $10, which may be included in some admission packages. *Always ask* whether parking is part of the package before you buy from Disney.

Park hours

Disneyland is open every day of the year, but operating hours vary widely. Call for the information that applies to the time frame of your visit (☎ 714-781-4565). You can also find exact open hours, ride clo-sures, and show schedules online at www.disneyland.com.

Generally speaking, the park is open from 9 a.m. or 10 a.m. to 6 p.m. or 7 p.m. on weekdays, fall to spring; and from 8 a.m. or 9 a.m. to midnight or 1 a.m. on weekends, holidays, and during summer vacation periods. If you'd like to receive a copy of the park's "Vacation Planner" brochure to orient yourself before you go, call ☎ 800-225-2024.

Buying in advance can be an enormous timesaver. If you plan to arrive during a busy time (when the gates open in the morning or between 11 a.m. and 2 p.m.), purchasing your tickets in advance and getting a jump on the crowds at the ticket counters is your best bet. You can buy your tickets through the Disneyland Web site, at Disney stores through-out the United States, or by calling the mail-order line (☎ 714-781-4043). Many area hotels also sell tickets (including whatever special deal is being offered at the time) through an arrangement with Disney.

Theart of the (package) deal

If you intend to spend two or more nights in Disney territory, investigat-ing the available package options can pay off. Start by contacting your hotel (even those in Los Angeles or San Diego) to see whether it offers Disneyland admission packages. Some of the inclusive airline vacation packages include admission to Disneyland.

In addition, check with the official Disney agency, **Walt Disney Travel Co.** (☎ 800-225-2024 or 714-520-5060; www.disneyland.com), whose pack-ages are value-packed time- and money-savers with lots of built-in flexibil-ity. You can log on to the Web site and click on "Book Your Vacation" to peruse package details, take a virtual tour of participating hotel proper-ties, and get online price quotes for customized, date-specific packages.

Hotel choices range from the official Disney hotels to one of 35 neighbor hotels in every price range (Chapter 18 has our hotel recommendations). A wide range of available extras includes admission to other Southern California attractions, guided tours (such as **Universal Studios** or a Tijuana shopping trip), and behind-the-scenes Disneyland tours, all in limitless combinations. Rates are highly competitive, especially consider-ing that each package may include multiday admission, early park entry, and free parking (if you choose a Disney hotel), plus keepsake souvenirs and coupon books. If you want to add air transportation or car rental, the Disney Travel Co. can make those arrangements, too.

Getting to Disneyland

Disneyland is located in the heart of Anaheim in Orange County, about 30 miles south of Los Angeles and 98 miles north of San Diego. To get there from either city, follow I-5 until you see signs for Disneyland; dedicated off-ramps from both directions lead directly to the park's parking lots and surrounding streets.

If you'd rather wing it, **Los Angeles International Airport (LAX)** serves as the region's major airport. It's about 30 miles away from the park. You can rent a car at the airport and drive to Anaheim, or you can take advantage of the many public-transportation services at LAX. Note that there are a number of shuttles just for Disneyland. They cost around $20, but haggling can be done.

If you'd rather fly directly into Anaheim from another state or another California city, the nearest airport is **John Wayne International Airport** in Irvine. It is 15 miles from Disneyland at the intersection of I-405 and Highway 55 (☎ **949-252-5200**; www.ocair.com). Most national airlines and major rental-car agencies serve the airport. To reach Anaheim from the airport, rent a car and take Highway 55 east and then I-5 north to the Disneyland exit.

You can also catch a ride with **American Taxi** (☎ **888-482-9466**), whose cabs queue up at the Ground Transportation Center on the lower level; reservations are not necessary. Expect the fare to Disneyland to run about $26. If only two of you are making the trip, though, consider using **Super Shuttle** (☎ **800-BLUE-VAN**; www.supershuttle.com), which charges $10 per person. Advance reservations are recommended.

Before you pay for a taxi or shuttle service, ask if your Anaheim hotel offers airport transportation when you make your reservation.

Driving to Disneyland

Remember to take rush hour into consideration if you're driving to the park. The park opens fairly early — 9 a.m., in some cases — so, if you're going to be there, ticket in hand, when the gates swing open, you need to leave the L.A. area perhaps as early as 7 a.m. If you leave later, you may get stuck in traffic.

Parking

The parking is now a slightly more complicated concern at Disneyland. Before California Adventure was built, it was all pretty straightforward. Visitors simply parked in a very large lot, with designated areas named after Disney characters, serviced by a tram. But the lot became California Adventure, so now it's a whole new parking experience.

Regulars feel that the **Mickey and Friends parking structure** (perhaps the largest indoor parking lot in the country) is the best bet. It's well lit and easily accessible. However, it is also the first choice of everyone coming to the park, so you are going to have to contend with lines. Still, it's better than the **Timon and Simba lots,** which use a tram to ferry visitors to the parks. But the Timon and Simba lots are better than the **Pumba lot,** which is strictly for overflow and doesn't currently have any kind of transport. If you use the latter, prepare for a long walk (though it might be a good place to go if you fear waiting in car lines more than walking).

Chapter 18

Where to Stay and Dine in Disneyland

In This Chapter

▶ Getting a "Good Neighbor Package" hotel deal
▶ Picking the right hotel, from budget to upscale to "castle-themed"
▶ Finding decent dining spots inside the parks
▶ Munching on authentic Cajun in Downtown Disney

*H*ere we give our advice on where to stay in and around the parks, plus tips on the best places to eat to fuel yet another day of Disneyland fun.

Where to Stay

There's a funny story about Disneyland. Back when Uncle Walt built his park, he knew that people would want to stay nearby, so he built a hotel, the **Disneyland Hotel,** inside the park. The park and hotel were a success, but Disney, in perhaps his only misstep, only bought enough land for his more-or-less immediate purposes. As a result, Disney lost business to savvy hotel owners who put up motel lodges right at the very edges of the park. Disney corrected this error when he created Walt Disney World in Florida by buying up pretty much all the land for several states in every direction from the main park.

Up until recently there was only one Disney-associated hotel, along with a whole bunch of tacky motor courts (many of which were themed to seem associated with Disney — "Fairy Tale Village," say, or "Robin Hood Courts"). Now, there are three (but only three) Disney-located and Disney-run hotels, but loads of nonaffiliated accommodations lie just at the outskirts of the park, mostly of the chain variety; you can more or less close your eyes and pick one and not go wrong. In fact, many of the hotels outside the property are very nice indeed — a Hilton, a Sheraton, a Doubletree — and they cost about the same as Disney's sensational **Grand Californian** (though they pale in comparison).

Disney has a relationship with a number of hotels in the area. Together they offer a package called the "Good Neighbor Package." You can purchase Disneyland tickets from the participating hotel at the regular price, thus saving yourself from having to stand in potentially very long lines at the parks. If Disney is offering any special ticket discounts during the time of your stay, the hotels will offer the same discount. (You must be staying at these hotels to purchase tickets from them.)

One of the advantages to staying at a Disney Resort hotel is that guests at Paradise Pier and the Grand Californian have their own entrance to California Adventure, thus saving them time in line — plus park guests have unlimited in-and-out privileges, so cranky kids (and adults) can take midday breaks at the hotel.

Disneyland hotels

For a breakdown of what the $ symbols mean, see Chapter 9, p. 81.

Disney's Grand Californian
$$$ **Disneyland**

The Grand Californian is a thing of lavish and loving beauty, a drop-dead-gorgeous hotel that has been painstakingly researched and designed. Styled to evoke Yosemite's landmark Ahwahnee Hotel (it's the "Mock-wahnee"), it has incredible period detail, from the cavernous, multistoried lobby with the giant, roaring fireplace, right down to the door fixtures and even the trash cans in each room. All the Grand Californian lacks is the patina of age. The first hotel ever built within the actual confines of the Disneyland park (well, within California Adventure, which the hotel adjoins through a special entrance), the Grand Californian is the luxury Disney Resort hotel. It's an increasingly rare hotel that invites guests to hang around the lobby and enjoy its cushy chairs, fireplace, and nightly piano player. Several times a day, a storyteller thrills kids with campfire tales; this charming, free service is just one of many kid-friendly activities (not to mention the three fun pools). The rooms are Arts and Crafts smashes, with nature themes (branches and leaves), lush amenities, and even a lack of maid carts in the hallways (baskets deliver the fresh linens in the morning). All of the rooms have robes, cribs, irons and boards, and duel vanities. The beds are comfy and firm, but the towels could be a bit softer, to tell the truth, and the bathrooms in standard rooms could be bigger. Aren't we ungrateful? In truth, we love this place to pieces — Disney should be justly proud of themselves.

Note: Rooms overlooking the California Adventure are the most desirable; other rooms overlook Downtown Disney (which could make for some noise at night, although it's all closed up by midnight) and the monorail (which closes with the parks and isn't too noisy).

1600 S. Disneyland Dr., Anaheim. ☎ *714-956-6425. Fax: 714-300-7300.* www. disneyland.com. *Parking: free self-parking, and valet ($24). Rack rates: $275–$340.*

Disneyland Hotel
$$–$$$ **Disneyland**

The Disneyland Hotel is the original Disney hotel, bless its heart, and for a while, it was the only Disney hotel. It was once so very, very grand and fun to stay at, but now that we've seen the Grand Californian, it's hard to come back. The renovated rooms have a vague Fantasyland theme, with Cinderella's castle on the (blonde-wood two-poster) headboards, glow-in-the-dark Tinkerbelles around the tops of the walls, armoires with sketches of the original Disneyland on them, and Mickey hands supporting the bathroom sconces. The lobby has been renovated as well, with new marble and TVs for cartoon watching. Though whimisical, all of this is still just a bit more grownup than a hotel that ought to be geared for kids should be. (They have weekday newspaper delivery for adults, but where's the kiddie love? A video arcade isn't enough.) There is still a Peter Pan–themed pool area, complete with water slide and pirate ship. Note that rooms in the Bonita tower are the largest and quietest.

1150 Magic Way, Anaheim. ☎ *714-956-6425. Fax: 714-956-6597.* www.disneyland.com. *Parking: free self-parking, and valet ($24). Rack rates: $225–$270.*

Disney's Paradise Pier
$$–$$$ **Disneyland**

This hotel, the second of the Disneyland hotels and the smallest of the three (500 rooms), has the lowest profile. But it does have its own entrance into California Adventure. Basically, the only reason to stay here is, well, because the other Disney hotels are full. There's nothing *wrong* with it; it even has a theme, finally, if you can call something as vague as "ocean fun" a theme. Renovated rooms (which seem larger than some at the Grand Californian) have a sort of beachy vibe with nautical fittings, bleached wood, striped fabrics, and a disturbing bubble-print carpet. The lobby has a (deliberate) ocean smell, and there is a kiddie TV room decorated to evoke the beach with beige carpet, beach chairs, and the TV monitor (that runs nonstop cartoons) encased in a giant painting of a sandcastle. The third-floor pool is rooftop, with a water slide, which is kind of cool, but it pales next to the pools at its sibling hotels.

1717 S. Disneyland Dr., Anaheim. ☎ *714-956-6425. Fax: 714-776-5763.* www.disneyland.com. *Parking: free self-parking, and valet ($24). Rack rates: $195–$245.*

Hotels outside the parks

Some hotels offer free shuttles to the park, whereas others are on the Anaheim Resort Transit line (ART), a shuttle service that picks up at clearly marked stops near or at hotels and goes to Disneyland, returning regularly from the Disneyland main shuttle drop-off area. The shuttles run every 20 minutes along Ball Road, Katella Avenue, and Harbor Boulevard. Rates are $3 for unlimited rides all day; children 9 and under ride free. Tickets are available at hotels along the routes and at the shuttle drop-off in Disneyland. Call **888-364-ARTS** or check on the Web page www.atnetwork.org/art_routes.html for more details.

Depending on season and availability, the rack rates can be deeply discounted. Be sure to check online and/or by telephone to get the best deal possible.

Anaheim Plaza Hotel & Suites
$–$$ Anaheim

Don't be put off by the initial appearance; from the outside this hotel complex looks like an unappealing strip mall. There is a lot going on here, especially since it's set on 9 acres, which provides plenty of lawn space for playing, not to mention an Olympic-size swimming pool. Inside there's a surprisingly large marble lobby with a small business center, bar, and Mexican-themed grill where kids under 9 eat free, plus a pool table that children can use.. The good-sized rooms are in two-story, garden-style bungalows which make the place feel more like Hawaii than Orange County. Rooms come with microwave, coffee makers, and wet bars; ground-floor accommodations have enclosed patios, whereas second-floor ones come with balconies. And it's just across the street from Disneyland Resort. A laundry room with dry cleaning is very handy.

1700 S. Harbor Blvd. ☎ *800-631-4144 or 714-772-5900. Fax 714-772-8386. www. anaheimplaza.com. Parking: free self-parking. Rack rates: $69–$139.*

Best Western Anaheim Stardust
$ Anaheim

This Best Western is right off the I-5, two (admittedly long) blocks from Disneyland, but right on the ART line. Hot breakfast is served free every morning, and basic but reliable and clean rooms come with microwave, coffee maker, sink, and fridge, plus "stardust" in every room — glow-in-the-dark stars on the walls and ceiling. Add in the nice, large, sunny pool and Jacuzzi, and you have a family vacation motel.

1057 W. Ball Rd. ☎ *800-222-3639 or 714-774-7600. Fax: 714-353-6953. www.anaheim stardust.com. Parking: free self-parking. Rack rates: $59–$99.*

Candy Cane Inn
$–$$ Anaheim

In the previous section, we talk about those fairy-tale-themed motor courts that sprang up near the park in the years after Disneyland was built. The Candy Cane Inn is more or less their heir. It is a sweet, family-run place, and there is something to be said for staying in a place that tries to look like an old cartoon village (complete with cobblestones, balconies, flowers, and vines), and certainly it's a fun and friendly place. Excessively floral in décor (though that could change as the owner's wife says she's bored with the flowers), they did recently add new carpeting and tile in the rooms, plus other bits and bobs of upgrades, like spa-quality amenities, grind-and-brew coffee makers, complimentary in-room breakfast (as opposed to competitors who have continental breakfasts in the lobby), and there are plans for a small workout room and Internet access by autumn 2004. The inn has two "premium" rooms with queen-size, instead of double, beds. With a little pool (and a kiddie wading pool), it feels more like a retreat than one would expect of a place smack dab on a major boulevard. Because it's independent, you will have to pay a bit more than you would for a room at its chain-hotel neighbors.

1747 S. Harbor Blvd., Anaheim. ☎ *800-345-7057 or 714-774-5284. Fax: 714-772-1305.* www.candycaneinn.net. *Parking: free self-parking. Rack rates: $77–$134.*

Castle Inn & Suites
$–$$ Anaheim

Over-the-top, "ye olde tyme castle" theme for the exterior (which we can't help but love), but the burgundy-and-blue rooms come with modern amenities — remote-control TV (well, they didn't have those in medieval times), minifridges, coffee makers, and Pizza Hut delivery. Stained-glass windows, Gothic statues, and a knight's armor decorate the lobby — teens will roll their eyes at the kitsch, but younger kids will love it. Pool, whirlpool, and a children's wading pool compound the fun. There's Internet access in the gift shop, which offers free coffee if you show your room key. The gift shop also sells inflatable water wings for youngsters to use in the pool. Walking distance to ART stop.

1734 S. Harbor Blvd., Anaheim. ☎ *800 227-8530 or 714-774-8111. Fax: 714-956-4736.* www.castleinn.com. *Parking: free self-parking. Rack rates: $82 –$132.*

Holiday Inn Anaheim at the Park
$$ Anaheim

This Holiday Inn is the most upscale, non-Disney hotel on our list. Although it's only a couple of minutes down from the park, the hotel does offer a shuttle. Rooms are large, all designed in a sort of hotel-generic décor, but they feel like they are constructed with good-quality wood (not like a veneer pasteboard, let's say). Bathrooms are also bigger than those found in some of the more moderately priced hotels. They are adding high-speed Internet access. Basically, you pay for more space and somewhat better amenities. The pool in the newly designed tropical courtyard is bigger (and open 24 hours) than those found at similar lodgings. A limited spa offers workouts, massages, and the like; the workout room is also open 24 hours. The hotel does offer "kids suites," with bunk beds and a queen bed, and kids under 9 eat for free in the cafe. Still, this hotel is better suited for grownups visiting the park who want only a certain amount of childhood fun — a resort hotel without a theme or any kind of Disney stamp. ART stops here.

1221 S. Harbor Blvd., Anaheim. ☎ *800-545-7275 or 714-758-0900. Fax: 714-553-1804.* www.holiday-inn.com. *Parking: free self-parking. Rack rates: $110–$150.*

Park Inn Anaheim
$ Anaheim

Of all the many hotels on Harbor Boulevard this is the only one that has any kind of interesting architecture — a sort of old-world Tudor design (okay, prefab, but still) rather than the typical concrete block. All the rooms are scheduled to undergo major renovation, as may the entire hotel itself. We sincerely hope they don't mess with the structure itself. The rooms are adequately sized. All of the rooms come complete with microwaves and a small fridge, which makes this a very fine choice for families looking to save some money on dining. There is a terrace-level pool and a hot tub on the third story, more or less facing Disneyland. Millie's coffee shop (reviewed below) delivers as room service. This is an extremely friendly place (winner of the 2002 President's Award for customer service), with a fireplace in the lobby. Walking distance to ART stop and fairly close to the resort. See below for their sister hotel.

1520 S. Harbor Blvd., Anaheim. ☎ ***800-670-7275*** *or 714-635-7275. Fax: 714-635-7276.* www.parkinn-anaheim.com. *Parking: free self-parking. Rack rates: $79–$99.*

Tropicana Inn & Suites
$–$$ Anaheim

This is the Park Inn's sister hotel. It's been newly and nicely renovated in warm Mediterranean colors, with nearby Millie's also providing room service. There is a pretty pool with wood-beamed huts for shade and an oversized Jacuzzi that can seat up to 12. Two gift shops can supply you with everything you might need, including extra T-shirts for messy kids, toys, snacks, and light reading materials. Like its sibling, clean and pleasant, with friendly helpful staff. Walking distance to ART stop and resort entrance.

1540 S. Harbor Blvd. ☎ ***800-828-4898*** *or 714-635-4082. Fax: 714-635-1535. Parking: free-self parking. Rack rate: $139 (but there are probably special deals galore).*

Where to Dine

Because the area outside the parks is littered with generic chain restaurants, the same types you have too many of in your own hometown, we urge you (with a few exceptions listed below) to eat at the big dining/entertainment/shopping complex known as Downtown Disney if you don't eat at the parks themselves. Although Downtown Disney is part of the Disneyland Resort, it has no entrance fee and no gate, so it's considered to be "outside the parks." Anyone who wants to leave the resort to visit Downtown Disney can have his or her hand stamped for re-entry to the parks. Downtown Disney is not cheap (if that's a concern, go to Denny's), but the choices are so much better. Hotel shuttles will take you near the shopping area, if not right to it, so it's easy enough to go to and from a nap in your hotel room to dinner in Downtown Disney.

If you want to save some money, especially when your hotel room has a fridge and/or microwave (like many of those outside the park), there is a Vons supermarket located on the corner of Chapman Avenue and Haster Street — about a half-mile from Disneyland. Stock up on breakfast items, and maybe even some easy dinner items, to save time in lines and money at the park. You can't bring food into the park, but many a parent has snuck in some snacks, and you can too.

Dining inside the parks

Most dining facilities inside Disneyland are overrated, overcrowded, and overpriced, redeeming themselves only by convenience. (The exceptions are the offerings at **Downtown Disney** and **California Adventure;** we talk more about these facilities later in this section.) It's not as bad as the days when Twinkies and "space punch" (and not much else) were served over in Tomorrowland, but hamburgers and carbs still rule the day. While the food works as fuel, it hardly works as haute cuisine (and don't get us started on those fake beignets offered in New Orleans Square). On the other hand, it tickles us that giant dill pickles are still inexplicably offered as snacks at stands in Adventureland and the Bountiful Valley Farm section of California Adventure. Here are some noteworthy exceptions worth seeking out:

✔ Disney has made an effort of late to accommodate those guests who want to eat healthier. There are several fresh fruit and vegetable carts (albeit not cheap) scattered throughout Disneyland (we spotted them on Main Street and in Adventureland and Critter Country) offering melon, pineapple, grapes, and assorted raw veggies and dip, along with kosher pickles, bottled water, and that healthy beverage, Coca-Cola.

✔ Atkins-style eaters will appreciate the Bengal Barbeque with a choice of fish, chicken, beef, or veggie kabobs served with (salty/sugary) sauces. Hardcore anti-carbists can forego the basting or order the bacon-wrapped asparagus: quick, cheap (by Disneyland standards) protein pick-me-ups.

✔ Scattered throughout Disneyland — but thankfully plotted on the official park map — are **churro carts,** named for the absolutely addictive cylindrical Mexican doughnuts they sell beginning at 11 a.m.

✔ On one hand, the **Blue Bayou** restaurant meticulously re-creates a classic New Orleans veranda, complete with lush, vine-wrapped ironwork, lazily chirping crickets, and (nonalcoholic) mint juleps. Its misty, sunless atmosphere comes from being literally inside the Pirates of the Caribbean ride, so boatloads of pirate-seeking parkgoers drift by during your meal. Opinions are sharply divided on the food. We say, come here at lunch, which has more and cheaper options than the overpriced dinner (including an authentic Monte Cristo sandwich), but if you really want quality New Orleans–style food, you should go to **Ralph's Jazz Café** in Downtown Disney.

✔ **Rancho del Zocalo Mexican** restaurant in Frontierland serves grilled meat and fish tacos, tri-tip and barbequed chicken, and it's actually pretty darn good Cali-Mex-style food.

✔ For more healthy snack options, head to Adventureland for refreshments at the **Tiki Juice Bar** and the **Indy Fruit Cart,** which both offer tropical juices and unembellished fresh fruit for a natural sugar boost and more diet-friendly options.

✔ The **Royal Street Veranda** in New Orleans Square offers imitation beignets, as well as some decent (if hardly authentic) gumbo in a sourdough bowl.

✔ Finally, you can get fairly decent coffee, cappuccino, and iced java drinks at Disneyland in the Blue Ribbon Bakery on Main Street. Stands throughout D'land offer frozen and hot mochas along with hot cappuccinos. The coffee cart at California Adventure is really good, but why don't they have a beatnik coffeehouse in the SF section?

The bulk of your eating, if possible, should be done at **California Adventure,** where the options are better in terms of quality and crowds. If you have the Hopper Pass (see chapter 17 for more on passes), consider coming over here, especially if you are an adult who doesn't want hot dogs. Even the fast food seems a bit more inventive and interesting in California Adventure. Among the highlights is the **Golden Vine Winery,** which offers two dining options: a more casual and delicious little trattoria downstairs and a formal dining room upstairs that offers *prix fixe tasting menus* (menus providing a fixed-price sampling of food). Both are surprising entries in an amusement park. They are actual mature dining options that serve excellent grownup food. Patronize them, please, so that there is a chance that more such ventures will be added in the future. Sitting on the edge of a mock harbor is the **Pacific Wharf Café,** which is modeled after those ubiquitous tourist-trap restaurants found at Fisherman's Wharf in San Francisco. It's not a bad choice: You can get real sourdough bread (made on park premises; afterward, you can go over to the Boudin Bakery and watch loaves bake) and clam chowder — have yours served in a sourdough bowl. **Cocina Cucamonga Mexican Grill** offers decent Mexican food with fresh tortillas made on the premises. A visit to the tortilla press is riveting fun for small children.

Breakfast places fill up as soon as the park opens. Because these facilities are expensive and uninspired, we say skip them; have some cereal before you arrive, and get right to the rides. In fact, try to avoid prime eating hours as much as you can.

Downtown Disney

You really can't go wrong dining at one of the restaurants in Downtown Disney unless, of course, you are on a strict budget. In which case you may want to resort to the fast-food/chain-restaurant options, or even the supermarket suggestion we describe on p. 301. Downtown Disney is located outside the resort (although it's considered part of it), but you may walk through it to get to Disneyland (on the left) or California Adventure (on the right), depending on your arrival point. Downtown Disney has no entrance fee and no gate, but you will have to pay for parking if you drive.

In addition to the restaurants listed below, you can also try the theme restaurants **(ESPN Zone, House of Blues, Rainforest Café).** All the restaurants have outdoor balcony or patio seating facing the Downtown Disney traffic, so the people-watching potential is very high.

Catal & Uva Bar
$$–$$$ MEDITERRANEAN

This restaurant, one of two Patina Group restaurants (the Patina Group was founded by the creator of L.A.'s Patina, which is considered one of the best restaurants in town) here in Downtown Disney, specializes in coastal Mediterranean dishes such as bouillabaisse, cassoulet, braised lamb, lots of rotisserie items, and light pastas. It's set in a lovely two-story space, with a Deco façade and a strong wood décor that emphasizes a wine and harvest theme. The first floor features casual dining; the second floor offers more-formal dining. Outside, the Uva Bar is a circular, casual cafe area right smack in the middle of Downtown Disney. The latter is oddly kid friendly (with chicken tenders that got rave reviews), though the wine list and tapas selection will continue to please the adults.

1510 Disneyland Dr., Anaheim. ☎ *714-774-4442. Main courses: $8.50–$24.50. Open: daily 8 a.m.–10 p.m. AE, MC, V.*

La Brea Bakery
$–$$ CAFE

The original La Brea Bakery is just that — a bakery, in Los Angeles, on La Brea. There, Nancy Silverton nearly single-handedly brought about a revolution of sorts, bringing the concept of artisan bread to the masses. Or so it became, when she turned her bakery into a conglomerate and household name. The bread here is indeed amazing, as are the pastries.Sadly, the Mediterranean–style, mayoless tuna sandwich on olive breadisn't very good, so stick with the grilled sandwiches with ham or turkey and cheese or the (breadless) salads, which fare far better. Desserts are spectacular, as they should be, since Ms. Silverton is also a pastry chef of renown. (We found the old-fashioned chocolate-chip cookies old and stale, but maybe it was a bad day.) Consider, even as an adult, trying the amazing mac and cheese from the kids' menu. And some claim the fries are the best they've eaten. Breakfast here can run about $15 a person, but it's a nice place to have a sit-down breakfast. There's also a walk-up window with a full range of coffee drinks, sandwiches, pastries, and salads, all of which cost a bit less than the sit-down service.

1556 Disneyland Dr., Anaheim. ☎ *714-490-0233. Main courses: $8.50–$30. Open: Mon–Fri 8 a.m.–10 p.m., Sat–Sun 8 a.m.–11 p.m. AE, DC, DISC, MC, V.*

Napa Rose
$$$$ CALIFORNIA CUISINE

This is Very Important Dining, with a price tag to match, but what a treat. Take in the floor-to-ceiling stained glass, the ceiling mural, the fireplace, and so on. Clearly, you're meant to think that you're in the heart of California wine country, where they take wining and dining very seriously, indeed. Menus change seasonally, but here are some highlights from the most recent winter list: scallops with a sauce of lemon, lobster, and vanilla; pheasant with merlot-date essence; truffled risotto cake stuffed with fontina cheese with rock shrimp bolognese. Wasted on children, you say? Perhaps, but note that they have a children's menu with buttered noodles, quesadillas, and pizzas. There are 22 sommeliers, so you can guess what the wine list looks like. This would be a wonderful restaurant no matter where it was located.

1600 S. Disneyland Dr., in the Grand Californian Hotel. ☎ 714-956-6755. Reservations required. Main courses: $23.50–$34.50. Open: daily 5:30–10:00 p.m., Sun brunch 11 a.m.–2 p.m. AE, MC, V.

Naples Ristorante e Pizzeria
$$ ITALIAN

This restaurant, the other of the two Pinot Group eateries here, lands squarely in fancy pasta land in a space that has a decidedly California décor. The restaurant features a large outdoor patio, a bright, colorful ambience, and a very fun atmosphere.

1510 Disneyland Dr., Anaheim. ☎ 714-776-6200. Main courses: $10.95–$14.50. Open: Sun–Thurs 11 a.m.–10:30 p.m., Fri–Sat 11 a.m. to midnight (note that closing hours are often based on how busy they are that particular night). AE, MC, V.

Napolini
$ ITALIAN

This is the takeout arm of **Naples Ristorante e Pizzeria** and is located right next door. It features "regular" pizza by the slice or pie (as opposed to its sister establishment's thin-crusted pies) that can be topped with a selection of meats and veggies. Salads, calzone, pastas, and sandwiches are hearty, trad Italian deli style and can be eaten at the few tables inside or taken outside to the tables there. Sodas, juice, water, and prepackaged salads and sandwiches can also be purchased out of the self-serve case. There is, however, only one restroom for each gender, so the wait for the facilities can be a drag.

1550 Disneyland Dr., Anaheim. ☎ 714-776-6200. Main courses: $2–$10. Open Mon–Sun 11 a.m.–11 p.m. AE, DC, DISC, MC, V.

Ralph Brennan's Jazz Kitchen
$$$ CREOLE/CAJUN

This is the best restaurant in Downtown Disney. New Orleans comes to Disney — well, it already did, over at the park in the New Orleans

Square — in the form of a building inspired by Royal Street in the French Quarter. The "Brennan" in the name is that of the finest New Orleans restaurant family. Start with a minisampler of soup, with perfect gumbo, and then move on to the fried soft-shell crabs, if in season, or the filet mignon Rockefeller, if not. The latter floats on a sauce of butter and pernod, with sautéed spinach flecked with bacon, and buttermilk mashed potatos piped into oyster shells. If it's lunchtime, get the *couchon de lait* (Cajun roast pork) po' boy sandwich, or better still, the barbecue shrimp, which is actually done in a peppery butter sauce and demands to be soaked up with French bread. The jambalaya, gumbo, and seafood are all heavenly. They are also fattening, but who cares, you're on vacation. Which brings us to dessert: Try the Bananas Foster (prepared tableside), or the decadent chocolate bread pudding. Live music nightly.

1590 S. Disneyland Dr., Anaheim. ☎ *714-776-5200. Main courses: $12.99–$23.99. Open: Sun–Thurs 10 a.m.–10 p.m., Fri–Sat 10 a.m.–11 p.m. AE, MC, V.*

Tortilla Jo's
$–$$ MEXICAN

Yet another offering from the Patina Group's acclaimed chef Joachim Splichal, this Mexican restaurant features casual dining with tableside guacamole service and a takeaway window with tasty, tasty tacos and sides. It's a colorful, fun, excellent value for families. Adults without kids will find quiet places to sit on the upstairs patios.

1510 Disneyland Dr. ☎ *714-535-5000. Main courses: $8.95 –$17.95. Open Sun–Mon 11 a.m.–10 p.m., Fri–Sat 11 a.m.–11 p.m. AE, DC, DISC, MC, V.*

Dining outside the parks
Outside the park, your dining is largely limited to either familiar chains (McDonald's, Denny's) or unreliable hotel coffee shops. The following are the best of the rest.

Casa Garcia
$–$$ Anaheim   MEXICAN

This family-style Southern California Mexican restaurant is located in a strip mall about a half-mile from Disneyland. The award-winning menu covers the ground from shrimps *al mojo de ajo* (in garlic sauce) to taco combo platters to Texas barbecue pork ribs. Casa Garcia is a local favorite (always a good sign), with a casual cafe style. Come early because there will be a line for dinner. But it's also open for breakfast!

531 W. Chapman Ave., Anaheim. ☎ *714-740-1108. Main courses: $5.95–$14.95. Open: daily 8 a.m.–10 p.m. AE, DC, MC, V.*

Millie's

$–$$ Anaheim   HOME COOKING

Skip the nearby Denny's and IHOP and come here for some seriously good home cooking. For breakfast, we insist on the "world-famous" cinnamon rolls. Omelets are fresh and fluffy and come with fresh biscuits and buttermilk gravy. For dinner, try the pot roast — for $10 you get a huge portion of falling-apart meat (no knife required!) served over carrots and potatoes (both mashed and otherwise) with soup or salad and cornbread. One portion may serve an entire family unless your family includes a whole lot of teenagers. Force yourself to eat dessert; try the Oreo fudge berry sundae.

1480 S. Harbor Blvd. (next to the Park Inn, which uses the restaurant for room service). ☎ *714-535-6892. Main courses: breakfast $5–$8, lunch and dinner $8–$15. Open: 6 a.m. to midnight daily. AE, DC, DISC, MC, V.*

Pho Republic Noodles and Grill

$–$$ VIETNAMESE

Vietnamese food is lighter than Thai food, emphasizing grilled meats, fresh herbs, raw vegetables, and rice noodles, usually in the form of the national soup *pho* (pronounced "fuhrrr"). A bowl of steaming, flavorful broth piled with thin noodles is served with a choice of beef or chicken and shrimp, and a plateful of basil, mint, and bean sprouts, plus sauces for seasoning your bowl your way. Another favorite is the "see-through egg roll" (*goi cuon*) — meat and veggies wrapped in a thin rice-paper crepe. Pho Republic is upscale, reasonably priced, kid friendly (if you have adventurous eaters), and is just a mile from Disneyland.

30 S. Anaheim Blvd. ☎ *714-999-1200. Main courses: $6.99–$24.94 (served for two people). Open: daily 10 a.m.–10 p.m. AE, MC. V.*

Chapter 19

Exploring the Disneyland Resort

Disneyland is no longer just Disneyland; it is now the **Disneyland Resort,** which encompasses Walt's original amusement park and the ambitious new theme park **California Adventure.** It also includes three resort hotels (reviewed in Chapter 18) and a new shopping/dining/entertainment district, **Downtown Disney.** Downtown Disney is located outside the resort (although it's considered part of it), but you may walk through it to get to Disneyland (on the left) or California Adventure (on the right), depending on your arrival point. Downtown Disney has no entrance fee and no gate, but you have to pay for parking if you drive. Anyone who wants to leave the Disneyland Resort to visit Downtown Disney can have a hand stamped for readmittance to the parks (for more on Downtown Disney, see Chapter 18). Here's your guide to exploring the resort's rides and attractions.

The first thing you notice about the parks is that they're clean. Really clean. The parks are so clean that someone once did a study to find out how long a piece of paper remains on the ground at Disneyland. Although we can't remember the exact number of seconds, it is just that — seconds.

Rides get the occasional facelift to take advantage of new technology, replace a tired joke, or just follow along with modern sensibilities. (For a brief time in the 1980s, there was an attempt to add some live figures to the rides; we had a knight suddenly come to life and wave an ax in our direction on the Haunted Mansion ride, a heart-stopping moment. The idea was quickly abandoned.) Political correctness has most affected the **Pirates of the Caribbean,** which used to show pirates chasing comely lasses and one pirate being chased by a homely woman. Now, the pirate being chased holds a pie, and the woman is trying to catch the thief. But the ride is worth taking over and over to catch all the little details, jokes, and insider bits (discussed exhaustively on the Internet, naturally) — the older and longer the ride, the more the Disney design team (the Imagineers) is likely to add funny, knowing details.

 Disneyland will get a lot crazier starting May 5ʰ, 2005, when the "Happiest Homecoming on Earth" kicks off for the park's 50th Anniversary. Plan accordingly, watch for deals and special events, and brace yourself for the crowds.

The Lowdown on Visiting Disneyland

This section could also be called "things we've learned over the years that can make your trip to the Disneyland Resort as hassle-free as possible." (There are, as you can imagine, entire Web sites devoted to this stuff.) Here are some tips:

✔ **Wear comfortable shoes.** You'll spend many hours walking, standing, and putting lots of strain on your legs and feet. Running shoes or tennis shoes are best. Open-toed shoes are fine, especially on hot days; just make sure that they support your feet.

✔ **Expect a dramatic temperature drop after dark, even in summer.** Bring a sweatshirt or jacket, and perhaps even long pants; you can store them in a locker, leave them in the car, or tote them in a backpack. Too many visitors show up in shorts and tank tops only to discover at 10 p.m. that they're freezing their buns off!

✔ **Don't forget bare necessities** such as sunscreen (the park gets a lot of direct sun); camera film (more than you think you'll want; film costs more in the park than outside it) and spare batteries; extra baby supplies; bottled water or a sports bottle that you can refill at drinking fountains; and snacks. Although anything that you may forget is available for purchase inside Disneyland, you'll cringe at the marked-up prices.

✔ **Purchase tickets in advance** via the Internet (www.disneyland.com) or phone (☎ 714-781-4400), or through your hotel; not only do Disney Resort hotels sell tickets, so do many area hotels through an arrangement with Disney. Buying beforehand saves you from standing in what can be long and slow ticket lines. Packages are also offered through the official Disney agency **Walt Disney Travel Co.** (☎ **800-225-2024** or 714-520-5050; www.disneyland.com). Go to the Web site and click on "Buy Vacation Packages Online" to see package details and get online price quotes for customized, date-specific packages.

Disneyland for the little ones

It's a given that all children love, or will love, Disneyland, right? Wrong. Some rides may simply be too intense (fast, dark, subtle) for certain ages or personalities. We strongly urge you to seriously consider your own child's individual tastes, phobias, and neuroses before treating your tyke to this fabulous, but pricey, destination. What may be fine for some eight-year-olds might not be for others, whereas many a four-year-old has spent the day crying, ruining what should have been a magical vacation. Don't worry; they all grow up to enjoy it, so just wait another year or two. It will still be here, and better than ever.

Disney's own rules and regulations do some natural weeding out, as most of the rides have some sort of age or height restrictions. For most attractions, you have to be 7 years or older to ride alone. For the more active, high-speed rides, such as **Space Mountain, Splash Mountain,** and **Big Thunder Mountain Railroad,** kids are required to be at least 40 inches high and 3 years old. You can get small fry measured at certain locations, have their hands stamped to show that they're at least 40 inches tall, and then not worry about height restrictions for the rest of the day.

If you have small kids with you, concentrate on **Fantasyland** (behind Sleeping Beauty Castle), a kids' paradise with fairy-tale-derived rides such as **King Arthur Carousel, Dumbo the Flying Elephant, Mr. Toad's Wild Ride, Peter Pan's Flight, Alice in Wonderland, Pinocchio's Daring Journey,** and the Disney signature ride **It's a Small World.** Elsewhere in the park, little ones will enjoy clambering through **Tarzan's Treehouse,** racing around **Tom Sawyer's Island,** following the **Many Adventures of Winnie the Pooh,** and doing space wheelies on **Rocket Rods,** which is tamer than the name implies (not worth a long wait for grownups). **Mickey's Toontown** is a wacky, gag-filled world inspired by the *Roger Rabbit* films, featuring endless amusement for young imaginations. Over at California Adventure, the **A Bug's Land** section has several benign rides designed just for the little ones, but they're so darn clever, adults won't be bored riding them.

Disneyland for those with disabilities

Travelers who have disabilities are treated very, very well at Disneyland. Of course, crowds may make it difficult to maneuver at times, and the parks themselves can be formidably large. Those concerns aside, if you're disabled, you are given royal treatment; however, the old policy of "line-jumping," wherein disabled guests (especially those in wheelchairs) were taken to the front of the line, has been discontinued (we suspect too many people abused the privilege). Rides that require nimbleness in boarding are halted if need be to ease passage for those requiring help. So when your "Doom Buggy" stops in the Haunted Mansion, odds are that it's because ride operators are helping a disabled person board or disembark. And there are special parade-viewing areas for those in wheelchairs. If you have any questions, or special needs, do contact Guest Relations at ☎ **714-781-7290.**

Parade and show-going smarts

The park's parades and shows draw huge crowds into relatively small areas. Parades usually run twice a day, in the late afternoon and midevening. If a parade doesn't interest you, make a point to steer clear of the parade grounds during and immediately after the parade. You can use this time to take advantage of shorter ride lines in Frontierland **(Big Thunder Mountain Railroad),** Tomorrowland **(Space Mountain),** and New Orleans Square **(Haunted Mansion** and **Pirates of the Caribbean).** Note that the parades for the 2005 50th Anniversary are expected to be the park's biggest ever.

Let's Go to Disneyland!

You've done your homework, you've packed the right park-going clothes and accessories, and you have a game plan in order. Now it's time to hit the parks.

Tickets, tours, and getting in

Plan to get to the gates of either park a few minutes, at least, before opening. If you're driving there, you may want to get an early start because you need to take into account early-morning rush-hour traffic, the drive itself, the parking, and the walk to the gate from the parking lot, all before 9 a.m. The extra time spent getting there may be reason enough to stay in the Anaheim area.

The **ticket booths** are located precisely between the entrances to Disneyland and California Adventure (one on the left, the other on the right), but you won't need to stand in those lines if you follow our advice and buy your tickets before you get to the park.

Before you get to the ticket booths in the center plaza between Disneyland and California Adventure, you will be funneled through a gate and your bags searched. They will be searched again before you enter the parks themselves. Depending on crowd size, this can add some time to your wait.

Get off the tram at Downtown Disney and walk away from the park, toward the Disneyland Hotel (or self-park in the Downtown Disneyland lot instead of the theme park lots). On your right will be the Monorail Station and booth where you can buy tickets to Disneyland. The Monorail will drop you off in Tomorrowland. By using this entrance to Disneyland, you can beat the crowds and avoid the long lines — though your bags will still be searched.

The free, automated **FastPass** system, one of the finer innovations in recent Disney history, allows you to get advance tickets to certain rides. Get your FastPass tickets at the FastPass machines located at or near the entrances to the attractions where the pass is offered. (Look for signs

Private tours and walks

If you want a super-ultra (or -califragilisticexpialidocious) visit to Disneyland, consider a tour. For $75 per hour, with a four-hour minimum, plus admission, you can get a private tour of Disneyland with a guide. Other special tours include the 2½-hour tour of the park, with special FastPasses for two rides, and tastes of Disneyland. This tour costs an extra $25 per person on top of the admission fee. "A Walk in Walt's Footsteps" includes a guide taking you for a peek into the lobby of Club 33 and a private lunch on the patio of the Gallery, Walt's personal apartment at Disneyland. This tour is an additional $49 per person, lasts 3½ hours, and is not recommended for children under 5.

directing you to the FastPass queue, not the Standby queue; it can be a bit confusing, so read the signs carefully, or just ask about it.) You will receive one FastPass ticket for each **Disneyland** Resort admission ticket, which you simply insert into a FastPass machine to get a FastPass ticket. You're assigned a one-hour window of time during which you can board the attraction, usually 45 to 90 minutes later. During this time, you can go on some other rides or have a snack. When you return during your appointed time, you get to bypass the regular line and more or less hop right on the ride. Not all rides have this option, but the most popular ones in both Disneyland and California Adventure do. Note, however, that you are only allowed one FastPass at a time. So, for example, if you get a pass for the Haunted Mansion, you have to use it before you can collect one for the Pirates of the Caribbean. While this system doesn't eliminate lines entirely — after all, other people have the same return time as you — it does help you do the park more efficiently. Just remember that Disney allows only a limited number of people to be in the FastPass queue at the same time. And did we mention that it's *free?*

Which park should you visit first? Disneyland, of course. It's the real reason, perhaps the only reason, you're here at all. And if you had to pick one, just one, park to visit, it would be that one. So let's go there first.

Disneyland

It's billed as the "Happiest Place on Earth," and although we can't confirm this claim (there are places in Bali that are very happy, indeed), we have to admit that we get happy just writing "Disneyland."

As the clock strikes 9 a.m., the gates open, and the crowd floods into the park. You start on **Main Street,** the famous two-thirds replica of an ideal American small town — mid-19th-century Mark Twain with a little Beaver Cleaver thrown in. (Actually, all buildings in the park are two-thirds size to help make kids feel at ease and adults feel sentimental.) We urge you, even if you have never been here before, not to linger — while you dally, the lines are getting longer and longer.

But here's what you see as you race past. (You'll see it in more detail when you return later.) You first pass through the **Town Square,** where you are likely to get immediately distracted as various Disney characters are there for greeting and photo-taking. Stop for a photo op if you must, but plenty more characters pop up later, we promise.

 The rest of the street contains stores offering Disney merchandise. We suggest that you hold off buying any stuff until later because you don't want to schlep packages around with you — although, stores and kiosks all over the park offer **free delivery of merchandise to your hotel** if you're staying in the Disney Resort.

"Steamboat Willie," the first Mickey Mouse cartoon (and thus, The One That Started It All), plays in a theater here, as does "Great Moments with Mr. Lincoln," an animatronic show wherein the Great Emancipator delivers some of his best-known lines. It's hokey, but when Disney tried to close it, protests were loud and long.

We also like the **General Store,** which has a couple of checkerboards and old-fashioned wall-mounted phones on which you can eavesdrop on an 1890s party-line conversation. Truth be told, it thrills us that these little low-tech moments still exist.

Main Street feeds into the central area of Disneyland, from which several main "lands" branch off — **Fantasyland, Tomorrowland, Frontierland, Adventure Land, New Orleans Square, Critter Country,** and **Mickey's Toontown** — rather like the fingers on a hand. Where you go at this point depends on your preferences. In the following section, we detail each area, highlighting the most popular rides, to help you decide which you should target first.

 From experience, we can say that among the most perennially popular rides park-wide are the **Pirates of the Caribbean, Haunted Mansion, Indiana Jones Adventure, Space Mountain,** and **Roger Rabbit's Car Toon Spin.** All of these rides currently offer FastPass service.

Adventureland

If you turn to your left after you enter the more-or-less main hub of Disneyland, you enter Adventureland. This section of Disneyland is all jungle-themed. Here you can find the **Jungle Cruise,** where hilarious and pun-addicted "guides" take you on a jungle journey that is noted more for its terrible jokes than its thrills — everyone adores it, even if they won't admit it; **Indiana Jones Adventure,** where visitors ride in a bouncy jeep and follow Indy's adventures — it's high-tech and for the short-attention-span generation, not for the faint of stomach; and the **Enchanted Tiki Room,** one of the oldest rides in the park, where the birds sing words and the flowers bloom — it's considered terribly dated by some, and adorable by others.

The former Swiss Family Robinson treehouse, now **Tarzan's Treehouse,** is a giant fake tree that kids can "climb" — actually, take stairs — and wander through while admiring Tarzan's home-decorating skills.

New Orleans Square

Adventureland leads directly to this little bit of the French Quarter. It is copied so perfectly that many people who then visit the real McCoy can't help but say "it looks just like Disneyland," when, in fact, it's the other way around.

Here you can find the **Pirates of the Caribbean,** where animatronic pirates make war on, raid, and destroy a Spanish Creole village. One of the first of the fancy rides in the park, it's hilarious and still the gold standard, even if the effects are slightly dated. It's one of the longer rides too, close to 15 minutes long. Because it's in the dark and features steep drops, explosions, and gunfire, it may be too intense for young kids. In the **Haunted Mansion,** you walk and ride through a house where ghosts are running amok; when we were very small and this was very new, we were terrified to go on it, but we ended up laughing our heads off and demanding an instant repeat visit. It may still be too much for some youngsters, even though the ride has jokes galore.

Note that each year, starting in early October through late January, the Mansion gets a total makeover (which causes the ride to be closed for some weeks on either end), turning it into a *Nightmare Before Christmas*–themed ride. This elaborate redo includes new figures in each room, new narration, amazing exterior decorations, and piped-in Christmas "scare-ols" that play during the wait in line to get in. Each year, the décor differs in some way. We are traditionalists, so even though the new setup is the usual extraordinary Disney creative effort, we prefer the Mansion the usual way. But most guests (to say nothing of avid fans of the movie) don't share our opinion, based on the long lines this time of year. The park also has a rush of guests on Friday and Saturday nights, when collectible *Nightmare* pins are released (a new one every week for 13 weeks) — hey, you gotta collect something.

While you're in New Orleans Square, look to the right of the Blue Bayou restaurant. See a discreet #33 on a door? That's the entrance to the exclusive **Club 33;** for a hefty $7,500 fee, plus $2,250 annual dues, members get year-long free admission to the park and a chance to wine and dine (this is the only place within Disneyland where alcohol is served) amid the ambience of a gracious, wood-paneled, English gentlemen's club.

Frontierland

From the **Pirate Ship,** where you clamber around on a galleon, you have access to **Tom Sawyer Island** via motorized rafts; it's one of the few totally low-tech areas remaining in the park. It just got a facelift, but it remains almost entirely the same, which comes as a great relief for those of us who mourn the passing of classics. Kids can climb rock towers, shimmy across suspension bridges, wiggle through secret passages and tight caves — the latter can be genuinely creepy thanks to the low lighting — and otherwise run around like crazy.

Other attractions include the **Mark Twain Riverboat,** which cruises around Tom Sawyer Island. **Big Thunder Mountain Railroad** is a popular runaway-train-themed roller coaster. There was a fatal accident on it recently, but the park went to great lengths to ensure this attraction is safe again.

Frontierland is also the home of an old-fashioned shooting gallery and the long-running **Golden Horseshoe Stage** (burlesque/vaudeville revue fun), which is noted for being a good place to park your grandparents, or anyone else looking to take a load off.

Critter Country

We loved the old-time **Country Bear Jamboree** animatronic show and blame the failure of the movie for its recent teardown. In its stead is another bear attraction, **The Many Adventures of Winnie the Pooh.** Wags refer to this as "the never-ending rave of Pooh," and when you experience the weird plot and dream sequences, as Pooh goes through a blustery day, then overindulges in honey and experiences hallucinations of heffalumps as a result, you'll understand why. It's adorable, though. Parents beware; as soon as you step off this ride you will be by surely the most lethal spot in the park — **Pooh Corner,** a candy store stuffed with every kind of sugary confection you can imagine. And this right after a ride that shows the fun one has after consuming too much sugar!

Critter Country still houses **Splash Mountain,** a combination log-flume ride, which ends with one heck of a steep drop — prepare to get wet — and the animatronic retelling of Uncle Remus tales. Newly relocated, the

Close encounters with Pluto

Of course, we all want our picture taken with Mickey (well, we want *ours* with Pluto), even if we're too cool to admit it. Disney characters pop up all over the park all day long, but they are most commonly found in the Town Square, as you enter the park, and in front of Sleeping Beauty Castle.

Be aware, even if your children are not, that there are real people in those (rather heavy) outfits. So in expressing your enthusiasm at the sight of them, try not to maul them (you'd be surprised how many people do). Even if you do play rough, you won't be allowed to manhandle Mickey for very long for each character has a plainclothes handler nearby, keeping an eye on encounters to make sure that the love fests don't turn into wrestling matches.

Davy Crockett Explore Canoes (formerly known as the Indian Canoes: there's that political correctness again), where guides force unsuspecting tourists to paddle canoes around the island. ("You pay that much to get in and they expect you to row?" we've heard at least one guest complain.)

Fantasyland

You can creep up on this section around the back via Frontierland or through **Sleeping Beauty Castle,** one of the two main landmarks of the park (the other being the Matterhorn). The fairy-tale castle (styled after Mad King Ludwig's Neuschwanstein Castle in Bavaria) is the perfect central meeting place for a family or group that has been split up.

Fantasyland got a major facelift right before the 1984 Olympics. Although the exteriors of the rides look better as a result, some of them lost a little bit of the magic, most noticeably **Alice in Wonderland** (your caterpillar-shaped buggy takes you on a tour of highlights from the movie), which seems to rely more on Day-Glo-painted cheap paper and cardboard cutouts than mannequins and the like (a problem found in many a newer or updated ride). Other rides include the justly popular **Mr. Toad's Wild Ride,** wherein, like Toad himself, you "drive" a car in a decidedly unsafe and highly amusing way; **Peter Pan's Flight,** where a pirate-ship-shaped buggy flies through highlights from the story (though as we wrote this, it was closed for yet another set of renovations: as we didn't like the last way they redid the ride, we have hopes they are restoring some of the fun that went out of it); **Snow White,** the fairy tale, which lost some of its power to scare thanks to the pre-1984 remake; and **Pinocchio's Daring Journey,** which was added during the '84 refurbishment, and which gets few riders. **Dumbo the Flying Elephant** allows you to fly around and around a pole in a small elephant (it's way more amusing than it sounds, especially because you can control the elephant, making it move up and down), and the spinning teacups in the **Mad Tea Party** have caused generations to puke. The **Storybook Land Canal Boats** take you on a journey past all sorts of (we admit it) adorable little replica settings from famous tales. (We so wish we could get out and play with them.)

After you leave the main Fantasyland area — with the Alice ride on your right — you can either ride the **Matterhorn** (the park's first roller coaster, which is still a stomach-turning thrill, even if it does seem a bit tame compared with the wild rides at more conventional amusement parks), or head to your left and see if you dare take on **It's a Small World,** one of the first "new," fancy attractions added in 1966. It's hard to recall what a big deal this was for so many years. In many ways, it's Dante's Inferno, as you travel through several circles of hell in the form of internationally dressed dolls who move their heads and click their eyes, and mouth the words to *that song,* which will never, ever again leave your head. Don't say you weren't warned.

Growing up in SoCal, we always believed the Tomorrowland side of the Matterhorn ride gave a faster, more wickedly twisting ride. Does it? Most likely not, but the lines are usually shorter on that side.

Mickey's Toontown

If you move to the left of Small World in Fantasyland, you will come to the entrance to **Mickey's Toontown,** the first major addition to the park in many a decade. Modeled after the animated world in the movie *Who Framed Roger Rabbit?,* it's largely aimed at the younger Disney visitor. They can bounce in **Goofy's Bounce House,** ride a junior-size roller coaster, stroll through **Mickey and Minnie's** homes, or take on **Roger Rabbit's Car Toon Spin** (essentially, the same wacky idea as the Mr. Toad ride, only these cars can spin 360 degrees, if you choose). Only the latter really appeals to grownups, although there are plenty of visual gags throughout the area to help while away the time.

Tomorrowland

On the other side of the Matterhorn from Fantasyland is Tomorrowland, which got a total makeover recently, a process that is still somewhat ongoing. This is the area that causes most boomers dismay because it has undergone the most changes over the years. Originally, it was Walt's favorite area of the park for it was his vision of the future — remember, this was back in the 1950s, when said future was exciting, and we would all have flying cars by the year 2000. But that sort of vision naturally has a built-in obsolescence. Over the years, a number of rides and attractions have been phased out (R.I.P.: House of Tomorrow, the People Mover, the Skyway Trams), converted (people still mourn the loss of Journey Through Inner Space, also known as the Shrinking Ride, which was converted into **Star Tours,** wherein riders get to have George Lucas–designed fun with C3PO — not for the faint of stomach), or just restyled (the beloved Mission to Mars is now called the **Astro Orbitor,** even though it's still pretty much rocket ships whirling around a pole). The recent makeover abandoned the admittedly dated look for a more H.G. Wells version of the future — and how's that for irony, to go to the 1890s for a futuristic look?

Anyway, in addition to the attractions mentioned already, here you can find **Space Mountain,** an indoor roller coaster made all the more vomit-inducing because it's entirely in the dark. (As we go to press, the ride was closed for renovations and due to reopen in 2005 for the 50th anniversary). You'll also find a 3D production (originally the Michael Jackson *Captain Eo* movie, it's currently *Honey, I Shrunk the Audience*) and **Autopia,** where you drive a miniature sports car around a bucolic highway (kids love this early chance at "driving" and the "license" they get during their wait in line). The eight submarines of the Submarine Voyage ride have been decommissioned, and it's still unclear what will be done with the giant submarine lagoon. This is also the area where you can catch the **monorail,** still perhaps the longest in the United States, which takes you to and from Downtown Disney.

California Adventure

Ah, now we come to the "new" park, which opened to great fanfare in 2001. The first major new development at Disneyland since, hmm,

Look ma — no lines!

That's what *you* think. Nearly every Disney ride is fiendishly designed to look as if there is no line in front of it — either by having the line snake in such a way that its true length is obscured, or by having most of it hidden inside the ride structure itself. You walk up and think, "Hey, there's no line. Let's try this ride!" only to get inside and find out there are quite a few people and a lengthy wait ahead of you. It's a clever psychological trick that we fall for *each and every time*.

The upside is that many of the newer rides have some kind of visual device — little sights, details, or other amusements (talking cars before Autopia, say, or a "set" that makes you think you are "backstage" at Roger Rabbit) — that can help while away the time. It's a good idea to bring a book or a magazine just in case. If you have kids in tow, make sure that they also have a book or comic to keep themselves occupied while they wait.

maybe Toontown — except this is so much bigger. (Toontown was just a new land; this is a whole new park.)

After we have been going on — and on and on and on — about the general overall perfection of Disney, we now have to say California Adventure may have been a major misstep. And, unless you get one of those multiday Hopper Passes (see p. 291), you can safely save your money and skip the California Adventure park.

Don't get us wrong; it's gorgeous. Disney design could produce no less. Every detail, as always, is extensively researched and exquisite. But did you notice the name? Do you know what the theme is? That's right: California. It's a mini version of California in (do we really need to point this out?) *California.* It boasts a mock version of Yosemite, a highly stylized version of San Francisco, and a wishful-thinking version of Hollywood Boulevard. You, the visitor, may well go, during the same day, from the real Hollywood Boulevard to the cartoon version here. And while this may be terrific for prompting discussions of the platonic ideal and archetypes, it just doesn't sit well as an amusement park, or at least not as an amusement park based in, let's just mention it again, *California.*

But never mind that. A more egregious sin is that the entire park lacks the same magic of Disneyland — which is, after all, based on mythologies or faraway lands and times rather than a re-creation of something that lies right outside the gates. Consequently, it's artificial in a Vegas way, not in a Disney dazzle way. Plus, it's a much more generic amusement park; there aren't many rides for the space, and those that are here often disappoint or are completely ordinary. To be fair, though, Disney has added some newer attractions much more in keeping with what we've come to expect from their creative teams, and the reception has been so good there are probably more on the way. Still, the park seems less efficiently laid out; after a couple of waits in line and a walk from one section to another, you've used up a couple of hours with little to show for it.

Which is not to say that there isn't plenty to enjoy at CA (get the initials?), but it's still more a stroll-around-and-admire park than an amusement park (much better for adults weary of lines or rides in general). And if the place didn't cost a whole separate expensive admission, we would probably think more kindly of it than we do. Which is where that Hopper Pass comes in; it pays for itself in just a couple days of Disneyland admission alone. With it, families can take advantage of the better food options in California Adventure and the smaller crowds.

Oh, yeah, the smaller crowds. As of this writing, it's clear that California Adventure is a bit of a bust. On a recent trip, admittedly a cold fall day, we found the park nearly deserted. And even when the crowds picked up a few days later, attendance was well below that of Disneyland. Disney continues to make some modifications, but it also conducted a Gallup poll to see if respondents would miss California Adventure were it gone for good (we participated in the poll), which just can't be good. Still, the economic repercussions from 9/11 cannot be discounted, and the park may find its footing again just as other tourism attractions rebound.

You enter California Adventure through a replica of the Golden Gate, serenaded from loudspeakers by wacky versions of California-centric tunes (expect lots of Beach Boys and Jan and Dean), which play rather strangely on drizzly days. When you enter the park, you can fan out (the park more or less is in a circle, surrounding a mini San Francisco Bay) as you see fit.

Golden State

The Golden State area of California Adventure is sort of a catchall for the beauty of California. It features some lovely — and entirely uninteresting for kids — exhibits on state produce and farming (actually in keeping with the original Disney gestalt). Here, also, is the **Grizzly River Run,** a thoroughly enjoyable water ride; expect to get either somewhat damp or soaked through. It's easily spotted, thanks to the 110-foot rock formation in the shape of California's own bear. **The Redwood Creek Challenge Trail,** newly rethemed with a *Brother Bear* tie in, is part of a kid's playground area that lets little ones run around, climb on ropes or rock-climbing walls, and just generally get their ya-yas out in an area designed to look like Yosemite ("oh, it's *faux*-semite," observed one attendee). For the New Age kid in all of us, there is a stage show led by a "shaman" and a cave where you can place your hand in a magical spot and be assigned an animal "spirit guide."

Also featured in the Golden State area of California Adventure is the **Soarin' Over California** ride. Riders pile into rows of seats that are lifted up so that they may sway and tilt, hang-glider style, in front of an IMAX-type film. It's one of the better rides, but it's prone to long lines, and it's a tad disappointing if you thought you were going to do more actual hang-gliding-type activity.

For the adults, there is honest-to-gosh wine tasting at the **Golden Vine Winery,** where you can learn about wine-making (right out of Napa Valley) and even taste the juice of the grape. There is also a replica of the **rotunda of San Francisco's Palace of Fine Arts** (it serves the same purpose as Cinderella's Castle: It's a good meeting spot) and a copy of the **Pacific Wharf,** where you can watch bread being made or, better still, a tortilla-making machine in action (and you get a free tortilla).

A Bug's Land

They took out one of our favorite California Adventure attractions — we whine a lot, don't we? — but in its place added this thoroughly successful return to pure Disney form, an entire little land inspired by *A Bug's Life*. In addition to insect-themed gardens, rides, and shows (**"It's Tough to Be a Bug!,"** a 3D movie, and **"Ugly Bug Ball,"** a live show for kids), **Flik's Fun Fair** within A Bug's Land contains several rides for younger kids ("No scary tunnels," said one three-year-old happily. "Disneyland's too scary and dark.") The best of these is **Heimlich's Chew Chew,** in which riders coast on a mechanical version of our favorite Teutonic caterpillar as he makes his way through fruit and vegetables, many of which give off distinctive odors as he munches along. The Bug's Land area is designed with large plants and big walls so even adults feel like a tiny bug. This is exactly the kind of magic we have come to expect from Disney.

Paradise Pier

This is essentially Disney's version of a traditional amusement park, which is to say a little bit of a letdown, precisely because it's just a basic spin on the ordinary. It's "carnival central," with the sort of rides that fly around on chains or whiz into the air and generally make you sick to your stomach. It's nothing you haven't ridden before and, as such, it's hardly a must-do. But then again, how lovely it is that in this manic, high-tech, short-attention-span world there are still kids who get thrilled riding a merry-go-round or Ferris wheel. In between the rides are lots of gaily-colored restaurants and cartoon-styled toy shops (the dino selling sunglasses does just that — sell sunglasses, we mean; they don't sell dinosaurs, more's the pity).

Hollywood Pictures Backlot

This is possibly the most dubious portion of the park, where the sinful, back-stabbing business of show is turned into wacky fun. Sure, the whole point of Disneyland is product-placement tie-ins, but the tie-ins here seem even more grotesque and shameless. (ABC soap operas have a major presence. Need we say more?)

We mention how very odd it is to see this highly stylized, cartoon version of Hollywood Boulevard (which, as we've mentioned elsewhere in this book, has no real association with Hollywood the motion-picture industry), but it pales in comparison to the sensations experienced when riding the **Superstar Limo,** wherein you enjoy the whole panoply of stardom, from your agent bossing you around, to *papparazzi* flashing their bulbs, to seeing your visage on a billboard (and you get waved at by cardboard representations — what, animatronics are too expensive? — of such ABC and Disney stars as Tim Allen and Whoopi Goldberg).

This place touts a value system that is even grosser than those telling little girls that someday their prince will come. Otherwise, there isn't much to do, although the **Muppet 3D Adventure** is sweetly enjoyable.

The big new attraction here is the **Hollywood Tower of Terror.** The anticipation builds as you wait in line inside what appears to be a crumbling replica of the Chateau Marmont hotel in Hollywood. After a short wait you step inside a dusty library circa 1939 and watch a short version of the *Twilight Zone* TV series explaining the legend of the Hollywood Tower Hotel. Back in line again, you wind your way through the destroyed hotel to the elevator, where you are belted into a metal cage with 15 other riders. ***Spoiler ahead:*** You think you're about to take the elevator up, but instead, you are already 13 flights up, so you go *down* (way down, below street level, since Disney couldn't build as tall as they'd requested). You're weightless three or four times before landing. Our verdict: It's terrific (and we don't like rides like this one bit), even better the second time because you know what to expect, but it's also too intense for most kids. Please, treat timid children to some cotton candy instead. (Seriously, we saw parents forcing their scared, screaming toddlers into the ride, and we worry about the therapy bills.)

Use a FastPass on Tower of Terror; if you don't, you'll go up a flight of stairs and back down again while the gloating FastPasses wind through a line half the length of yours. If you can't beat 'em, join 'em.

Part VII
The Part of Tens

The 5th Wave   By Rich Tennant

"I appreciate that our room is so near the ocean
I can hear the waves crashing, but I had to get
up to go to the bathroom 6 times last night."

In this part . . .

Every *For Dummies* book has the funny, quirky Part of Tens. Here our part includes the best places in Los Angeles to spot celebrities, the ritziest places you probably can't afford, and — for when you need a break from the glitz and glamour — the spots where you think you're anywhere else but in L.A.

Chapter 20

Top Fifteen Places to Spot Celebrities

*B*e honest: You want to see a star. It would be at least moderately satisfying to return home and say, "Hey, guess who was *right next to me* at the gas station?" It may even be a major reason for your trip to L.A. And surely, you think, the ground is thick with them. Well, that's true, but then again, they aren't going to the tourist sites — how often do you visit the ones in your own hometown? And you can buy one of those outdated Maps to the Stars' Homes, if you want to waste your money. We say forget it. Instead, listen up, *People* fans. Here are some tried-and-true Star Hangouts and some surefire ways to track those pesky famous folks in their natural habitat. Just remember that stalking is a crime . . .

Runyon Canyon

Runyon Canyon is a nice and sometimes trying hike in Hollywood. But if the beautiful people can climb it, so can you! In one day, Drew Barrymore, Cameron Diaz, and someone who looks like Lucy Liu's agent were there. A trifecta of Angels. Almost. But every day, there are celebs, famous faces devoid of makeup and hidden beneath baseball caps, hauling their tracksuit-clad bods up the steep trails, hollering at their off-leash pound dogs.

Just north of Franklin Ave. at Poinsettia Place.

Laurel Canyon Dog Park

Los Angeles has a few off-leash, fenced-in dog parks, but this one is the most popular. On any given day, you can always spot some WB star, or even someone like Julia Roberts or Justin Timberlake, letting their dog have a nice constitutional or other social outing, sometimes without ever getting off their cell phones.

8260 Mulholland Dr. (west of Laurel Canyon), Los Angeles.

Newsroom Cafe

The Newsroom Cafe offers a nice, friendly atmosphere. This restaurant serves affordable health food the way you want it, complete with Hollywood stars sipping their fresh-squeezed juice at the table next to you. Can you say Keanu? We saw Kato Kalin, and Drew lunching with Adam Sandler, all on the same visit, so there.

120. N. Robertson Blvd. ☎ *310-652-4444.*

Nobu

At Nobu, you get delicious sushi, perfect martinis, and Dirk Diggler (also known as Mark Wahlberg). All Mark, all the time. Okay, also Cindy Crawford and husband, Gillian Anderson, Kelly Lynch, Adam Duritz from the Counting Crows, and a smattering of big Hollywood executives. And that was just one evening!

3853 Cross Creek Rd. at the Pacific Coast Highway, Malibu. ☎ *310-317-9140.*

Westside Pavilions Supermarket

Well, the stars have to eat too, you know, and they can't always do it at Nobu. This is the supermarket to the stars — mainly TV stars in a big rush. Look near the "15 items or less" checkout stand to see Jenny McCarthy, David Schwimmer (those sunglasses don't fool anyone), and Suzanne Pleshette, who have all pushed their own carts around this chain supermarket. Faye Dunaway insists that the store carry her favorite maple-flavored bacon.

Santa Monica Boulevard, at Robertson Boulevard.

Supermarkets usually have a good stock of stars, so you may want to check out these stores also:

- ✔ **Gelsons** in Pacific Palisades (15424 W. Sunset Blvd.) has had Kate Capshaw, Steven Spielberg, and Tom Hanks stroll their aisles, while the one in Hollywood (5877 Franklin Ave.) is where platinum-record-selling musicians and character actors and big-name stars like Naomi Watts and Tim Roth shop, plus it was the local market for

Brad and Jennifer until they decamped for Beverly Hills (though *shhh,* they still have a home/retreat in this neighborhood). Tim Roth and the Red Hot Chili Peppers fill their baskets.

✔ Both **Bristol Farms** in West Hollywood (9039 Beverly Blvd. and 7880 W. Sunset Blvd.) — where Drew Barrymore and the Pitt-Aniston family shop — have high star-spotting quotients.

✔ **Vicente Foods** (12027 San Vicente Blvd.) in Brentwood is a likely spot for a variety of family-oriented celebs, such as Brooke Shields, though you may be surprised if we include Angelina Jolie among them.

Rexall Drugs

Just your average corner chain drugstore, except this one is well known throughout L.A. as the place to go for drugstore-brand cosmetics. On any given day, keep your eyes peeled for the likes of Drew Barrymore, Sarah Michelle Geller, Courtney Love, Jodie Foster, Rose McGowan, and more, all searching for the right shade of lipstick.

8490 Beverly Blvd.

Coffee Bean and Tea Leaf

This coffeehouse is located next to designer shopping in trendy Sunset Plaza (itself a highly predictable celeb locale). Location is everything, as they say. It's an easy place to spot a favorite celebrity sucking down a frothy drink or fat-free latte. There are too many stars to name, but we can start with Brad Pitt and Britney Spears. Throw in just about every *Friend,* maybe an N'Syncer or two, and you get the picture.

8591 Sunset Blvd. `http://coffeebean.com`.

Other places to catch a star getting caffeinated:

✔ Cameron Diaz and Portia DiRossi like to munch out and load up on coffee drinks at **Kings Road Cafe** (8361 Beverly Blvd.).

✔ The **Starbucks** in Malibu (30765 Pacific Coast Hwy.) is famous for Barbra Streisand/James Brolin sightings, along with Goldie Hawn, Kurt Russell, and Kate Hudson appearances. You may even see Tommy Lee or Pamela Anderson, perhaps even together.

Skybar at the Mondrian Hotel

This spot, which was once a hangout for George Clooney, has been way too publicized to keep the major stars coming, but the minor stars haven't gotten the memo yet. Besides, with the beautiful view and poolside service from beautiful young waitresses, you'll feel like a star. Isn't that enough?

8440 Sunset Blvd., West Hollywood. ☎ *323-848-6025.*

L.A. Lakers at the Staples Center

Oh, yes. L.A. loves the Lakers. Celebrities love the Lakers. But you won't find them in the nosebleed seats. Bring a pair of binoculars, point them down toward the floor, and you may see the likes of Jack Nicholson, Dyan Cannon, Charlie Sheen, Will Smith and Jada Pinkett Smith, Demi and Ashton, Leo and Giselle, Brad and Jen, and Matthew Perry and whoever.

1111 S. Figueroa St., Downtown. ☎ *213-742-7300.* www.staplescenter.com.

Fred Segal Stores

Be afraid, be very afraid. They're here, and they want that overpriced little black blouse you have in your hands. Go for lunch at the restaurant and casually glance to your left to figure out if you know that person from TV, movies, magazines, or radio. Or just camp out in the parking lot the week before the Oscars and watch the stars parade by in a buying frenzy, searching for shoes, suits, dresses, accessories, and gift items for winners and losers.

8100 Melrose Ave. in West Hollywood; Broadway and Fouth Street in Santa Monica.

The Lobby Bar at the Four Seasons Hotel

It used to be that you could see everyone in the world pass by the corner of Hollywood and Vine if you stood there long enough. Now, the Four Seasons in Beverly Hills features a constant stream of Hollywood and international famous faces. Is Mick Jagger well known enough for you?

300 S. Doheny Dr., Beverly Hills. ☎ *323-273-2222.* www.fourseasons.com.

The Polo Lounge at the Beverly Hills Hotel

It's a classic, and it still works, though you're more likely to spot "Old Hollywood" here than the young and tragically hip. Nancy Reagan likes to lunch here with her pals. Elizabeth Taylor is a customer, as well.

9641 Sunset Blvd., Beverly Hills. ☎ *310-276-2251.* www.beverlyhillshotel.com.

Chateau Marmont

All of "New Hollywood" can be found at this gothic noir Hollywood hotel. Hang out in the lobby (get a drink) or the pretty public grounds and spot Nicole Kidman, Michael Stipe of R.E.M., Ben Stiller, and many more, around for anything from a day's magazine shoot to a long-term stay.

8221 Sunset Blvd., Beverly Hills. ☎ *323-656-1010.* www.chateaumarmont.com.

Ago

Celebs like Sean Penn, Gary Shandling, and the late Marlon Brando have been seen here, a traditionally fertile ground for celeb-watching, maybe because it's owned by two celebs (they do seem to travel in packs), Robert De Niro and Christopher Walken. It's also famous as the place where Quentin Tarantino punched out producer Don Murphy.

8478 Melrose Ave.

The Ivy

Honestly, who *doesn't* eat here? Lazy *papparazzi* know all they have to do is camp across the street from this Industry restaurant, and they will have some kind of shot within hours. They get so blasé that they won't lift their cameras unless it's someone bigger (and we mean fame-wise, not size-wise) than Randy Jackson. The star wattage could be as high as Julia and Madonna, or down to Geri Halliwell and George Michael. Either way, book a table but be discreet with the neck craning.

113 N. Robertson, West Hollywood. ☎ *310-274-8303.*

Chapter 21

Eight Places You Can't Afford

. . . .

In This Chapter

▶ Dining with an Iron Chef
▶ Schmoozing at the Golden Globes
▶ Splurging on celebrity haircuts and eyebrows
▶ Staying in classy digs

. . . .

Sad but true, Los Angeles is a money-hungry, money-happy, money-making city with a lot of wealthy people. Come on, it's *Hollywood*, after all. Those movie stars have to spend those $20-million salaries (and those sitcom stars their $750,000 per episode) somewhere, don't they?

Where can you and I go to feel like the super-rich do, if only for an hour or two? Here are a few places to check out if you're happy with your APR rate on your worn-out credit card.

Matsuhisa

Forget about not being able to afford this wonderfully creative sushi restaurant; you won't even be able to get a table — but if you call way in advance and can be happy eating before 7 p.m. or after 10 p.m. (an exaggeration, but you *must* have a reservation), go for it. The fish and the service are so great that you won't mind too much when you get the bill. And, if you have enough of their unique and dee-licious martinis, you might not mind at all.

129 N. La Cienega Blvd., Beverly Hills. ☎ *310-659-9639.* www.nobumatsuhisa.com.

Nobu

This is the sister restaurant to Iron Chef Nobuyuki's Matsuhisa. It's a little easier to get a table here, in the more relaxed atmosphere of Malibu, but be prepared to eat, drink, be happy, and then get the bill. Hey, the rice is good and inexpensive . . . maybe you should go heavy on that. Nah, celebrate the good fortune that you found this spot as it's buried in the corner of a rustic but (you guessed it) pricey shopping mall for the Malibu set.

3853 Cross Creek Rd. at the Pacific Coast Highway, Malibu. ☎ *310-317-9140.* www. nobumatsuhisa.com.

The Golden Globe Awards

By far the most relaxed fun of all the awards shows (they serve lots of wine, and then Dick Clark televises this shindig), the Golden Globes is for the fancy-schmancy only. But you can check into the Hilton for the evening ($255 plus tax per night), dress up (Neiman Marcus is just down the street), drink up (a Heineken beer out of the minibar will set you back $6), and feel like a rich star all you want. Heck, you can even throw a tantrum when you don't win! The Golden Globes are held the third Sunday night in January.

Beverly Hilton, 9876 Wilshire Blvd., Beverly Hills. ☎ *310-274-7777.* www.thegolden globes.com.

Nonfat Yogurt with Hot Fudge at The Flowering Tree

Prices start at $4 for a small. It must be the homemade, nonfat, delicious hot fudge sauce that makes them so pricey. Okay, it's good and sorta good for you, but it's not like it's served with a complimentary engraved spoon from Tiffany's. What gives? No parking, either!

8253 Santa Monica Blvd., West Hollywood. ☎ *323-654-4332.*

Barney's of New York

The chic-est department store in town, this is a branch of the store so beloved by the fashionistas in New York City, laid out so that it looks like a veritable museum of clothes. We can't even afford the oxygen here. Armani, Vera Wang, Christian Louboutin shoes — it's all here, and it all costs a bundle.

9570 Wilshire Blvd., Beverly Hills. ☎ *310-276-4400.* www.barneys.com.

Sally Herschberger at John Frieda Salon

Sally Herschberger made her name when she gave Meg Ryan her adorable, shaggy blonde haircut. Colorist Lorri Goddard keeps Jennifer Aniston, Nicole Kidman, Kim Basinger, and a host of others in the pink (or rather, blonde or red or brown). There's a reason these gals and many, many others go to this chic salon — they can afford it, and they look like a million bucks afterward (arguably the best cuts and best colorists in town).

8440 Melrose Place, West Hollywood. ☎ *323-653-4040.* www.johnfrieda.com.

Eyebrows by Anastasia

Romanian immigrant Anastasia charges about three or four times what a regular brow wax costs, but she has shaped the errant brow of many a celeb, and with good reason — she's an artist. She dyes, she pulls, she plucks, she shapes, and she draws (all at a fast pace, but don't worry, she *so* knows what she's doing). The results are so stunning that you'll gladly hand out still more dollars for some of her equipment (pencils, gloss) to try to reproduce the effects at home.

438 N. Bedford Dr., Beverly Hills. ☎ *310-273-3155.* www.anastasia.net.

A Room at the Hotel Bel-Air

Flat-out beautiful, the Hotel Bel-Air is discreetly tucked away in the hills above Bel-Air, on several acres of enchanting grounds full of trees, greenery, swans, and bubbling water, with the kind of service you could grow so very accustomed to. Believe us when we say that if we could afford it (rooms start at $450 per night), we would say hang the cost. Perhaps it's just as well for if we got a room here, we would never leave. But there's no reason why you can't join us for a drink in the bar at the romantic restaurant and pretend that we're staying at the hotel.

701 Stone Canyon Rd., Los Angeles. ☎ *310-472-1211.* www.hotelbelair.com.

Chapter 22

Ten Places Where You Feel as if You're Not Even Near L.A.

• •

In This Chapter

▶ Horseback riding in pseudo-Montana

▶ Driving through not-quite-Colorado

▶ Dining in seemingly '60s Miami

▶ Reading in an almost-English rose garden

• •

S ure, some of these may be city landmarks, but these places are so unique that even natives can feel as if they are far, far away from the City of Angels.

The Apple Pan

This restaurant has been around since 1947. Even though The Gap, big bad malls, and pizza joints pop up all around it, the people find it and then flock here. Try the pie. Close your eyes, and chew slowly — you'll swear you're in Mayberry, RFD.

See map p. 121. 10801 W. Pico Blvd., West Los Angeles. ☎ **310-475-3585.**

Circle K Riding Stables

Take a horseback ride in Griffith Park. It's cheap ($20 for the first hour, $12 each additional and you get to take the well-behaved horse on the trail yourself), the people are nice, and the trail is lush and quiet — if you can pretend the white noise of the 134 Freeway (it's just at the beginning of the ride) is a river, you may think you're in Montana.

910 S. Mariposa St., Burbank. ☎ **818-843-9890.**

Topanga Canyon

Travel north along the Pacific Coast Highway a few miles past the Santa Monica Pier, and you'll feel like you're in Colorado — if Colorado had Pacific Ocean breezes. Topanga is full of happy old hippies and kind New Age types — and what's wrong with that? Peaceful, easy feelings abound, and all the folks you run into are happy to share the good vibrations with you as long as you stay within the speed limit.

While you're there, try the **Inn of the Seventh Ray** (128 Old Topanga Canyon Rd.; ☎ 310-455-1311). This health-food restaurant resides in a former church. The food is organically prepared, service is friendly, and the vibe is completely Topanga.

Chez Jay

This beachfront roadhouse opened in 1959. Chez Jay's mellow, laid-back atmosphere, sawdust-covered floors, portholes, and giant schooner wheel may make you think that you've stumbled into Miami in the '60s or arrived somewhere off the beaten path in Hawaii. After you get a high-caloric, sauce-heavy meal, you'll be convinced that you've left the city.

1657 Ocean Ave., Santa Monica. ☎ *310-395-1741.* www.chezjays.com.

The Getty Museum

Fine art, culture, class . . . this can't be L.A., right? Wrong.

See map p. 191. 1200 Getty Dr., Los Angeles. ☎ *310-440-7300.* www.getty.edu.

Beverly Hot Springs

Yes, *of course* steam rooms, facials, and ye olde cucumber and soy milk massages are all so very L.A., but you can really feel light-years away as you relax at the city's own natural hot spring. No, it wasn't built in the 1920s by L. B. Mayer for one of his pampered contract players. Mother Nature made this one for us eons ago. They've raised their prices considerably since the day it was a cheap, few-hours getaway and respite, but it's still worth it. (We could have put this in the Star-Spotting list, too. But be nice. No one wants to be gawked at when they are buck nekkid.)

308 Oxford Ave., Los Angeles. ☎ *323-734-7000.* www.beverlyhotsprings.com.

The Huntington Library, Art Collections, and Botanical Gardens

Six million books and a fabulous, not-so-secret, oh-so-serene Zen garden to read them in? Sipping English tea overlooking the rose garden? Books in L.A.? It can't be L.A. Well, it is, and it's a top attraction in Pasadena.

1150 Oxford Rd., Pasadena (San Marino). ☎ **626-405-2100.** www.huntington.org.

Matteo's

It's a little bit "Old Hollywood." It's a little bit Las Vegas. Either way, with the vintage booths and décor (including clown paintings by the late comedian Red Skelton), Matteo's is not today's Los Angeles. Think Dean Martin — this was one of his favorite Italian eateries.

2321 Westwood Blvd. between Olympic and Pico blvds., Los Angeles. ☎ **310-475-4521.** Closed Mon.

Self-Realization Fellowship Meditation Garden

This public meditation spot on the Pacific Palisades takes up several acres right along Sunset Boulevard as it winds down toward the Pacific. Wander through the park-like setting, complete with lake and dedicated to religious harmony, and wonder how the heck it came to be here. (You can find the answer in the bookshop; it was built by the late guru Yogananda and is on the site of the international headquarters for the yogi's Self-Realization Fellowship religious order.) You may also wonder how some of Gandhi's ashes came to be entombed here (a gift to the yogi). Say a little something to help the world become as peaceful as this place some day.

17190 Sunset Blvd. ☎ **310-454-4114.** Open: Tues@ndSat 10 a.m.–4 p.m., Sun 10 a.m.–4 p.m. Closed Mon.

The Blocks between MOCA and the Cathedral

Start at 250 Grand and walk from the Museum of Contemporary Art down past the Walt Disney Concert Hall, through the Music Center, and to Our Lady of the Angels Cathedral, at the corner of Temple. (Possibly stopping in at one or all of these places.) Art, culture, religion. Snacks. Haute cuisine. Drinks. Cutting-edge architecture. Huh. Just like a real urban center. In Downtown!

MOCA: 250 S. Grand Ave. and 152 N. Central Ave. ☎ **213-626-6222.** www.moca.org. *Walt Disney Concert Hall: 111 S. Grand Ave.* ☎ **323-850-2000.** www.musiccenter. org/wdch. *Our Lady of the Angels Cathedral: 555 W. Temple St.* ☎ **213-680-5200.** www.olacathedral.org.

Appendix

Quick Concierge

Fast Facts

AAA

National Hotline: ☎ 800-222-4537.
Internet: www.aaa.com. Roadside
Assistance in California: ☎ 800-400-4222.
Office locations: Westside (1900 S.
Sepulveda Blvd., near Santa Monica Blvd.,
Los Angeles, CA 90025; ☎ 310-914-8500;
Mon–Fri 9 a.m.–5 p.m.). Downtown (2601 S.
Figueroa St., near Adams Blvd., Los
Angeles, CA 90007; ☎ 213-741-3686;
Mon–Fri 9 a.m.–5 p.m.). Hollywood/
Wilshire (5550 Wilshire Blvd., between La
Brea and Fairfax, Los Angeles, CA 90036;
☎ 323-525-0018; Mon–Fri 9 a.m.–5 p.m.).

Ambulance

Dial ☎ 911.

American Express

Call ☎ 800-221-7282. Internet: www.
americanexpress.com. Office locations: Downtown (735 S. Figueroa St.,
Seventh Market Place, Los Angeles, CA
90017; ☎ 213-627-4800; Mon–Fri 9 a.m.–
6 p.m.). West Hollywood (8493 W. Third St.,
at La Cienega, Los Angeles, CA 90048;
☎ 310-659-1682; Mon–Fri 9 a.m.–6 p.m.,
Sat 10 a.m.–3 p.m.).

Area Codes

213: Downtown Los Angeles and vicinity.
310: West Los Angeles, Santa Monica,
Beverly Hills. **323:** Hollywood, Silverlake,
West Hollywood. **562:** Long Beach. **626:**
Pasadena. **661:** Palmdale, Newhall,
Lancaster. **714:** North and Central Orange

County. **752:** Ontario, Pomona, Riverside,
San Bernardino. **805:** Thousand Oaks,
Agoura. **818:** San Fernando Valley,
Burbank, Glendale. **909:** San Bernardino.

ATMs

ATMs are widely available at banks
throughout Los Angeles. The most popular networks are Cirrus (☎ 800-424-7787;
Internet: www.mastercard.com/
cardholderservices/atm/) and
Plus (☎ 800-843-7587; Internet: www.
visa.com/atms).

Babysitters

Babysitters Guild (6399 Wilshire Blvd.,
Suite 812, Los Angeles, CA 90048; ☎ 323-
658-8792; Mon–Fri 8 a.m.–3 p.m.). L.A.'s
largest and oldest babysitting service, the
Babysitters Guild was recently named
the city's best babysitting agency by *Los
Angeles* magazine. Sitters are at least 21,
speak English, and know how to drive;
some have CPR (cardiopulmonary resusci-
tation) training. They serve hotels all over
the city for $8 to $11 per hour (four-hour
minimum) plus gas and parking costs.

Business Hours

Banks: Mon–Fri 9 a.m.–6 p.m., Saturday
9 a.m.–1 p.m. Businesses: weekdays
9 a.m.–6 p.m. Stores/Shops: weekdays
9 a.m.–9 p.m., weekends 10 a.m.–6 p.m.

Camera Repair

There's a one-hour photo shop about
every 4 feet in Los Angeles, so getting
your pictures developed is nothing to

worry about. Getting your camera equipment repaired is another story. The biggest and best camera place in town is Samy's Camera in Hollywood. They're open 24 hours, so if they aren't convenient they can probably recommend someplace that is. Samy's Camera (431 S. Fairfax Ave., Hollywood, CA 90036; ☎ 323-938-2420; Internet: www.samys.com; open daily 24 hours).

Convention Centers

Los Angeles Convention Center (1201 S. Figueroa St., Los Angeles, CA 90015; ☎ 213-741-1151; Internet: www.lacclink.com). Anaheim Convention Center (800 W. Katella Ave., Anaheim, CA 92802; ☎ 714-765-8950; Internet: www.anaheim.net/conventioncenter/).

Credit Cards

American Express (☎ 800-221-7282). MasterCard (☎ 800-307-7309). Visa (☎ 800-336-8472).

Dentists

DentistReferral.com (☎ 888-343-3440; Internet: www.dentistreferral.com). 1-800-Dentist (☎ 800-336-8478); Internet: www.1800dentist.com).

Doctors

The "urgent care" facilities all over Los Angeles may be a better bet for minor emergencies or health-care issues than heading to the emergency room. These clinics require no appointments, and most accept the major health insurance plans. If you need a doctor but don't need a full-on hospital visit, check the Yellow Pages or ask your hotel concierge for an urgent-care facility near you.

Emergencies

For police, fire, and ambulance, dial ☎ **911**.

Hospitals

Westside: UCLA Medical Center (10833 Le Conte Ave., Los Angeles, CA 90095; ☎ 310-825-9111). St. John's (1328 22nd St., Santa Monica, CA 90404; ☎ 310-829-5511). Century City Hospital (2070 Century Park East, Los Angeles, CA 90067; ☎ 310-553-6211).

Hollywood/West Hollywood: Cedars-Sinai Medical Center (8700 Beverly Blvd., Los Angeles, CA 90048; ☎ 310-423-327). Los Angeles Children's Hospital (4650 W. Sunset Blvd., Los Angeles, CA 90027; ☎ 323-669-2178).

Downtown: Good Samaritan Hospital (1225 Wilshire Blvd., Los Angeles, CA 90017; ☎ 213-977-2121). City of Angels Medical Center (1711 W. Temple St., Los Angeles, CA 90026; ☎ 213-989-6100).

Hotlines

Los Angeles County Rape and Battering Hotline (☎ 310-392-8381). National Domestic Violence Hotline (☎ 800-799-7233). National Rape, Abuse, Incest Hotline (☎ 800-656-4673). National Suicide Prevention Hotline (☎ 800-784-2433). Los Angeles Suicide Prevention Center (☎ 310-391-1253 or 877-727-4747).

Internet Access and Cybercafes

Many hotels are wired for Internet access, but if you've left your laptop at home, Kinko's (☎ 800-2-KINKOS for the location nearest you) has Internet access, complete with high-speed computers for in-store use at 20¢ per minute, or $12 per hour prorated. The California Welcome Center in the Beverly Center (8500 Beverly Blvd., Los Angeles; ☎ 310-854-7616) provides free Internet access for travelers. Free Internet access is also available at the many branches of the Los Angeles Public Library (☎ 213-228-7000 for locations nearest you). To use their terminals, you must present a photo ID and sign up for a time slot. You are limited to two hours per day, in 30-minute blocks. The Santa Monica Public Library has four branches (☎ 310-458-8600 for locations nearest you) and provides free Internet access for an hour a day when you sign up for a library card. All you need for a library card is an ID that shows your address. If you prefer to gulp lattes while surfing the Web, Cyber Java (7080 Hollywood Blvd., Los Angeles; ☎ 323-466-5600) can set you up; terminals are $5 per half-hour or $9 per hour, from 7 a.m. to midnight. The Internet stations in the Knitting Factory's bar/restaurant (7021 Hollywood Blvd., Hollywood; ☎ 323-463-0204) are free of charge, but you have to order food or drink.

Liquor Laws

The legal drinking age in California is 21. Alcohol may be consumed only in establishments with liquor sales licenses (bars, restaurants, nightclubs, for example) between the hours of 6 a.m. and 2 a.m. Alcohol may be sold only between the hours of 6 a.m. and 2 a.m. Open containers are not allowed in public, either on the street or in a vehicle.

Mail

Downtown: Bunker Hill Station (300 S. Grand Ave., Los Angeles, CA 90071; ☎ 800-275-8777; Mon–Fri 8:30 a.m.–5:30 p.m.). Hollywood (1615 Wilcox Ave., Los Angeles, CA 90028; ☎ 323-464-2355; Mon–Fri 8:30 a.m.–5:30 p.m., Sat 8:30 a.m.–3:30 p.m.). West Hollywood (820 N. San Vicente, West Hollywood, CA 90069; ☎ 310-652-5435; Mon–Fri 8:30 a.m.–5:30 p.m., Sat 8 a.m.–2:30 p.m.).

Westside: Santa Monica (1248 Fifth St., Santa Monica, CA 90401; ☎ 310-576-6786; Mon–Fri 9 a.m.–6 p.m., Sat 9 a.m.–3 p.m.). Federal Building Westwood (11000 Wilshire Blvd., Los Angeles, CA 90024; ☎ 310-235-7443; Mon–Fri 7:30 a.m.–5:30 p.m.).

Maps

Good local maps can be found at most newsstands, many gas stations, or at the nearest AAA office.

Pharmacies

Santa Monica/Westside: Rite Aid (1808 Wilshire Blvd., Santa Monica, CA 90403; ☎ 310-829-3951; open 24 hours). Sav-On Drugs (12015 Wilshire Blvd., Los Angeles, CA 90025; ☎ 310-479-6500; Mon–Fri 9 a.m.–9 p.m., Sat 9 a.m.–7p.m, Sun 10 a.m.–6 p.m.).

West Hollywood/Hollywood: Sav-On Drugs (8491 Santa Monica Blvd., West Hollywood, CA 90069; ☎ 310-360-7303; Mon–Fri 8 a.m.–1 p.m., Sat–Sun 10 a.m.–8 p.m.). Rite-Aid Pharmacy (6130 W. Sunset Blvd., Los Angeles, CA 90028; ☎ 323-467-4201; open 24 hours).

Downtown: Rite-Aid (600 W. Seventh St., Los Angeles, CA 90017; ☎ 213-896-0083; Mon–Fri 9 a.m.–7 p.m., Sat 9 a.m.–6 p.m.).

Police

Call ☎ **911.**

Radio Station

You can find modern rock at KROQ-FM (106.7 FM), where they pretty much invented the term, pop hits at KISS FM (102.7), and classic rock at KLOS FM (95.5). Urban rules at KBT FM (100.3), and hip-hop is found at KPWR FM (105.9). The largest public radio station in L.A. is KCRW (89.9 FM), with NPR news and eclectic music. Regular news is at KFWB (980 AM), which also has traffic updates every ten minutes.

Restrooms

Los Angeles doesn't have the kind of public restrooms you'd find in London or Paris, but you can usually take advantage of the facilities at fast-food restaurants or some gas stations. In rare circumstances, you may be asked to buy something before using the restrooms — but isn't that a small price to pay for taking care of business?

Safety

While Los Angeles does have its dangerous parts of town, by and large the average tourist isn't going to be anywhere near those sections of town. If you're staying in Downtown or in a more seedy part of Hollywood, exercise a little extra caution at night, but in general your basic street smarts apply around these parts of town. Avoid dark places in the middle of the night unless you're with a big group. Use travel wallets rather than easily snatched purses. Generally, just keep your eyes open.

Smoking

Smoking is not allowed inside most public buildings, including airports, shopping malls, restaurants, bars, and nightclubs. Smoking is only allowed outdoors.

Taxes

The sales tax on most commonly purchased items (except for snack foods) is 8.25 percent in all of Los Angeles County. You pay additional taxes and fees for travel-related items such as rental cars and hotel rooms (from 12 to 18 percent in the Los Angeles area).

Taxis

Yellow Cab (☎ 800-200-1085). United Independent (☎ 800-411-0303). Independent Taxi (☎ 800-521-8294). Checker Cabs (☎ 800-300-5007).Cabs charge an airport fee of $2.50 in addition to their $2 pickup fee, $2 per mile charge, and additional charges when you get stuck in traffic, a common occurrence. It is customary to tip 10 to 15 percent.

Time Zone

Los Angeles is located in the Pacific Time Zone. California recognizes daylight saving time from late April through late October.

Tipping

You should generally tip bartenders 10 to 15 percent; bellhops at least $1 per bag, more if you have a lot of luggage or heavy bags; cab drivers 15 percent of the fare; chambermaids at least $1 per day; checkroom attendants at least $1 per garment; delivery drivers, 15 to 20 percent of the check; hairdressers and barbers 15 to 20 percent of the bill; waiters and waitresses 15 to 20 percent of the check; and valet parking attendants at least $1 per vehicle.

Transit Info

The city's buses, subways, and commuter rail system are all operated under the heading of "Metro," a cutesy name for the Los Angeles County Metropolitan Transportation Authority. Buses run on most major thoroughfares throughout the city. The one subway line runs from Downtown through Hollywood, past Universal Studios, and ends in North Hollywood in the San Fernando Valley. The Metro operates a few light rail lines, including the "Blue Line" from downtown to Long Beach and the "Green Line" that goes near the airport (but not right to it; see Chapter 10 for more on your transportation options from the airport). For schedules, routes, and fares call ☎ 800-COMMUTE or check the MTA Web site at www.mta.net.

Weather Updates

The best source for weather information is www.weather.com, the Web site operated by The Weather Channel. If you don't have Internet access, you can call ☎ 213-976-1212 for recorded information. It'll cost you $2, but you'll also get all the latest California Lottery draw results at the same time, so what the heck!

Toll-Free Numbers and Web Sites

Major car rental agencies

Advantage
☎ 800-777-5500
www.advantagerentacar.com

Alamo
☎ 800-327-9633
www.goalamo.com

Avis
☎ 800-331-1212 in Continental
United States
☎ 800-879-2847 in Canada
www.avis.com

Budget
☎ 800-527-0700
www.budgetrentacar.com

Dollar
☎ 800-800-4000
www.dollar.com

Enterprise
☎ 800-325-8007
www.enterprise.com

Hertz
☎ 800-654-3131
www.hertz.com

National
☎ 800-CAR-RENT (800-227-7368)
www.nationalcar.com

Payless
☎ 800-PAYLESS (800-729-5377)
www.paylesscarrental.com

Rent-A-Wreck
☎ 800-535-1391
www.rentawreck.com

Thrifty
☎ 800-367-2277
www.thrifty.com

Major hotel and motel chains

Best Western International
☎ 800-528-1234
www.bestwestern.com

Clarion Hotels
☎ 800-CLARION (800-252-7466)
www.clarionhotel.com

Comfort Inns
☎ 800-228-5150
www.hotelchoice.com

Courtyard by Marriott
☎ 800-321-2211
www.courtyard.com

Days Inn
☎ 800-325-2525
www.daysinn.com

Doubletree Hotels
☎ 800-222-TREE (800-222-8733)
www.doubletree.com

Econo Lodges
☎ 800-55-ECONO (800-553-2666)
www.hotelchoice.com

Fairfield Inn by Marriott
☎ 800-228-2800
www.marriott.com

Hampton Inn
☎ 800-HAMPTON (800-426-7866)
www.hampton-inn.com

Hilton Hotels
☎ 800-HILTONS (800-445-8667)
www.hilton.com

Holiday Inn
☎ 800-HOLIDAY (800-4654329)
www.basshotels.com

Howard Johnson
☎ 800-654-2000
www.hojo.com

Hyatt Hotels & Resorts
☎ 800-228-9000
www.hyatt.com

ITT Sheraton
☎ 800-325-3535
www.starwood.com

La Quinta Motor Inns
☎ 800-531-5900
www.laquinta.com

Marriott Hotels
☎ 800-228-9290
www.marriott.com

Motel 6
☎ 800-4-MOTEL6 (800-466-8356)
www.motel6.com

Quality Inns
☎ 800-228-5151
www.hotelchoice.com

Radisson Hotels International
☎ 800-333-3333
www.radisson.com

Ramada Inns
☎ 800-2-RAMADA (800-272-6232)
www.ramada.com

Red Carpet Inns
☎ 800-251-1962
www.bookroomsnow.com

Red Lion Hotels & Inns
☎ 800-547-8010
http://www.redlion.com/

Red Roof Inns
☎ 800-843-7663
www.redroof.com

Residence Inn by Marriott
☎ 800-331-3131
www.marriott.com

Rodeway Inns
☎ 800-228-2000
www.hotelchoice.com

Super 8 Motels
☎ 800-800-8000
www.super8.com

Travelodge
☎ 800-255-3050
www.travelodge.com

Vagabond Inns
☎ 800-522-1555
www.vagabondinn.com

Wyndham Hotels and Resorts
☎ 800-822-4200 in continental United
States and Canada
www.wyndham.com

Index

• *E* •

• *F* •

• *G* •

• N •

• O •

Accommodations Index

Restaurant Index

BUSINESS, CAREERS & PERSONAL FINANCE

0-7645-5307-0

0-7645-5331-3 *†

Also available:

- Accounting For Dummies †
  0-7645-5314-3
- Business Plans Kit For Dummies †
  0-7645-5365-8
- Cover Letters For Dummies
  0-7645-5224-4
- Frugal Living For Dummies
  0-7645-5403-4
- Leadership For Dummies
  0-7645-5176-0
- Managing For Dummies
  0-7645-1771-6

- Marketing For Dummies
  0-7645-5600-2
- Personal Finance For Dummies *
  0-7645-2590-5
- Project Management
  For Dummies
  0-7645-5283-X
- Resumes For Dummies †
  0-7645-5471-9
- Selling For Dummies
  0-7645-5363-1
- Small Business Kit For Dummies *†
  0-7645-5093-4

HOME & BUSINESS COMPUTER BASICS

0-7645-4074-2

0-7645-3758-X

Also available:

- ACT! 6 For Dummies
  0-7645-2645-6
- iLife '04 All-in-One Desk Reference
  For Dummies
  0-7645-7347-0
- iPAQ For Dummies
  0-7645-6769-1
- Mac OS X Panther Timesaving
  Techniques For Dummies
  0-7645-5812-9
- Macs For Dummies
  0-7645-5656-8
- Microsoft Money 2004 For Dummies
  0-7645-4195-1

- Office 2003 All-in-One Desk
  Reference For Dummies
  0-7645-3883-7
- Outlook 2003 For Dummies
  0-7645-3759-8
- PCs For Dummies
  0-7645-4074-2
- TiVo For Dummies
  0-7645-6923-6
- Upgrading and Fixing PCs
  For Dummies
  0-7645-1665-5
- Windows XP Timesaving
  Techniques For Dummies
  0-7645-3748-2

FOOD, HOME, GARDEN, HOBBIES, MUSIC & PETS

0-7645-5295-3

0-7645-5232-5

Also available:

- Bass Guitar For Dummies
  0-7645-2487-9
- Diabetes Cookbook For Dummies
  0-7645-5230-9
- Gardening For Dummies *
  0-7645-5130-2
- Guitar For Dummies
  0-7645-5106-X
- Holiday Decorating For Dummies
  0-7645-2570-0
- Home Improvement All-in-One
  For Dummies
  0-7645-5680-0

- Knitting For Dummies
  0-7645-5395-X
- Piano For Dummies
  0-7645-5105-1
- Puppies For Dummies
  0-7645-5255-4
- Scrapbooking For Dummies
  0-7645-7208-3
- Senior Dogs For Dummies
  0-7645-5818-8
- Singing For Dummies
  0-7645-2475-5
- 30-Minute Meals For Dummies
  0-7645-2589-1

INTERNET & DIGITAL MEDIA

0-7645-1664-7

0-7645-6924-4

Also available:

- 2005 Online Shopping Directory
  For Dummies
  0-7645-7495-7
- CD & DVD Recording For Dummies
  0-7645-5956-7
- eBay For Dummies
  0-7645-5654-1
- Fighting Spam For Dummies
  0-7645-5965-6
- Genealogy Online For Dummies
  0-7645-5964-8
- Google For Dummies
  0-7645-4420-9

- Home Recording For Musicians
  For Dummies
  0-7645-1634-5
- The Internet For Dummies
  0-7645-4173-0
- iPod & iTunes For Dummies
  0-7645-7772-7
- Preventing Identity Theft
  For Dummies
  0-7645-7336-5
- Pro Tools All-in-One Desk
  Reference For Dummies
  0-7645-5714-9
- Roxio Easy Media Creator
  For Dummies
  0-7645-7131-1

* Separate Canadian edition also available

† Separate U.K. edition also available

Available wherever books are sold. For more information or to order direct: U.S. customers
visit www.dummies.com or call 1-877-762-2974.
U.K. customers visit www.wileyeurope.com or call 0800 243407. Canadian customers visit
www.wiley.ca or call 1-800-567-4797.

SPORTS, FITNESS, PARENTING, RELIGION & SPIRITUALITY

0-7645-5146-9

0-7645-5418-2

Also available:
- Adoption For Dummies
  0-7645-5488-3
- Basketball For Dummies
  0-7645-5248-1
- The Bible For Dummies
  0-7645-5296-1
- Buddhism For Dummies
  0-7645-5359-3
- Catholicism For Dummies
  0-7645-5391-7
- Hockey For Dummies
  0-7645-5228-7

- Judaism For Dummies
  0-7645-5299-6
- Martial Arts For Dummies
  0-7645-5358-5
- Pilates For Dummies
  0-7645-5397-6
- Religion For Dummies
  0-7645-5264-3
- Teaching Kids to Read
  For Dummies
  0-7645-4043-2
- Weight Training For Dummies
  0-7645-5168-X
- Yoga For Dummies
  0-7645-5117-5

TRAVEL

0-7645-5438-7

0-7645-5453-0

Also available:
- Alaska For Dummies
  0-7645-1761-9
- Arizona For Dummies
  0-7645-6938-4
- Cancún and the Yucatán
  For Dummies
  0-7645-2437-2
- Cruise Vacations For Dummies
  0-7645-6941-4
- Europe For Dummies
  0-7645-5456-5
- Ireland For Dummies
  0-7645-5455-7

- Las Vegas For Dummies
  0-7645-5448-4
- London For Dummies
  0-7645-4277-X
- New York City For Dummies
  0-7645-6945-7
- Paris For Dummies
  0-7645-5494-8
- RV Vacations For Dummies
  0-7645-5443-3
- Walt Disney World & Orlando
  For Dummies
  0-7645-6943-0

GRAPHICS, DESIGN & WEB DEVELOPMENT

0-7645-4345-8

0-7645-5589-8

Also available:
- Adobe Acrobat 6 PDF
  For Dummies
  0-7645-3760-1
- Building a Web Site For Dummies
  0-7645-7144-3
- Dreamweaver MX 2004
  For Dummies
  0-7645-4342-3
- FrontPage 2003 For Dummies
  0-7645-3882-9
- HTML 4 For Dummies
  0-7645-1995-6
- Illustrator CS For Dummies
  0-7645-4084-X

- Macromedia Flash MX 2004
  For Dummies
  0-7645-4358-X
- Photoshop 7 All-in-One Desk
  Reference For Dummies
  0-7645-1667-1
- Photoshop CS Timesaving
  Techniques For Dummies
  0-7645-6782-9
- PHP 5 For Dummies
  0-7645-4166-8
- PowerPoint 2003 For Dummies
  0-7645-3908-6
- QuarkXPress 6 For Dummies
  0-7645-2593-X

NETWORKING, SECURITY, PROGRAMMING & DATABASES

0-7645-6852-3

0-7645-5784-X

Also available:
- A+ Certification For Dummies
  0-7645-4187-0
- Access 2003 All-in-One Desk
  Reference For Dummies
  0-7645-3988-4
- Beginning Programming
  For Dummies
  0-7645-4997-9
- C For Dummies
  0-7645-7068-4
- Firewalls For Dummies
  0-7645-4048-3
- Home Networking For Dummies
  0-7645-42796

- Network Security For Dummies
  0-7645-1679-5
- Networking For Dummies
  0-7645-1677-9
- TCP/IP For Dummies
  0-7645-1760-0
- VBA For Dummies
  0-7645-3989-2
- Wireless All In-One Desk Reference
  For Dummies
  0-7645-7496-5
- Wireless Home Networking
  For Dummies
  0-7645-3910-8

HEALTH & SELF-HELP

0-7645-6820-5 *†   0-7645-2566-2

Also available:
- Alzheimer's For Dummies
  0-7645-3899-3
- Asthma For Dummies
  0-7645-4233-8
- Controlling Cholesterol For Dummies
  0-7645-5440-9
- Depression For Dummies
  0-7645-3900-0
- Dieting For Dummies
  0-7645-4149-8
- Fertility For Dummies
  0-7645-2549-2

- Fibromyalgia For Dummies
  0-7645-5441-7
- Improving Your Memory For Dummies
  0-7645-5435-2
- Pregnancy For Dummies †
  0-7645-4483-7
- Quitting Smoking For Dummies
  0-7645-2629-4
- Relationships For Dummies
  0-7645-5384-4
- Thyroid For Dummies
  0-7645-5385-2

EDUCATION, HISTORY, REFERENCE & TEST PREPARATION

0-7645-5194-9   0-7645-4186-2

Also available:
- Algebra For Dummies
  0-7645-5325-9
- British History For Dummies
  0-7645-7021-8
- Calculus For Dummies
  0-7645-2498-4
- English Grammar For Dummies
  0-7645-5322-4
- Forensics For Dummies
  0-7645-5580-4
- The GMAT for Dummies
  0-7645-5251-1
- Inglés Para Dummies
  0-7645-5427-1

- Italian For Dummies
  0-7645-5196-5
- Latin For Dummies
  0-7645-5431-X
- Lewis & Clark For Dummies
  0-7645-2545-X
- Research Papers For Dummies
  0-7645-5426-3
- The SAT I For Dummies
  0-7645-7193-1
- Science Fair Projects For Dummies
  0-7645-5460-3
- U.S. History For Dummies
  0-7645-5249-X

Get smart @ dummies.com®

- Find a full list of Dummies titles
- Look into loads of FREE on-site articles
- Sign up for FREE eTips e-mailed to you weekly
- See what other products carry the Dummies name
- Shop directly from the Dummies bookstore
- Enter to win new prizes every month!

* Separate Canadian edition also available
† Separate U.K. edition also available

Available wherever books are sold. For more information or to order direct: U.S. customers visit www.dummies.com or call 1-877-762-2974.
U.K. customers visit www.wileyeurope.com or call 0800 243407. Canadian customers visit www.wiley.ca or call 1-800-567-4797.